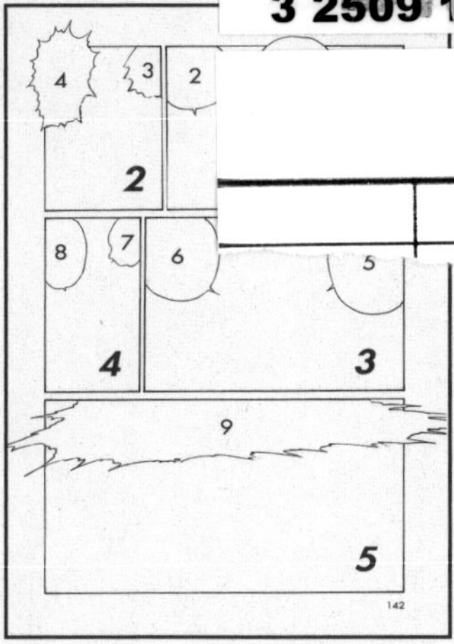
4
3
2
2
8
7
6
5
4
3
9
5
142

...the original Japanese comic format, this book reads from right to left—so action, sound effects and word balloons are completely reversed. This preserves the orientation of the original artwork—plus, it's fun! Check out the diagram shown here to get the hang of things, and then turn to the other side of the book to get started!

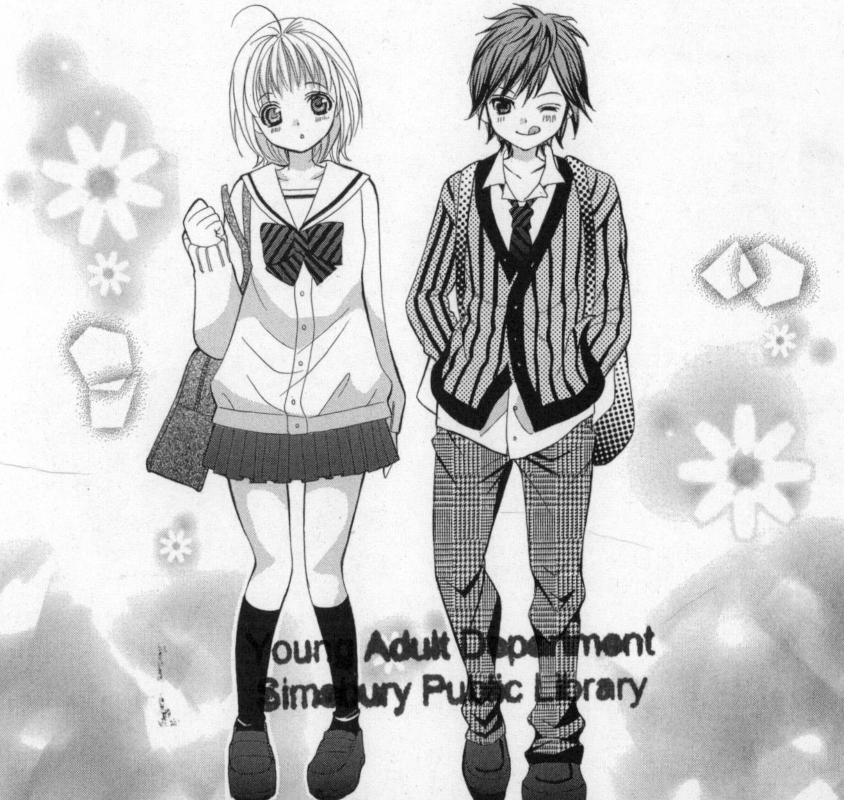

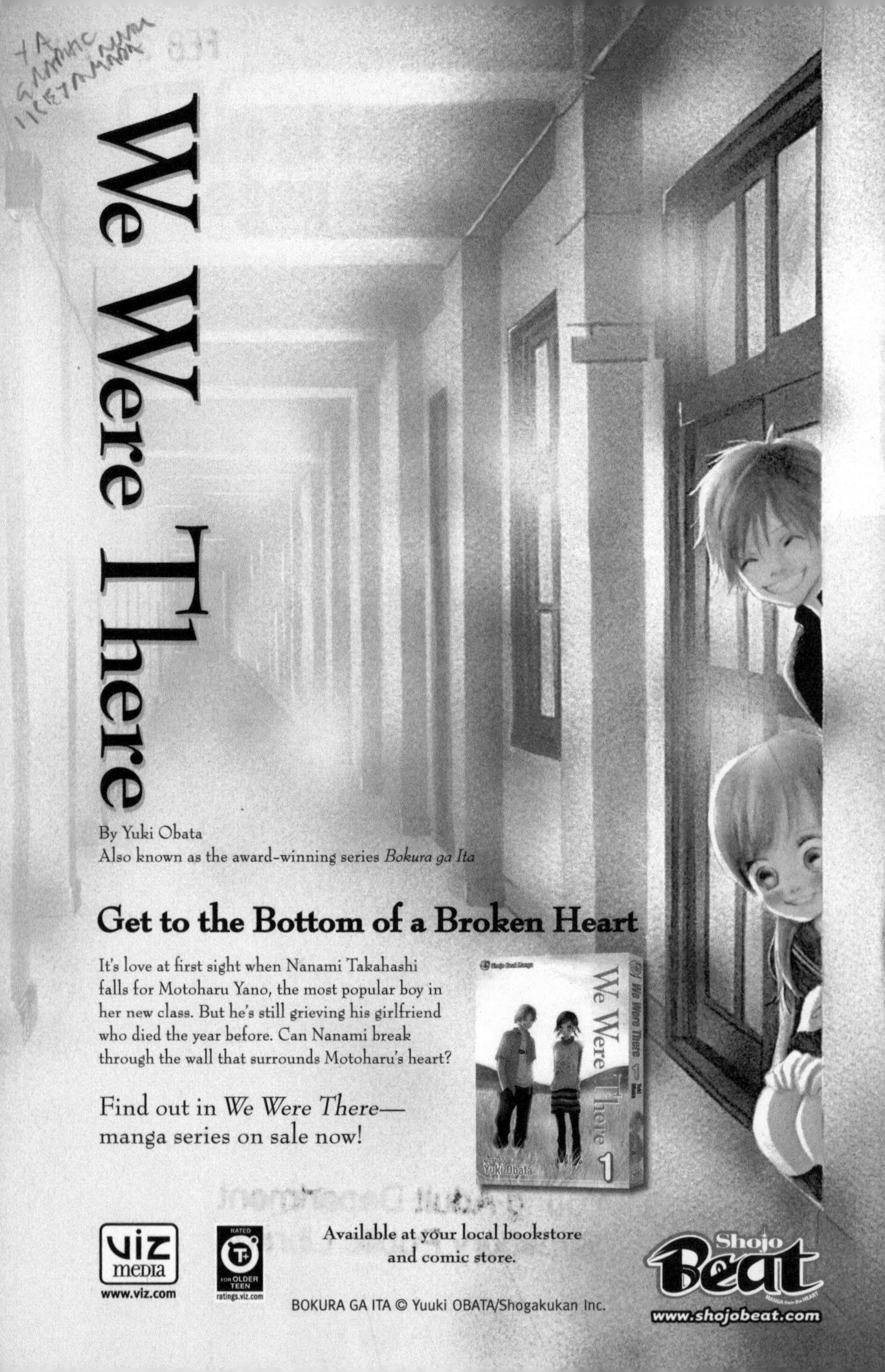
We Were There
By Yuki Obata
Also known as the award-winning series Bokura ga Ita
Get to the Bottom of a Broken Heart
It's love at first sight when Nanami Takahashi falls for Motoharu Yano, the most popular boy in her new class. But he's still grieving his girlfriend who died the year before. Can Nanami break through the wall that surrounds Motoharu's heart?
Find out in We Were There—manga series on sale now!
We Were There
Yuki Obata
1
viz media
www.viz.com
RATED T+ FOR OLDER TEEN
ratings.viz.com
Available at your local bookstore and comic store.
Shojo Beat
www.shojobeat.com
BOKURA GA ITA © Yuuki OBATA/Shogakukan Inc.

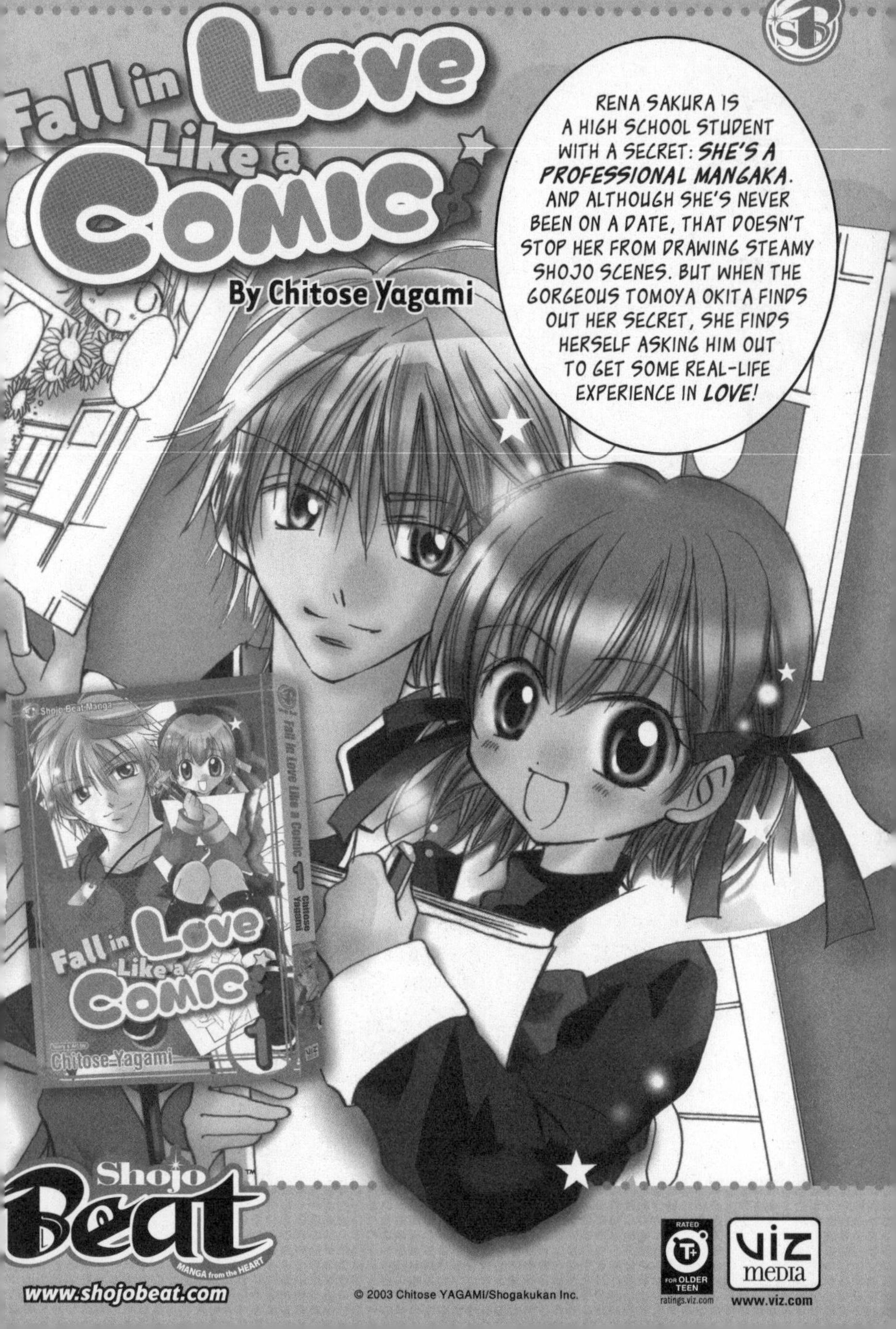

SO CUTE IT HURTS!!
Volume 3

Shojo Beat Edition

STORY AND ART BY
GO IKEYAMADA

English Translation & Adaptation/Tomo Kimura
Touch-Up Art & Lettering/Joanna Estep
Design/Izumi Evers
Editor/Pancha Diaz

KOBAYASHI GA KAWAISUGITE TSURAI!! Vol.3
by Go IKEYAMADA
© 2012 Go IKEYAMADA
All rights reserved.
Original Japanese edition published by SHOGAKUKAN.
English translation rights in the United States of America, Canada,
United Kingdom and Ireland arranged with SHOGAKUKAN.

Printed in the U.S.A.

Published by VIZ Media, LLC
P.O. Box 77010
San Francisco, CA 94107

10 9 8 7 6 5 4 3 2 1
First printing, October 2015

www.viz.com   www.shojobeat.com

CHARACTERS

Cross-dressing as her brother!

Nickname: Mego

Switched places at school!

Mitsuru wears bows! ☆

Cross-dressing as his sister!

Megumu Kobayashi (younger sister)
History nerd who loves video games. She likes Aoi.

Twins

Mitsuru Kobayashi (older brother)
Girls love him. Good in any sport. He falls in love with Shino.

They run into each other on the school roof

Enemies

Rescues her

Aoi Sanada
Strongest guy at school. Megumu accidentally kissed him, but he doesn't know it was her.

Azusa Tokugawa
School chairman's daughter, bully and fashion model.

Shino Takenaka
She's deaf. And she knows Aoi...?

STORY

★ Mitsuru and Megumu are twins. One day they switch places and go to each other's school for a week!

★ At Akechi Boys' High, Megumu falls in love with Aoi. When she discovers that Aoi gets so uncomfortable around women that he can't even touch them, she decides to keep cross-dressing so she can be with him. Meanwhile, Mitsuru falls in love with Shino when he stops Azusa from bullying her. And Aoi and Shino turn out to be siblings!

★ Then one day Azusa falls into a pit, and Mitsuru tries to help her get out. But he falls in the pit too and his wig comes off, so now Azusa knows Mitsuru is a boy.

★ At the same time, Megumu gets hurt when she stops some guys from ambushing Aoi. Aoi brings her to his place so he can treat her wounds and accidentally sees her changing, so now Aoi knows Megumu is a girl!

CONTENTS

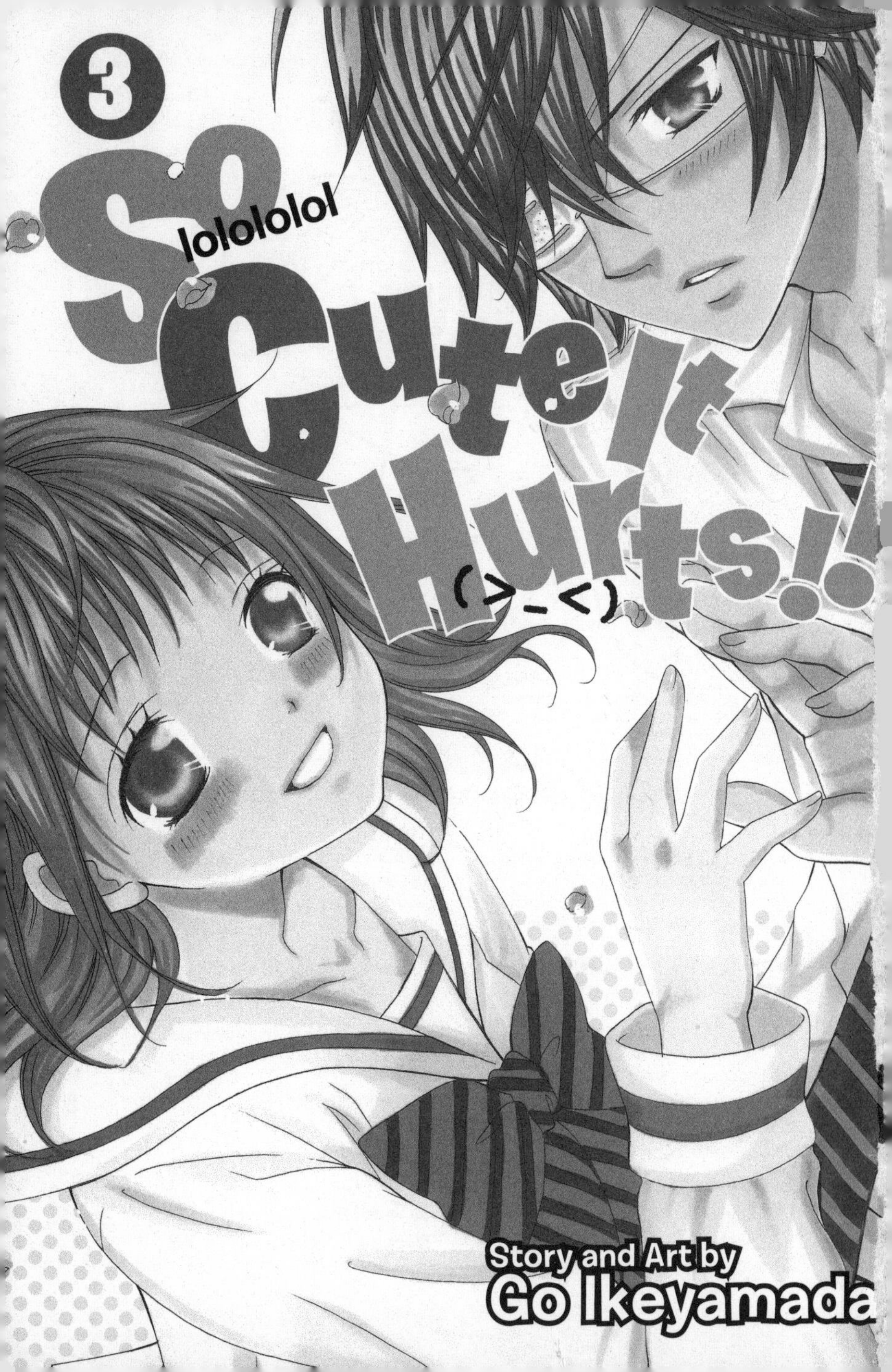
3
So Cute It Hurts!!
lololol
(>_<)
Story and Art by
Go Ikeyamada

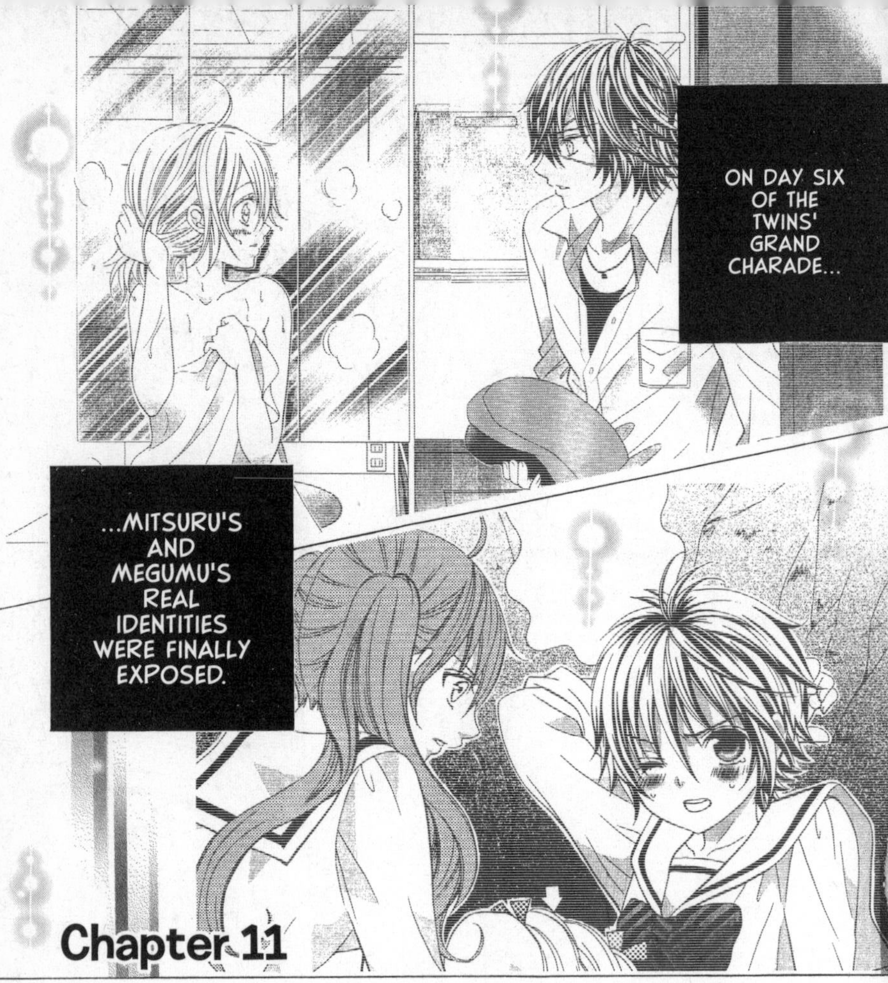
ON DAY SIX OF THE TWINS' GRAND CHARADE...
...MITSURU'S AND MEGUMU'S REAL IDENTITIES WERE FINALLY EXPOSED.

Chapter 11

HELLO.
I'M GO IKEYAMADA.
THANK YOU FOR PICKING UP VOLUME 3 OF *SO CUTE IT HURTS!!*, MY 46TH BOOK IN PRINT!!

THANKS TO EVERYONE, I WAS ABLE TO CELEBRATE MY 11TH YEAR AS A PROFESSIONAL MANGAKA. (*TEARS*) MY SINCERE GRATITUDE TO EVERYONE WHO HAS SUPPORTED ME!! DO KEEP ROOTING FOR ME!!

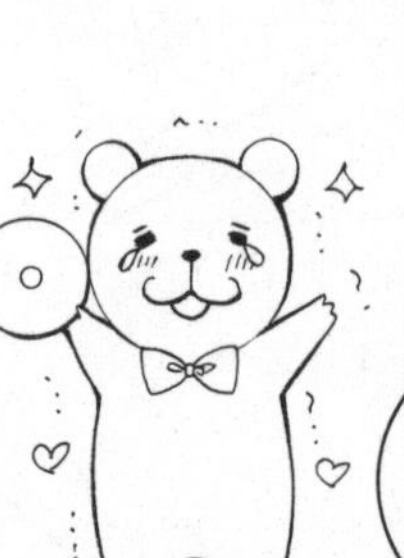

A SPECIAL VERSION OF THIS VOLUME IS ALSO ON SALE! IT COMES WITH **AN ANIME DVD!**
MY HOME IS SHOWN **FOR THE VERY FIRST TIME** IN THE EXTRAS. (*SMILE*)

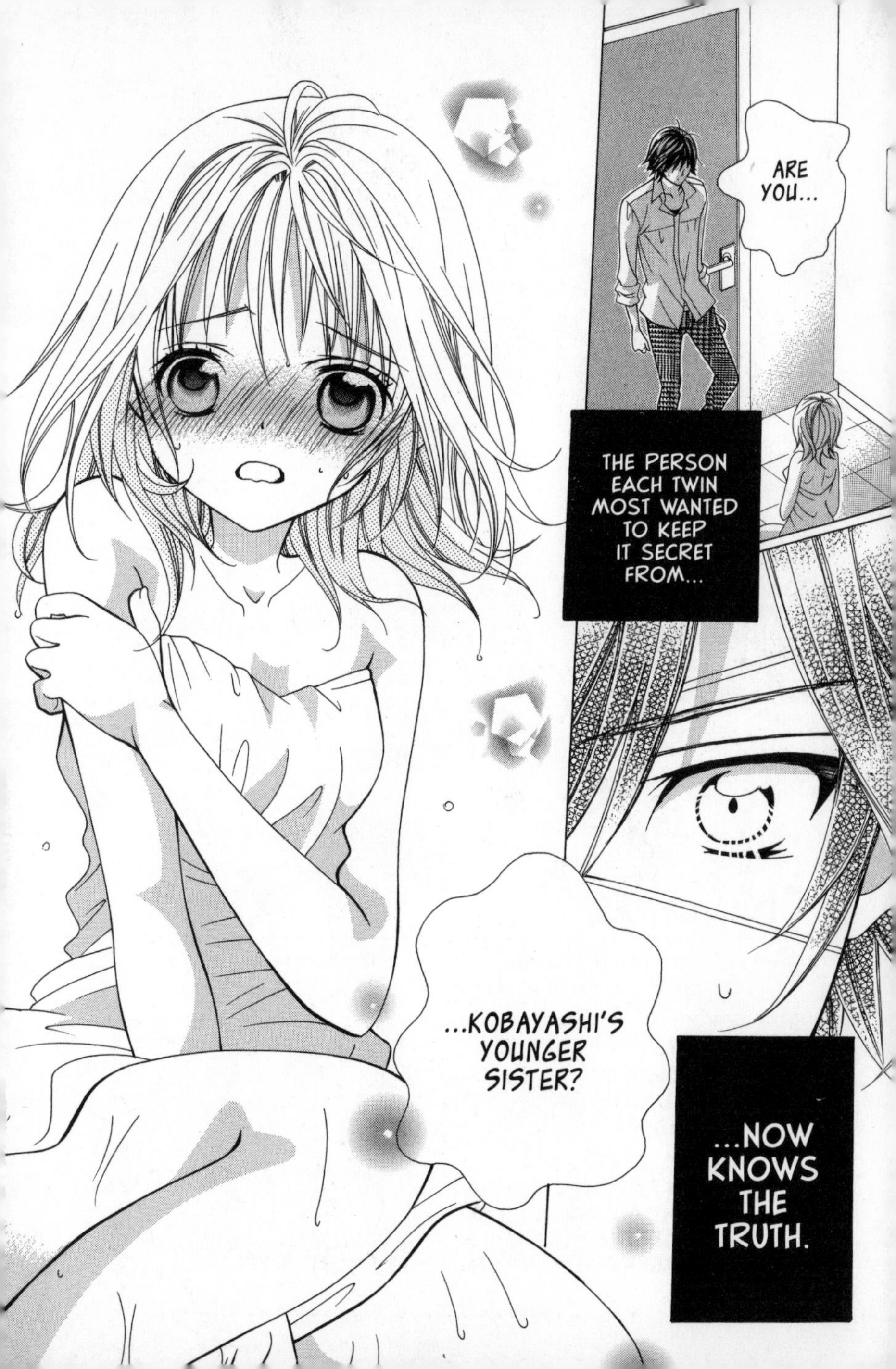
ARE YOU...
THE PERSON EACH TWIN MOST WANTED TO KEEP IT SECRET FROM...
...KOBAYASHI'S YOUNGER SISTER?
...NOW KNOWS THE TRUTH.

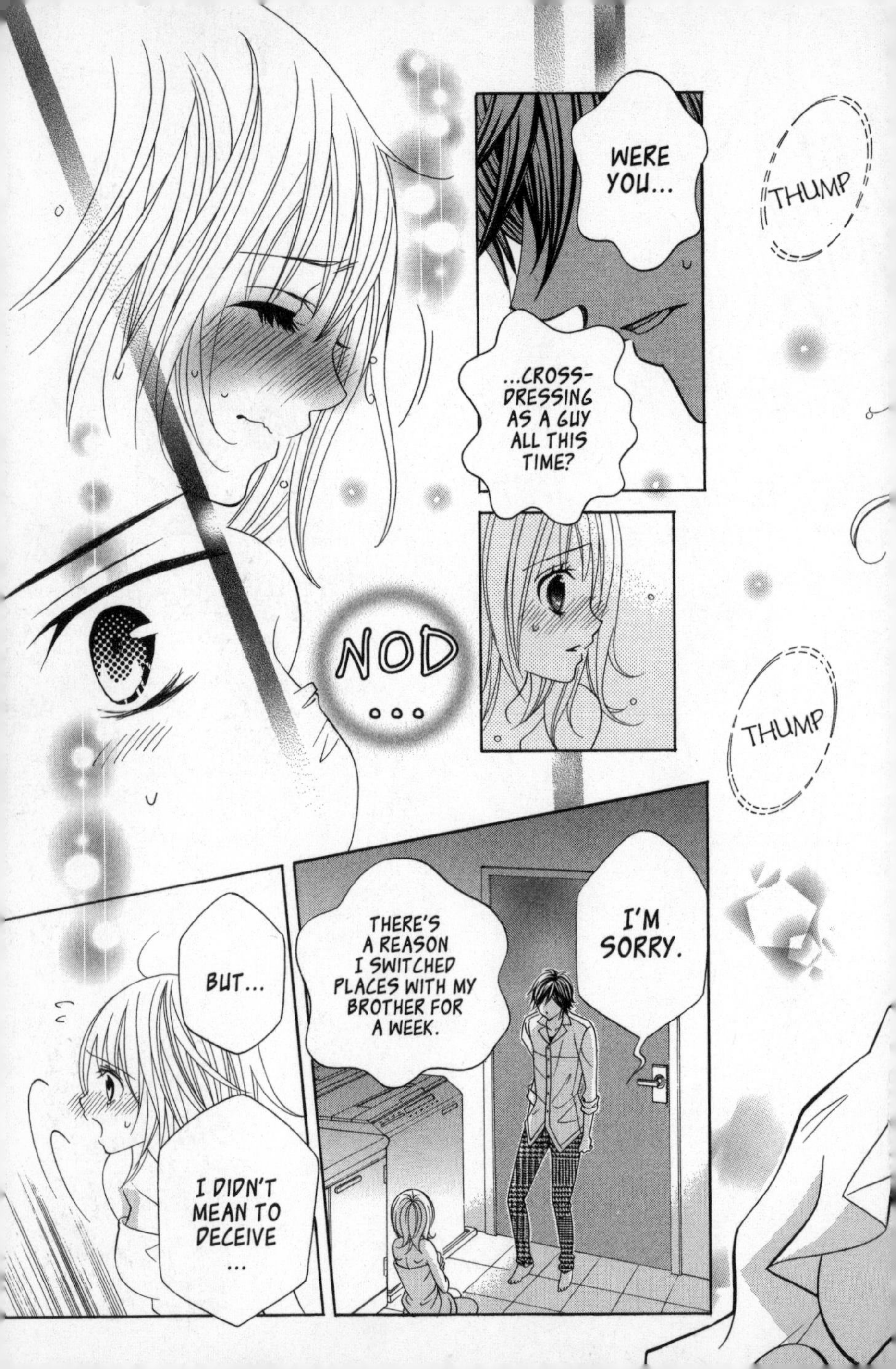
THUMP
WERE YOU...
...CROSS-DRESSING AS A GUY ALL THIS TIME?
THUMP
NOD ...
I'M SORRY.
THERE'S A REASON I SWITCHED PLACES WITH MY BROTHER FOR A WEEK.
BUT...
I DIDN'T MEAN TO DECEIVE ...

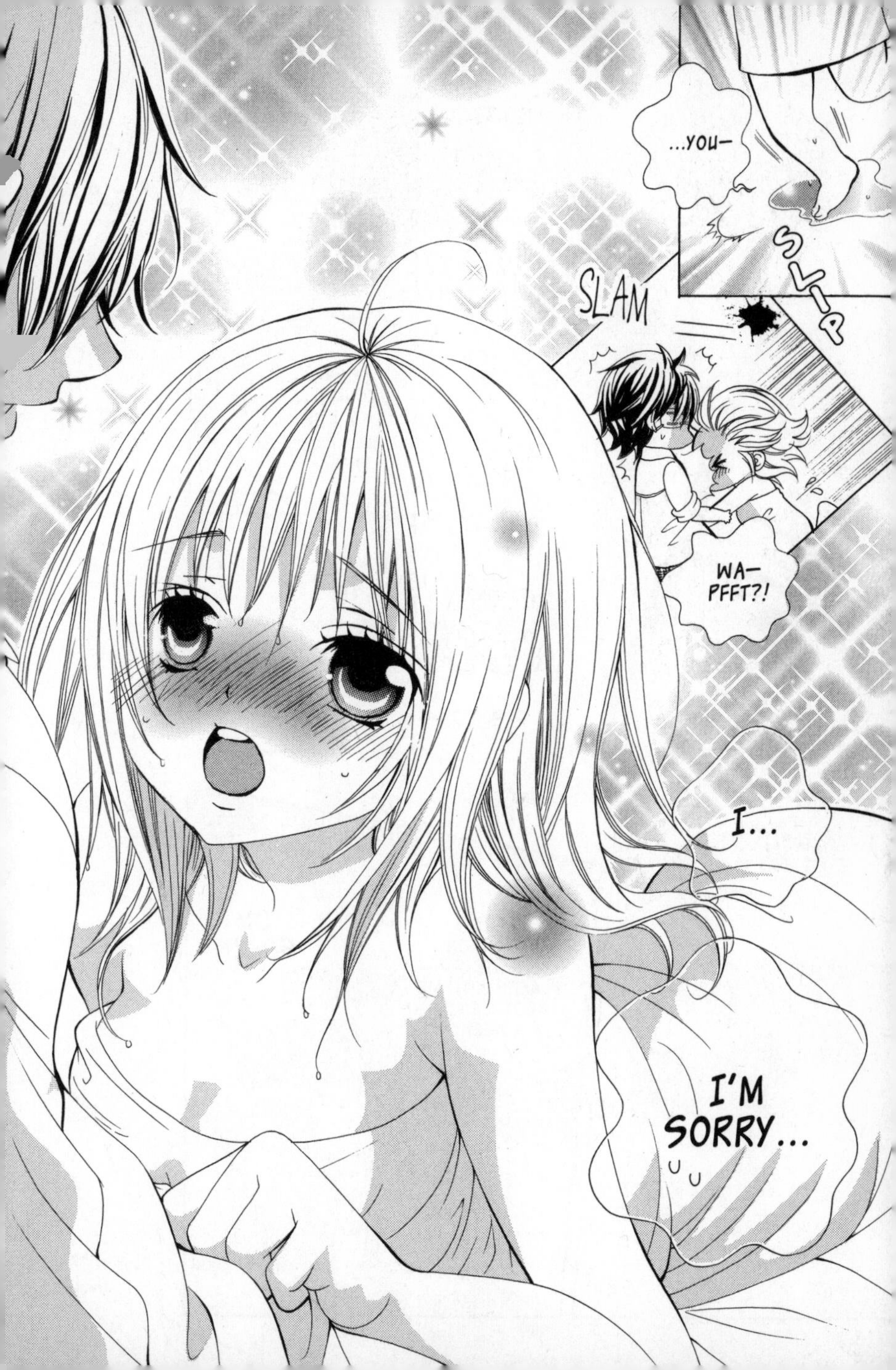
...YOU—
SLIP
SLAM
WA-PFFT?!
I...
I'M SORRY...

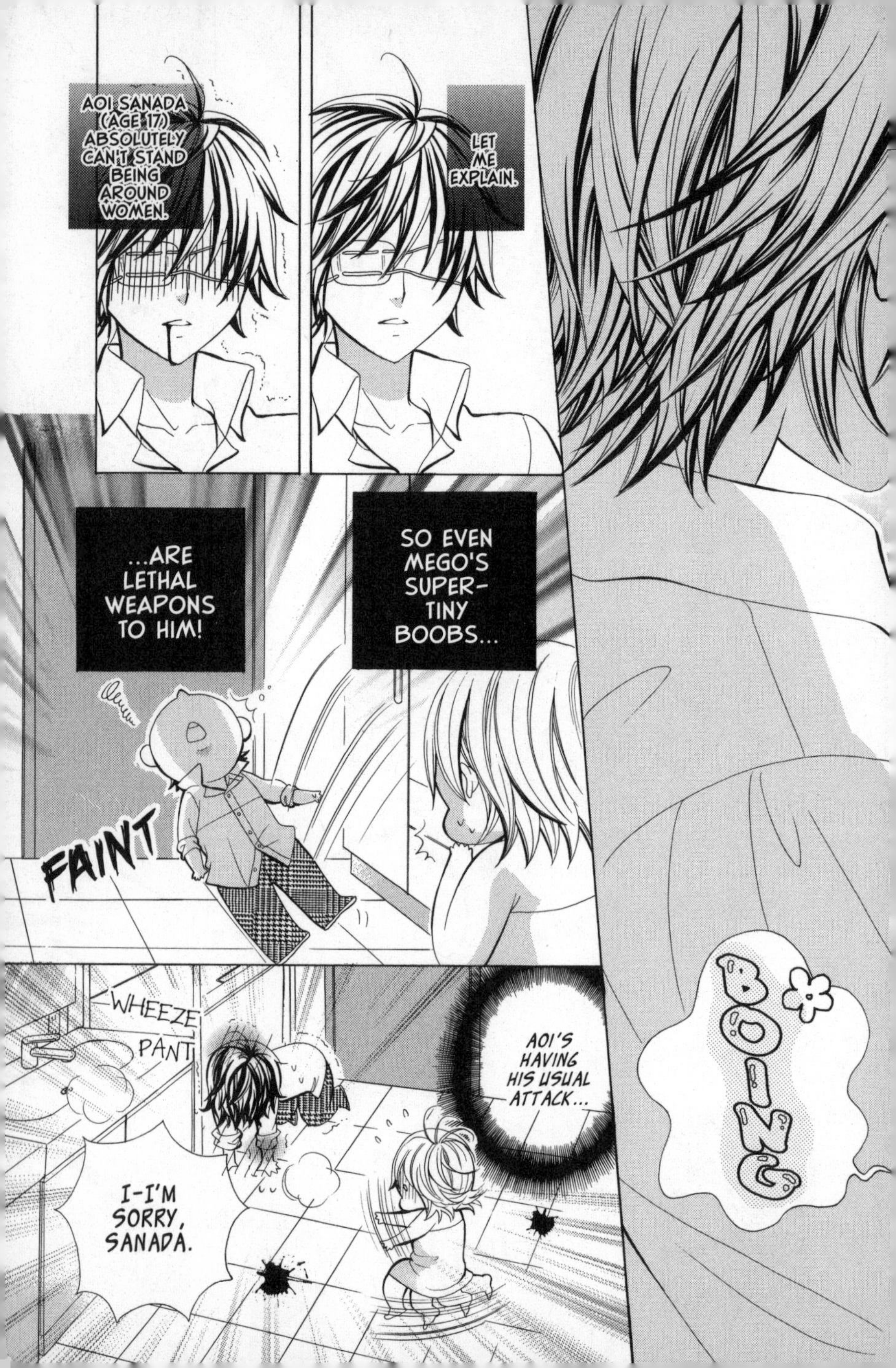
BOING
LET ME EXPLAIN.
AOI SANADA (AGE 17) ABSOLUTELY CAN'T STAND BEING AROUND WOMEN.
SO EVEN MEGO'S SUPER-TINY BOOBS...
...ARE LETHAL WEAPONS TO HIM!
FAINT
AOI'S HAVING HIS USUAL ATTACK...
WHEEZE
PANT
I-I'M SORRY, SANADA.

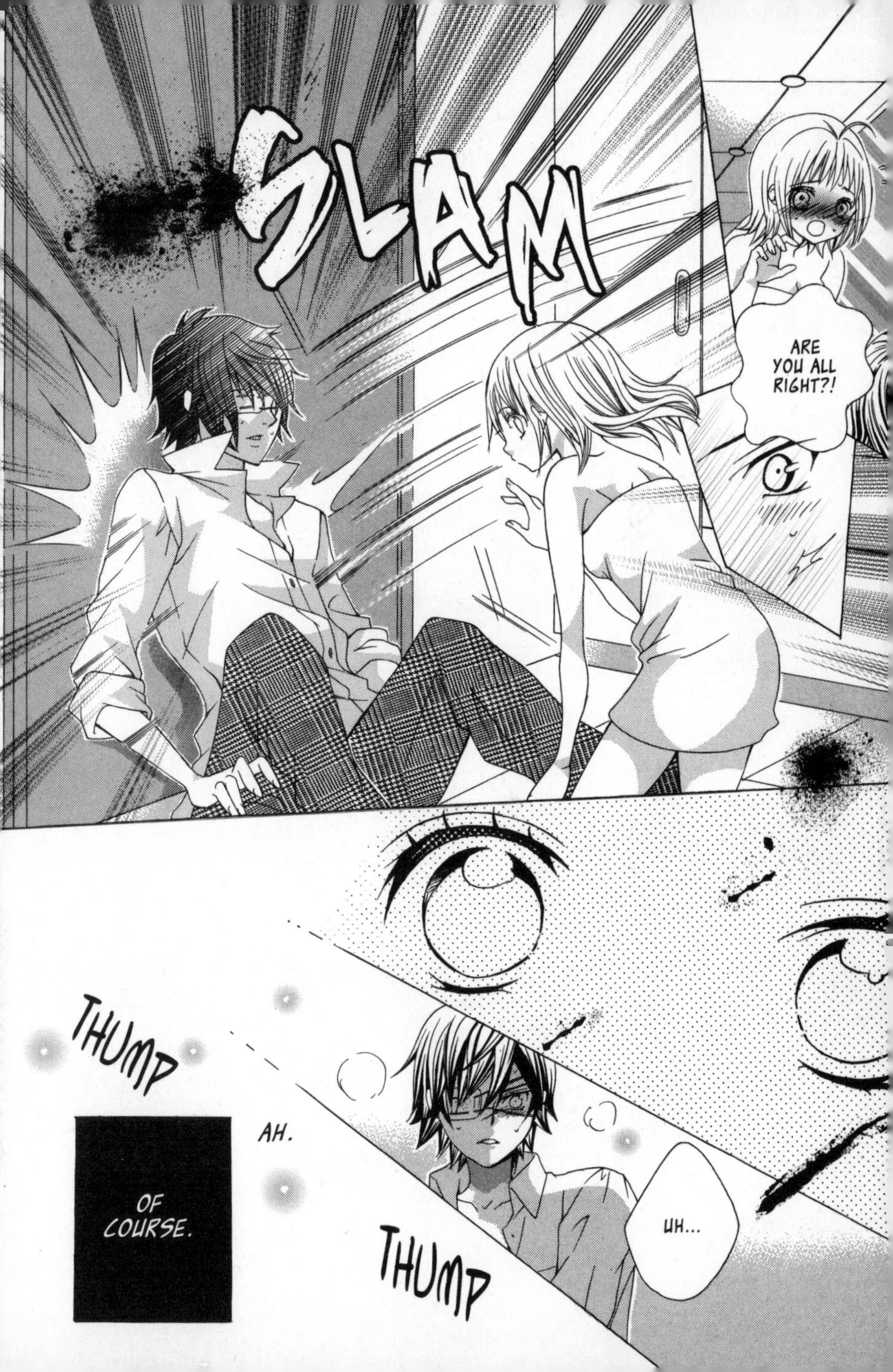
SLAM
ARE YOU ALL RIGHT?!
UH...
THUMP
AH.
THUMP
OF COURSE.

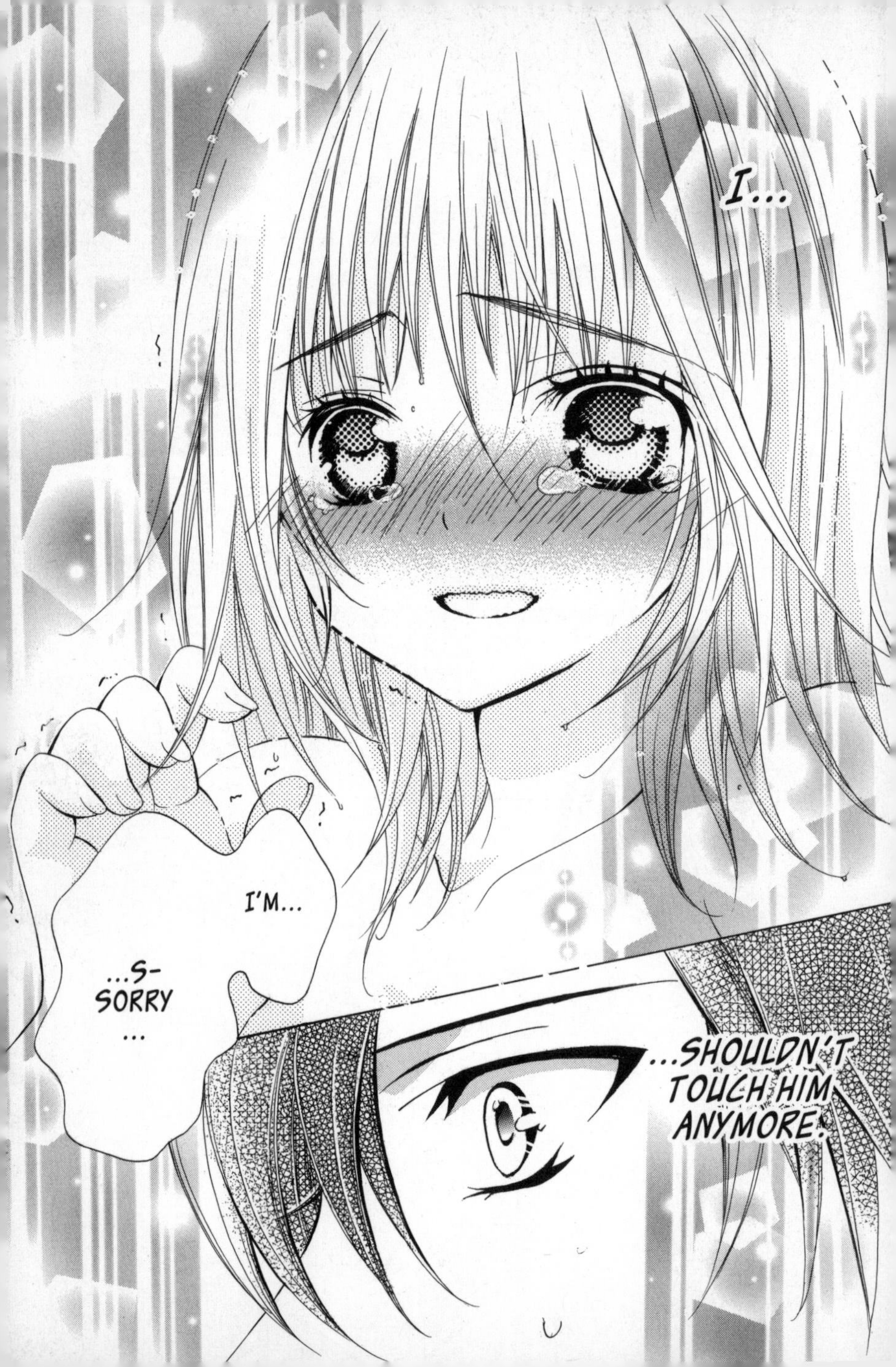
I...
I'M...
...S-SORRY...
...SHOULDN'T TOUCH HIM ANYMORE.

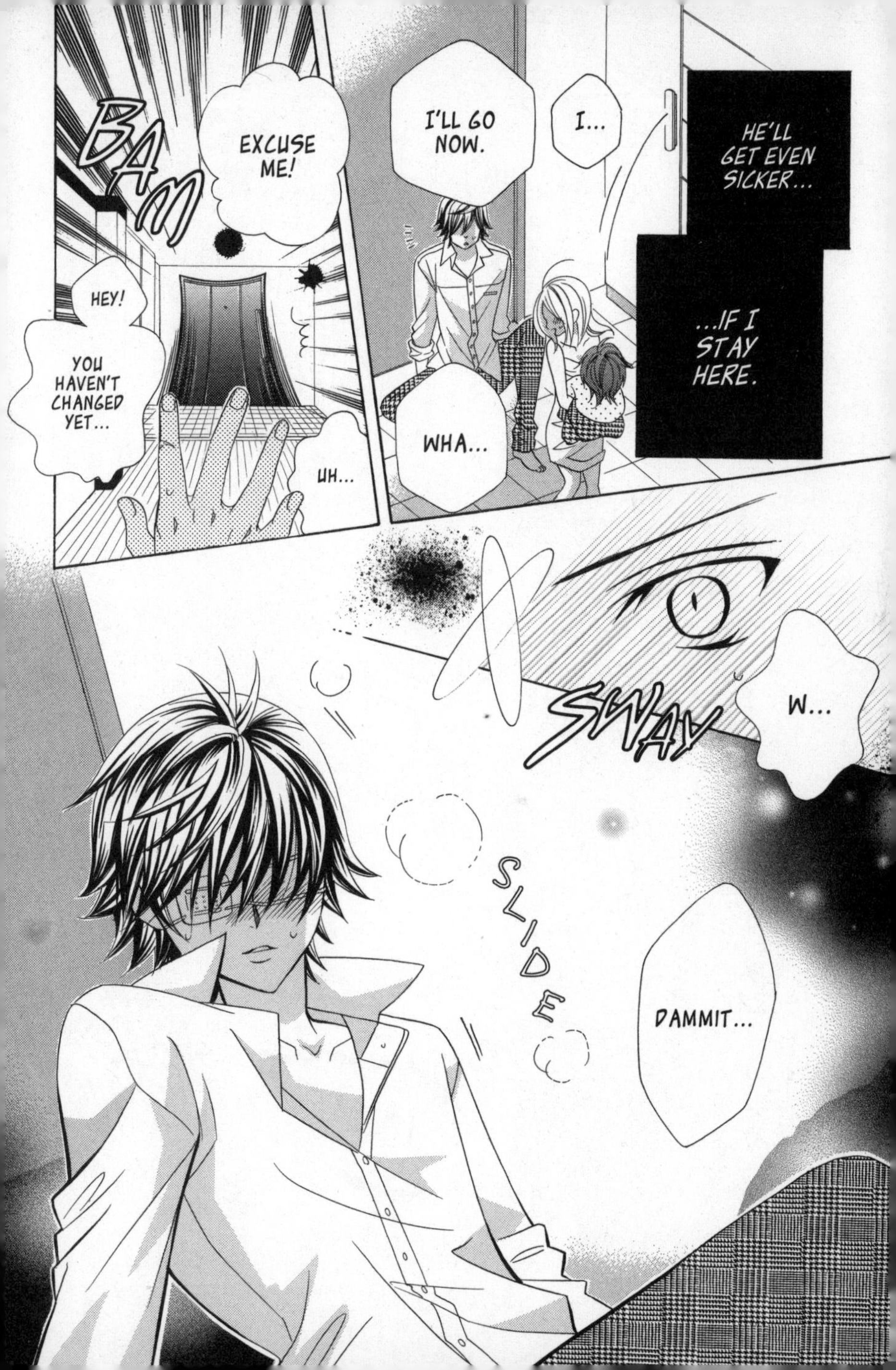
HE'LL GET EVEN SICKER...
I...
I'LL GO NOW.
...IF I STAY HERE.
WHA...
EXCUSE ME!
BAM
HEY!
YOU HAVEN'T CHANGED YET...
UH...
W...
SWAY
SLIDE
DAMMIT...

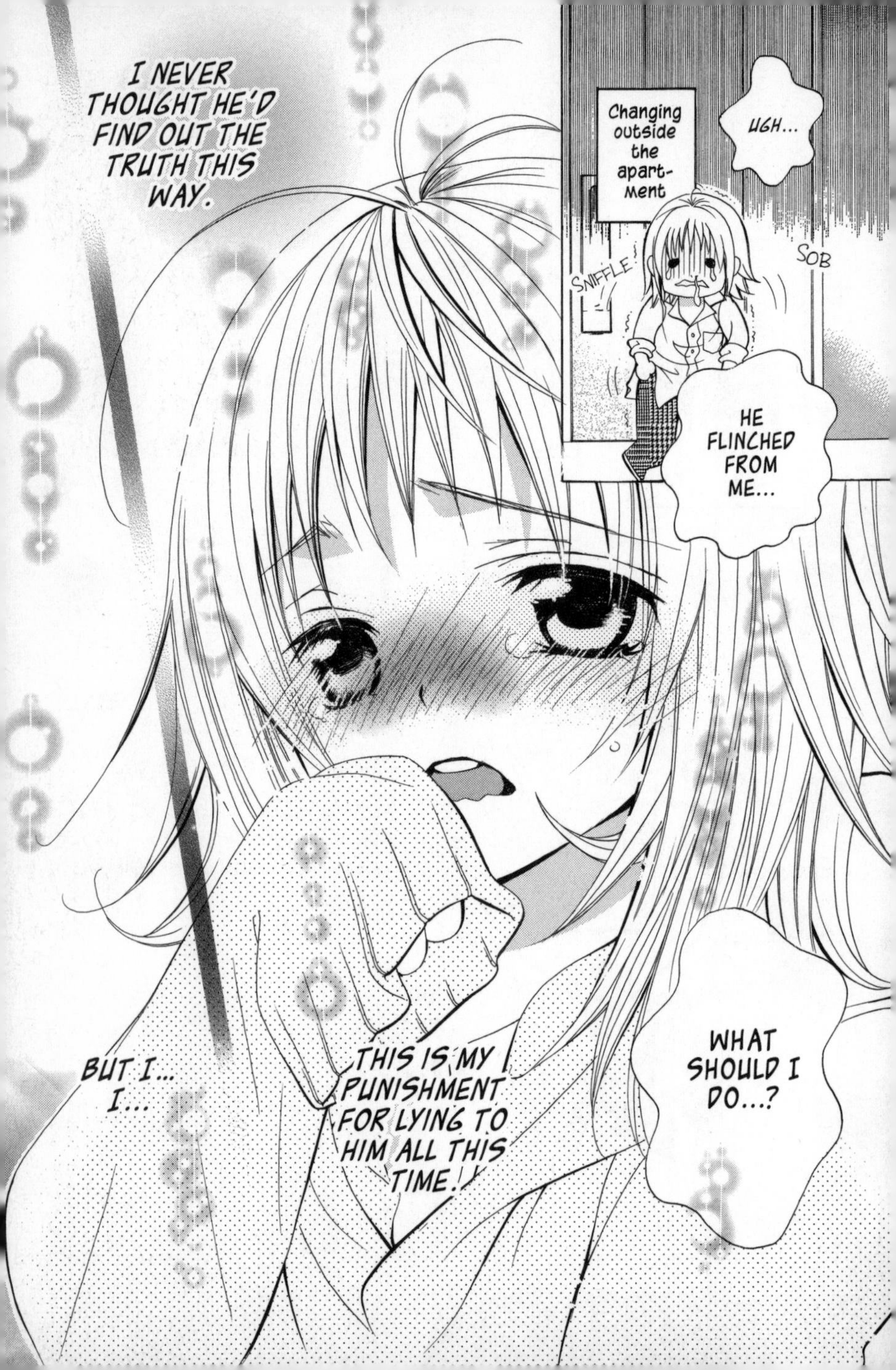
Changing outside the apartment
UGH...
SOB
SNIFFLE
HE FLINCHED FROM ME...
I NEVER THOUGHT HE'D FIND OUT THE TRUTH THIS WAY.
WHAT SHOULD I DO...?
THIS IS MY PUNISHMENT FOR LYING TO HIM ALL THIS TIME.
BUT I... I...

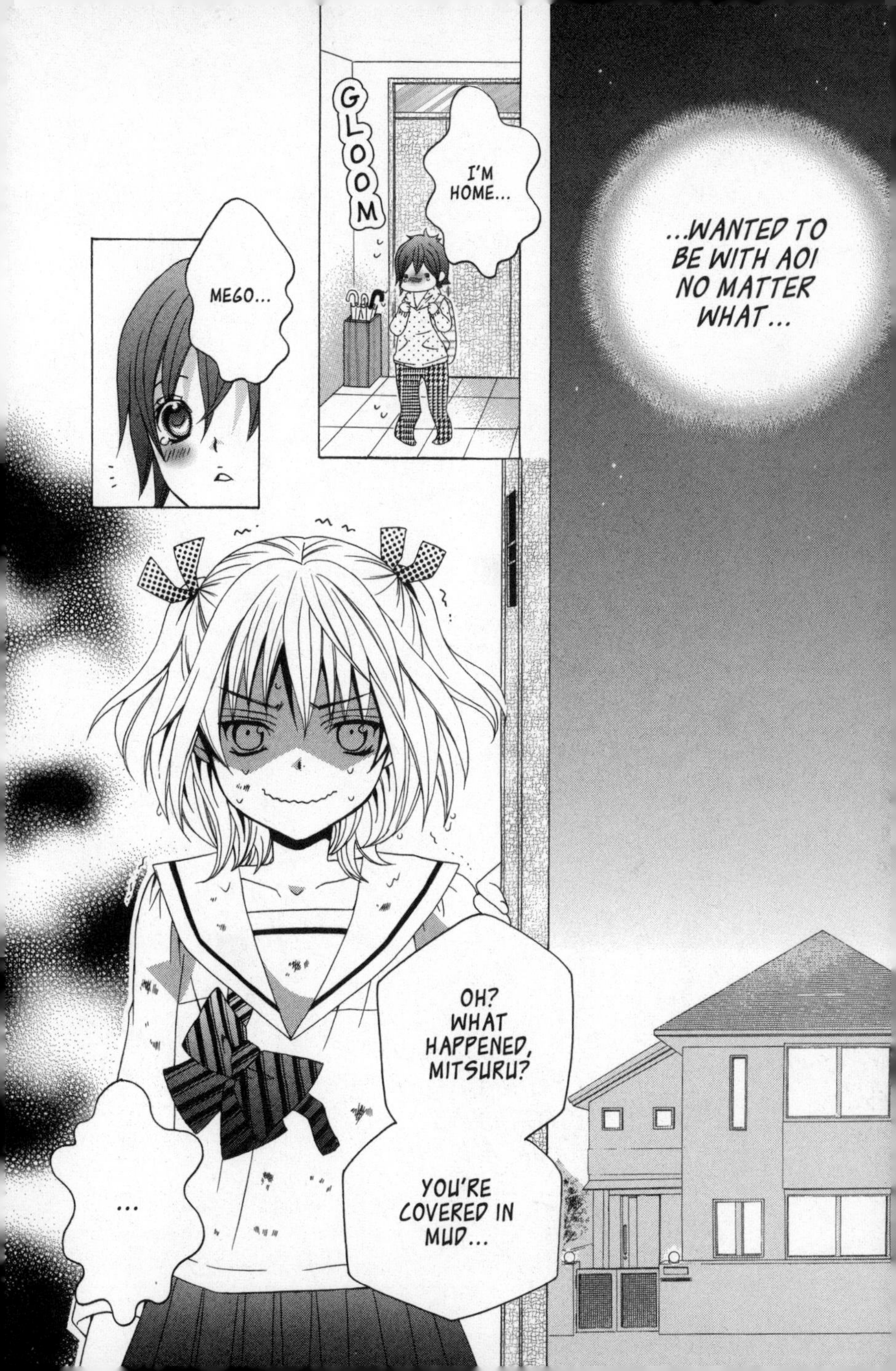
...WANTED TO BE WITH AOI NO MATTER WHAT...
I'M HOME...
GLOOM
MEGO...
OH? WHAT HAPPENED, MITSURU?
YOU'RE COVERED IN MUD...
...

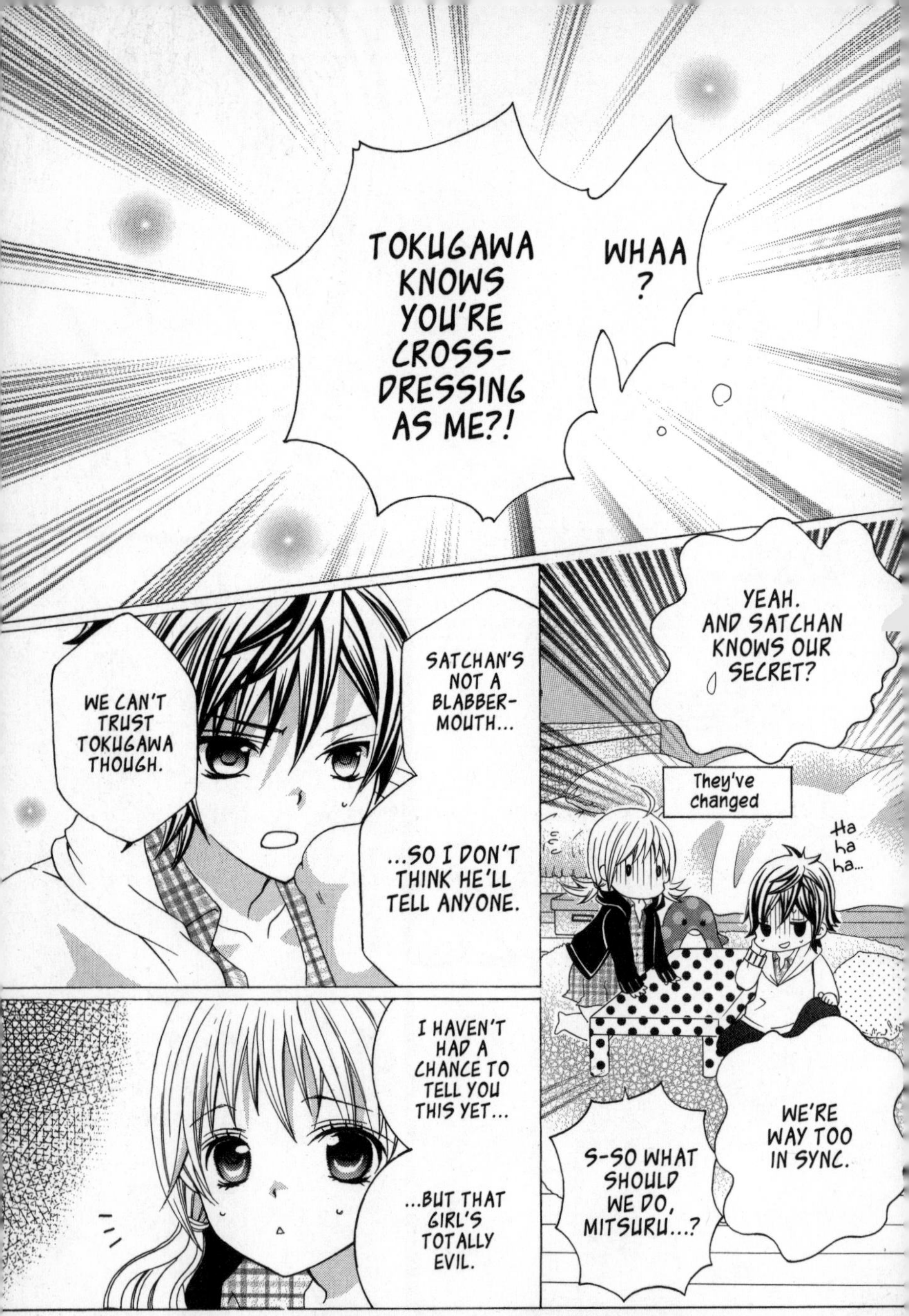
WHAA ?
TOKUGAWA KNOWS YOU'RE CROSS-DRESSING AS ME?!
YEAH. AND SATCHAN KNOWS OUR SECRET?
They've changed
Ha ha ha...
WE'RE WAY TOO IN SYNC.
S-SO WHAT SHOULD WE DO, MITSURU...?
SATCHAN'S NOT A BLABBER-MOUTH...
...SO I DON'T THINK HE'LL TELL ANYONE.
WE CAN'T TRUST TOKUGAWA THOUGH.
I HAVEN'T HAD A CHANCE TO TELL YOU THIS YET...
...BUT THAT GIRL'S TOTALLY EVIL.

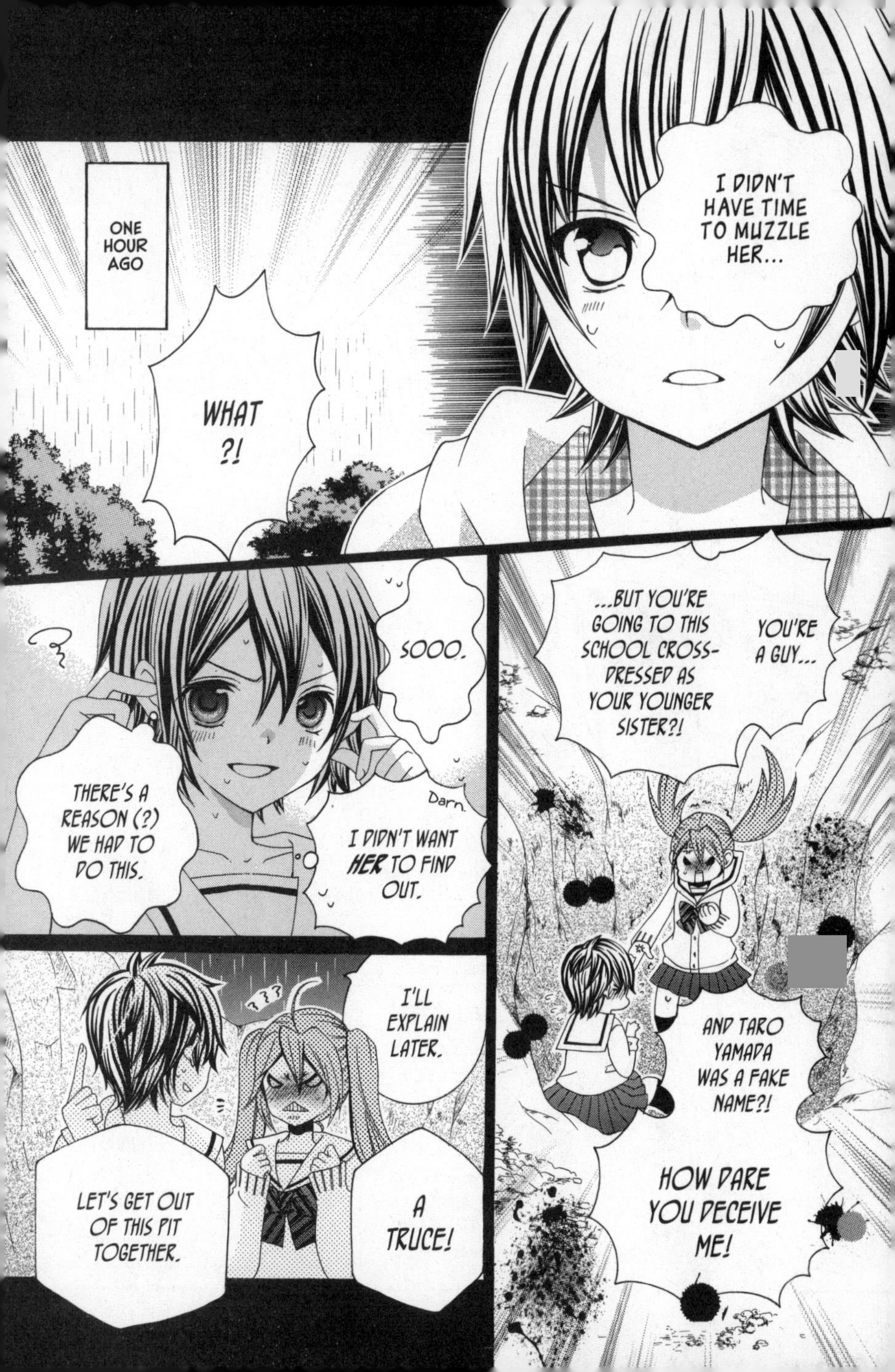
I DIDN'T HAVE TIME TO MUZZLE HER...
ONE HOUR AGO
WHAT ?!
YOU'RE A GUY...
...BUT YOU'RE GOING TO THIS SCHOOL CROSS-DRESSED AS YOUR YOUNGER SISTER?!
AND TARO YAMADA WAS A FAKE NAME?!
HOW DARE YOU DECEIVE ME!
SOOO.
Darn.
I DIDN'T WANT HER TO FIND OUT.
THERE'S A REASON (?) WE HAD TO DO THIS.
I'LL EXPLAIN LATER.
A TRUCE!
LET'S GET OUT OF THIS PIT TOGETHER.

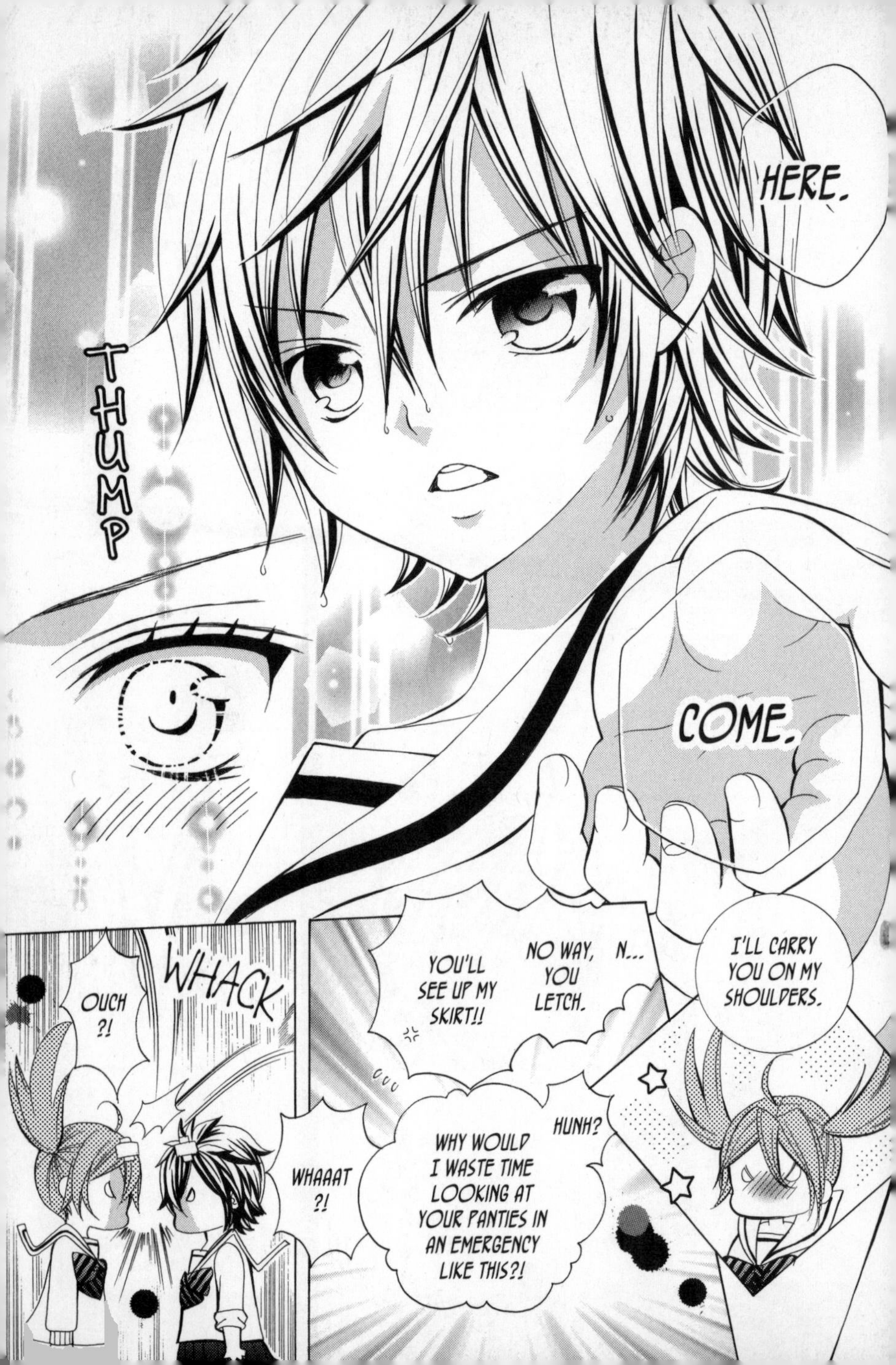
HERE.
COME.
THUMP
I'LL CARRY YOU ON MY SHOULDERS.
N...
NO WAY, YOU LETCH.
YOU'LL SEE UP MY SKIRT!!
HUNH?
WHY WOULD I WASTE TIME LOOKING AT YOUR PANTIES IN AN EMERGENCY LIKE THIS?!
WHAAAT ?!
WHACK
OUCH ?!

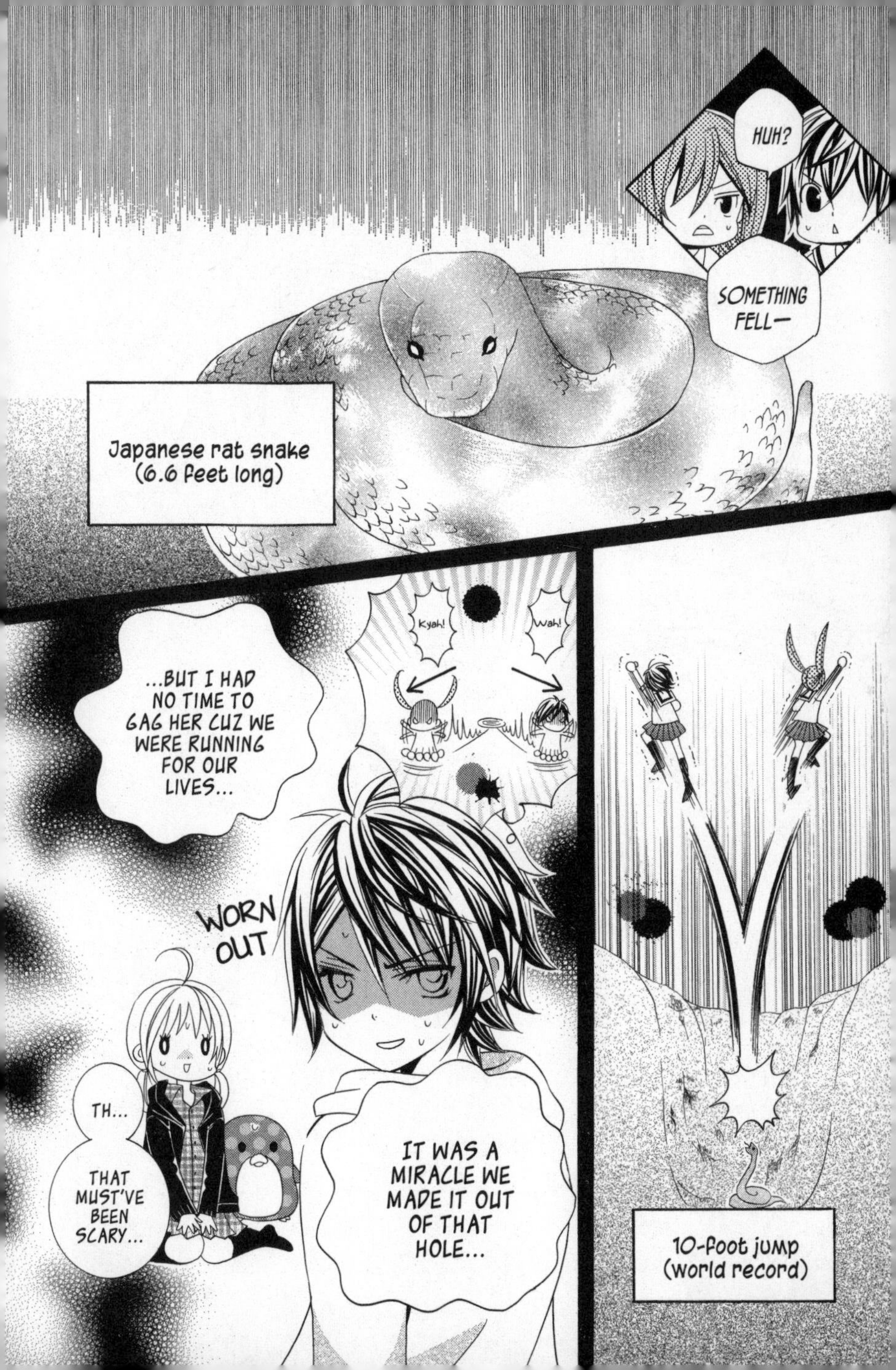
HUH?
SOMETHING FELL—
Japanese rat snake (6.6 feet long)
10-foot jump (world record)
Wah!
Kyah!
...BUT I HAD NO TIME TO GAG HER CUZ WE WERE RUNNING FOR OUR LIVES...
IT WAS A MIRACLE WE MADE IT OUT OF THAT HOLE...
WORN OUT
TH...
THAT MUST'VE BEEN SCARY...

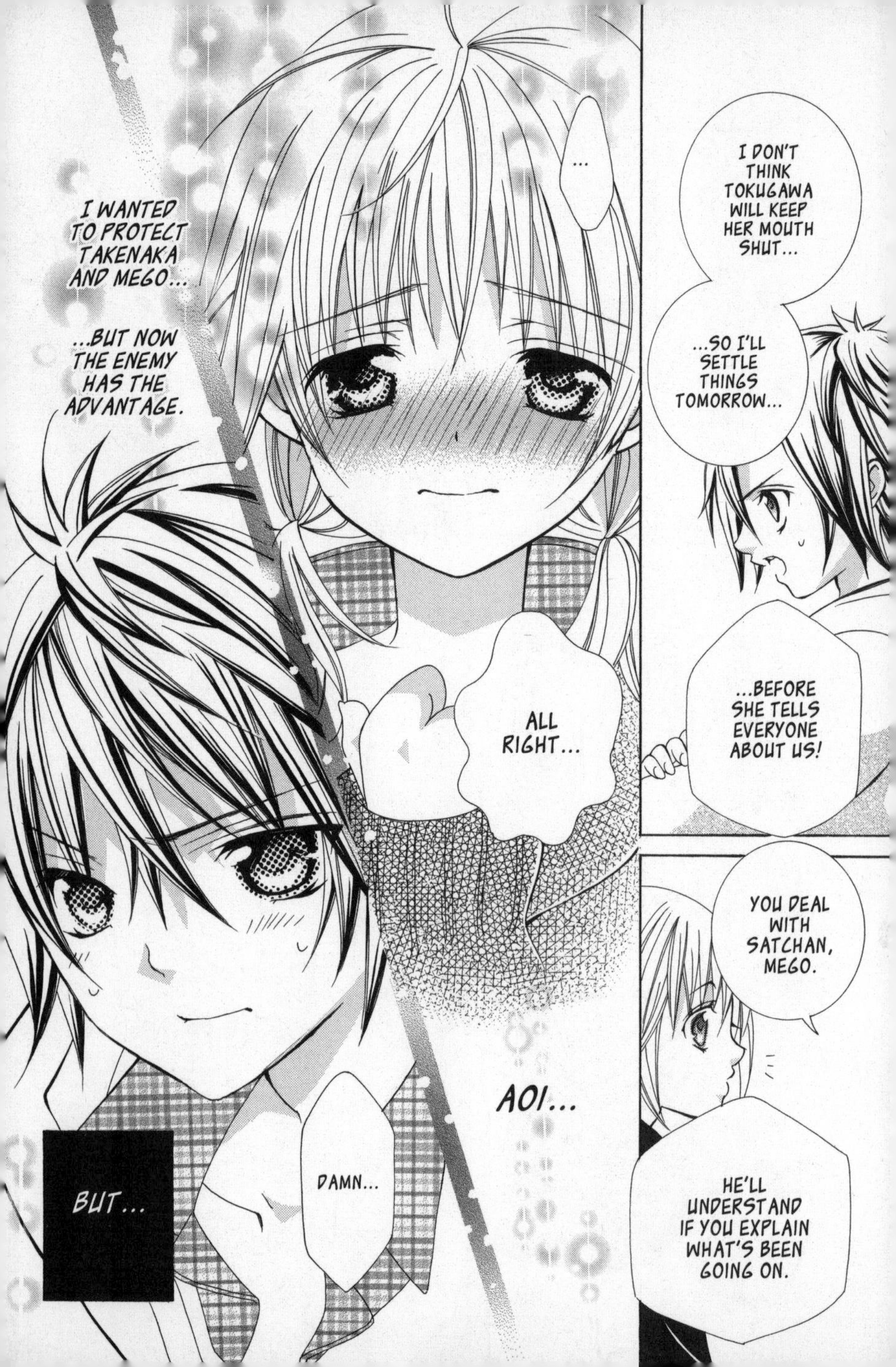
I DON'T THINK TOKUGAWA WILL KEEP HER MOUTH SHUT...
...SO I'LL SETTLE THINGS TOMORROW...
...BEFORE SHE TELLS EVERYONE ABOUT US!
YOU DEAL WITH SATCHAN, MEGO.
HE'LL UNDERSTAND IF YOU EXPLAIN WHAT'S BEEN GOING ON.
...
I WANTED TO PROTECT TAKENAKA AND MEGO...
...BUT NOW THE ENEMY HAS THE ADVANTAGE.
ALL RIGHT...
AOI...
DAMN...
BUT...

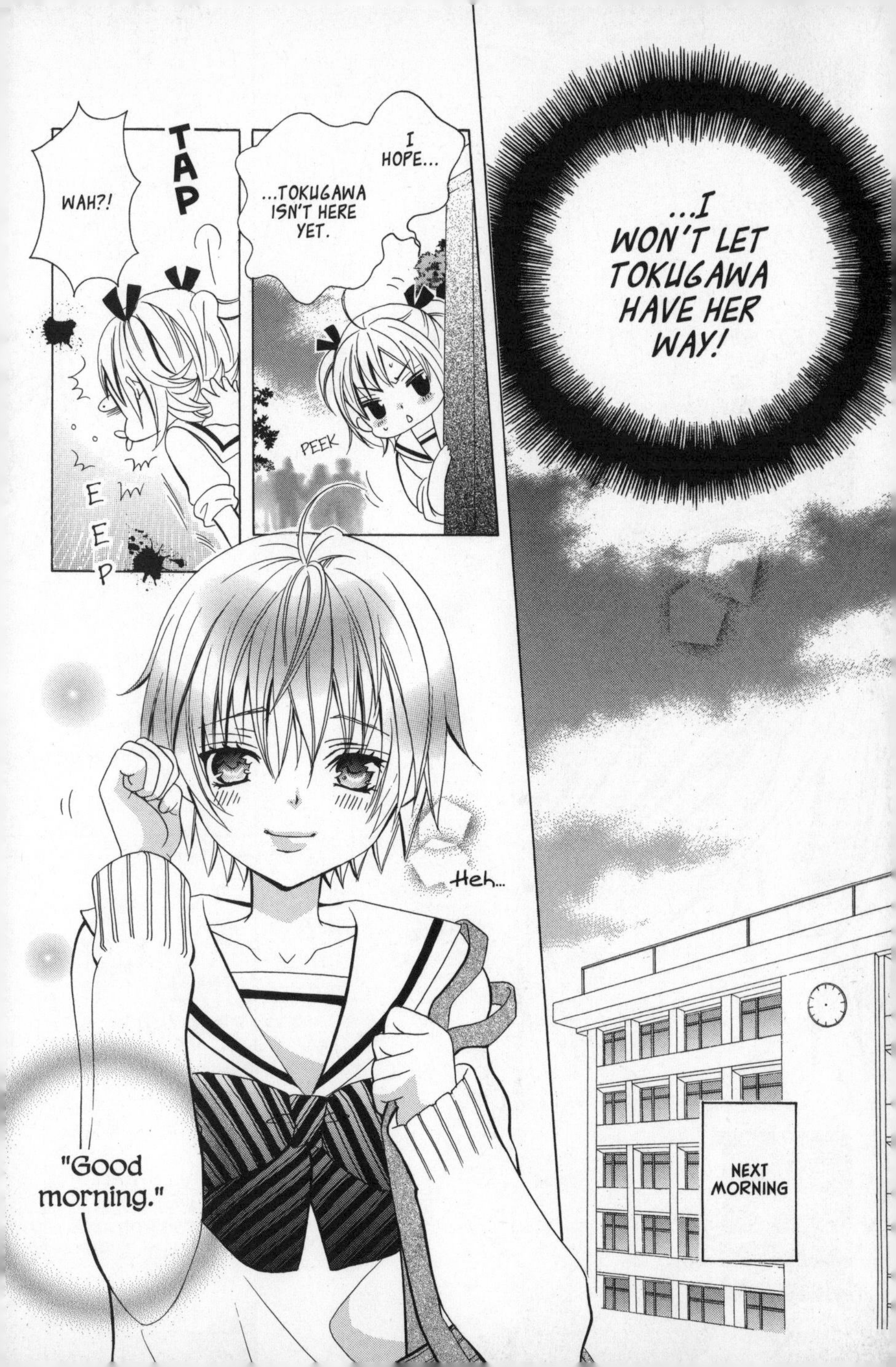
...I WON'T LET TOKUGAWA HAVE HER WAY!
NEXT MORNING
I HOPE...
...TOKUGAWA ISN'T HERE YET.
PEEK
TAP
WAH?!
EEEP
Heh...
"Good morning."

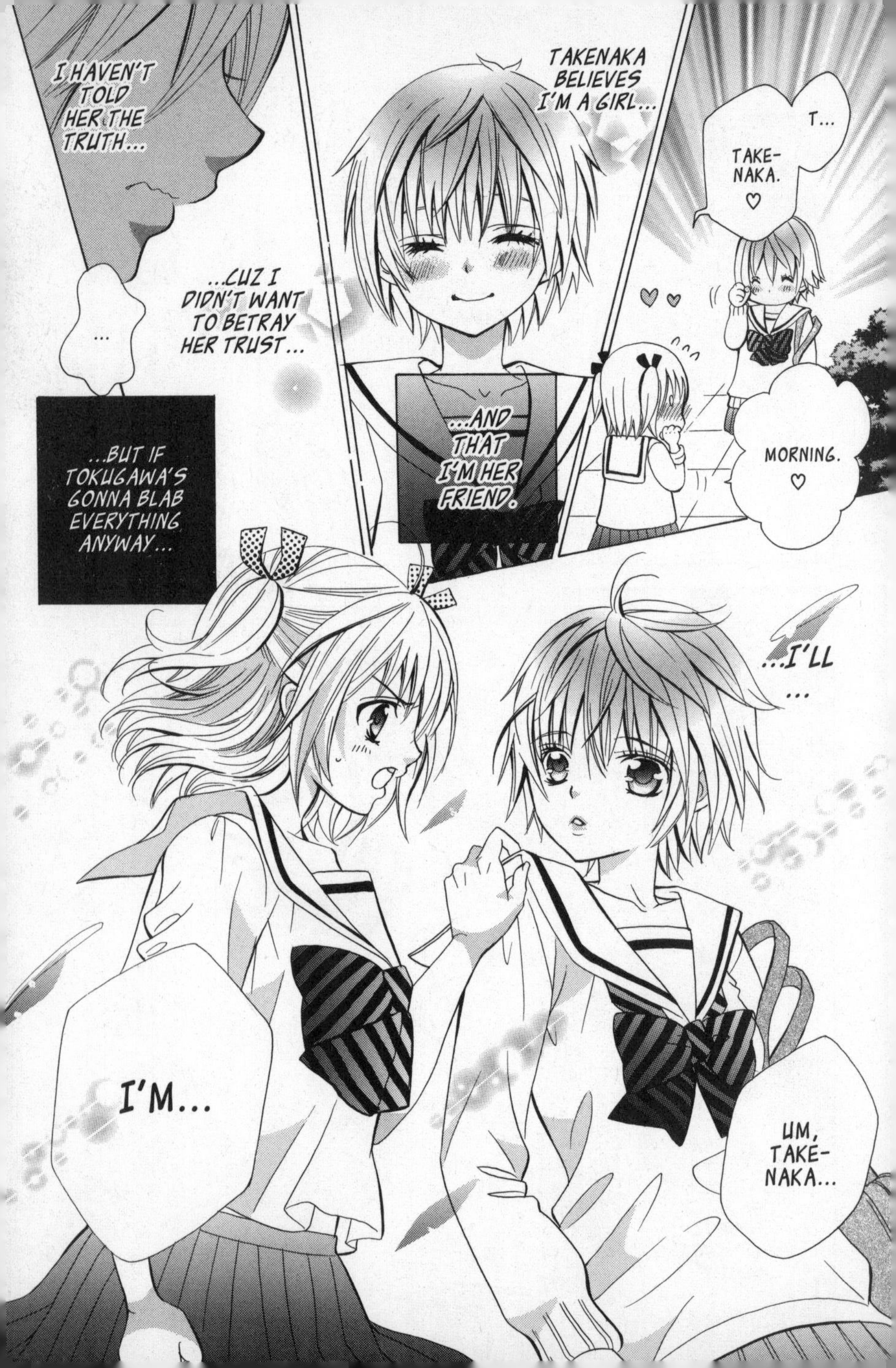
T...
TAKE-NAKA. ♡
MORNING. ♡
TAKENAKA BELIEVES I'M A GIRL...
...AND THAT I'M HER FRIEND.
I HAVEN'T TOLD HER THE TRUTH...
...CUZ I DIDN'T WANT TO BETRAY HER TRUST...
...
...BUT IF TOKUGAWA'S GONNA BLAB EVERYTHING ANYWAY...
...I'LL ...
UM, TAKE-NAKA...
I'M...

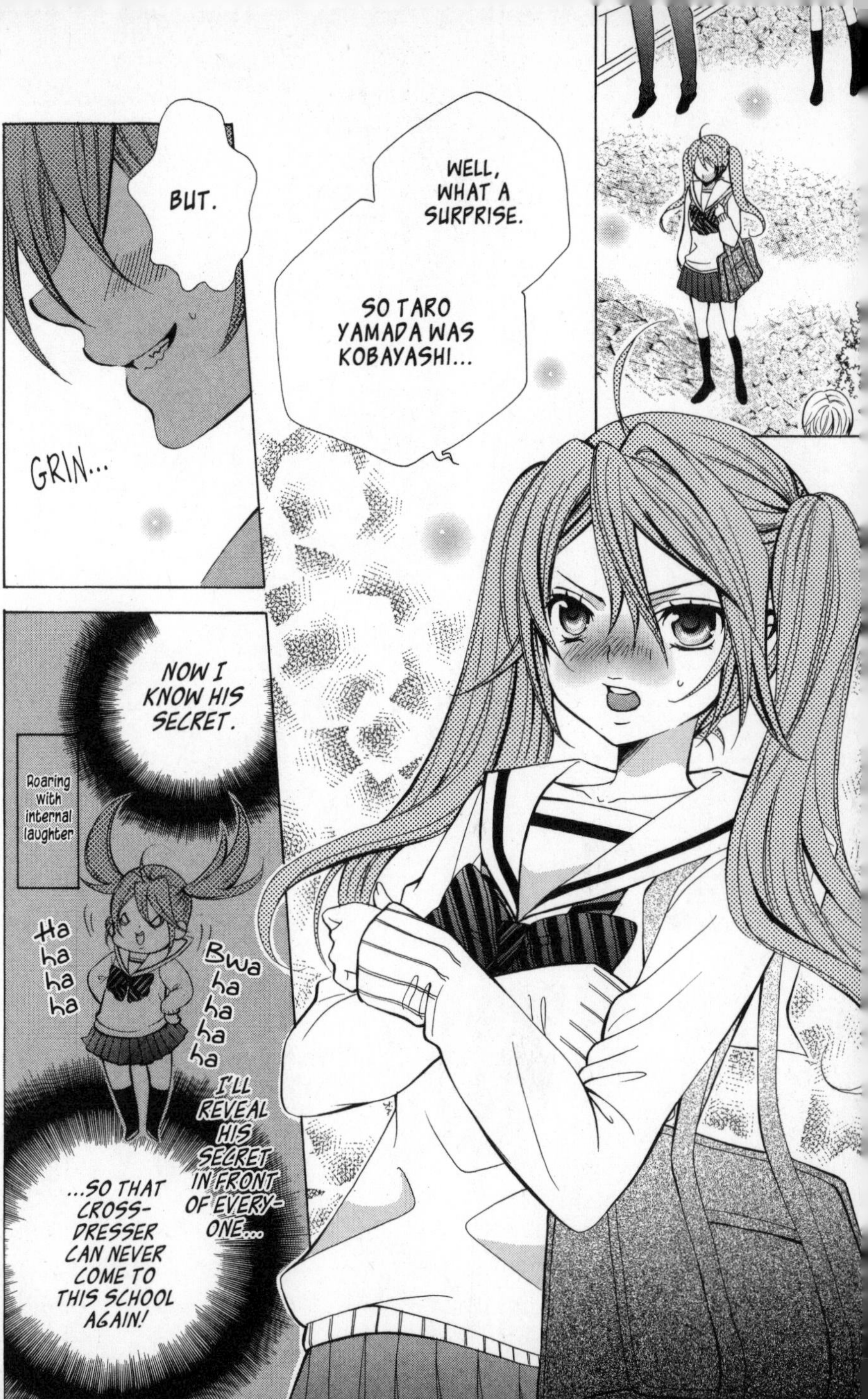
WELL, WHAT A SURPRISE.
SO TARO YAMADA WAS KOBAYASHI...
BUT.
GRIN...
NOW I KNOW HIS SECRET.
Roaring with internal laughter
Bwa ha ha ha ha ha
Ha ha ha ha
I'LL REVEAL HIS SECRET IN FRONT OF EVERY-ONE...
...SO THAT CROSS-DRESSER CAN NEVER COME TO THIS SCHOOL AGAIN!

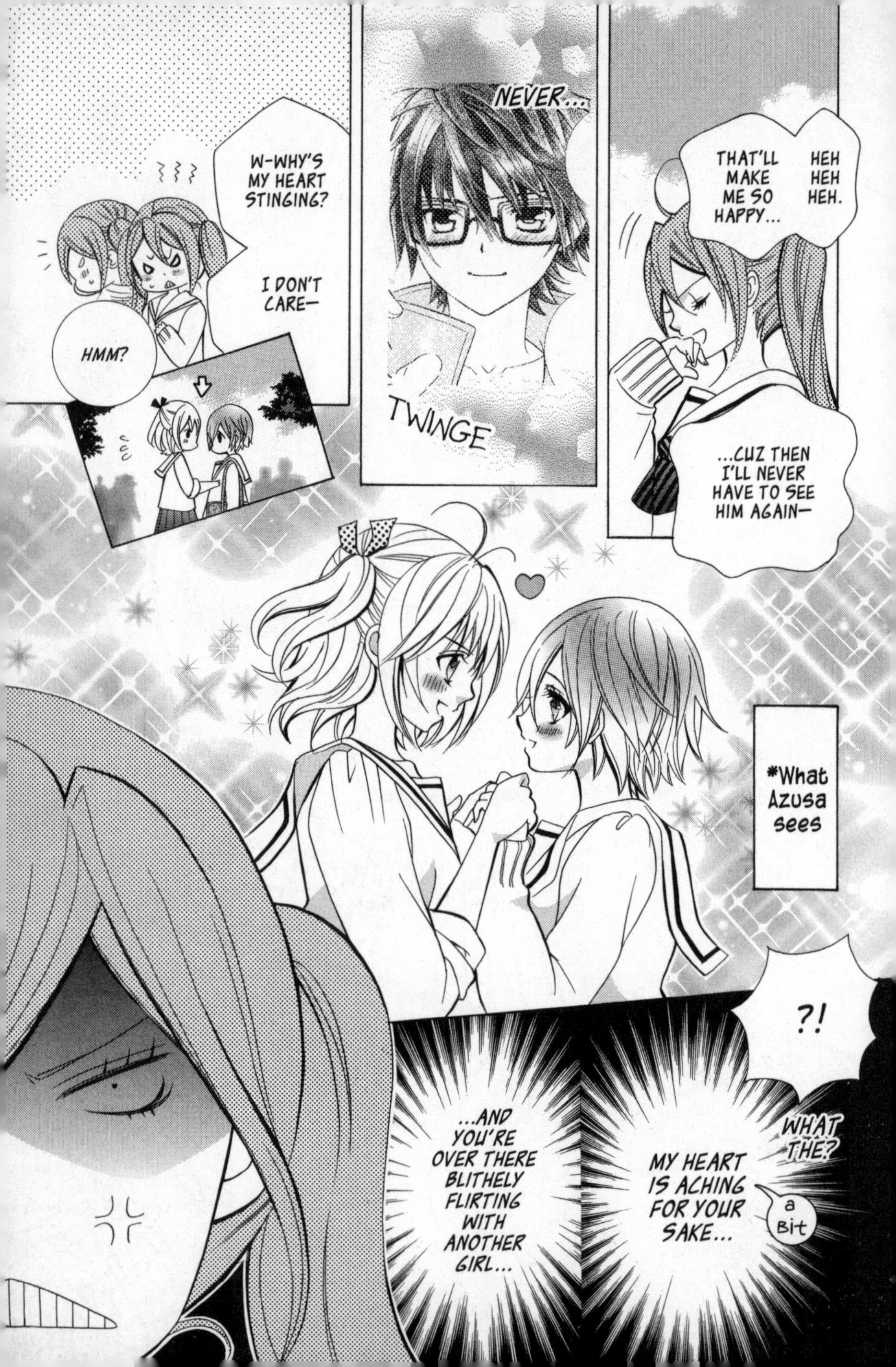
HEH HEH HEH.
THAT'LL MAKE ME SO HAPPY...
...CUZ THEN I'LL NEVER HAVE TO SEE HIM AGAIN—
NEVER...
TWINGE
W-WHY'S MY HEART STINGING?
I DON'T CARE—
HMM?
*What Azusa sees
?!
WHAT THE?
MY HEART IS ACHING FOR YOUR SAKE...
a Bit
...AND YOU'RE OVER THERE BLITHELY FLIRTING WITH ANOTHER GIRL...

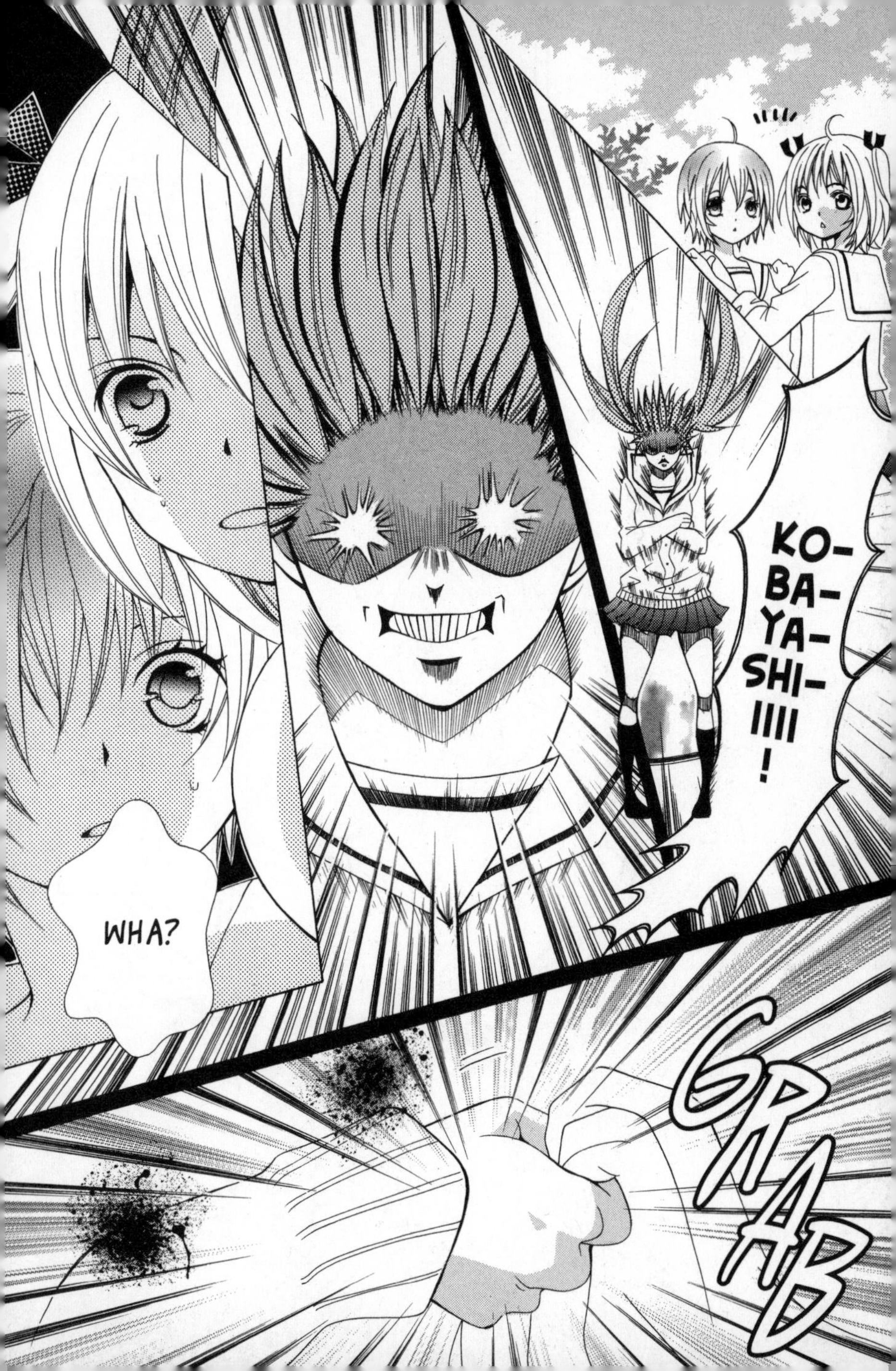
KO-BA-YA-SHI-IIIII!
WHA?
GRAB

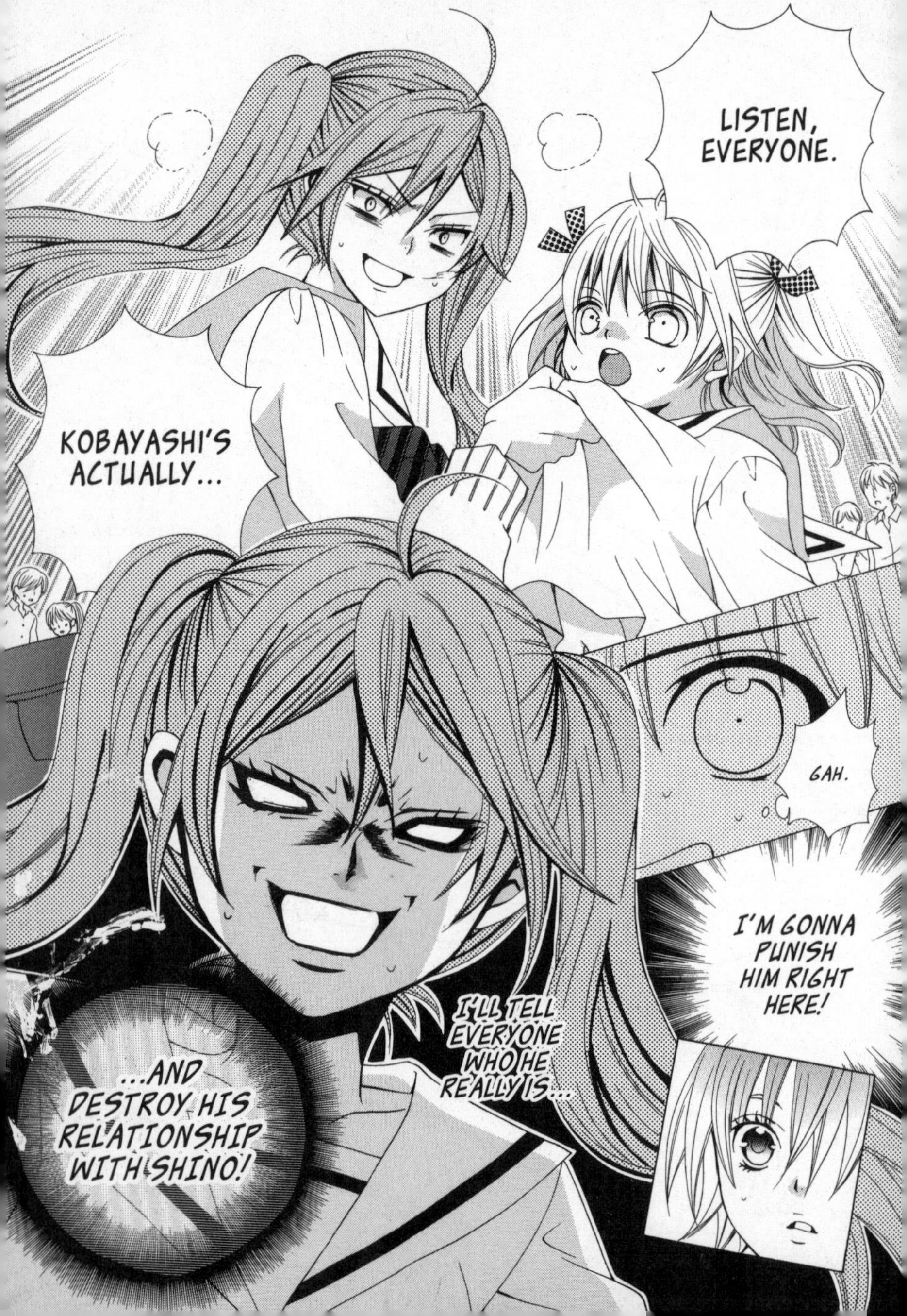
LISTEN, EVERYONE.
KOBAYASHI'S ACTUALLY...
GAH.
I'M GONNA PUNISH HIM RIGHT HERE!
I'LL TELL EVERYONE WHO HE REALLY IS...
...AND DESTROY HIS RELATIONSHIP WITH SHINO!

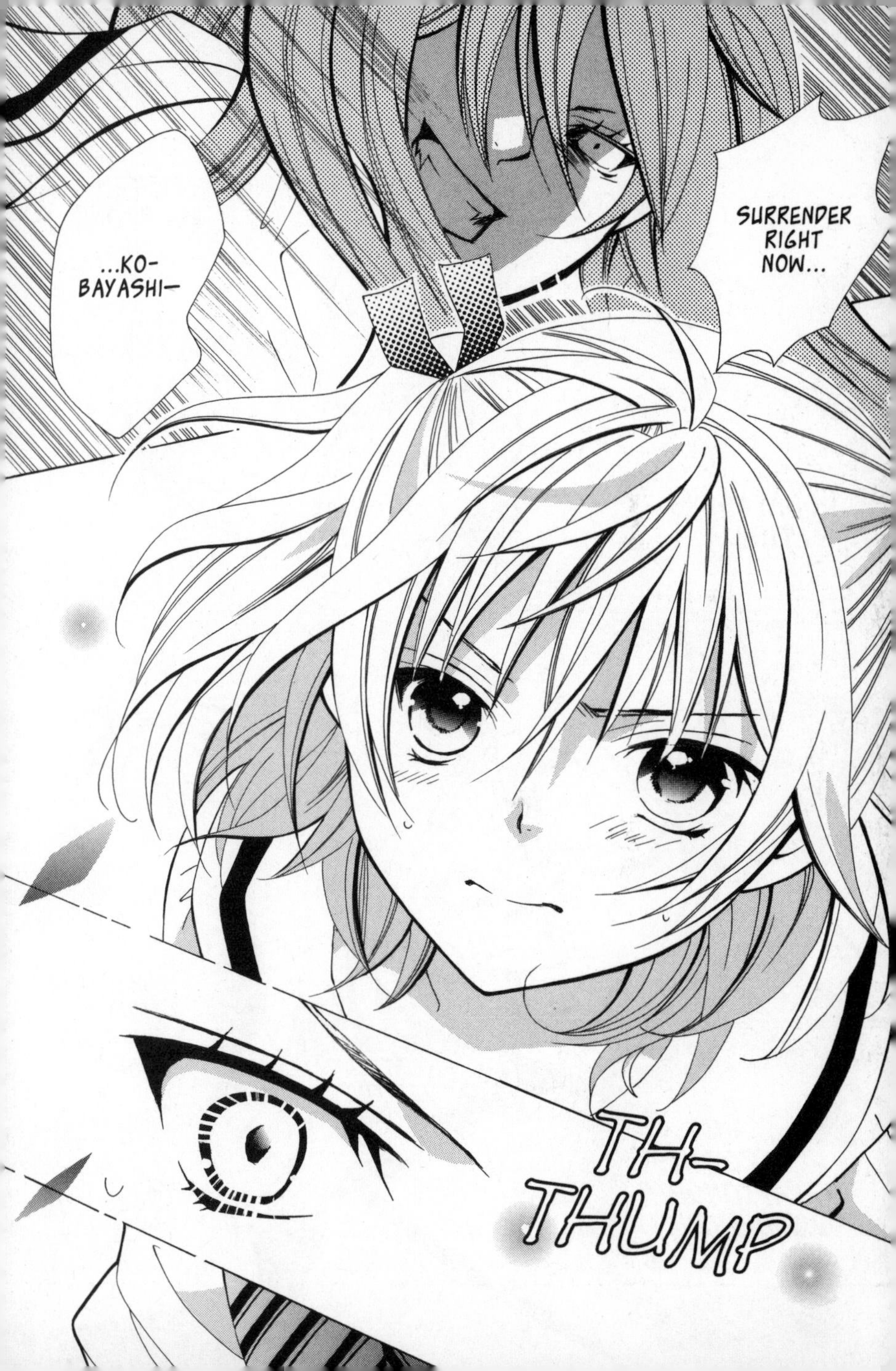
SURRENDER RIGHT NOW...
...KO-BAYASHI—
TH-THUMP

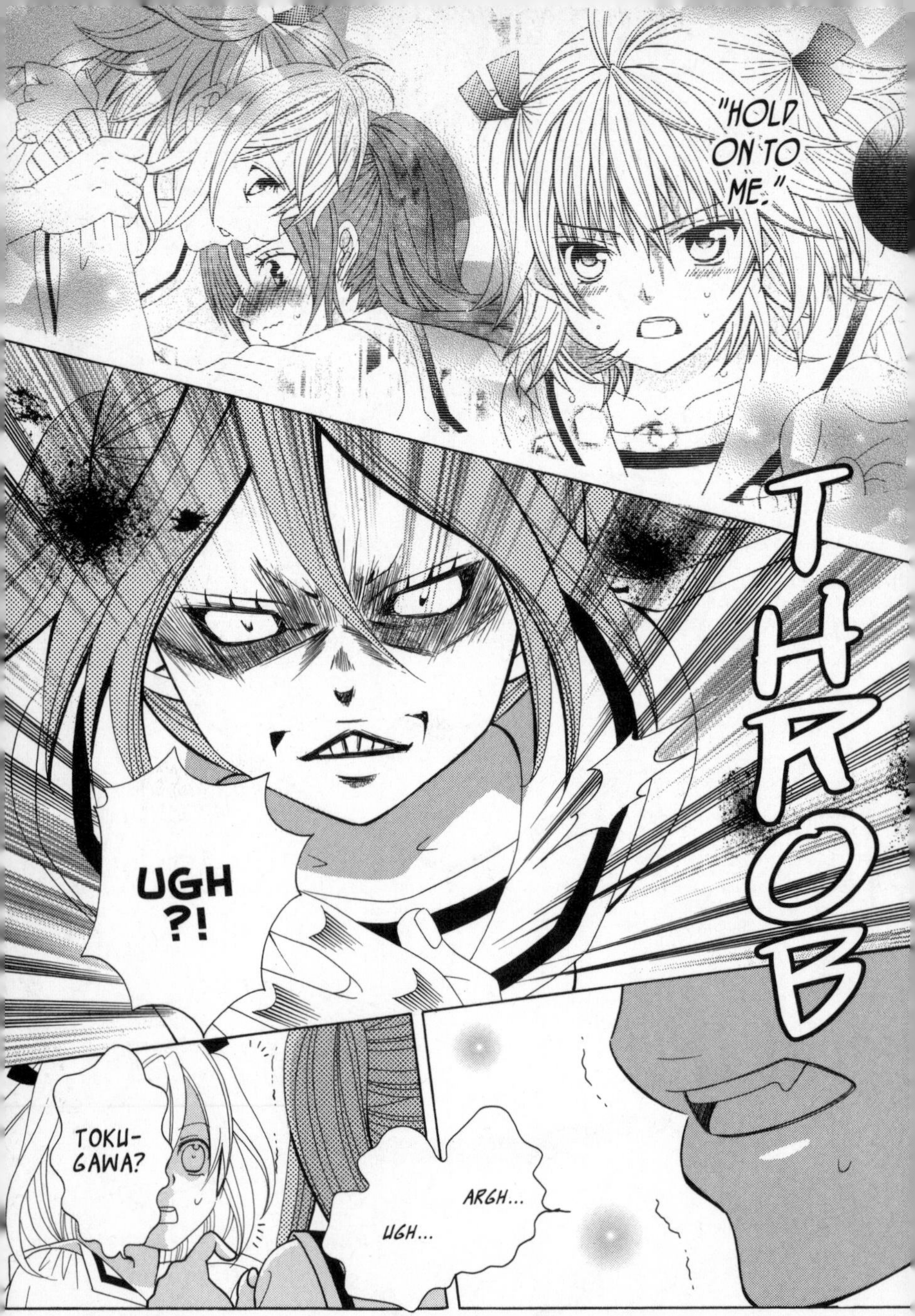
"HOLD ON TO ME."
THROB
UGH ?!
ARGH...
UGH...
TOKU-GAWA?

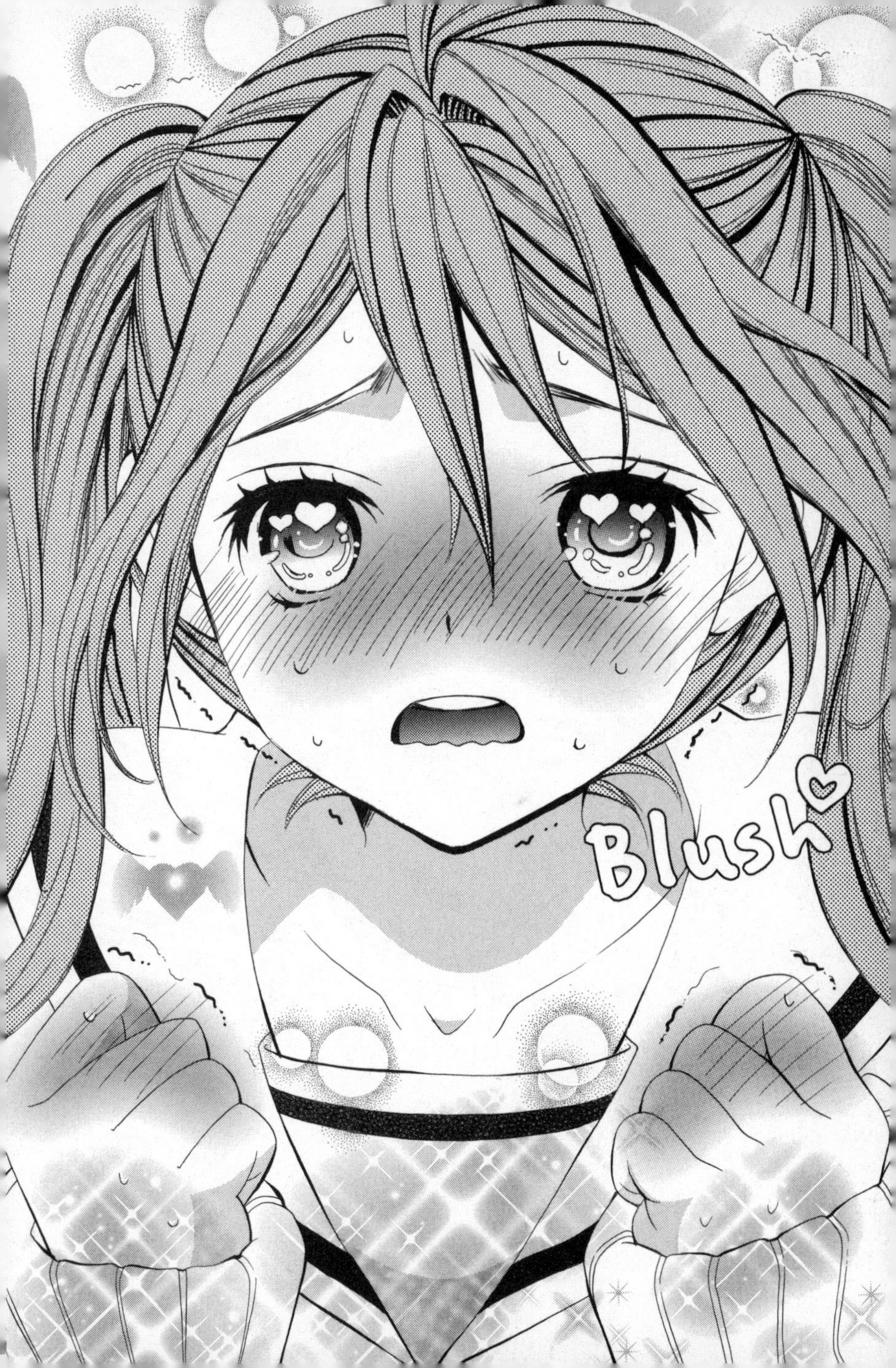
Blush

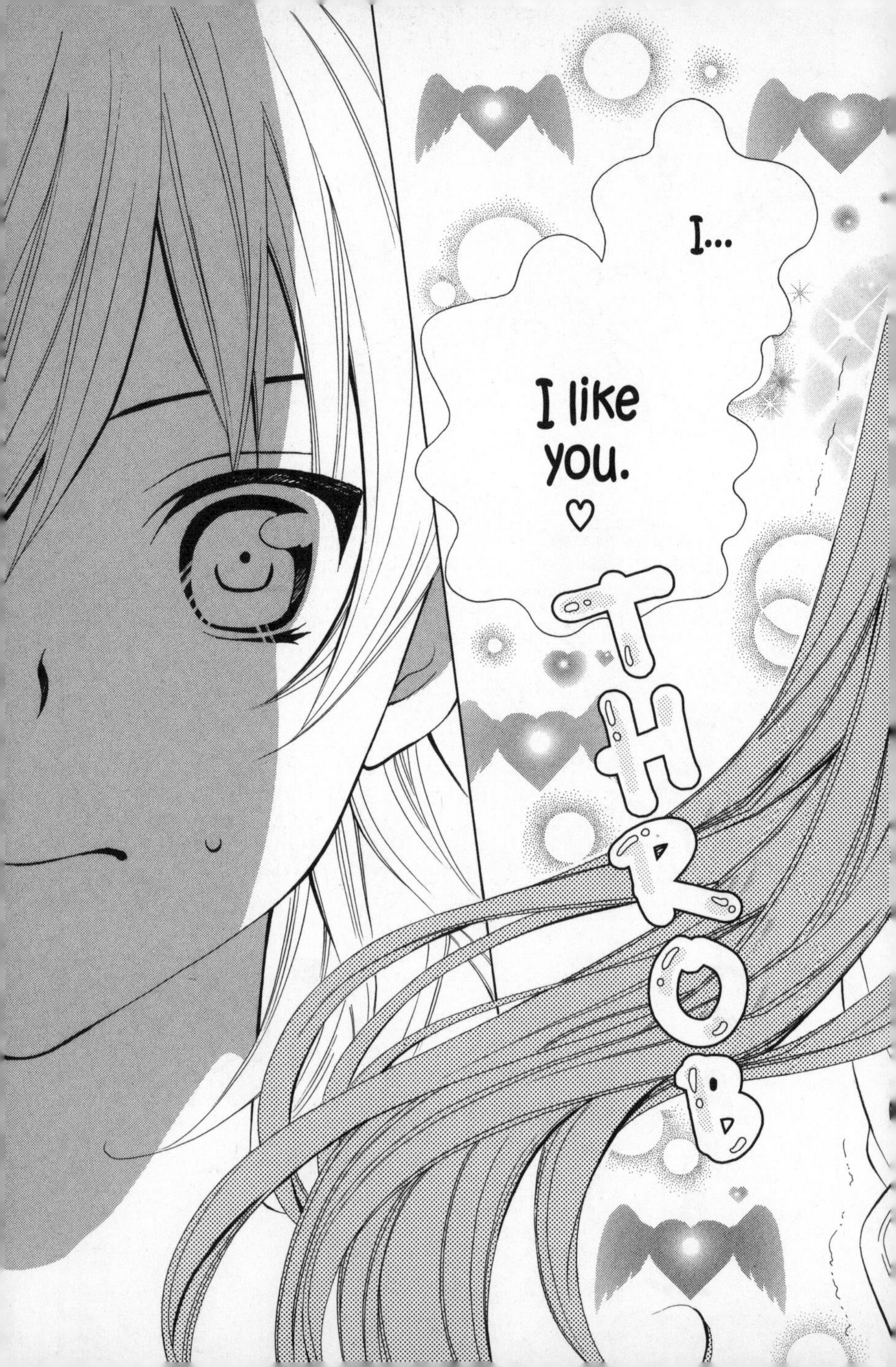
I...
I like you. ♡
THROB

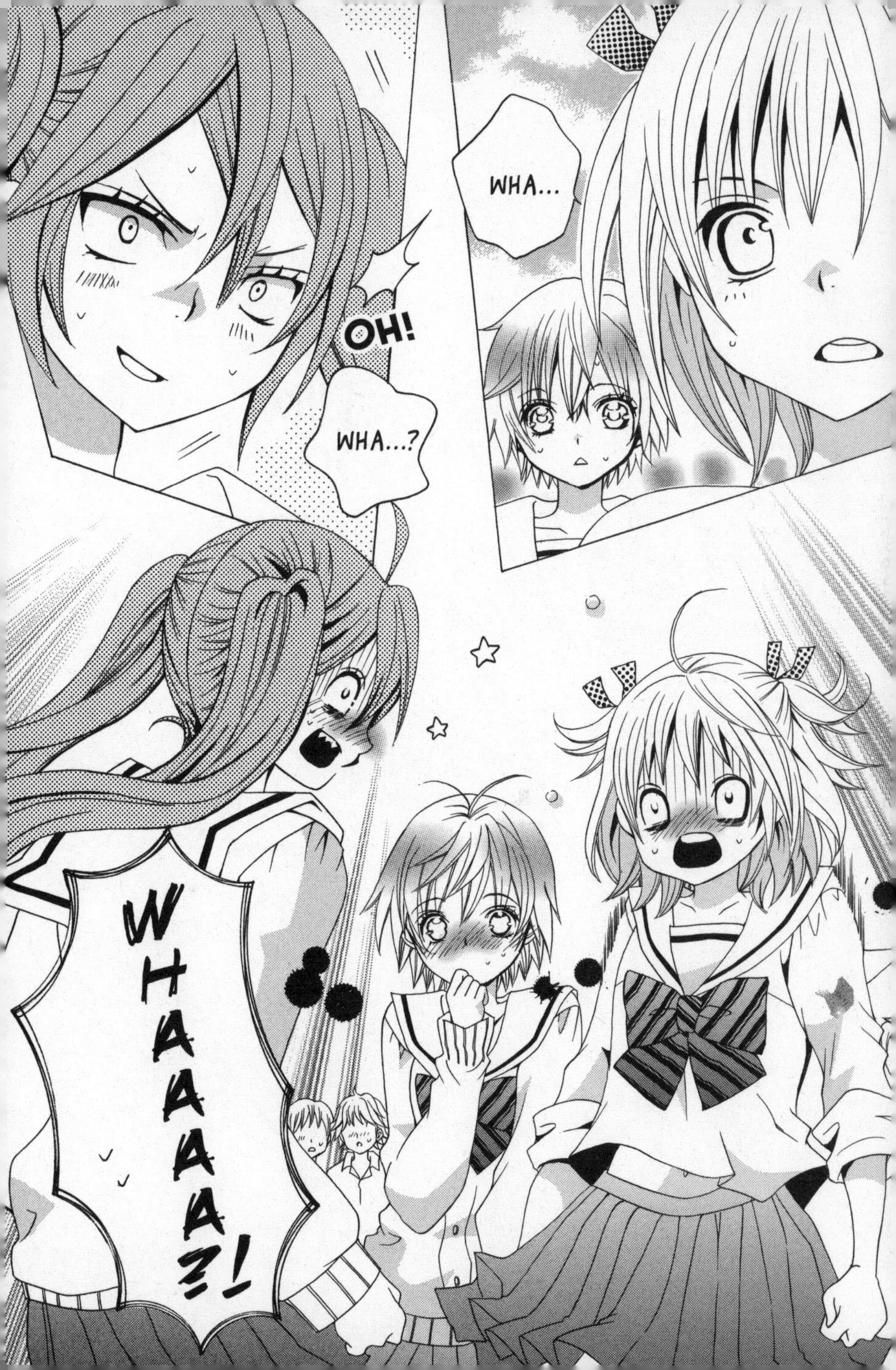
WHA...
OH!
WHA...?
WHAAAAAZ!

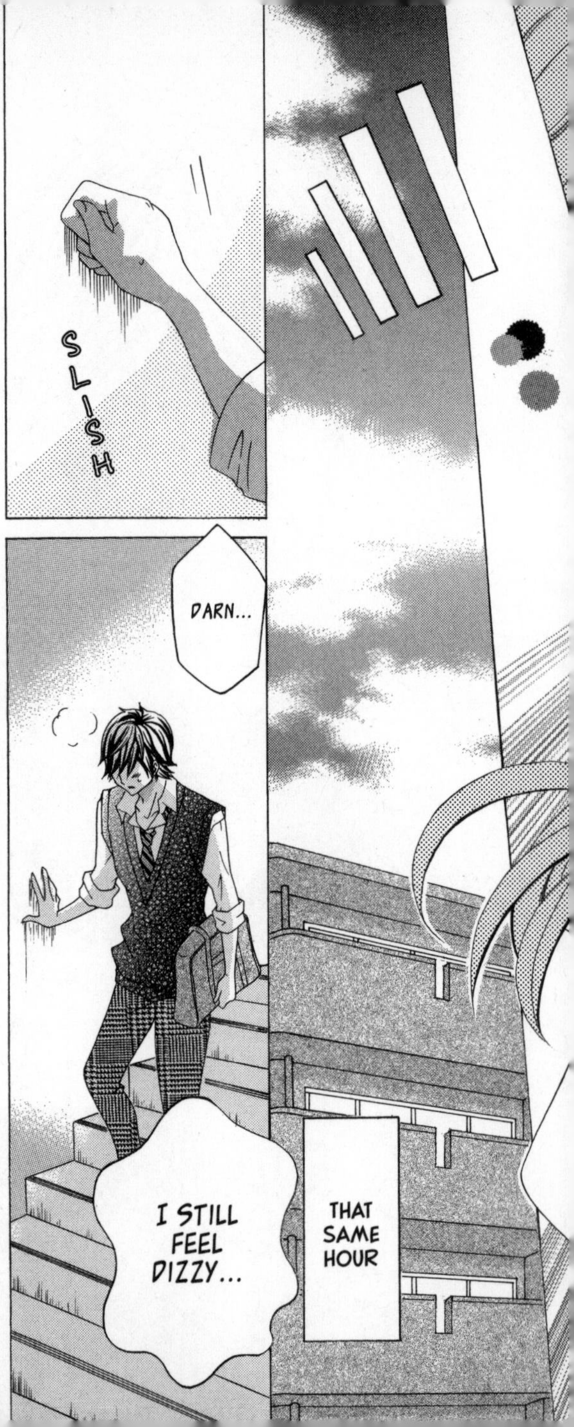
THAT SAME HOUR
SLISH
DARN...
I STILL FEEL DIZZY...

SPECIAL THANKS

Yuka Ito-sama,
Rieko Hirai-sama,
Kayoko Takahashi-sama,
Kawasaki-sama,
Nagisa Sato Sensei.

Rei Nanase Sensei,
Arisu Fujishiro Sensei,
Mumi Mimura Sensei,
Masayo Nagata-sama,
Naochan-sama,
Asuka Sakura Sensei,
and many others.

Bookstore Dan Kinshicho Branch, Kinokuniya Shinjuku Branch, LIBRO Ikebukuro Branch, Kinokuniya Hankyu 32-Bangai Branch.

Sendai Hachimonjiya Bookstore, Books HOSHINO Kintetsu Pass'e Branch, Asahiya Tennoji MiO Branch, Kurashiki Kikuya Bookstore.

Salesperson:
Mizusawa-sama

Previous salesperson:
Honma-sama

Previous editor:
Nakata-sama

Current editor:
Shoji-sama

I also sincerely express my gratitude to everyone who picked up this volume.

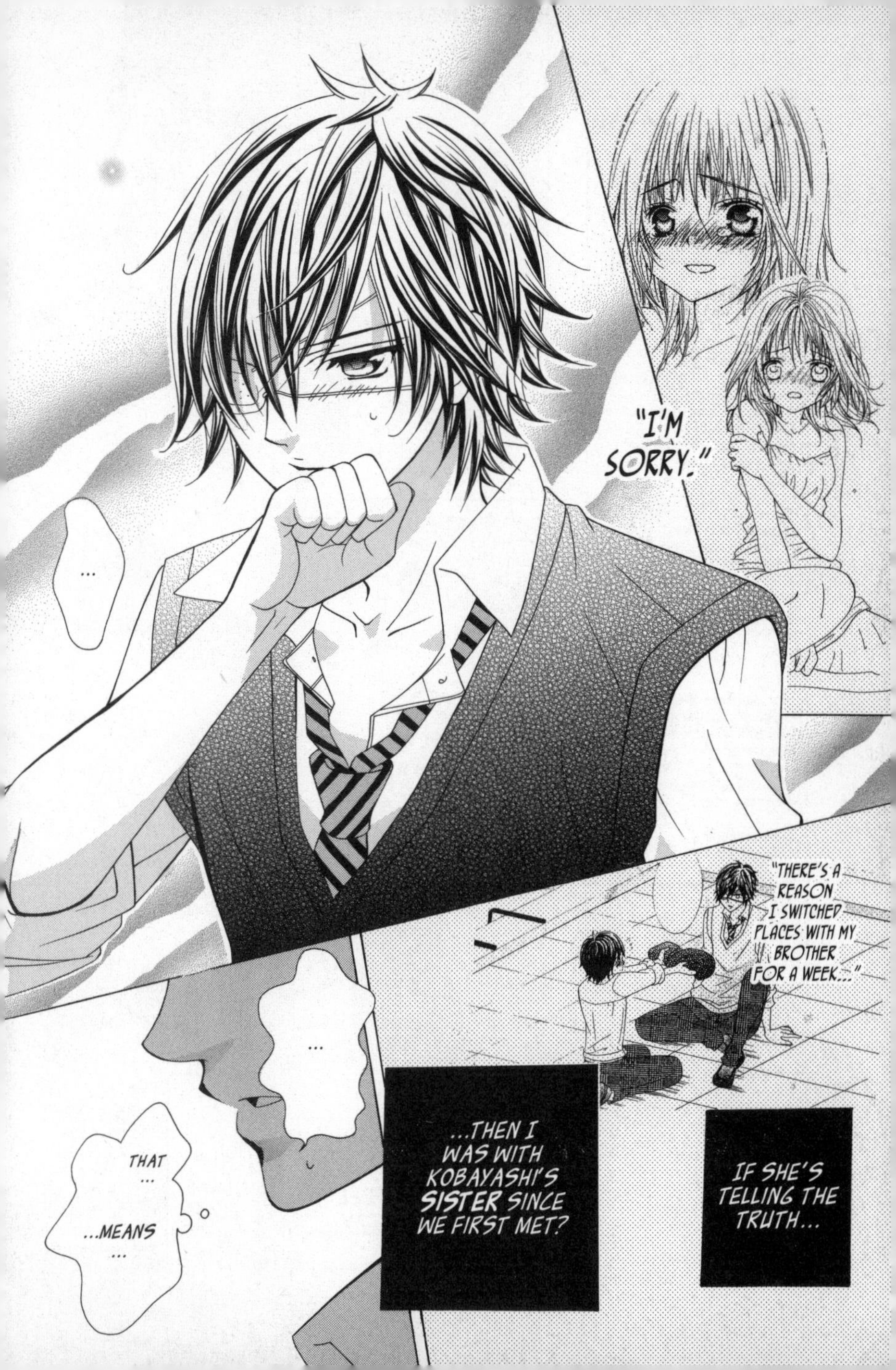
"I'M SORRY."
...
"THERE'S A REASON I SWITCHED PLACES WITH MY BROTHER FOR A WEEK..."
IF SHE'S TELLING THE TRUTH...
...THEN I WAS WITH KOBAYASHI'S SISTER SINCE WE FIRST MET?
...
THAT ... ...MEANS ...

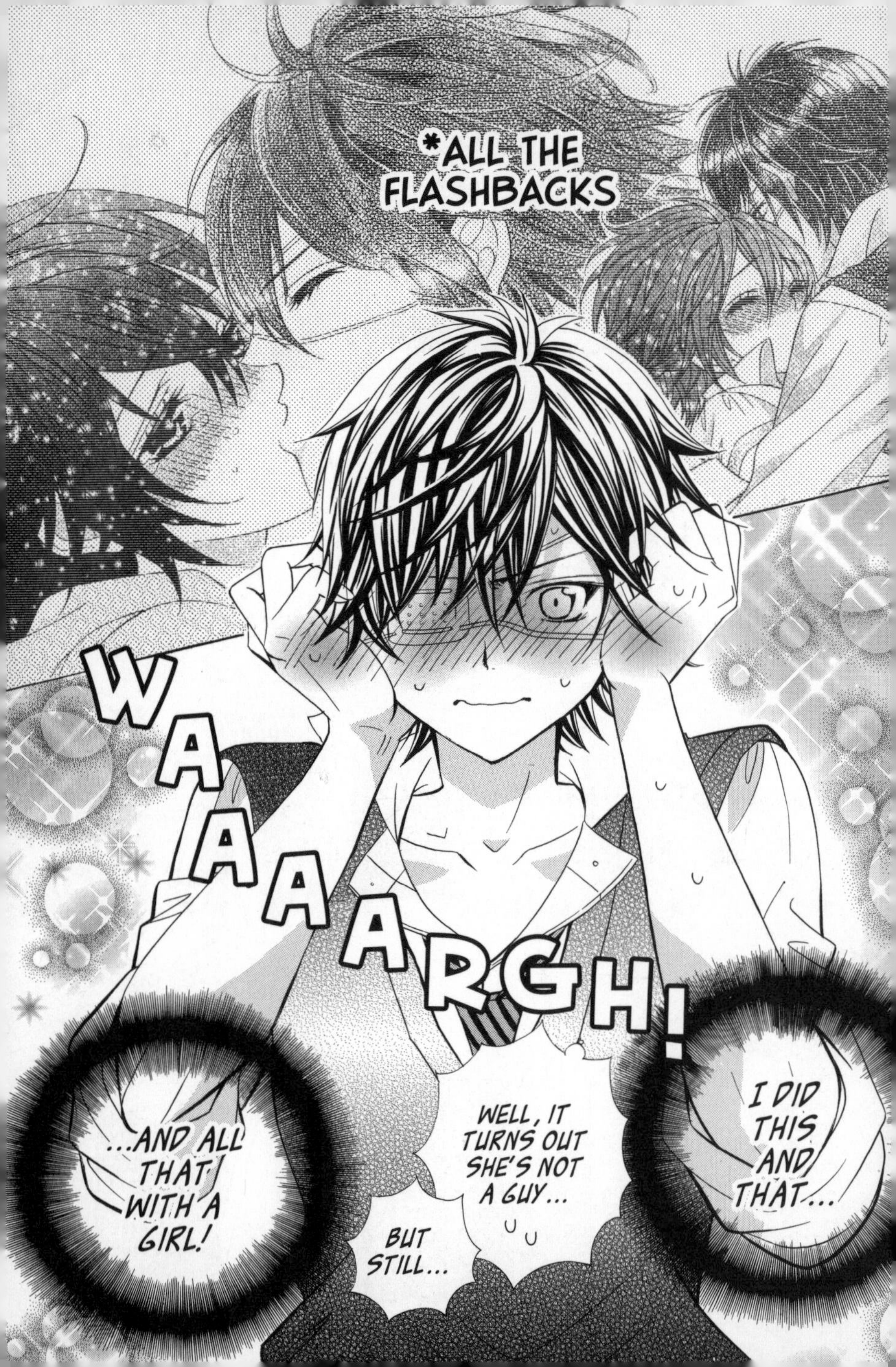
*ALL THE FLASHBACKS
WAAAAARGH!
I DID THIS AND THAT...
WELL, IT TURNS OUT SHE'S NOT A GUY...
BUT STILL...
...AND ALL THAT WITH A GIRL!

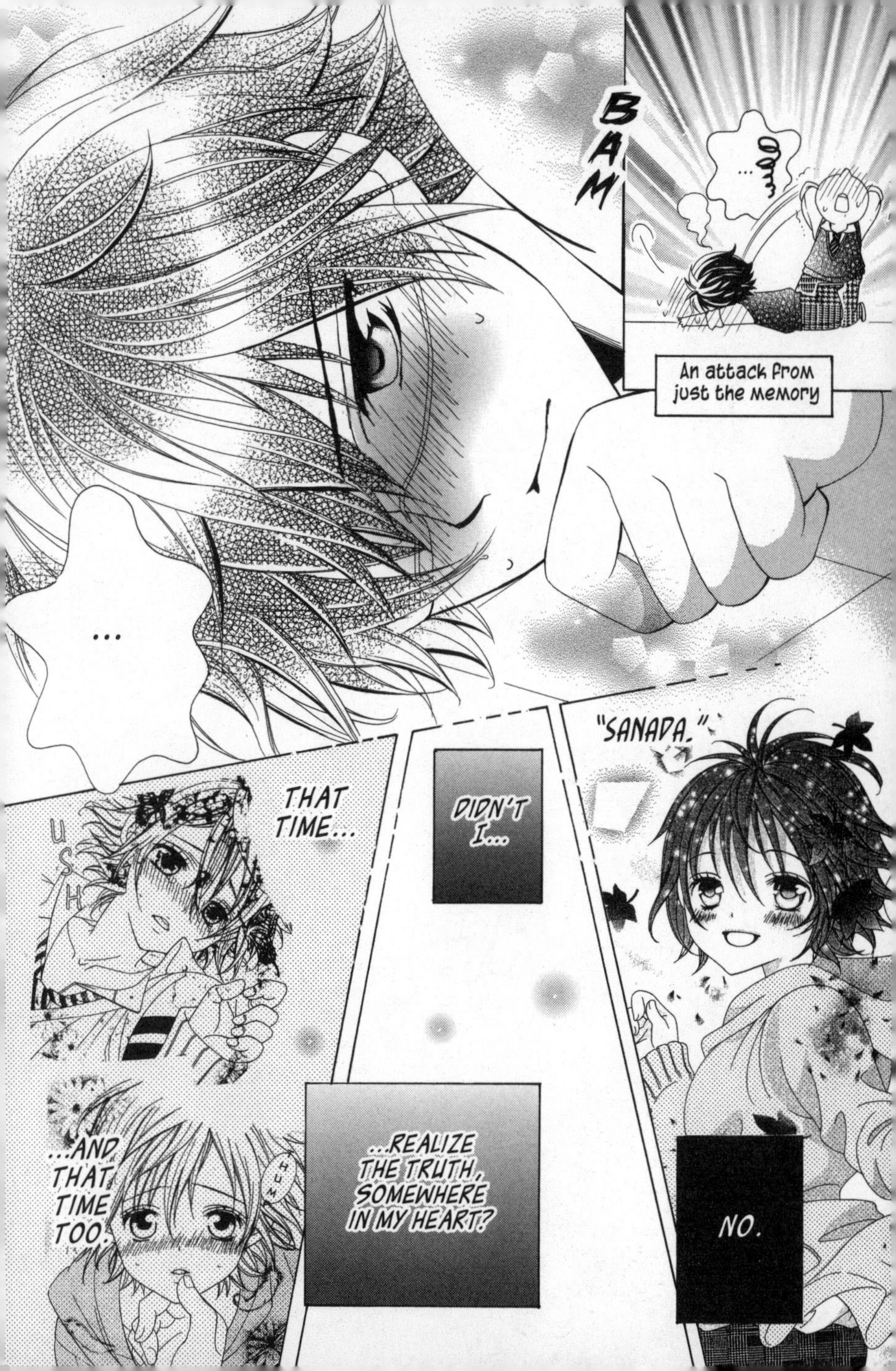
BAM
...
An attack from just the memory
...
"SANADA."
NO.
DIDN'T I...
...REALIZE THE TRUTH, SOMEWHERE IN MY HEART?
THAT TIME...
USH
...AND THAT TIME TOO.
HUM

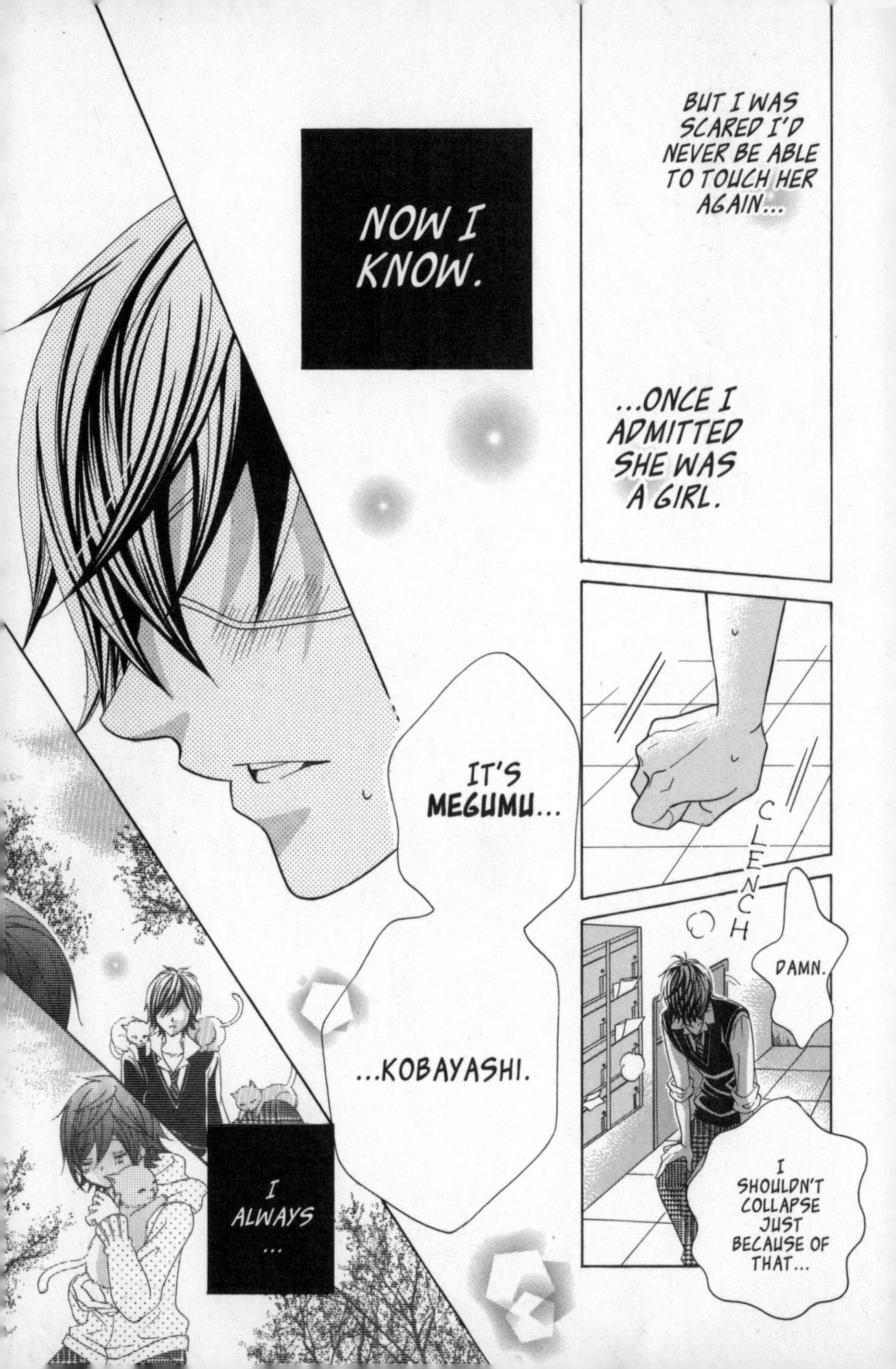
BUT I WAS SCARED I'D NEVER BE ABLE TO TOUCH HER AGAIN...
...ONCE I ADMITTED SHE WAS A GIRL.
CLENCH
DAMN.
I SHOULDN'T COLLAPSE JUST BECAUSE OF THAT...
NOW I KNOW.
IT'S MEGUMU...
...KOBAYASHI.
I ALWAYS ...

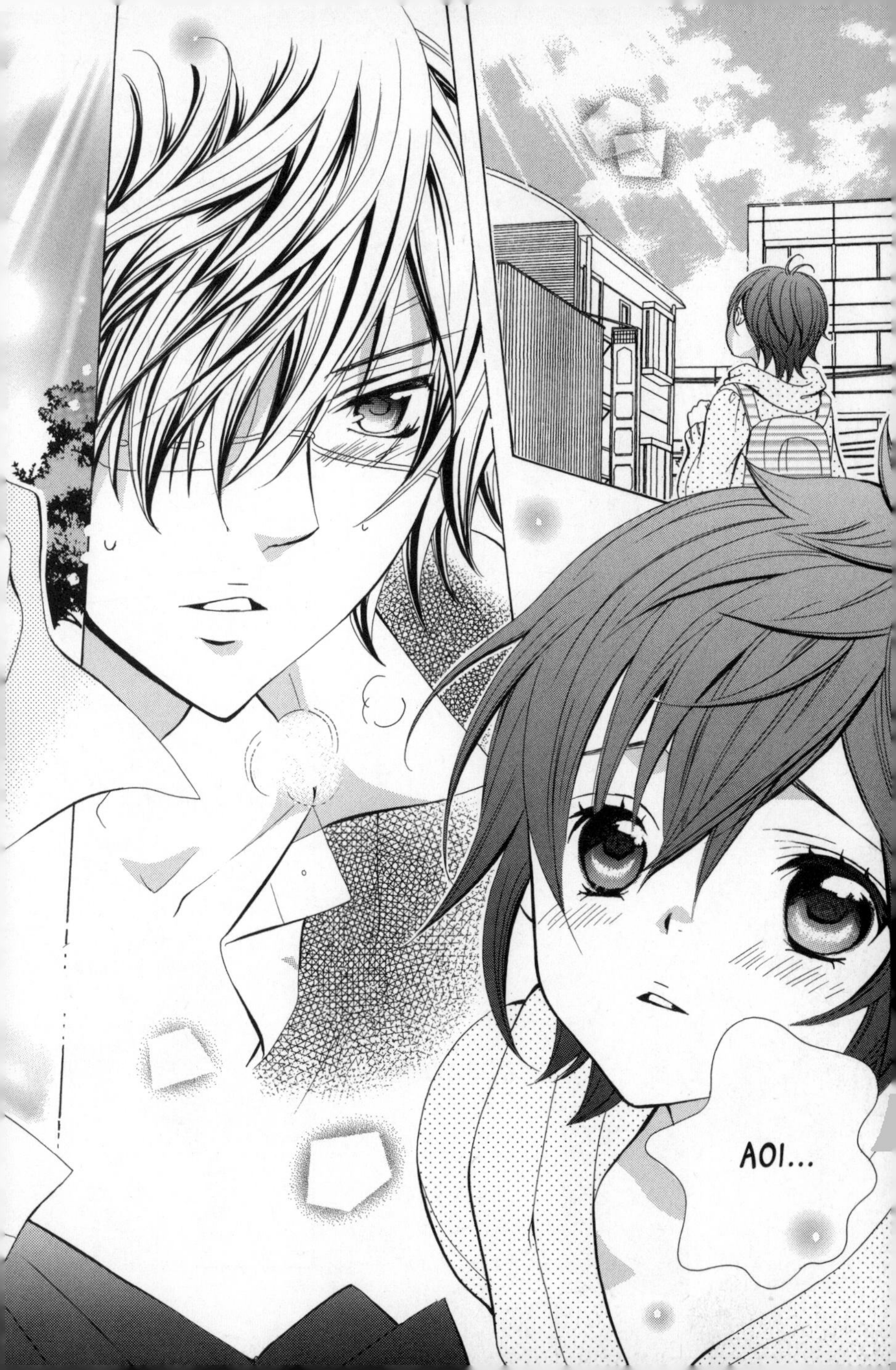
AOI...

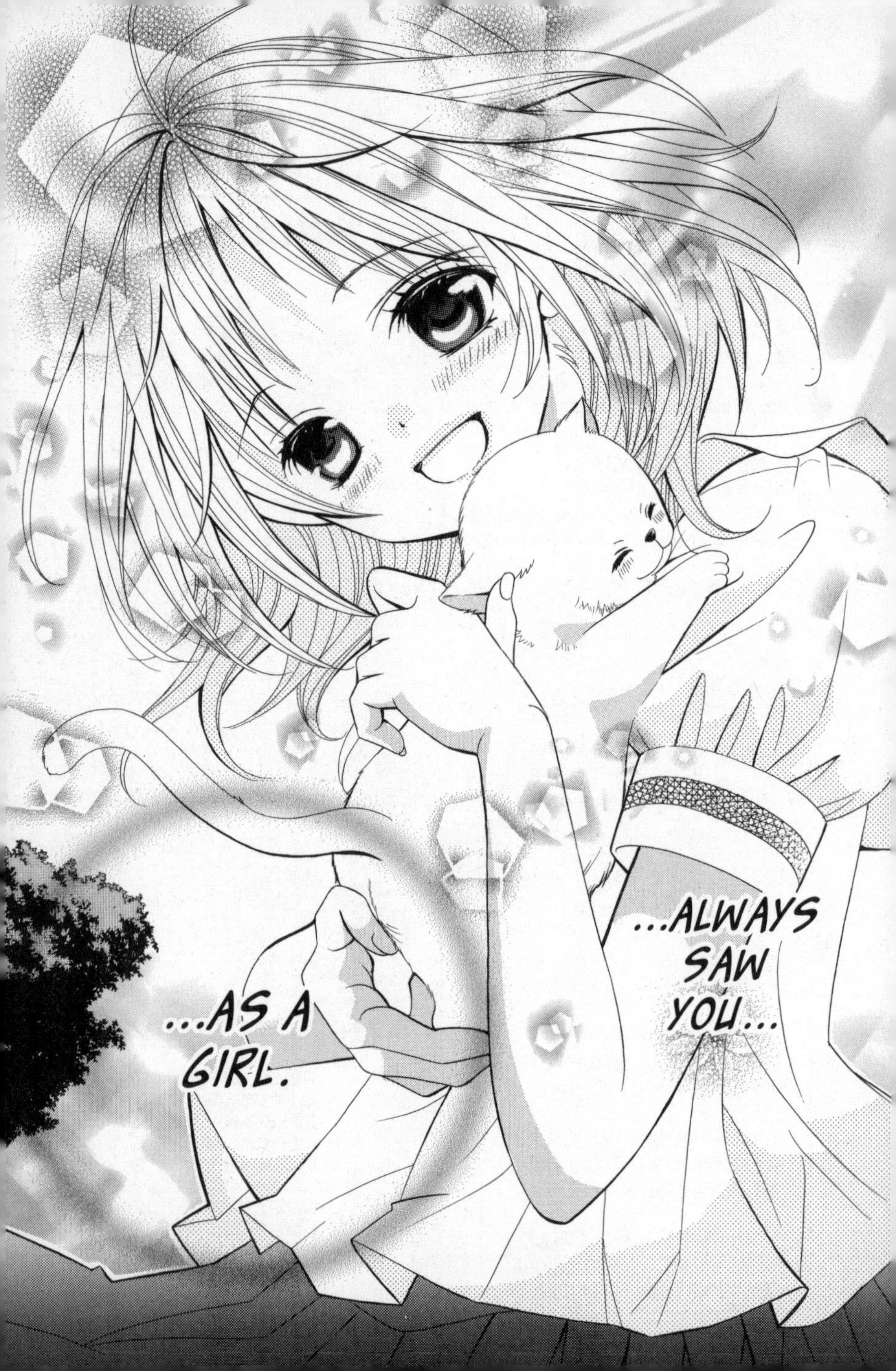
...ALWAYS SAW YOU...
...AS A GIRL.

SO CUTE! ANIME DVD!

AOI SANADA:
MR. DAISUKE ONO
SEBASTIAN FROM *BLACK BUTLER*
MIDORIMA FROM *KUROKO NO BASUKE*
SINBAD FROM *MAGI* AND OTHERS

MITSURU/MEGUMU KOBAYASHI:
MS. AYUMI FUJIMURA
MISAKI AYUZAWA FROM *MAID SAMA!*
HIKARU KAGEYAMA FROM *INAZUMA ELEVEN GO!*
MIX FROM *AQUARION: EVOL* AND OTHERS

AZUSA TOKUGAWA:
MS. AZUMI ASAKURA
SAYAKA HOSHINO FROM *SUKI DESU SUZUKI-KUN*
YUKIHO HAGIWARA FROM *THE IDOLMA@STER* AND OTHERS

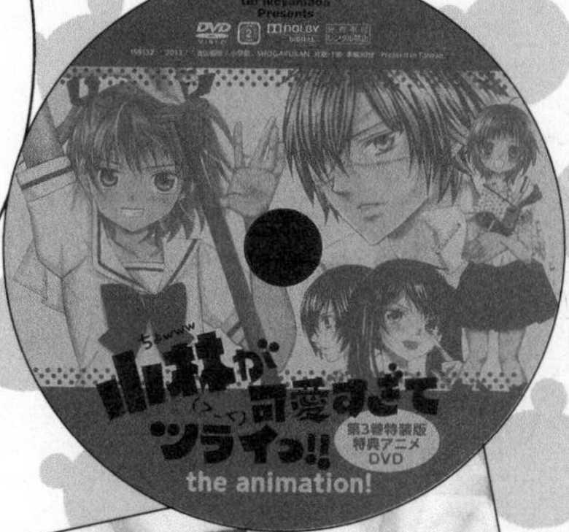
第3巻特装版
特典アニメ
DVD
the animation!

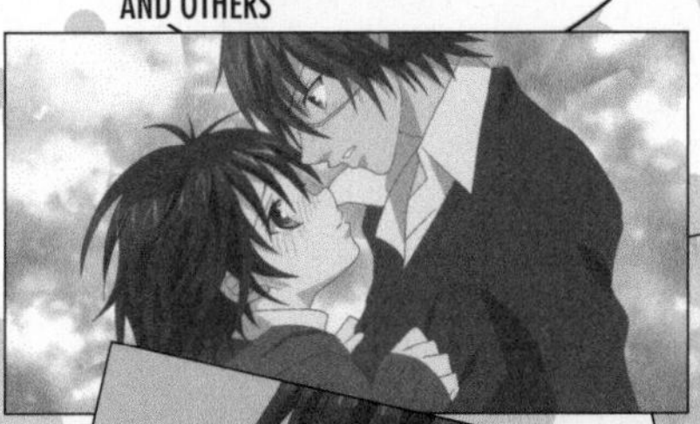

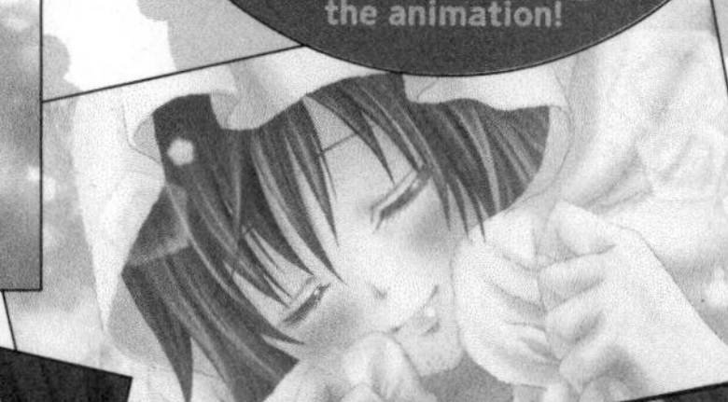

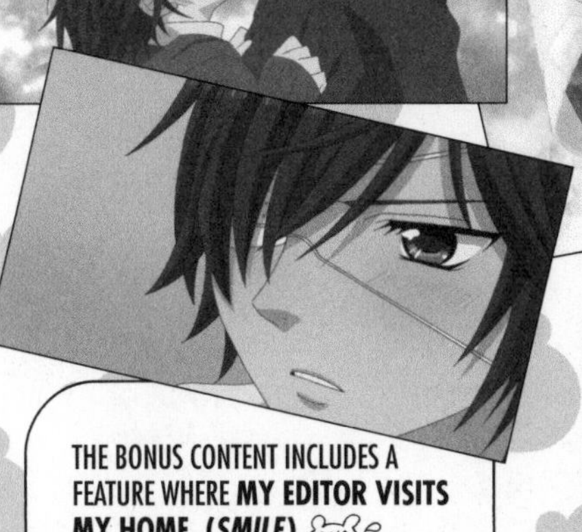

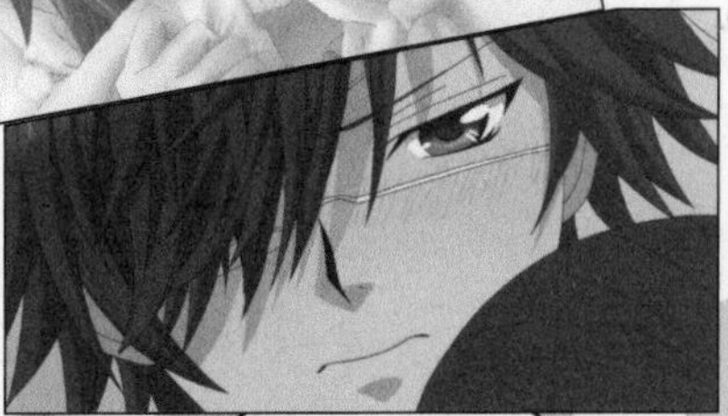

THE BONUS CONTENT INCLUDES A FEATURE WHERE **MY EDITOR VISITS MY HOME. (*SMILE*)**

(THIS IS THE FIRST TIME I'VE HAD A CAMERA IN MY STUDIO AND MY PRIVATE ROOM!)

I FOUND IT VERY EMBARRASSING BUT WE DID OUR BEST, SO I HOPE EVERYONE GETS A GOOD LAUGH OUT OF IT. LOL.

VOLUME 3 OF *SO CUTE!* COMES IN TWO VERSIONS IN JAPAN, THE REGULAR VERSION AND THE SPECIAL EDITION THAT INCLUDES THE ANIME DVD!
I'M REALLY HAPPY THE ANIME WAS MADE WITH A SPLENDID VOICE CAST. ♡♡
I HOPE YOU WATCH MEGO, MITSURU AND AOI MOVE AND SPEAK LIKE THEY'RE ALIVE (^0^) !!

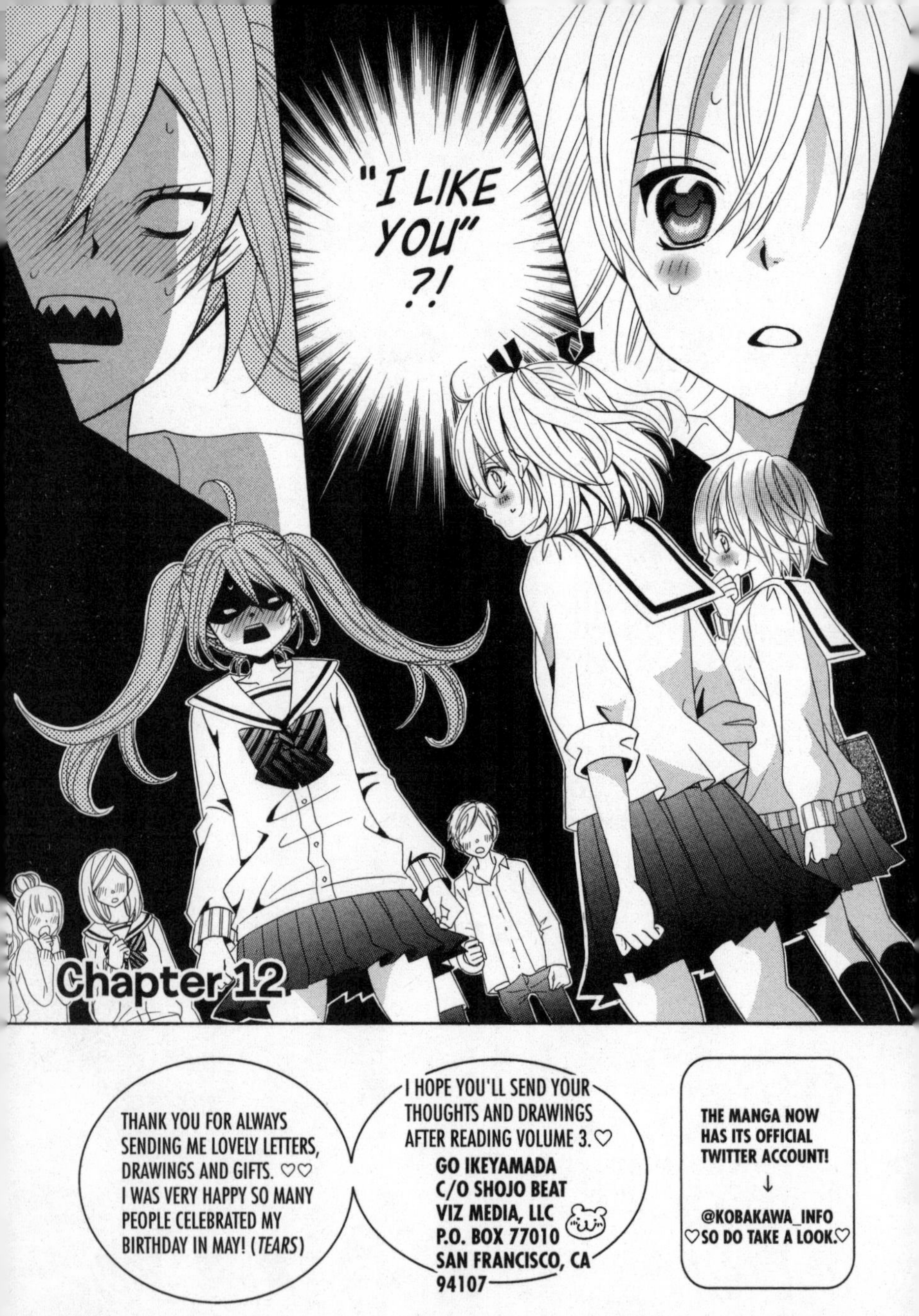
"I LIKE YOU" ?!
Chapter 12

THANK YOU FOR ALWAYS SENDING ME LOVELY LETTERS, DRAWINGS AND GIFTS. ♡♡ I WAS VERY HAPPY SO MANY PEOPLE CELEBRATED MY BIRTHDAY IN MAY! (*TEARS*)

I HOPE YOU'LL SEND YOUR THOUGHTS AND DRAWINGS AFTER READING VOLUME 3. ♡

GO IKEYAMADA
C/O SHOJO BEAT
VIZ MEDIA, LLC
P.O. BOX 77010
SAN FRANCISCO, CA
94107

THE MANGA NOW HAS ITS OFFICIAL TWITTER ACCOUNT!
↓
@KOBAKAWA_INFO
♡SO DO TAKE A LOOK.♡

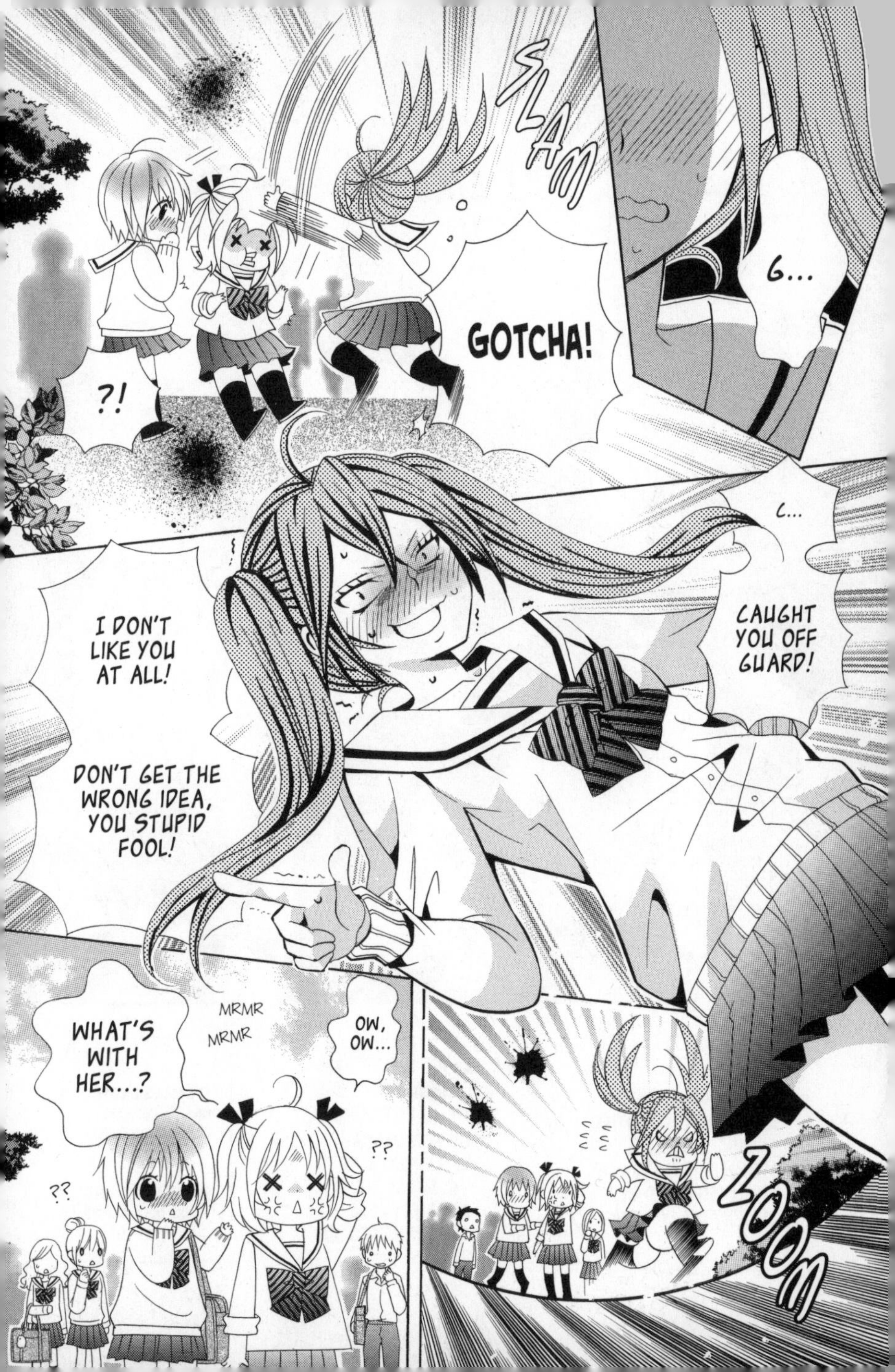
G...
SLAM
GOTCHA!
?!
C...
CAUGHT YOU OFF GUARD!
I DON'T LIKE YOU AT ALL!
DON'T GET THE WRONG IDEA, YOU STUPID FOOL!
ZOOM
OW, OW...
MRMR
MRMR
WHAT'S WITH HER...?
??
??

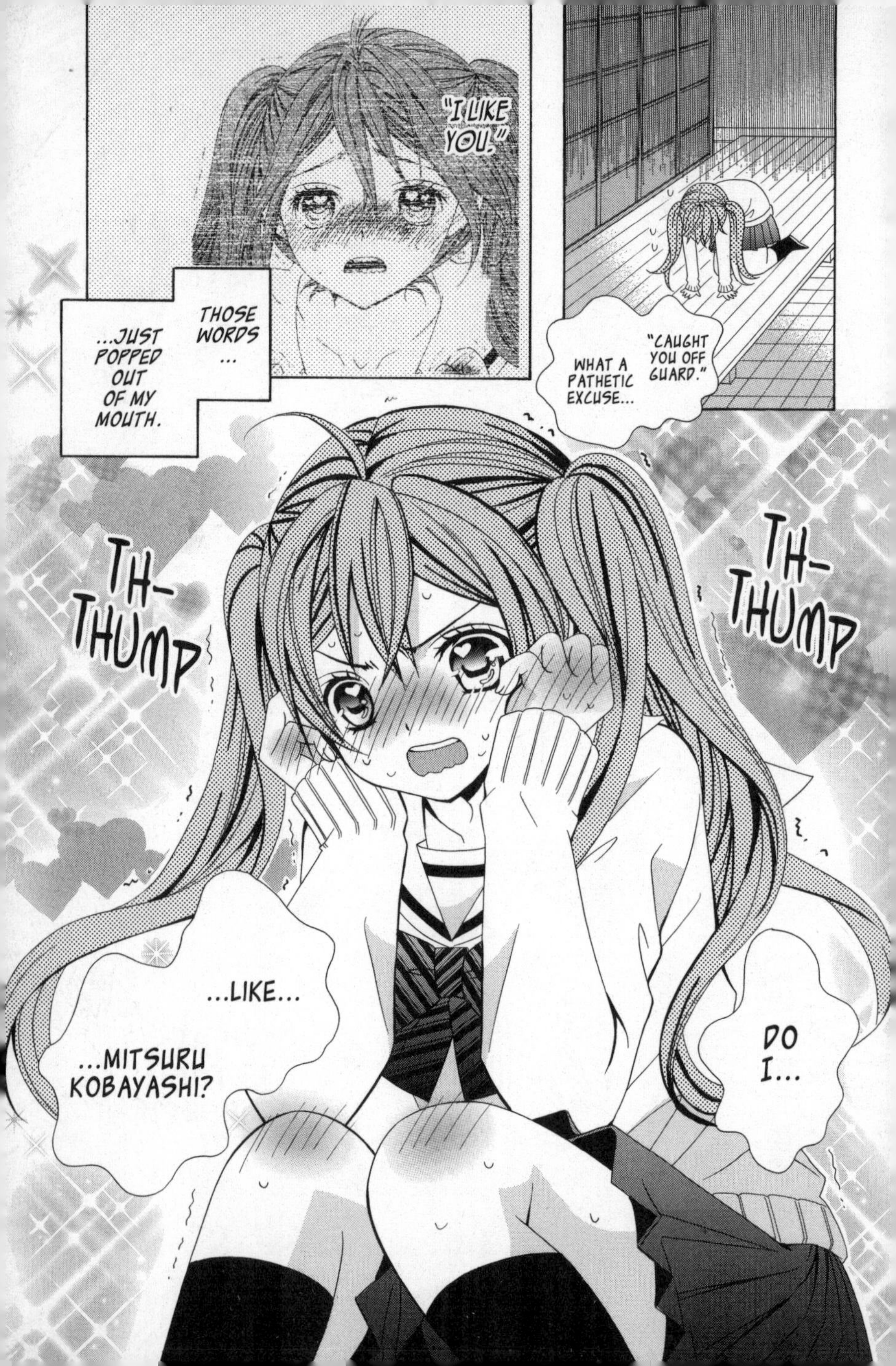
"CAUGHT YOU OFF GUARD."
WHAT A PATHETIC EXCUSE...
"I LIKE YOU."
THOSE WORDS ...
...JUST POPPED OUT OF MY MOUTH.
TH-THUMP
TH-THUMP
DO I...
...LIKE...
...MITSURU KOBAYASHI?

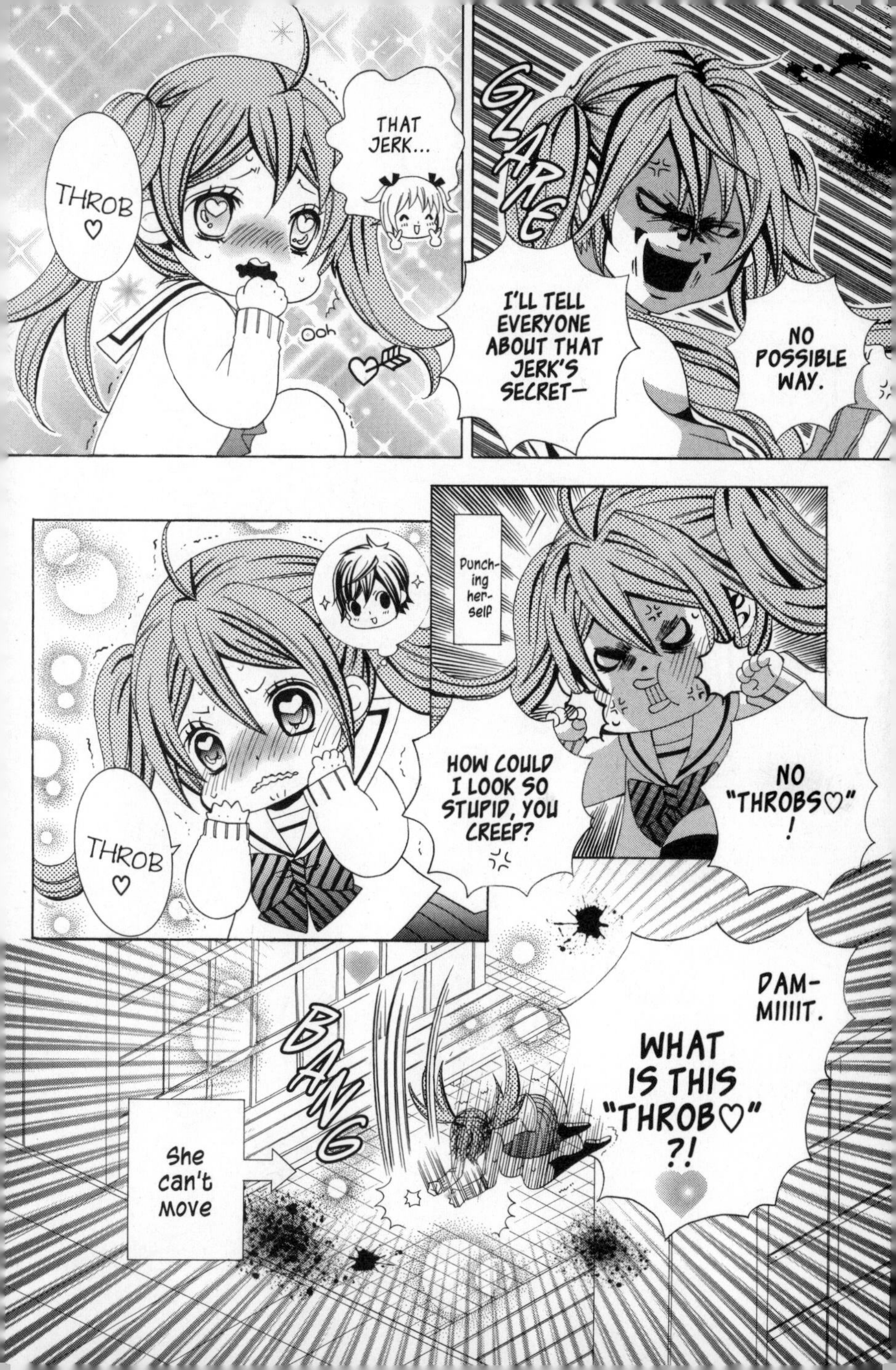
GLARE
NO POSSIBLE WAY.
I'LL TELL EVERYONE ABOUT THAT JERK'S SECRET—
THAT JERK...
THROB ♡
Ooh
Punching herself
NO "THROBS♡"!
HOW COULD I LOOK SO STUPID, YOU CREEP?
THROB ♡
DAM-MIIIIT.
WHAT IS THIS "THROB♡"?!
BANG
She can't move

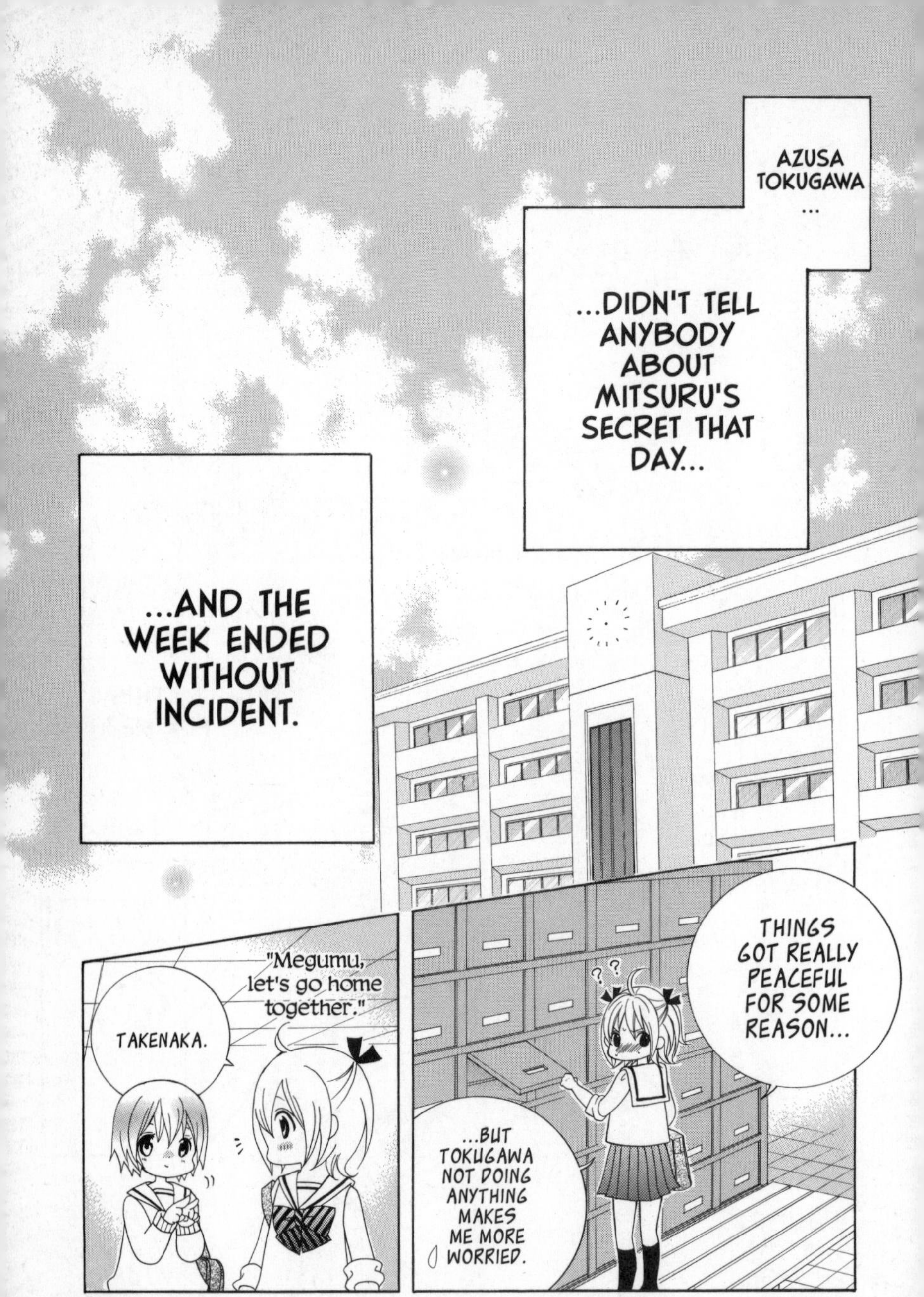
AZUSA TOKUGAWA ...
...DIDN'T TELL ANYBODY ABOUT MITSURU'S SECRET THAT DAY...
...AND THE WEEK ENDED WITHOUT INCIDENT.
THINGS GOT REALLY PEACEFUL FOR SOME REASON...
...BUT TOKUGAWA NOT DOING ANYTHING MAKES ME MORE WORRIED.
"Megumu, let's go home together."
TAKENAKA.

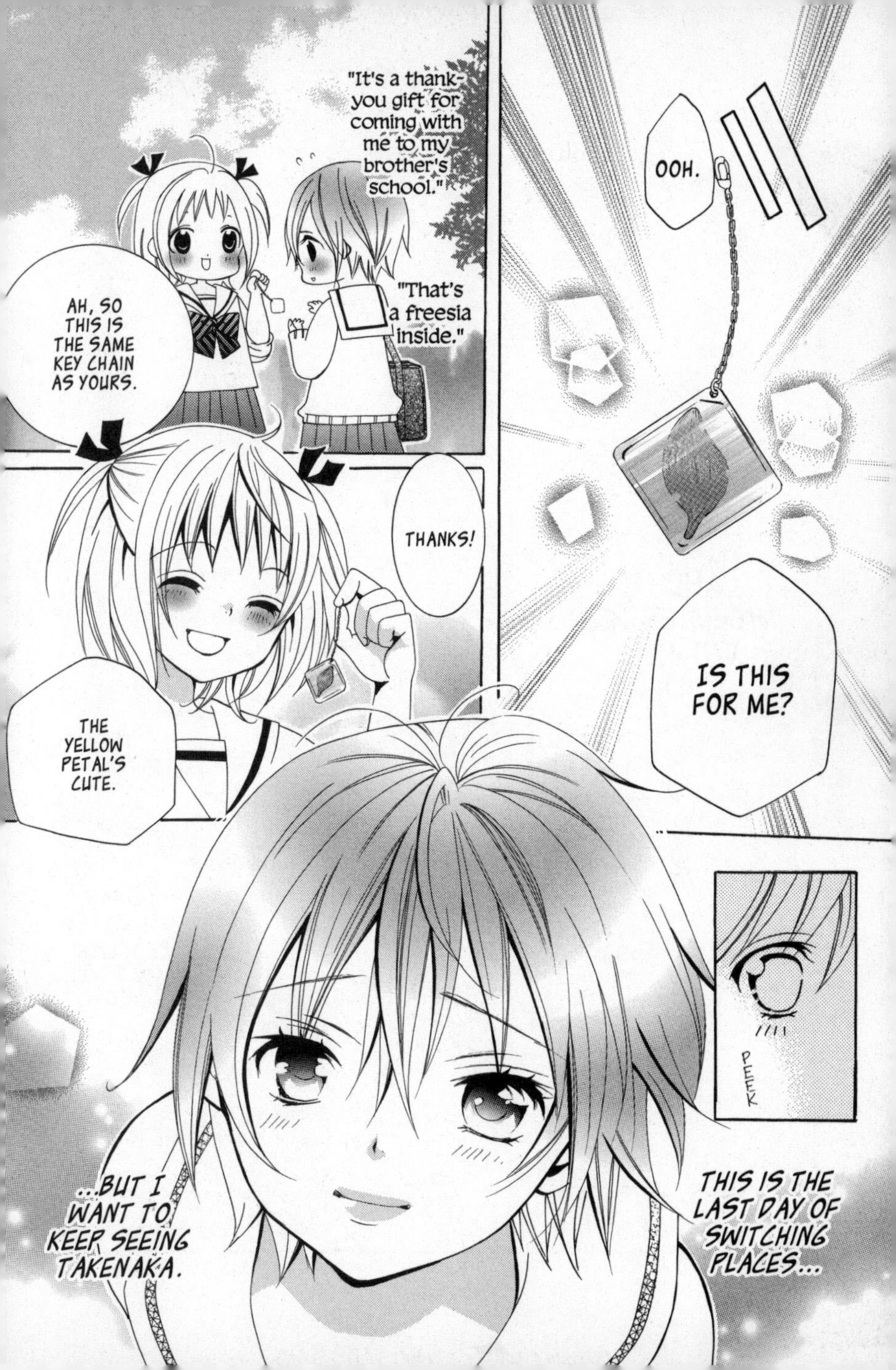
OOH.
IS THIS FOR ME?
"It's a thank-you gift for coming with me to my brother's school."
"That's a freesia inside."
AH, SO THIS IS THE SAME KEY CHAIN AS YOURS.
THANKS!
THE YELLOW PETAL'S CUTE.
PEEK
THIS IS THE LAST DAY OF SWITCHING PLACES...
...BUT I WANT TO KEEP SEEING TAKENAKA.

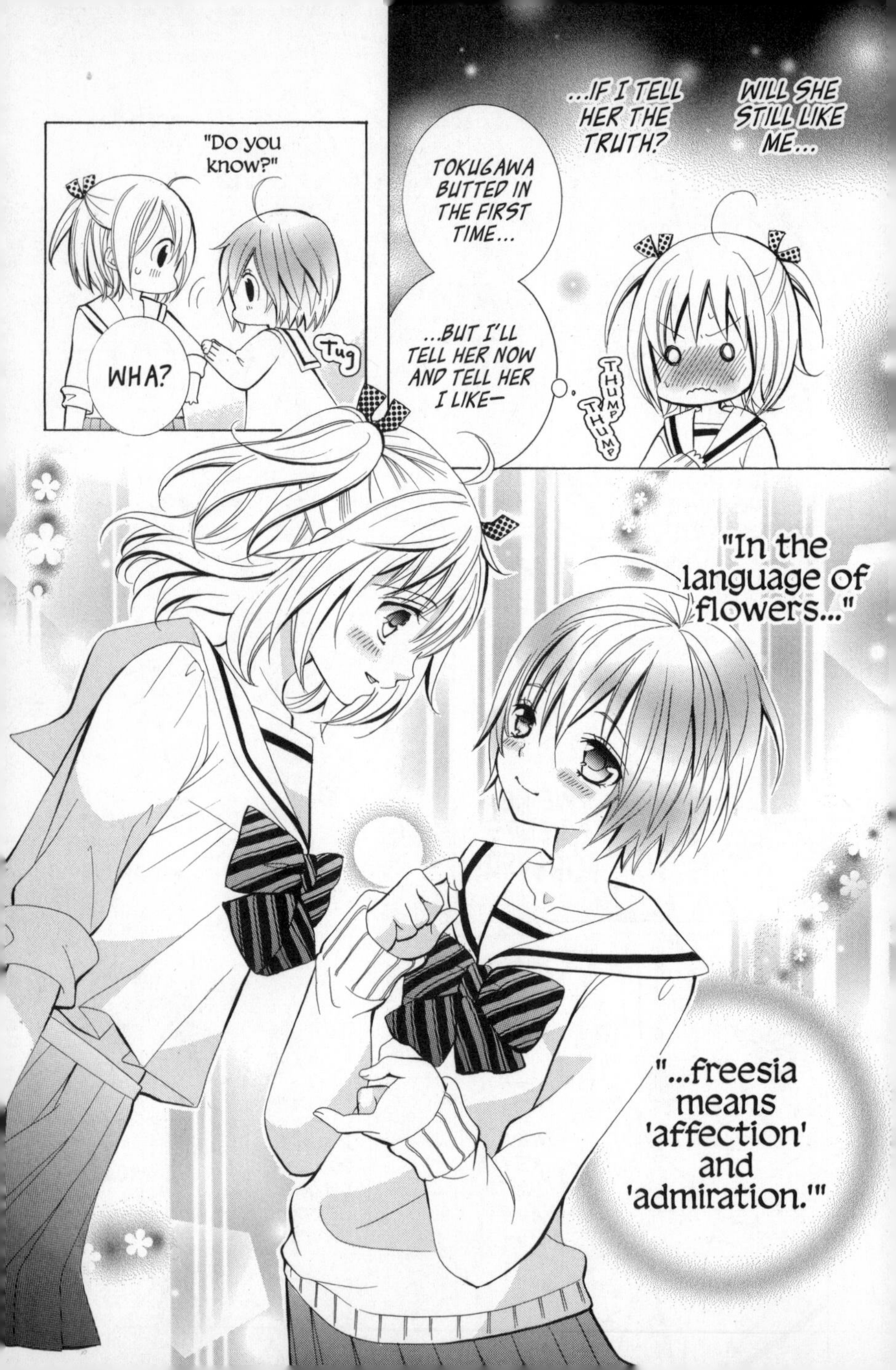
WILL SHE STILL LIKE ME...
...IF I TELL HER THE TRUTH?
TOKUGAWA BUTTED IN THE FIRST TIME...
...BUT I'LL TELL HER NOW AND TELL HER I LIKE—
THUMP THUMP
"Do you know?"
WHA?
Tug
"In the language of flowers..."
"...freesia means 'affection' and 'admiration.'"

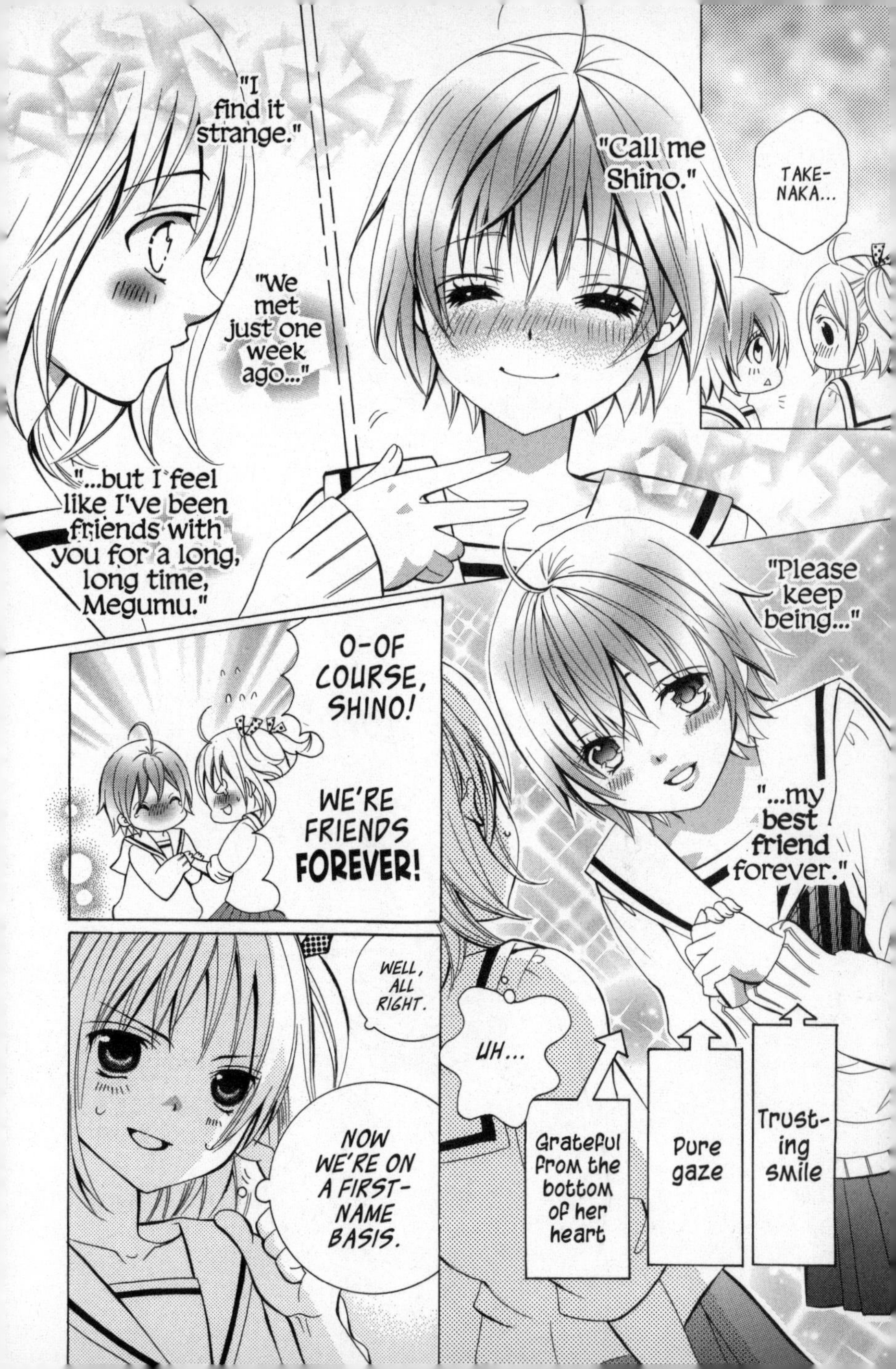
TAKE-NAKA...
"Call me Shino."
"I find it strange."
"We met just one week ago..."
"...but I feel like I've been friends with you for a long, long time, Megumu."
"Please keep being..."
"...my best friend forever."
Trust-ing smile
Pure gaze
Grateful from the bottom of her heart
UH...
O-OF COURSE, SHINO!
WE'RE FRIENDS FOREVER!
WELL, ALL RIGHT.
NOW WE'RE ON A FIRST-NAME BASIS.

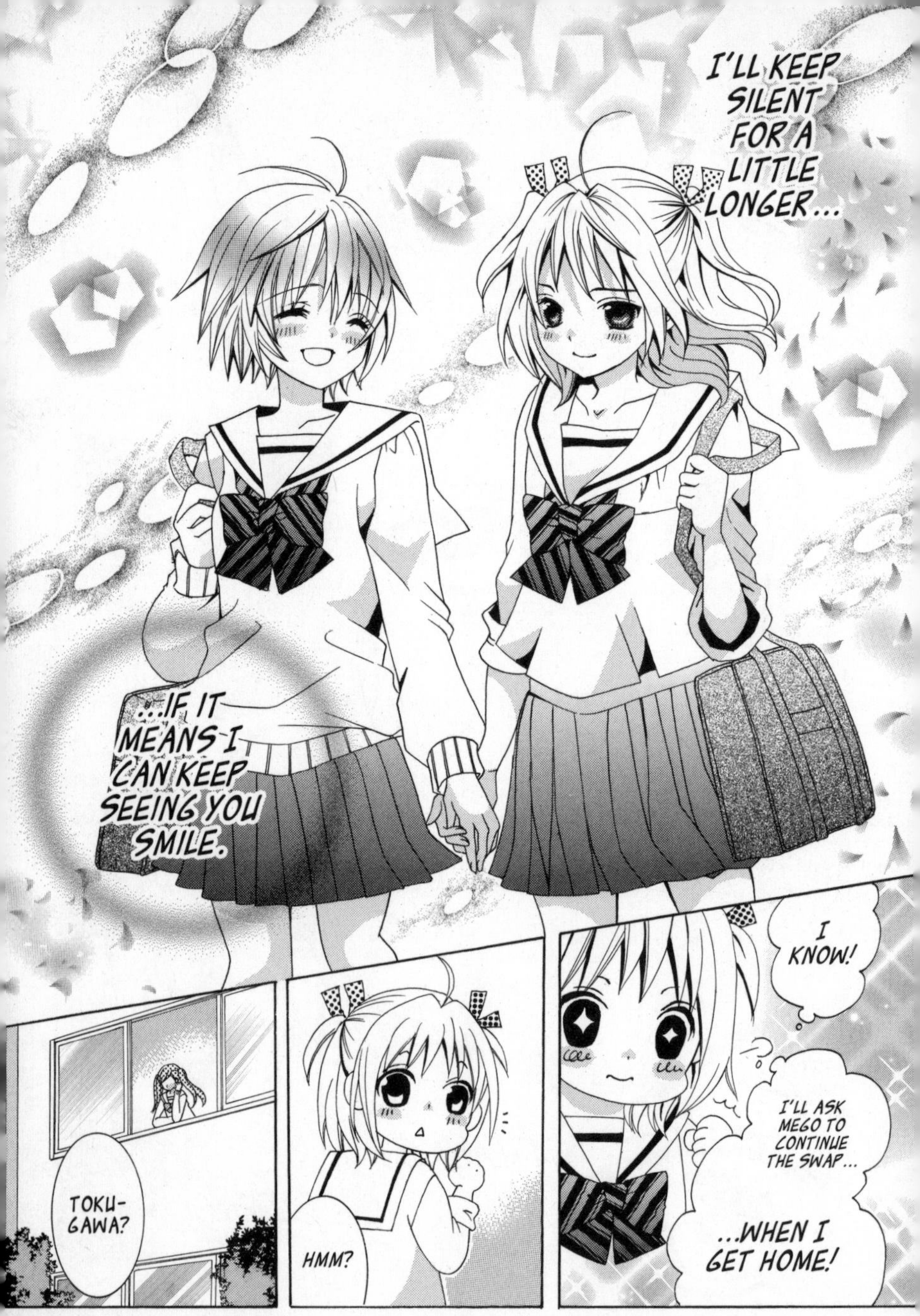
I'LL KEEP SILENT FOR A LITTLE LONGER...
...IF IT MEANS I CAN KEEP SEEING YOU SMILE.
I KNOW!
I'LL ASK MEGO TO CONTINUE THE SWAP...
...WHEN I GET HOME!
HMM?
TOKU-GAWA?

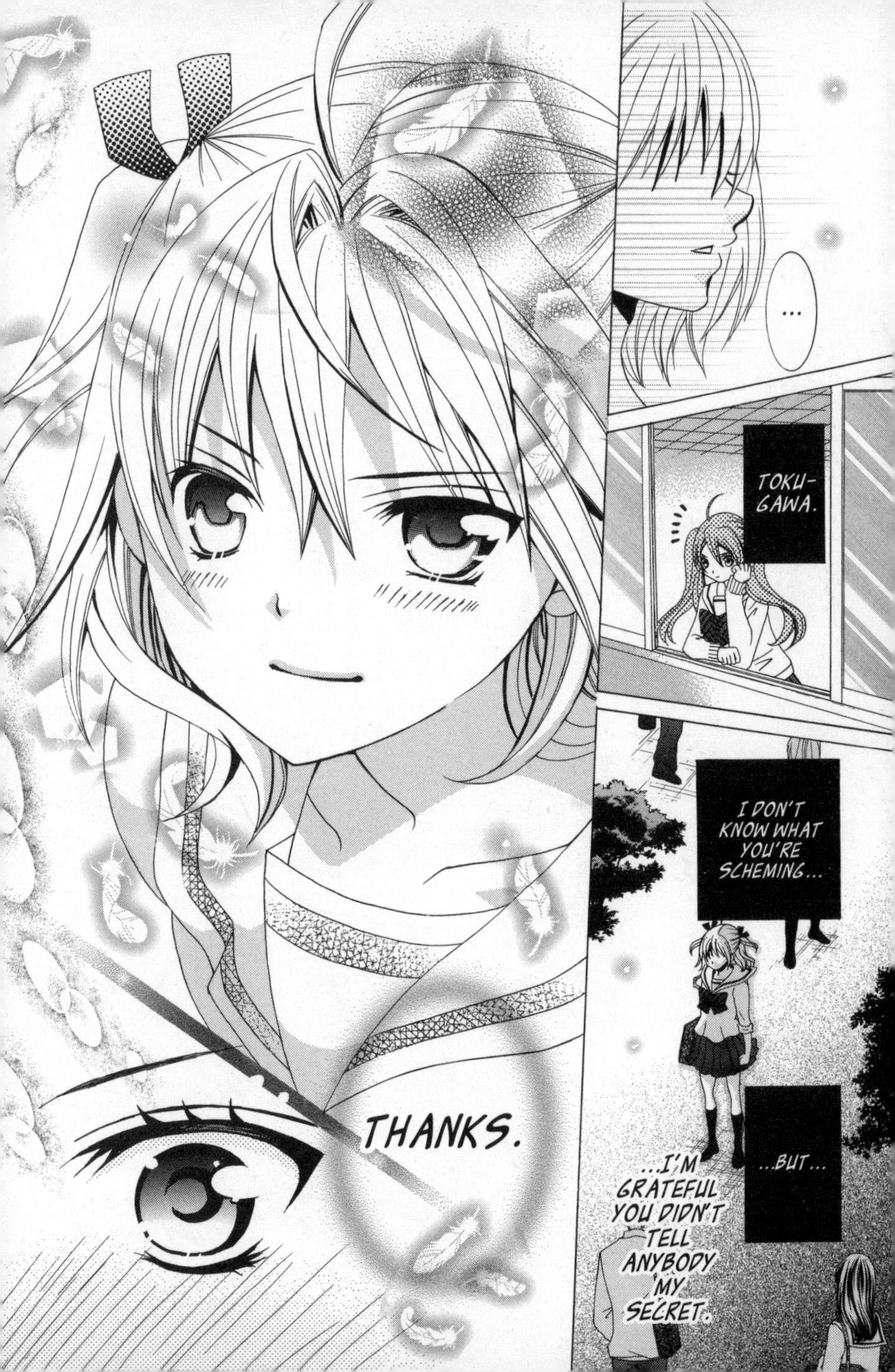
...
TOKU-GAWA.
I DON'T KNOW WHAT YOU'RE SCHEMING...
...BUT...
...I'M GRATEFUL YOU DIDN'T TELL ANYBODY MY SECRET.
THANKS.

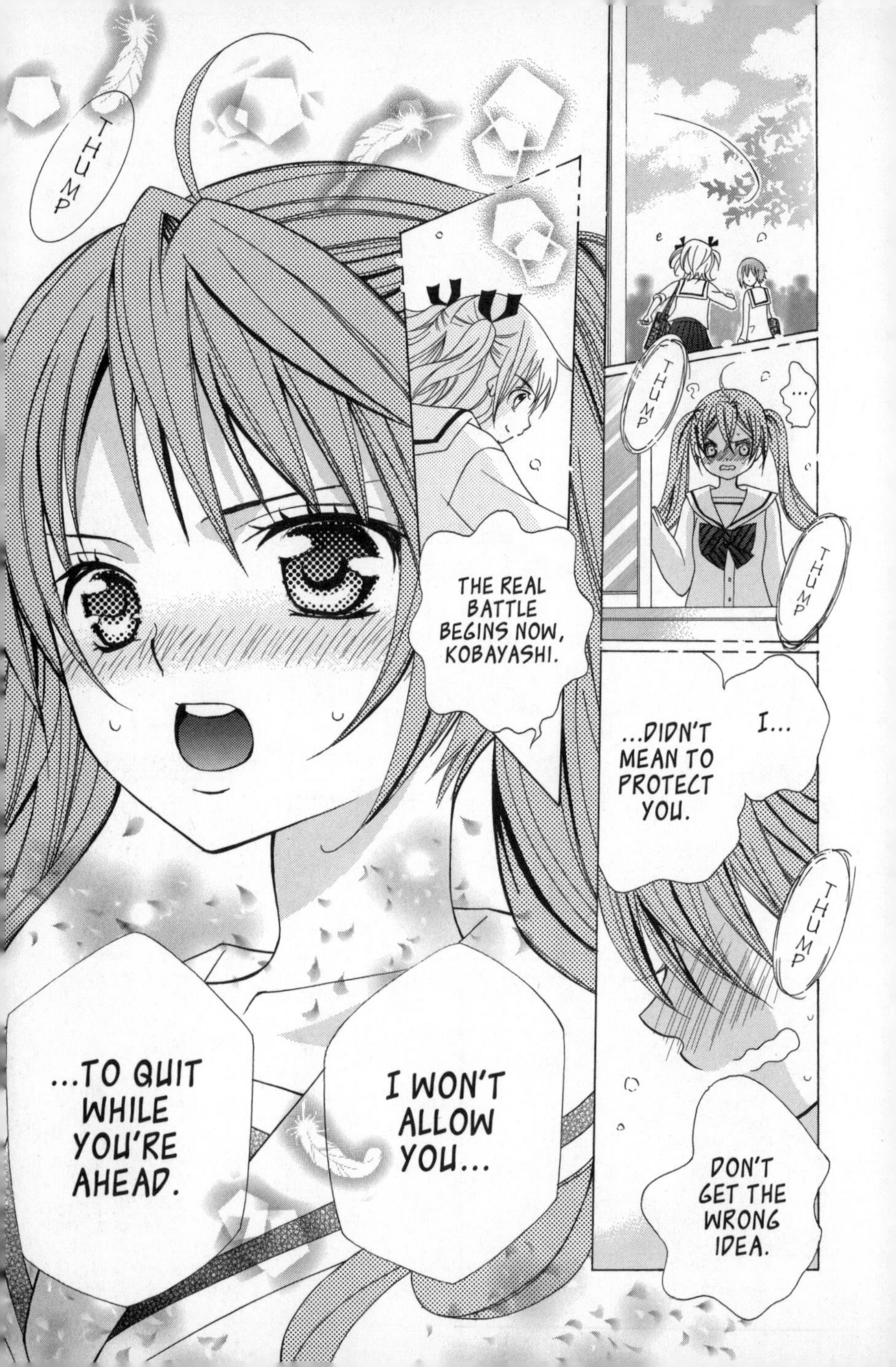
THUMP
...
THUMP
I...
...DIDN'T MEAN TO PROTECT YOU.
THUMP
DON'T GET THE WRONG IDEA.
THUMP
THE REAL BATTLE BEGINS NOW, KOBAYASHI.
I WON'T ALLOW YOU...
...TO QUIT WHILE YOU'RE AHEAD.

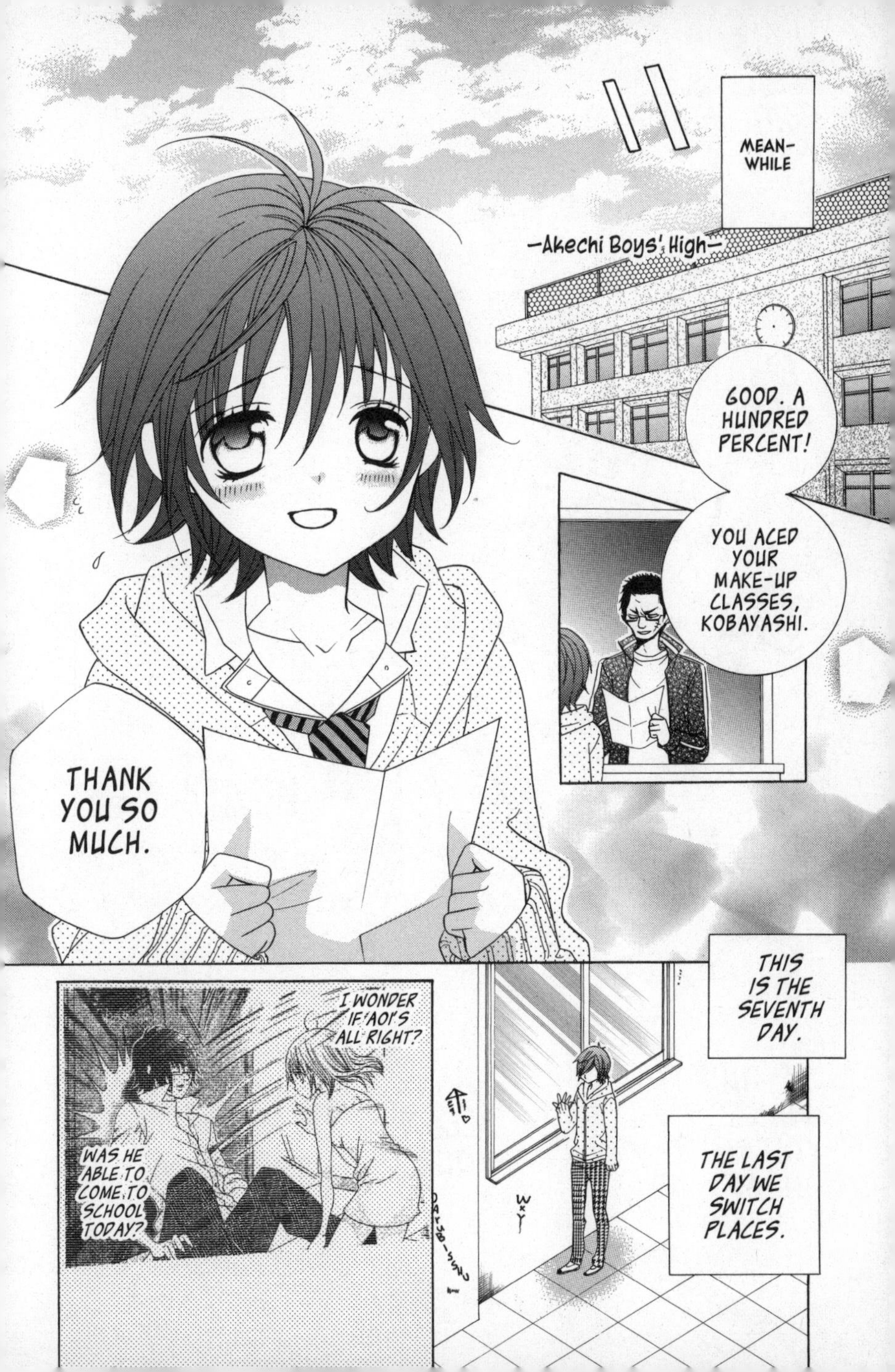
MEAN-WHILE
—Akechi Boys' High—
GOOD. A HUNDRED PERCENT!
YOU ACED YOUR MAKE-UP CLASSES, KOBAYASHI.
THANK YOU SO MUCH.
THIS IS THE SEVENTH DAY.
THE LAST DAY WE SWITCH PLACES.
I WONDER IF AOI'S ALL RIGHT?
WAS HE ABLE TO COME TO SCHOOL TODAY?

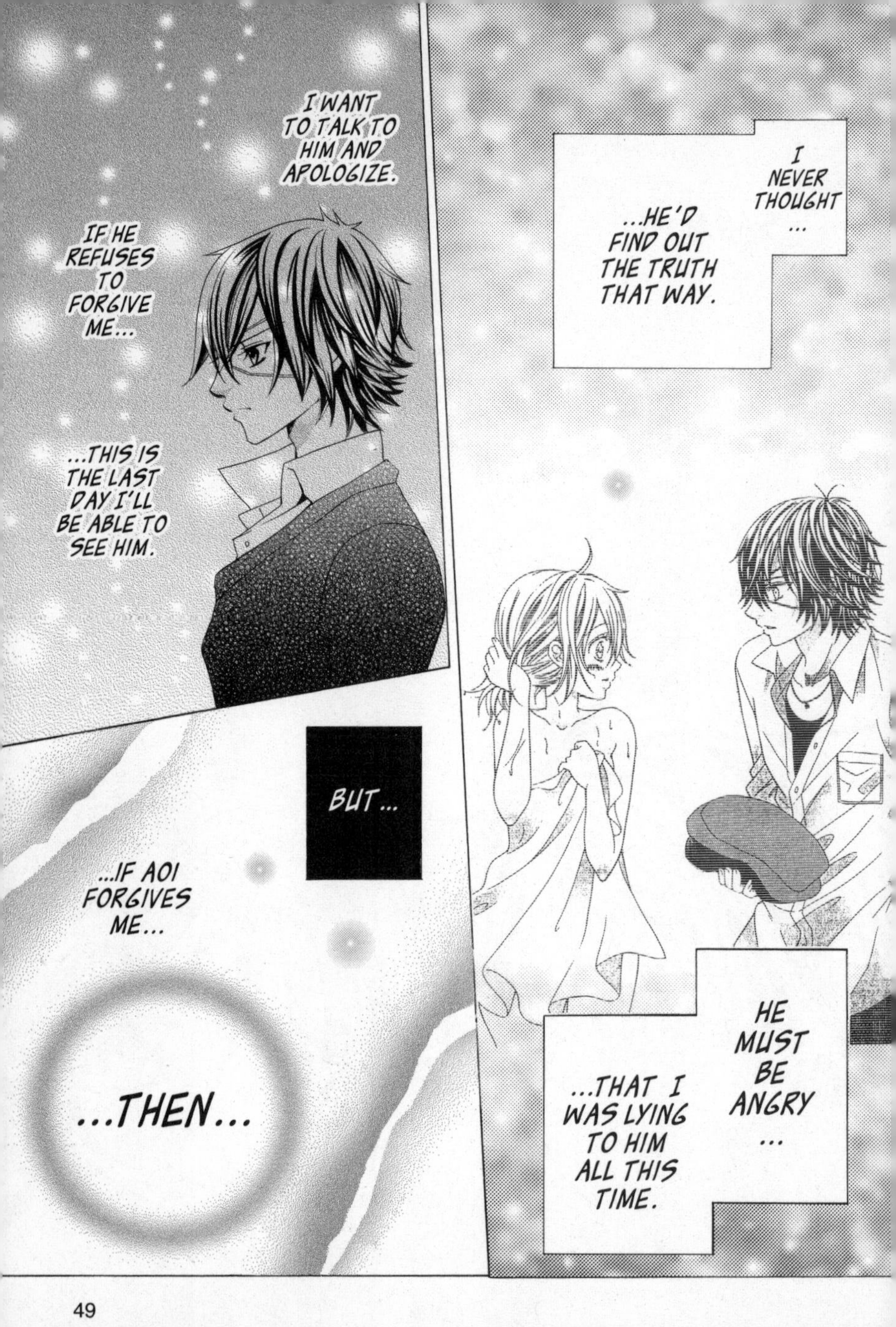
I NEVER THOUGHT ...
...HE'D FIND OUT THE TRUTH THAT WAY.
HE MUST BE ANGRY ...
...THAT I WAS LYING TO HIM ALL THIS TIME.
I WANT TO TALK TO HIM AND APOLOGIZE.
IF HE REFUSES TO FORGIVE ME...
...THIS IS THE LAST DAY I'LL BE ABLE TO SEE HIM.
BUT...
...IF AOI FORGIVES ME...
...THEN...

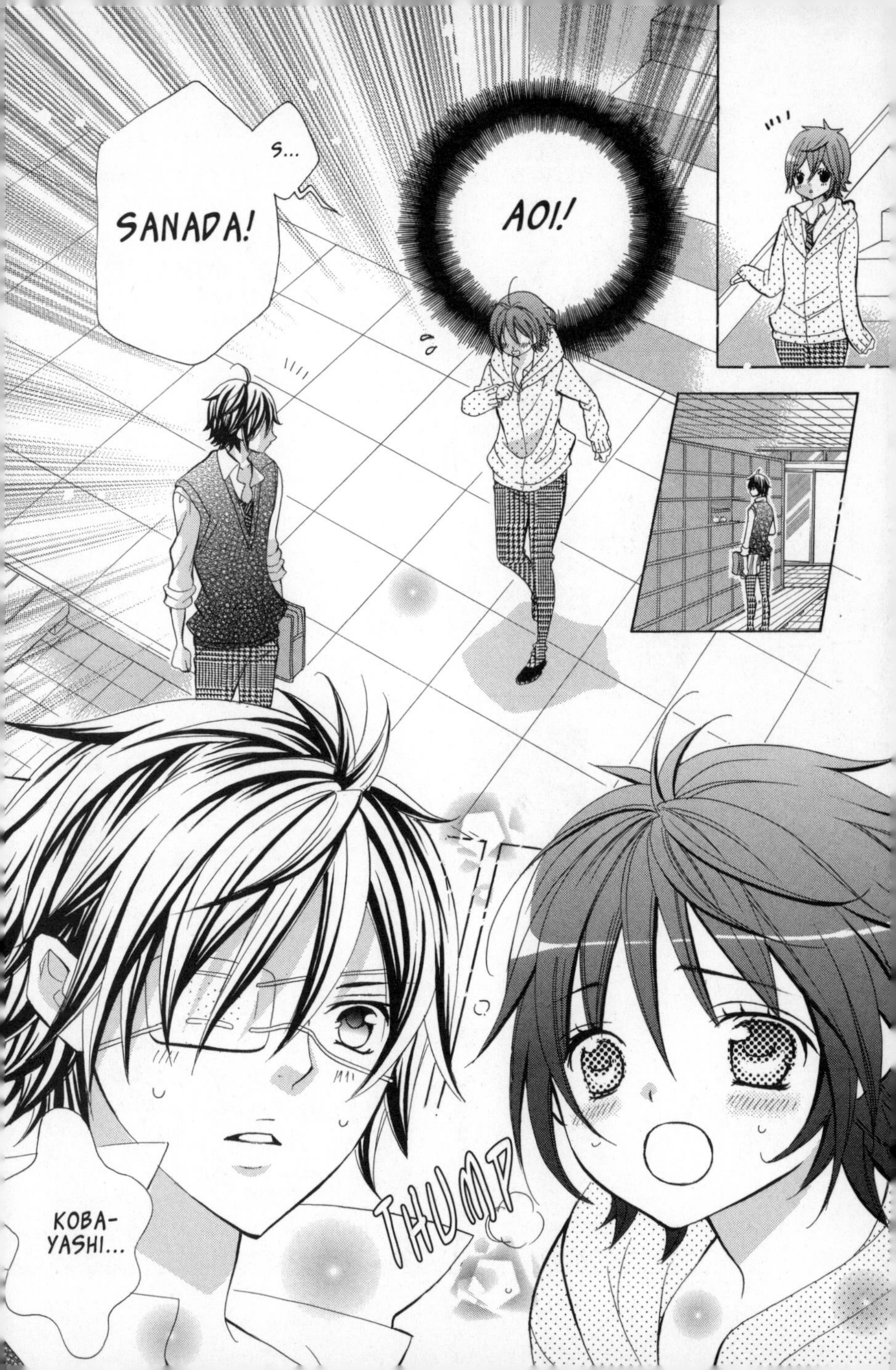
AOI!
S...
SANADA!
THUMP
KOBA-YASHI...

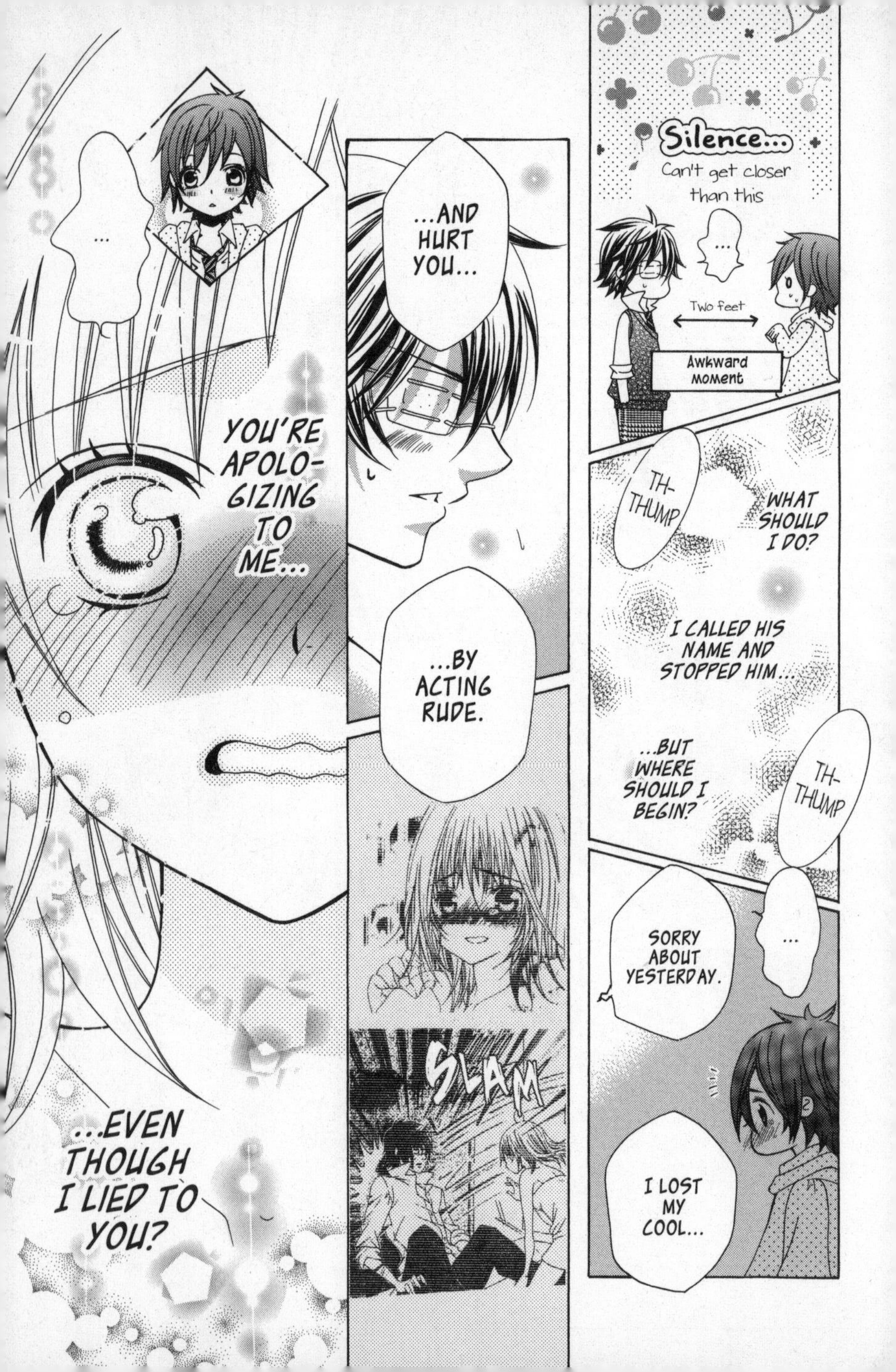
Silence...
Can't get closer than this
...
Two feet
Awkward moment
WHAT SHOULD I DO?
TH-THUMP
I CALLED HIS NAME AND STOPPED HIM...
TH-THUMP
...BUT WHERE SHOULD I BEGIN?
...
SORRY ABOUT YESTERDAY.
I LOST MY COOL...
...AND HURT YOU...
...BY ACTING RUDE.
SLAM
...
YOU'RE APOLOGIZING TO ME...
...EVEN THOUGH I LIED TO YOU?

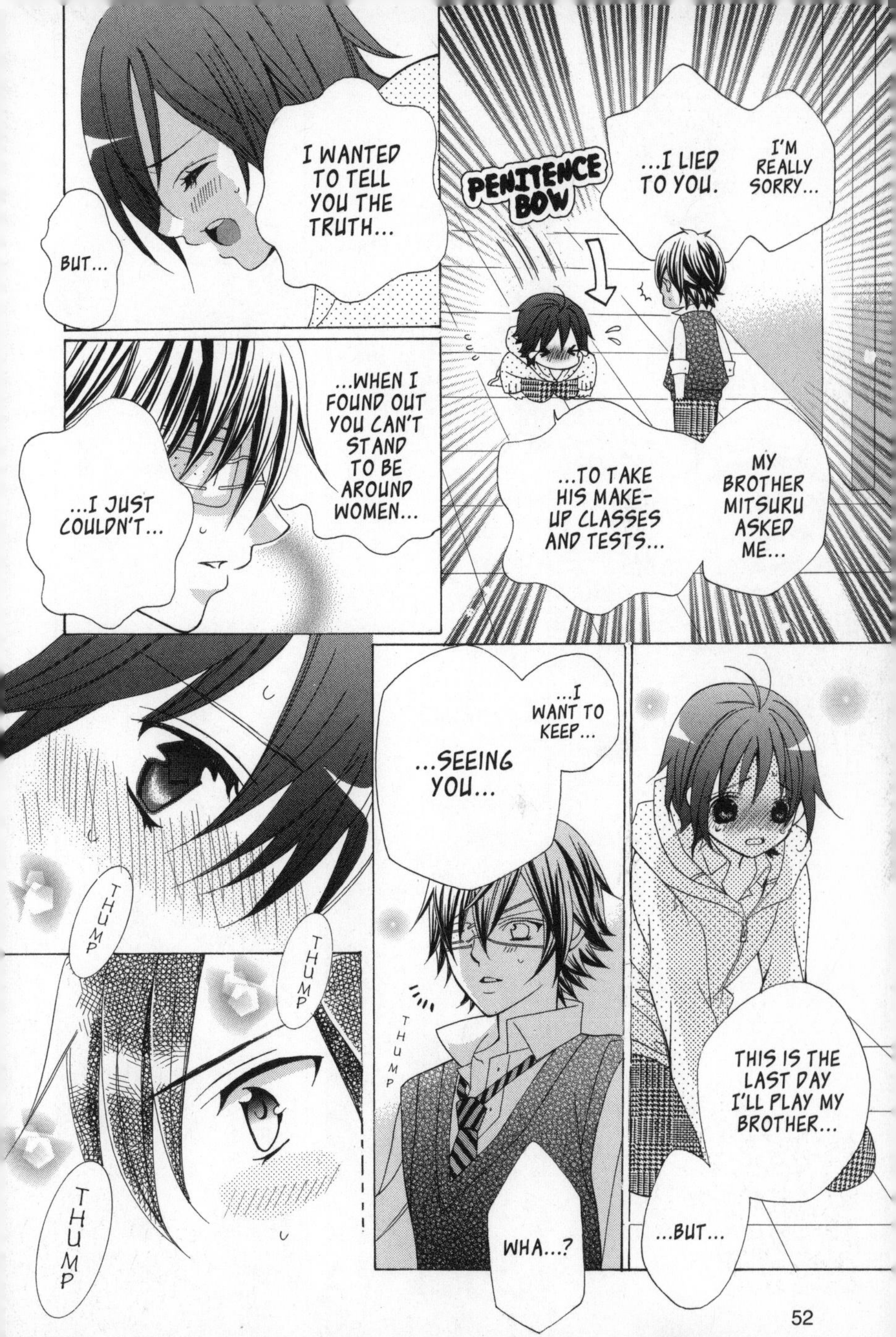
I'M REALLY SORRY...
...I LIED TO YOU.
PENITENCE BOW
MY BROTHER MITSURU ASKED ME...
...TO TAKE HIS MAKE-UP CLASSES AND TESTS...
I WANTED TO TELL YOU THE TRUTH...
BUT...
...WHEN I FOUND OUT YOU CAN'T STAND TO BE AROUND WOMEN...
...I JUST COULDN'T...
THIS IS THE LAST DAY I'LL PLAY MY BROTHER...
...BUT...
...I WANT TO KEEP...
...SEEING YOU...
WHA...?
THUMP
THUMP
THUMP
THUMP

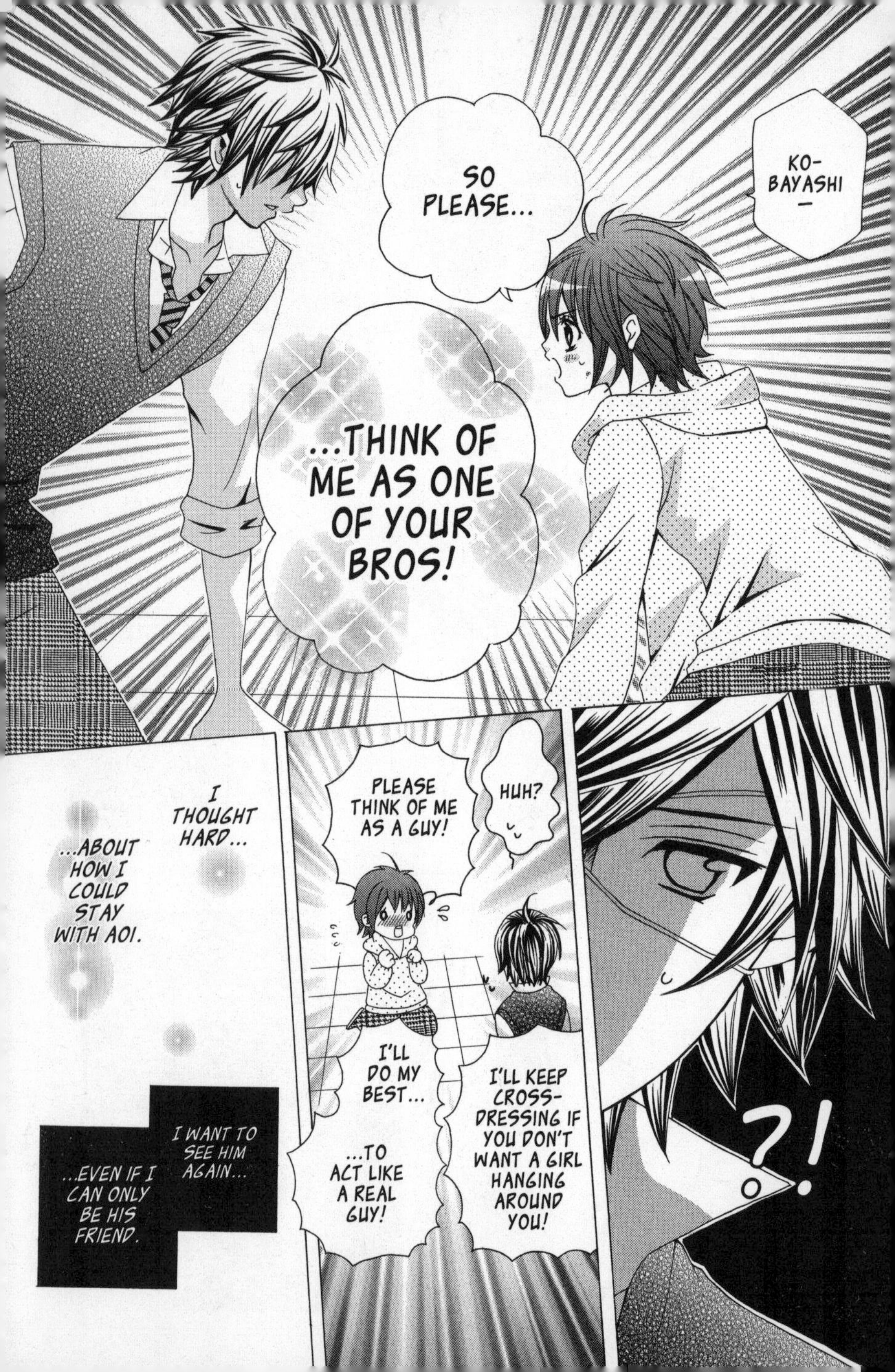
KO-BAYASHI—
SO PLEASE...
...THINK OF ME AS ONE OF YOUR BROS!
?!
PLEASE THINK OF ME AS A GUY!
HUH?
I'LL KEEP CROSS-DRESSING IF YOU DON'T WANT A GIRL HANGING AROUND YOU!
I'LL DO MY BEST...
...TO ACT LIKE A REAL GUY!
I THOUGHT HARD...
...ABOUT HOW I COULD STAY WITH AOI.
I WANT TO SEE HIM AGAIN...
...EVEN IF I CAN ONLY BE HIS FRIEND.

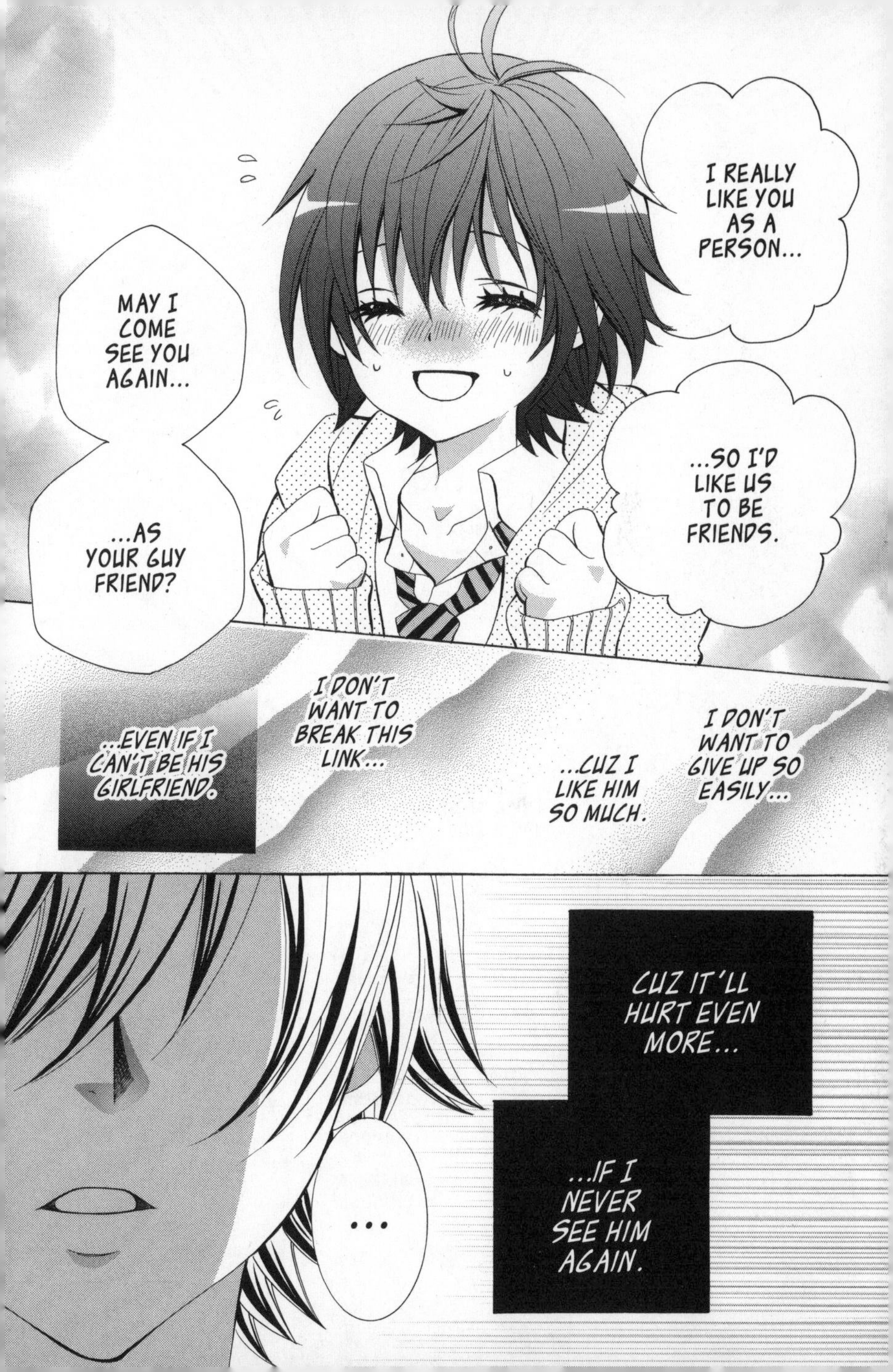
I REALLY LIKE YOU AS A PERSON...
...SO I'D LIKE US TO BE FRIENDS.
MAY I COME SEE YOU AGAIN...
...AS YOUR GUY FRIEND?
I DON'T WANT TO GIVE UP SO EASILY...
...CUZ I LIKE HIM SO MUCH.
I DON'T WANT TO BREAK THIS LINK...
...EVEN IF I CAN'T BE HIS GIRLFRIEND.
CUZ IT'LL HURT EVEN MORE...
...IF I NEVER SEE HIM AGAIN.
...

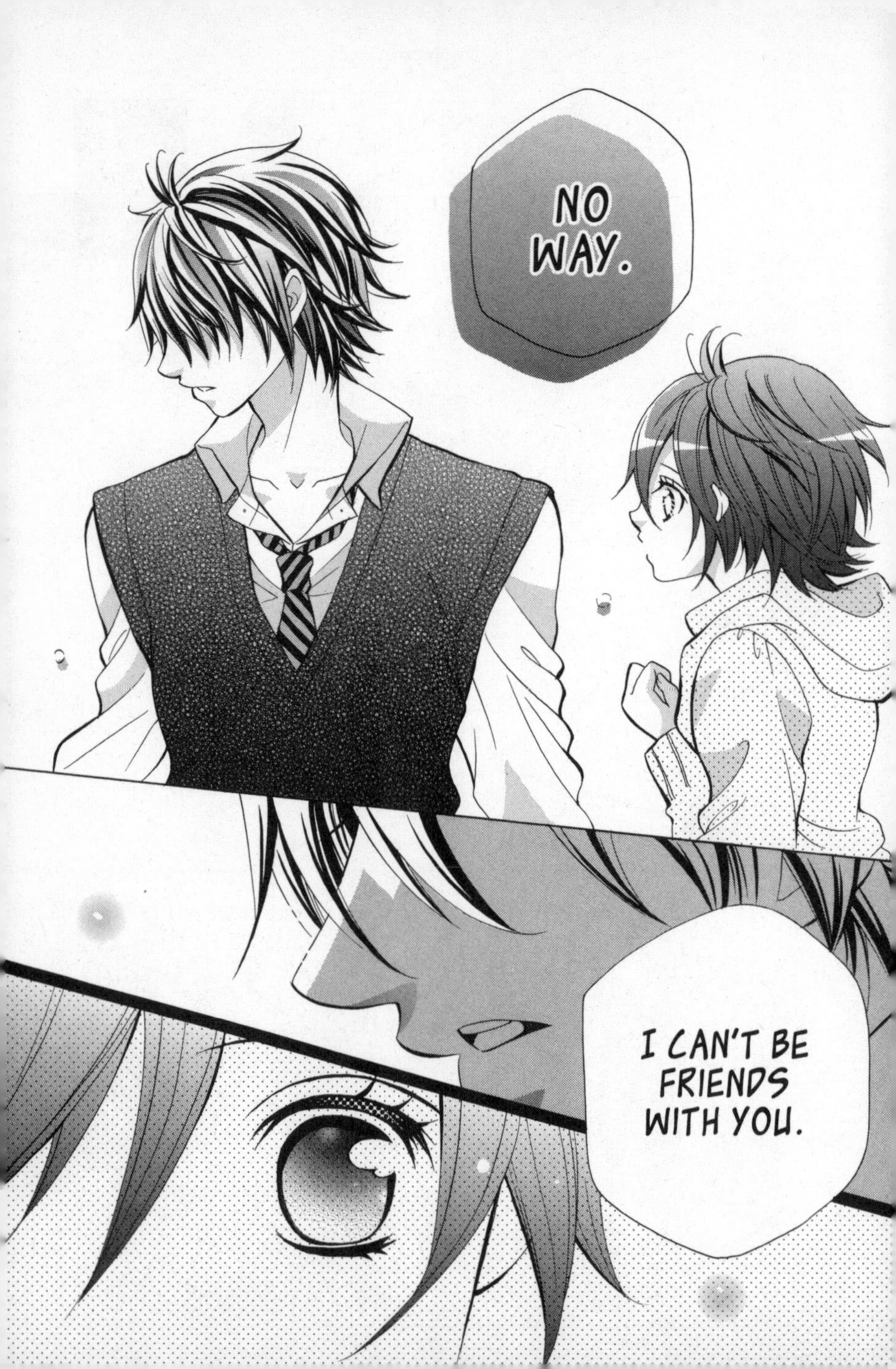
NO WAY.
I CAN'T BE FRIENDS WITH YOU.

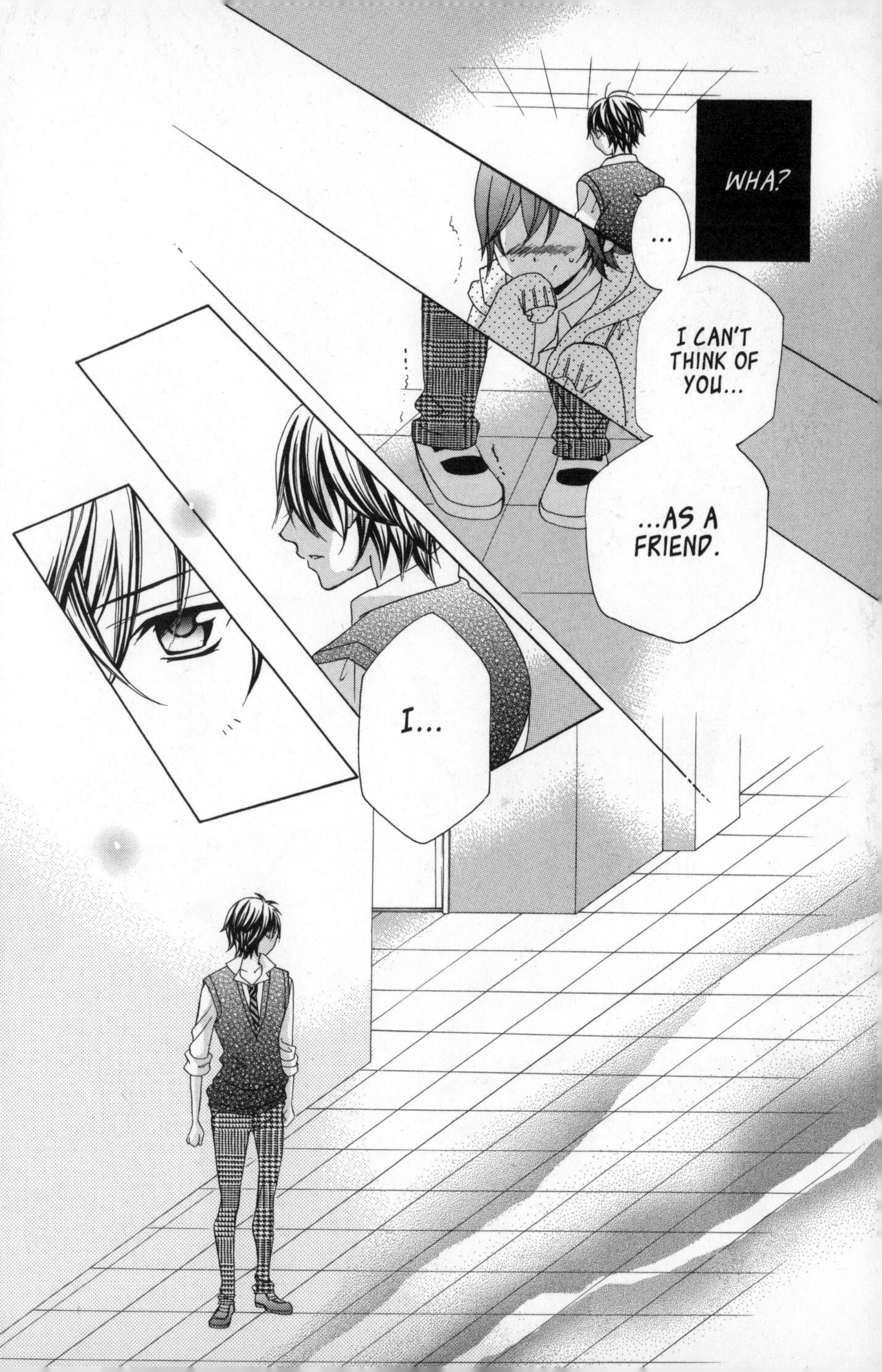
WHA?
...
I CAN'T THINK OF YOU...
...AS A FRIEND.
I...

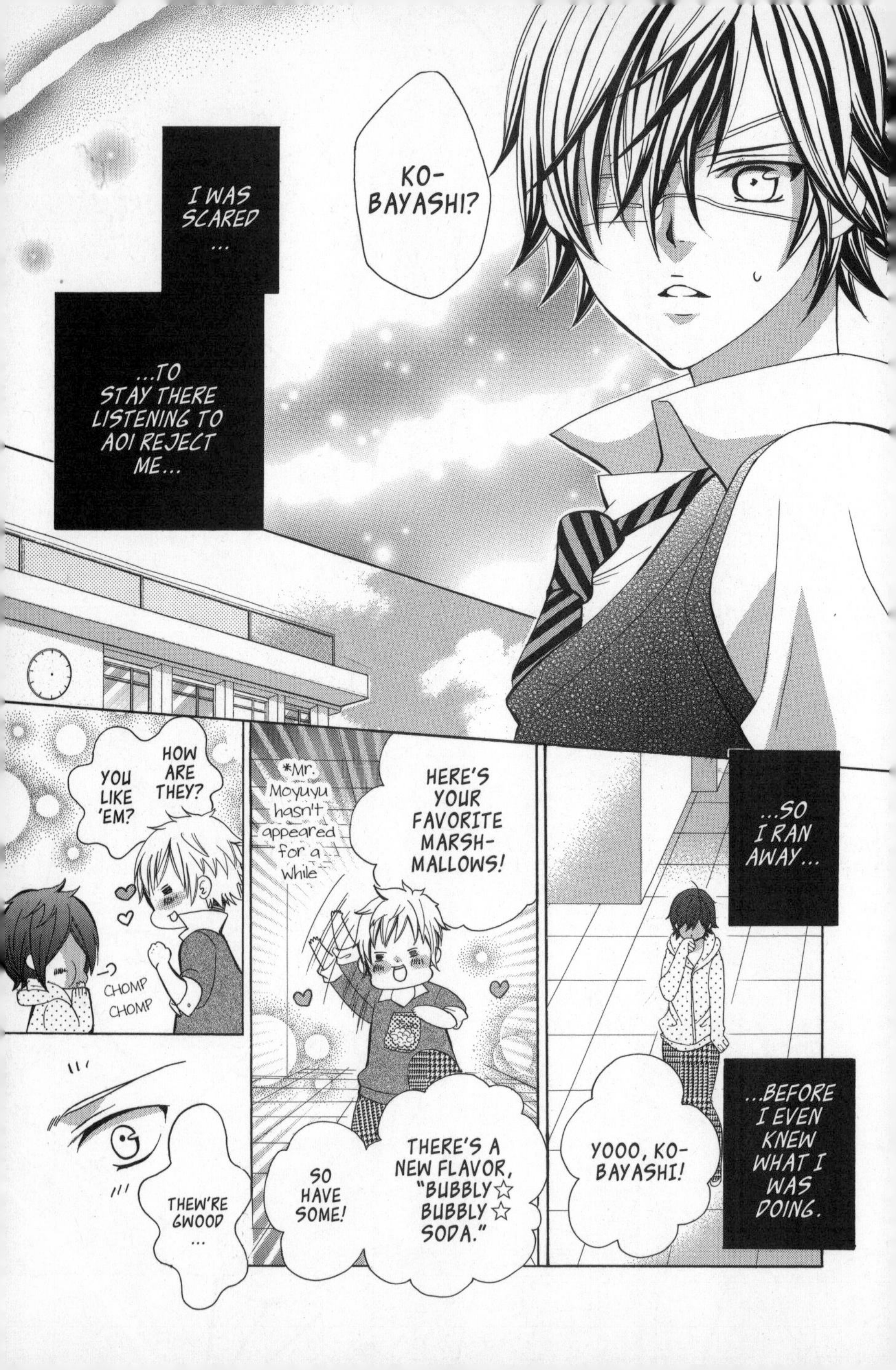
KO-BAYASHI?
I WAS SCARED ...
...TO STAY THERE LISTENING TO AOI REJECT ME...
...SO I RAN AWAY...
...BEFORE I EVEN KNEW WHAT I WAS DOING.
YOOO, KO-BAYASHI!
HERE'S YOUR FAVORITE MARSH-MALLOWS!
*Mr. Moyuyu hasn't appeared for a while
THERE'S A NEW FLAVOR, "BUBBLY☆ BUBBLY☆ SODA."
SO HAVE SOME!
HOW ARE THEY?
YOU LIKE 'EM?
CHOMP CHOMP
THEW'RE GWOOD ...

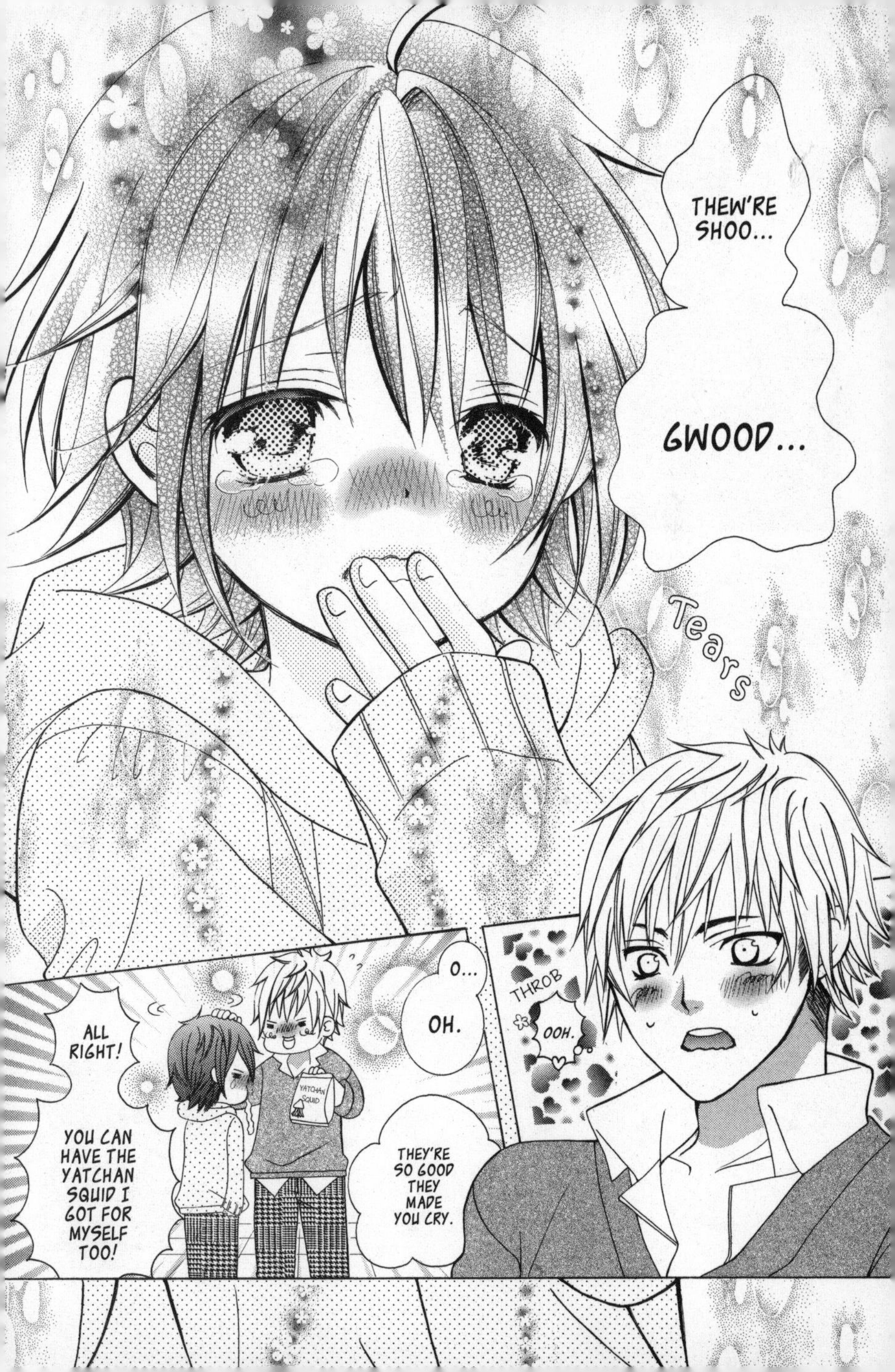
THEW'RE SHOO...
GWOOD...
Tears
THROB
OOH.
O...
OH.
THEY'RE SO GOOD THEY MADE YOU CRY.
ALL RIGHT!
YOU CAN HAVE THE YATCHAN SQUID I GOT FOR MYSELF TOO!
YATCHAN SQUID

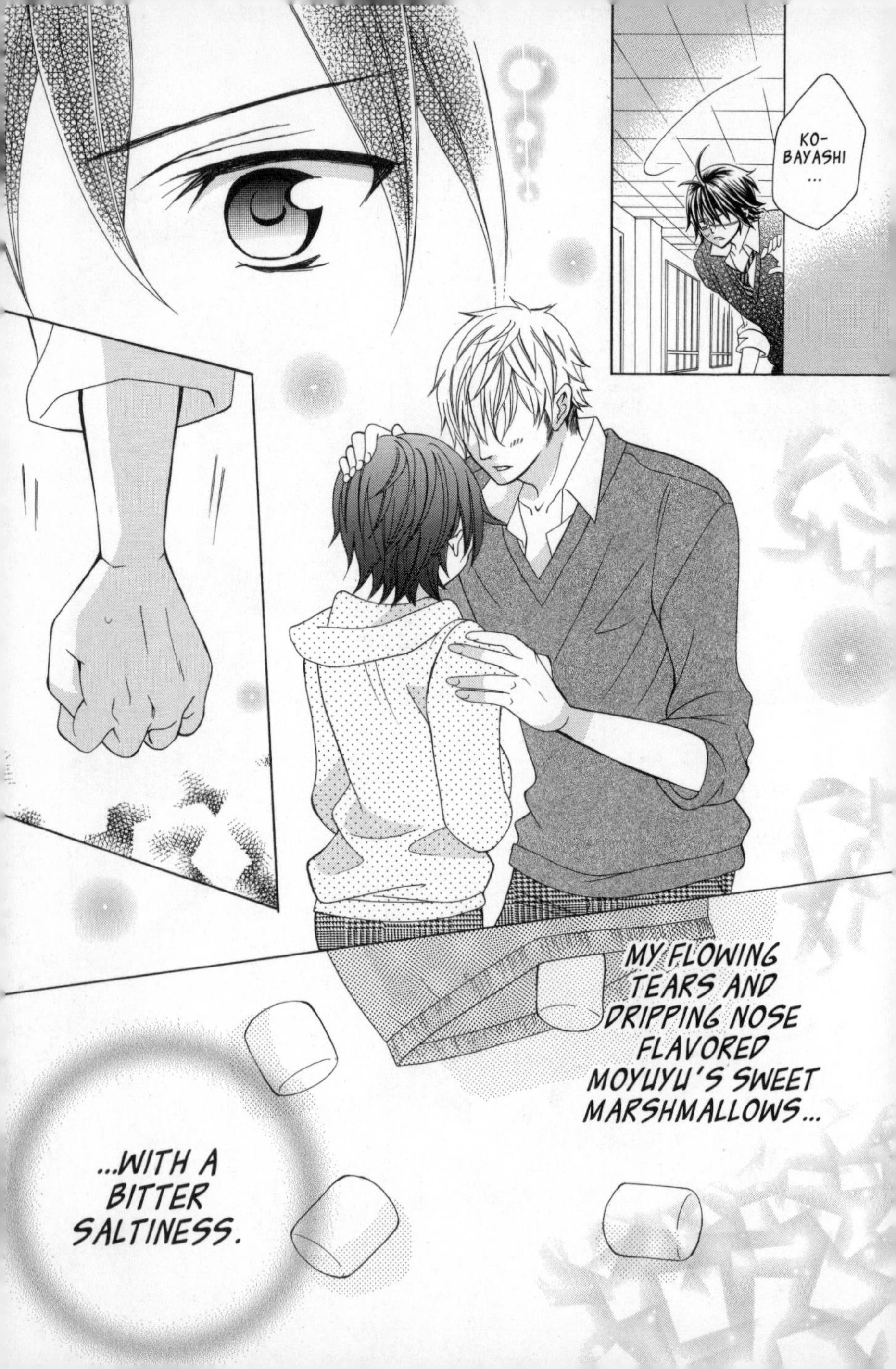
KO-BAYASHI ...
MY FLOWING TEARS AND DRIPPING NOSE FLAVORED MOYUYU'S SWEET MARSHMALLOWS...
...WITH A BITTER SALTINESS.

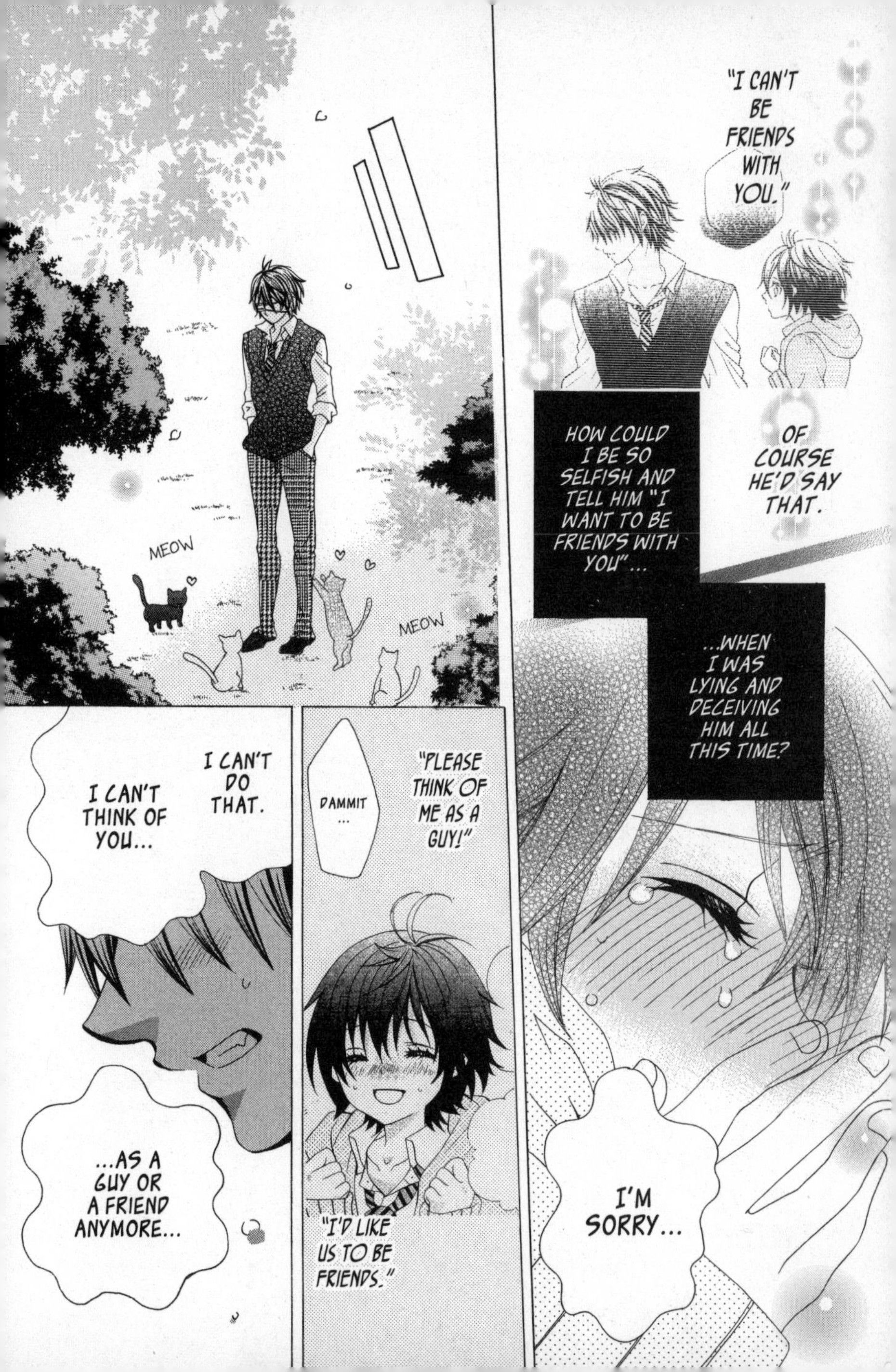
"I CAN'T BE FRIENDS WITH YOU."
OF COURSE HE'D SAY THAT.
HOW COULD I BE SO SELFISH AND TELL HIM "I WANT TO BE FRIENDS WITH YOU"...
...WHEN I WAS LYING AND DECEIVING HIM ALL THIS TIME?
I'M SORRY...
MEOW
MEOW
"PLEASE THINK OF ME AS A GUY!"
DAMMIT...
"I'D LIKE US TO BE FRIENDS."
I CAN'T DO THAT.
I CAN'T THINK OF YOU...
...AS A GUY OR A FRIEND ANYMORE...

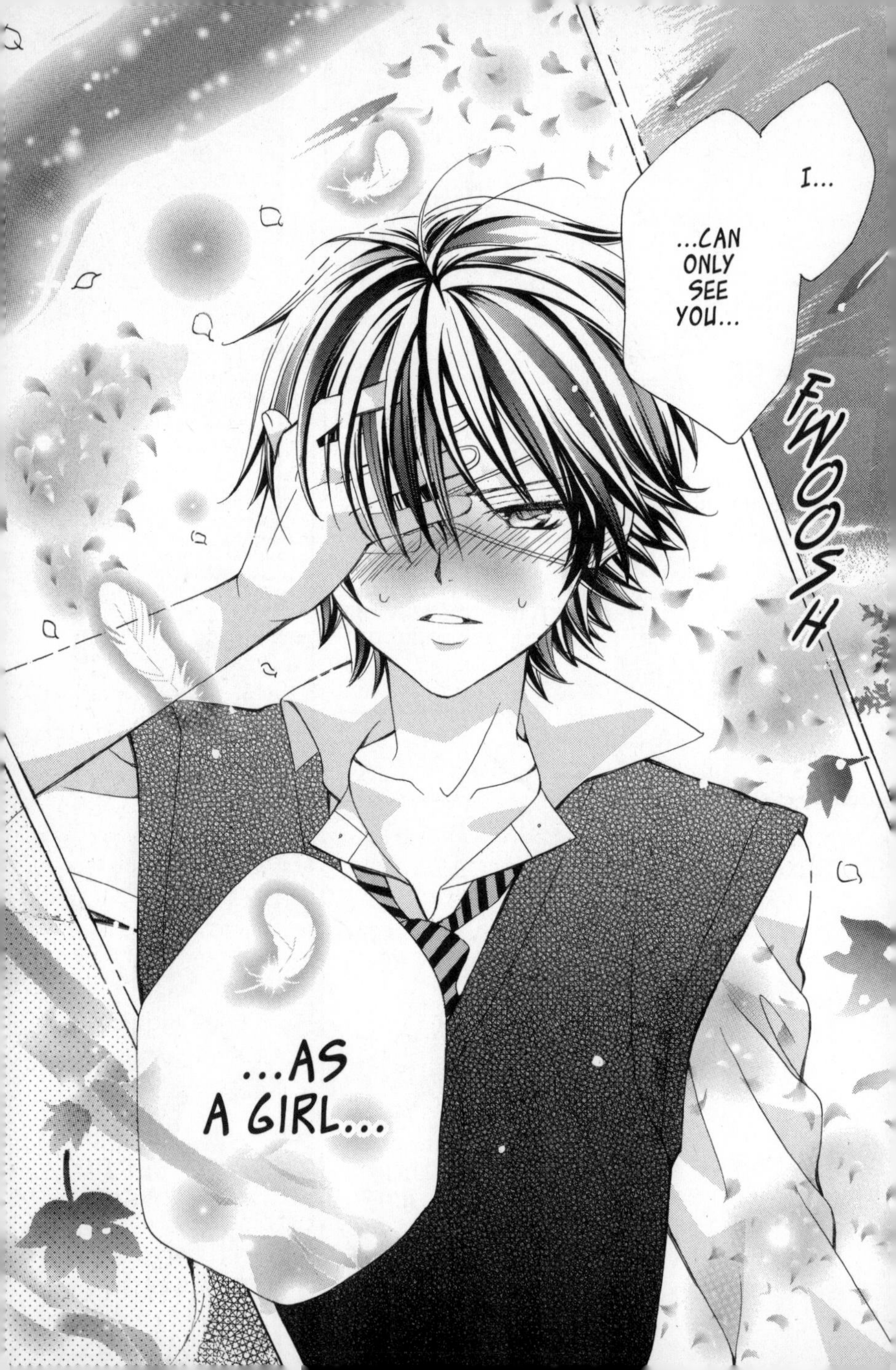
I...
...CAN ONLY SEE YOU...
FWOOSH
...AS A GIRL...

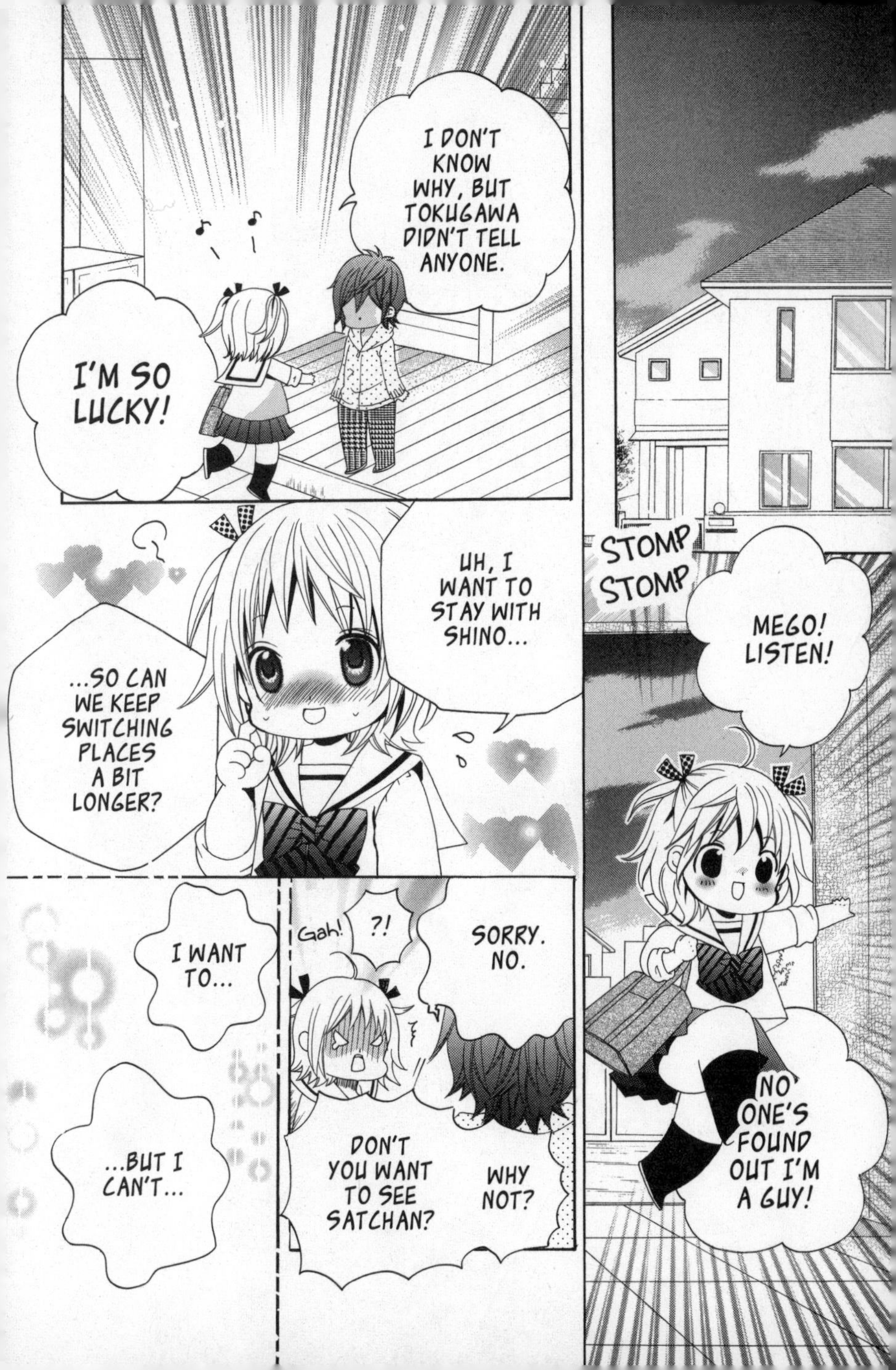
STOMP STOMP
MEGO! LISTEN!
NO ONE'S FOUND OUT I'M A GUY!
I DON'T KNOW WHY, BUT TOKUGAWA DIDN'T TELL ANYONE.
I'M SO LUCKY!
UH, I WANT TO STAY WITH SHINO...
...SO CAN WE KEEP SWITCHING PLACES A BIT LONGER?
SORRY. NO.
?!
Gah!
WHY NOT?
DON'T YOU WANT TO SEE SATCHAN?
I WANT TO...
...BUT I CAN'T...

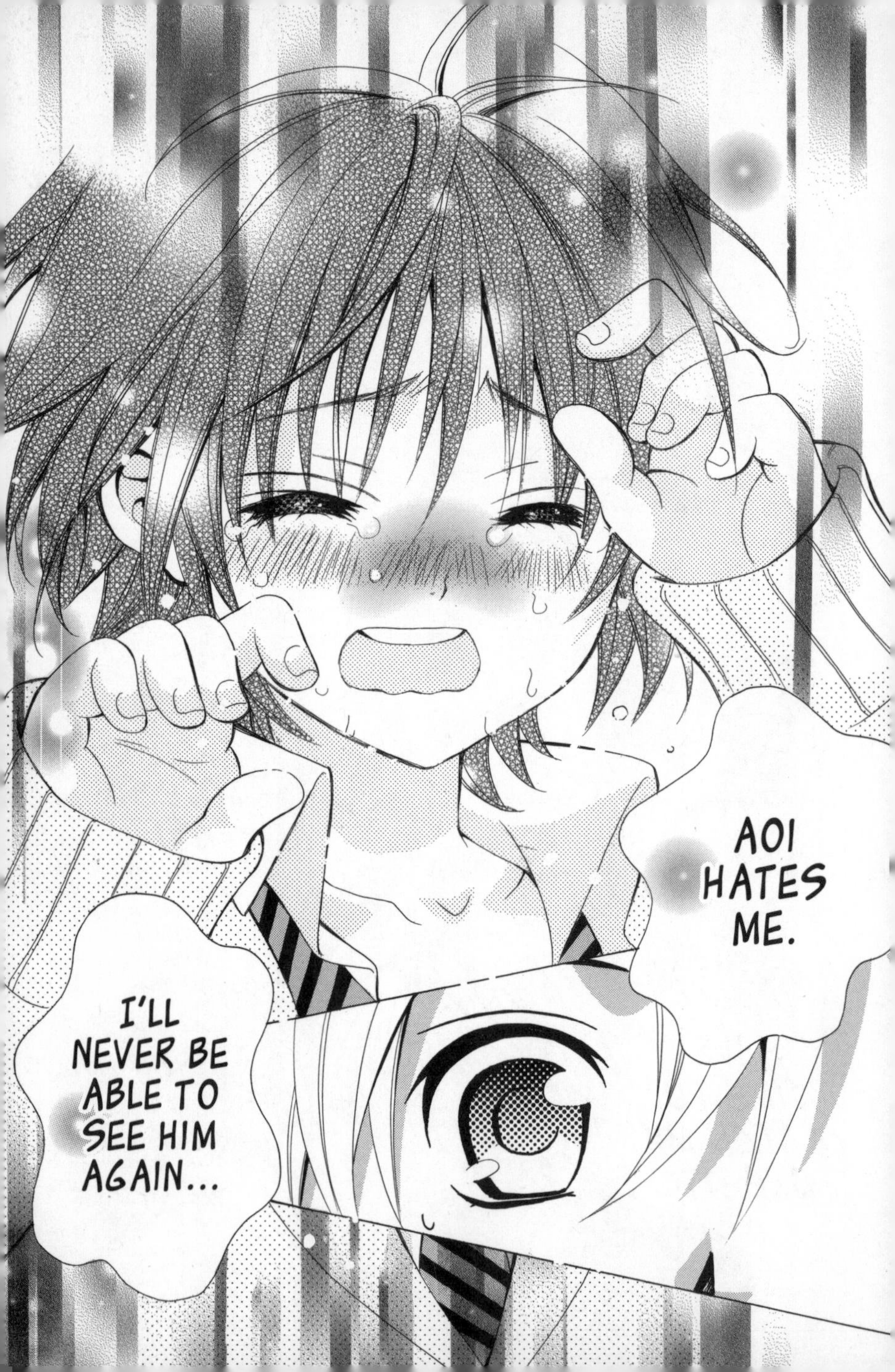
AOI HATES ME.
I'LL NEVER BE ABLE TO SEE HIM AGAIN...

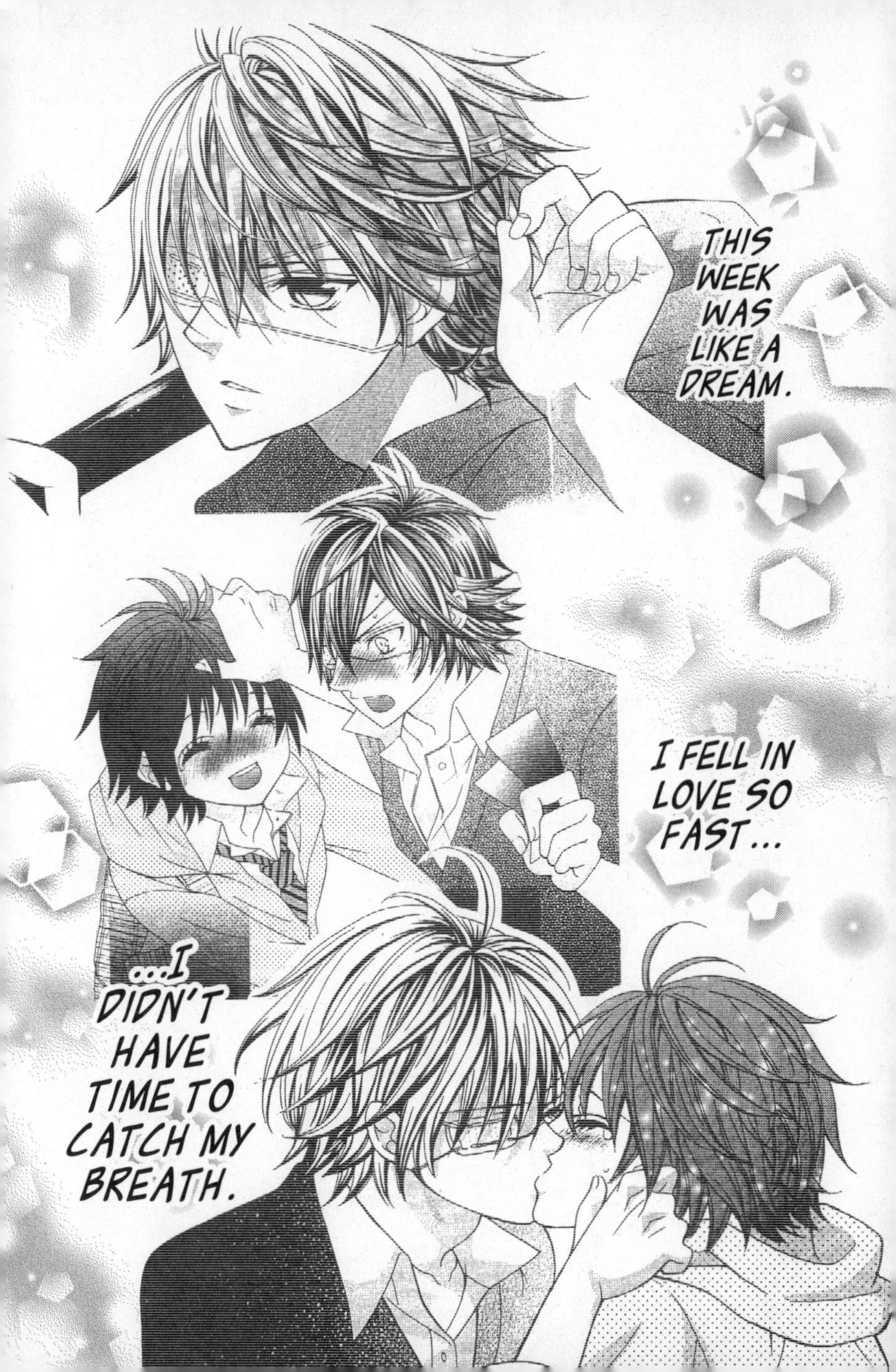
THIS WEEK WAS LIKE A DREAM.
I FELL IN LOVE SO FAST...
...I DIDN'T HAVE TIME TO CATCH MY BREATH.

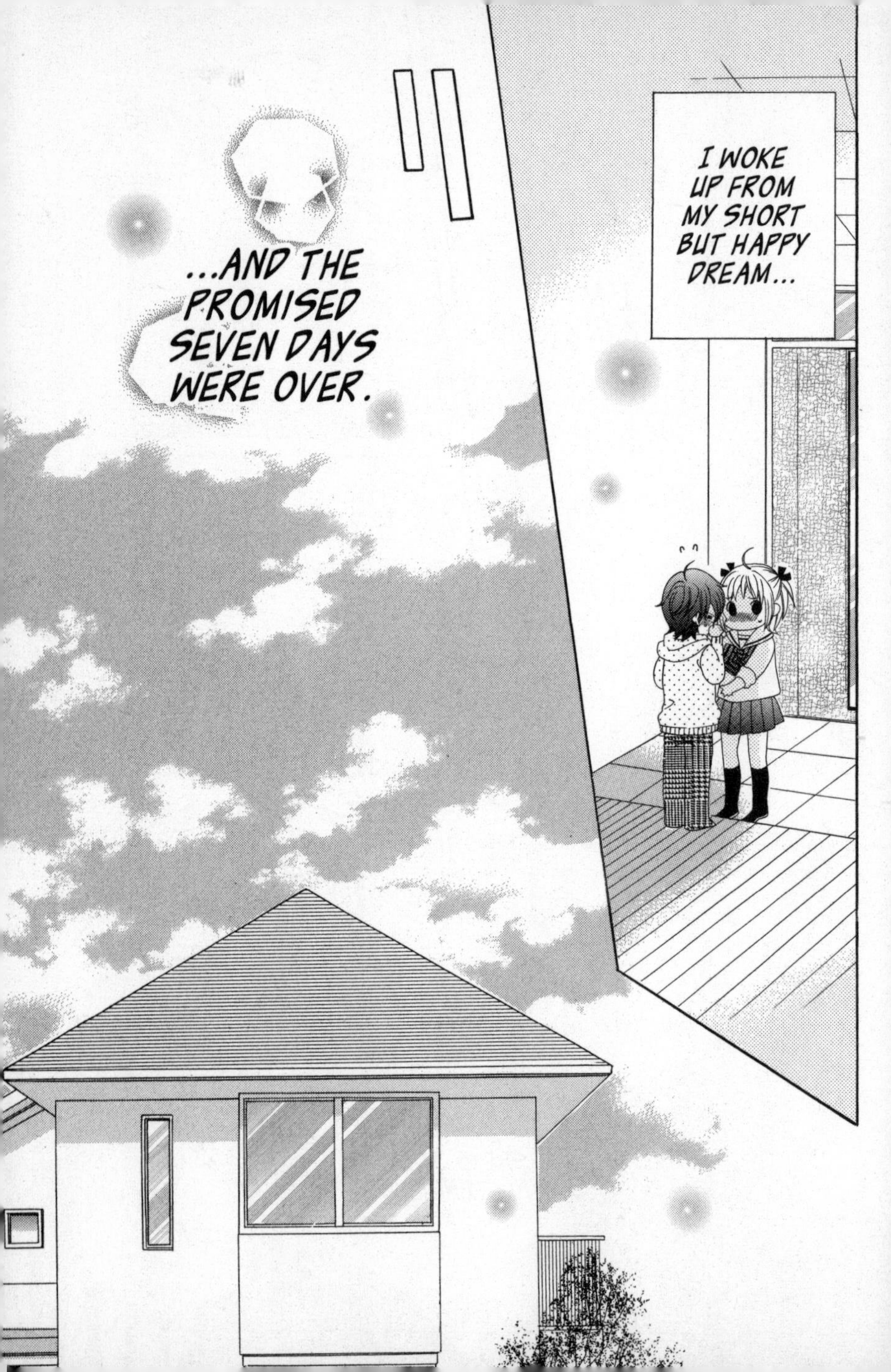
I WOKE UP FROM MY SHORT BUT HAPPY DREAM...
...AND THE PROMISED SEVEN DAYS WERE OVER.

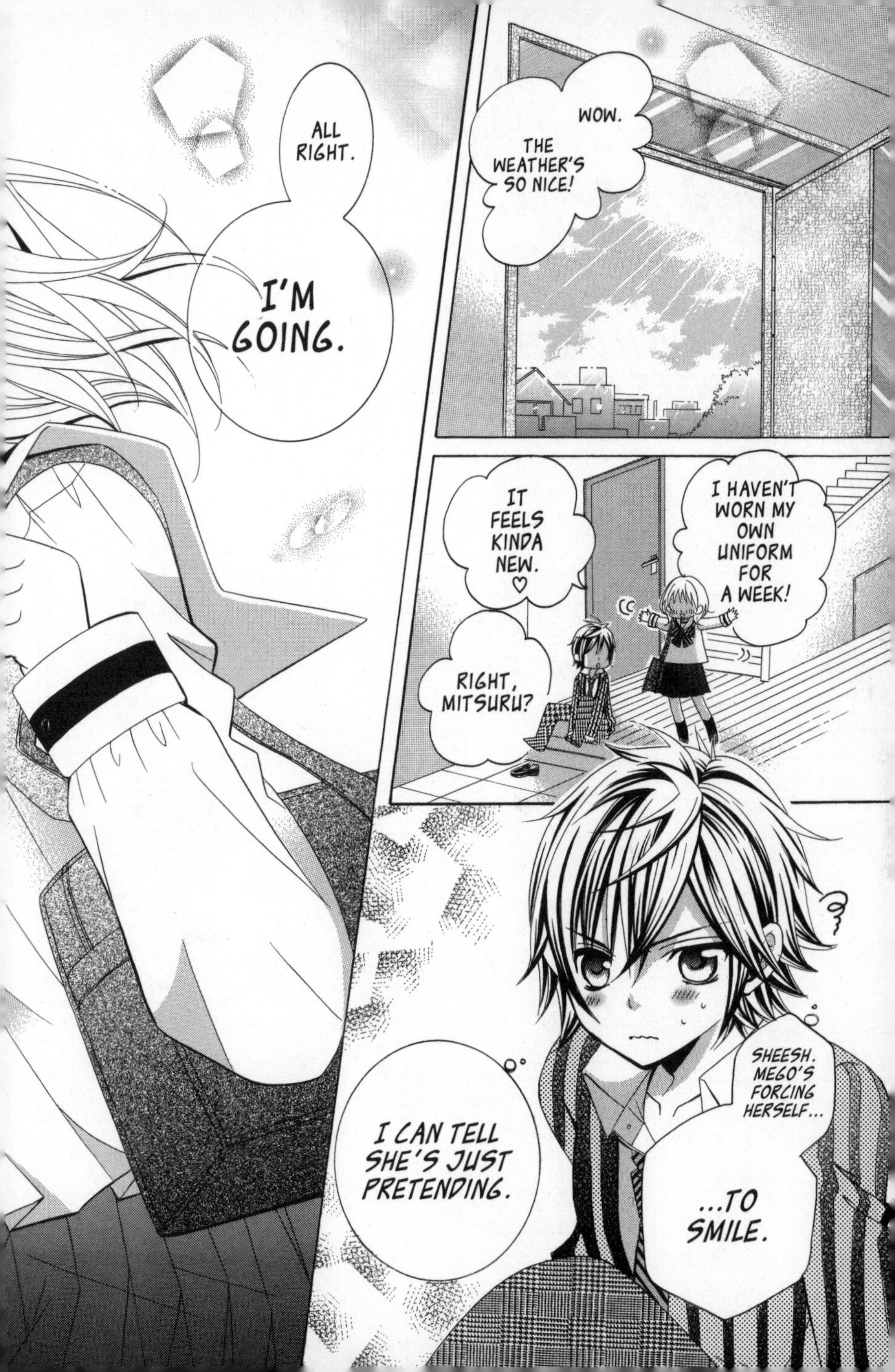
WOW.
THE WEATHER'S SO NICE!
I HAVEN'T WORN MY OWN UNIFORM FOR A WEEK!
IT FEELS KINDA NEW. ♡
RIGHT, MITSURU?
SHEESH. MEGO'S FORCING HERSELF...
...TO SMILE.
I CAN TELL SHE'S JUST PRETENDING.
ALL RIGHT.
I'M GOING.

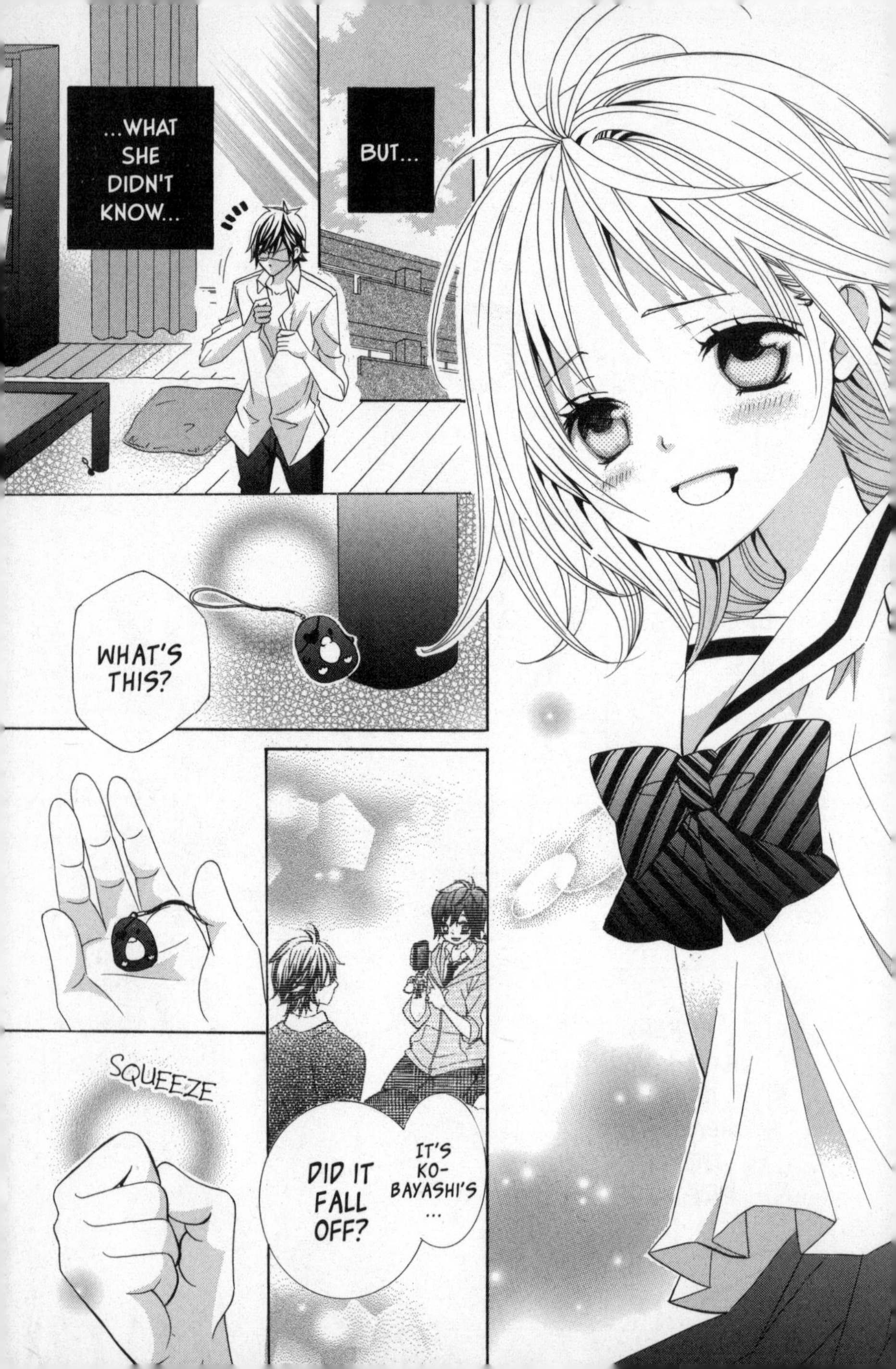
BUT...
...WHAT SHE DIDN'T KNOW...
WHAT'S THIS?
IT'S KO-BAYASHI'S...
DID IT FALL OFF?
SQUEEZE

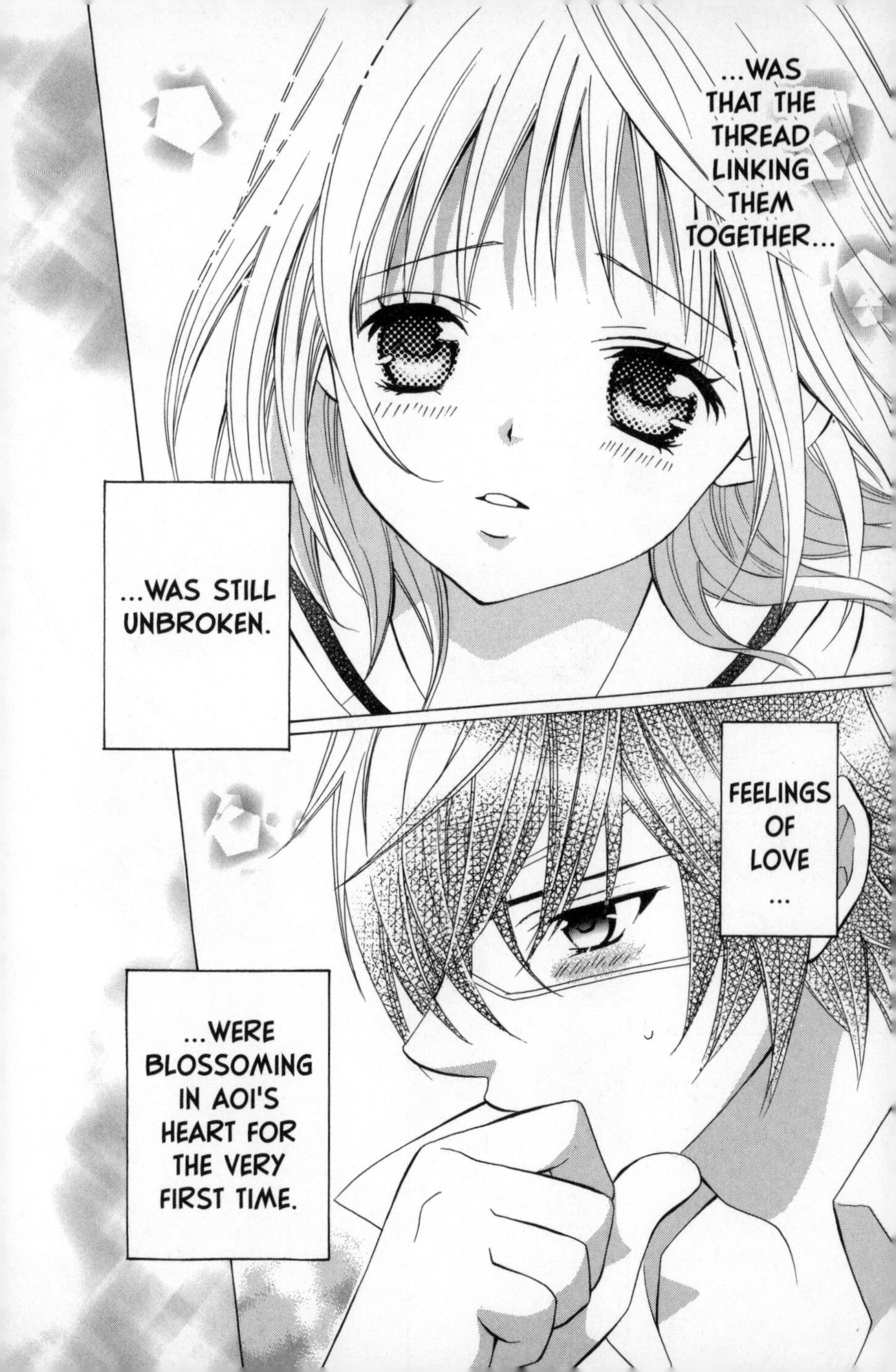
...WAS THAT THE THREAD LINKING THEM TOGETHER...
...WAS STILL UNBROKEN.
FEELINGS OF LOVE ...
...WERE BLOSSOMING IN AOI'S HEART FOR THE VERY FIRST TIME.

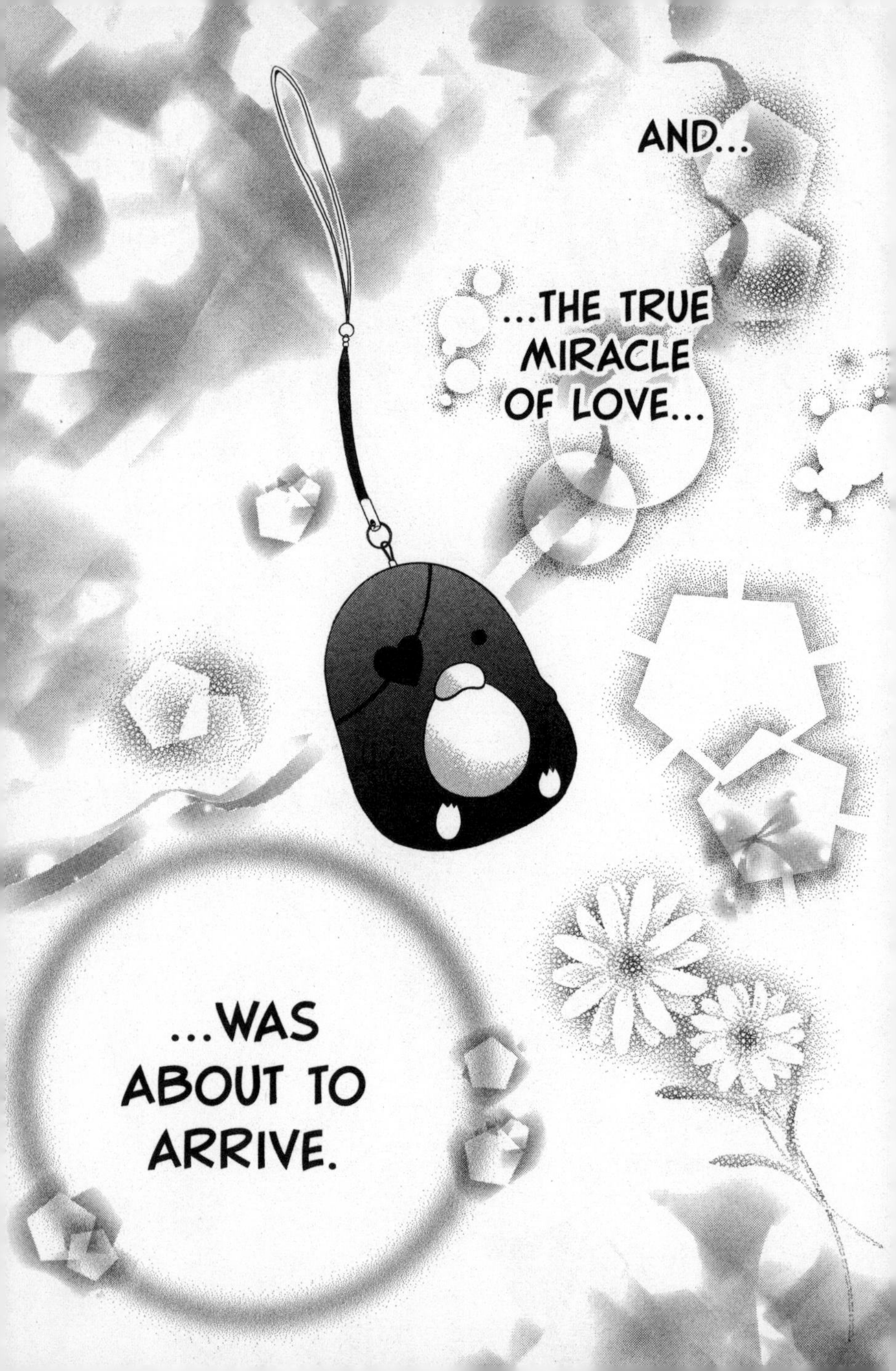
AND...
...THE TRUE MIRACLE OF LOVE...
...WAS ABOUT TO ARRIVE.

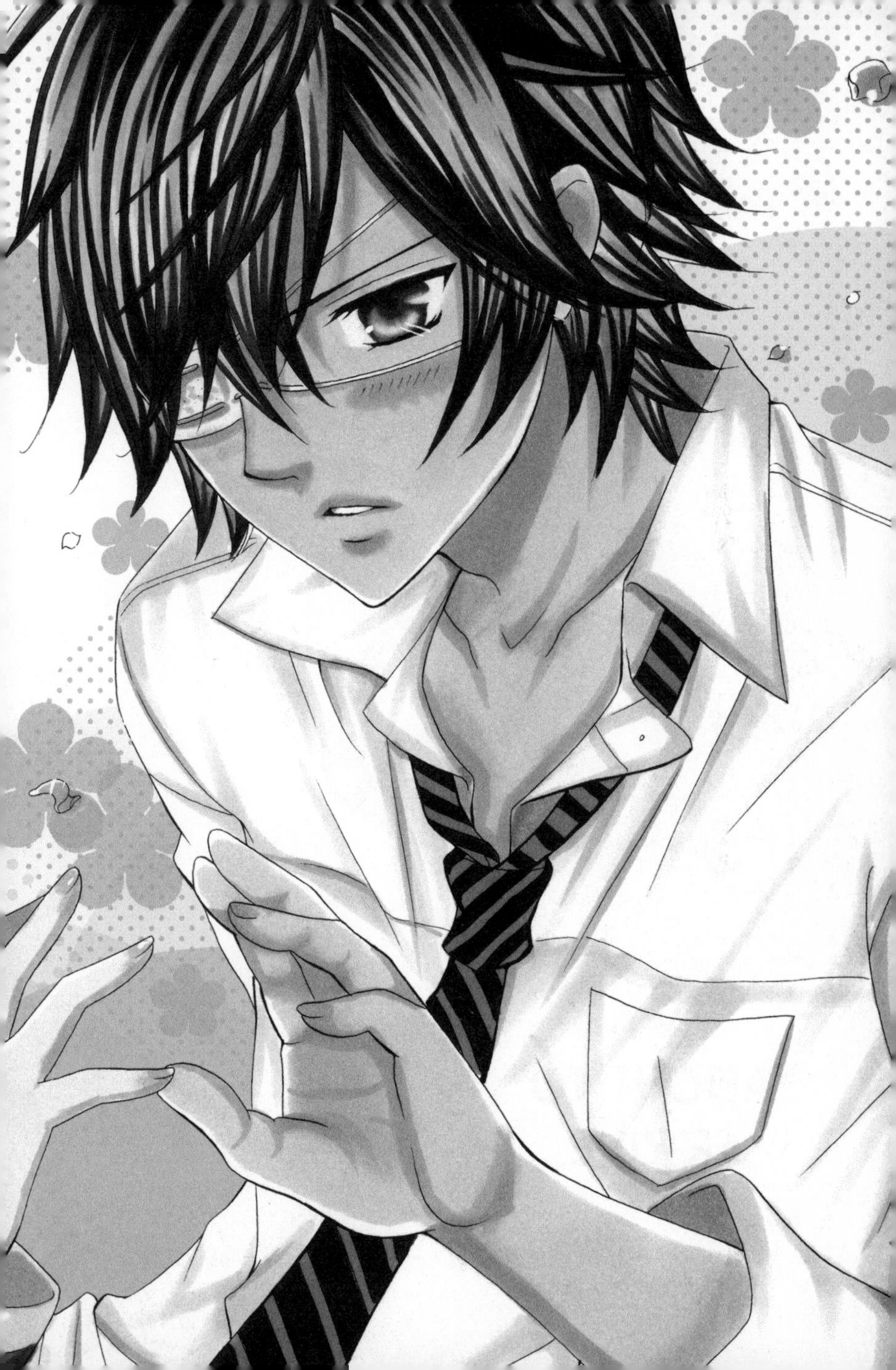

Chapter 13

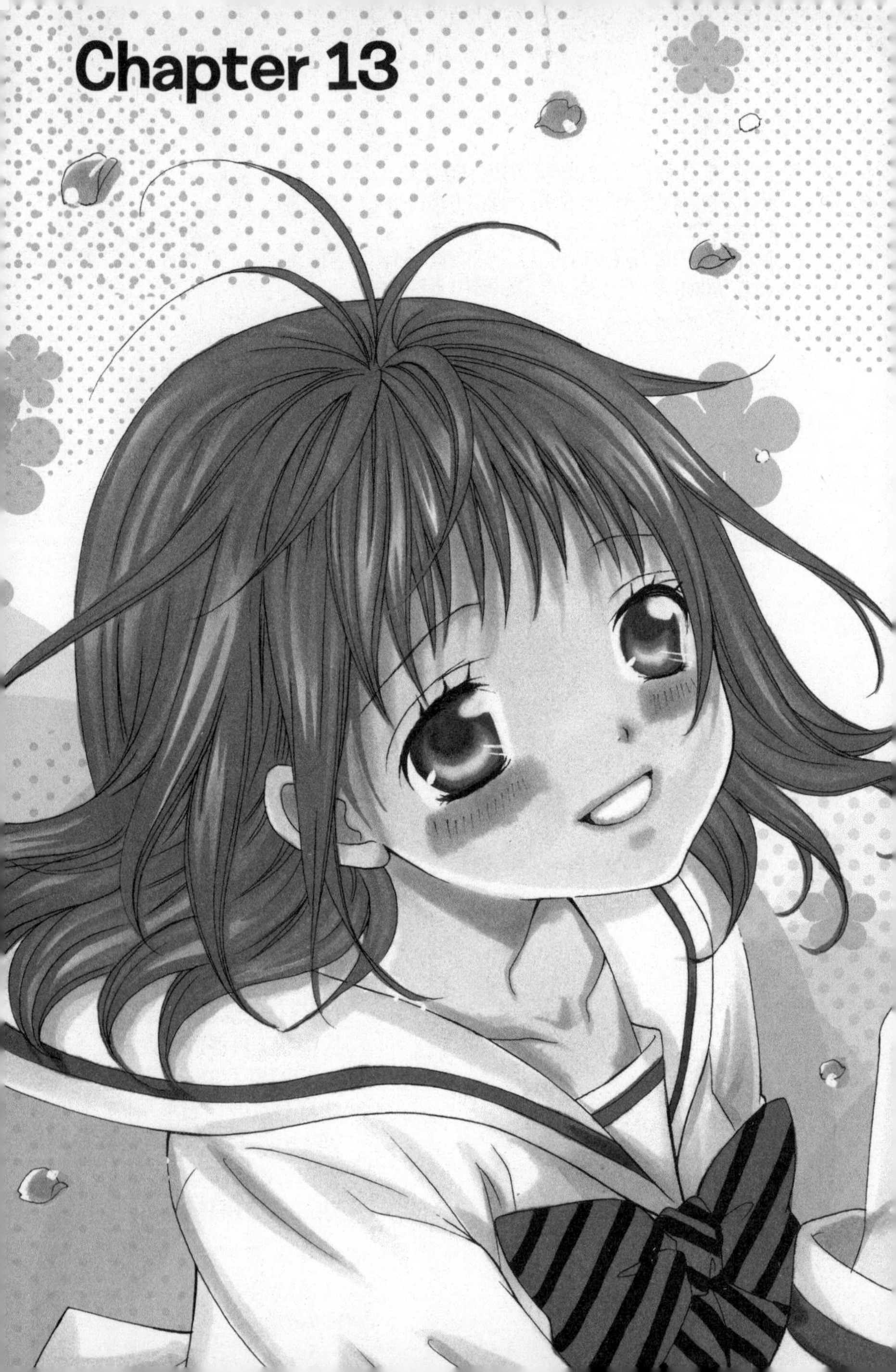

HERE ARE FUROKU AND OTHER ITEMS *SHO-COMI* MAGAZINE MADE FOR *SO CUTE!* THERE'RE LOTS OF FUROKU THAT ARE SO CUTE IT HURTS, LIKE A REUSABLE BAG, ZIP PACKS AND A SPARKLING DECO CASE, WHICH ALL FEATURE THE EYE-PATCH PENGUIN, THE *SO CUTE!* MASCOT.

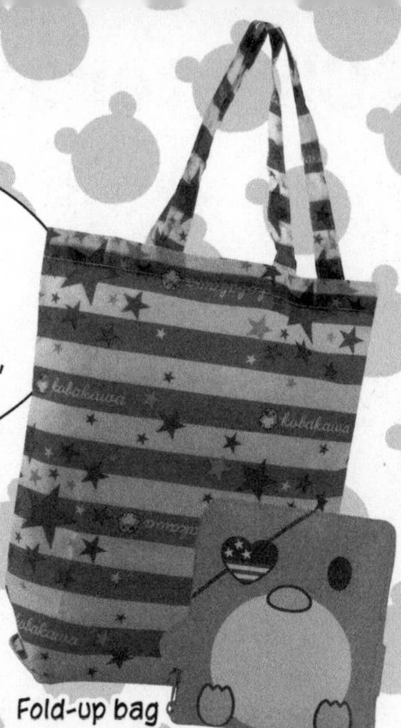
kobakawa
kobakawa

Fold-up bag

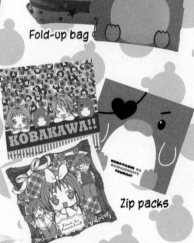

THE EXTRA-LARGE HANDKERCHIEF MEGO USES TO HIDE HER FACE IN CHAPTER 14 WAS ALSO MADE INTO A FUROKU! (*SMILE*)

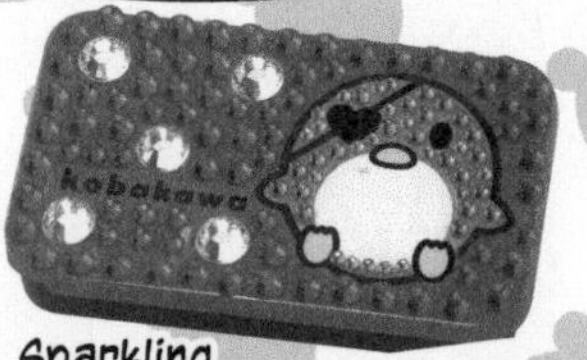
kobakawa

Sparkling deco case

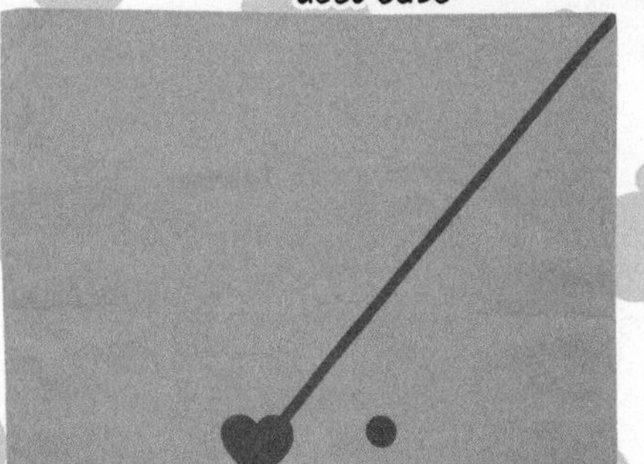

Large handkerchief

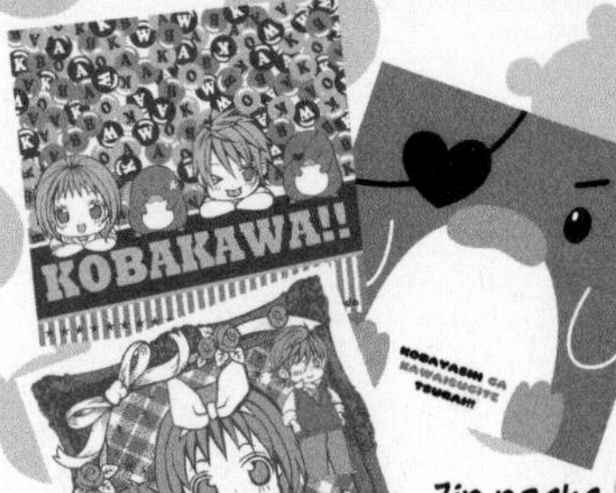
KOBAKAWA!!

Zip packs

THERE ARE GORGEOUS GIVEAWAYS AND MAIL-ORDER ITEMS AS WELL, SO CHECK OUT *SHO-COMI* AND OTHER OFFICIAL WEBSITES. ♡♡

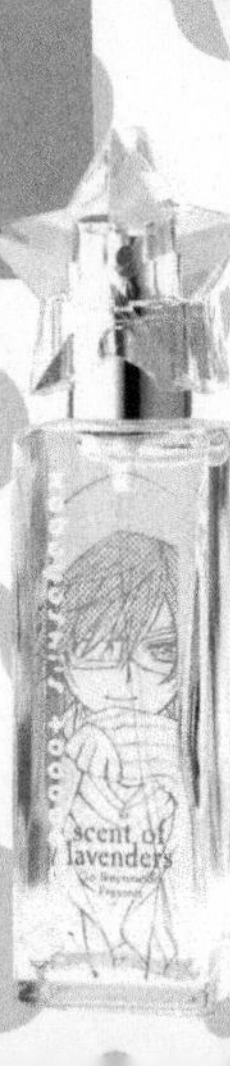
scent of lavenders

Perfume

AOI'S LAVENDER SCENT IS NOW A PERFUME. ♪♪ I LOVE THE COOL DESIGN THAT FEATURES AOI WEARING A HOODIE, WHICH HE DOESN'T WEAR TOO OFTEN. ♡♡

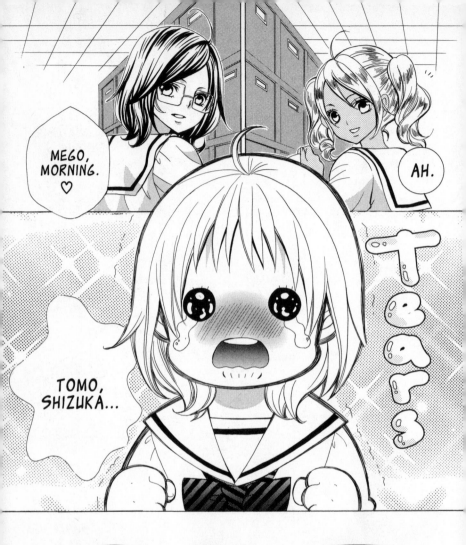

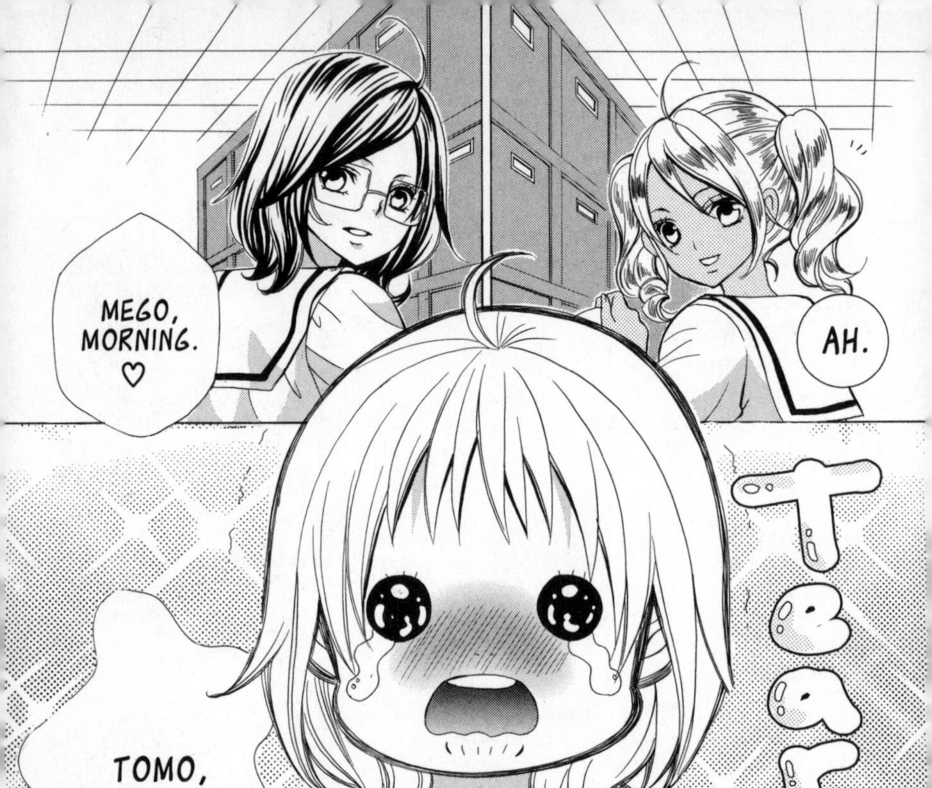
AH.
MEGO, MORNING. ♡
TEARS
TOMO, SHIZUKA...

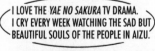

WHAT'S NEW

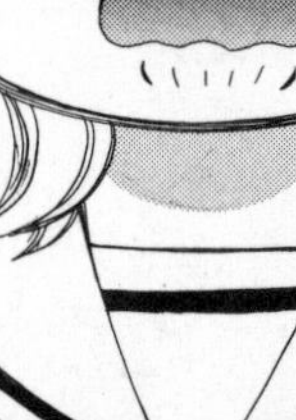

I WENT TO SEE SEXY ZONE LIVE! I WENT WITH MY ASSISTANTS DURING GOLDEN WEEK. SEXY ZONE AND THEIR FANGIRLS ARE ALL YOUNG AND CUTE AND SUCH EYE CANDY. ♡
I PASSIONATELY WROTE ABOUT THE SHOW IN MY BLOG. I HAD SO MUCH FUN!!
I WANT TO SHOUT "LOVE KENTY" ONCE MORE WHILE KENTO NAKAJIMA SINGS "CANDY!" (*SMILE*)

I LOVE THE *YAE NO SAKURA* TV DRAMA. I CRY EVERY WEEK WATCHING THE SAD BUT BEAUTIFUL SOULS OF THE PEOPLE IN AIZU.

THE *BAD BOYS* J TV DRAMA THAT STARRED "LOVEHOLIC SENPAI" (KENTO NAKAJIMA) HAS ENDED, BUT I'M VERY, VERY HAPPY THEY'RE MAKING IT INTO A MOVIE! TAMAMORI-KUN WILL STAR IN THE *PINTOKONA* TV DRAMA THIS SUMMER! I LOVE THE MANGA, SO I'M REALLY LOOKING FORWARD TO THE DRAMA!! (^0^)

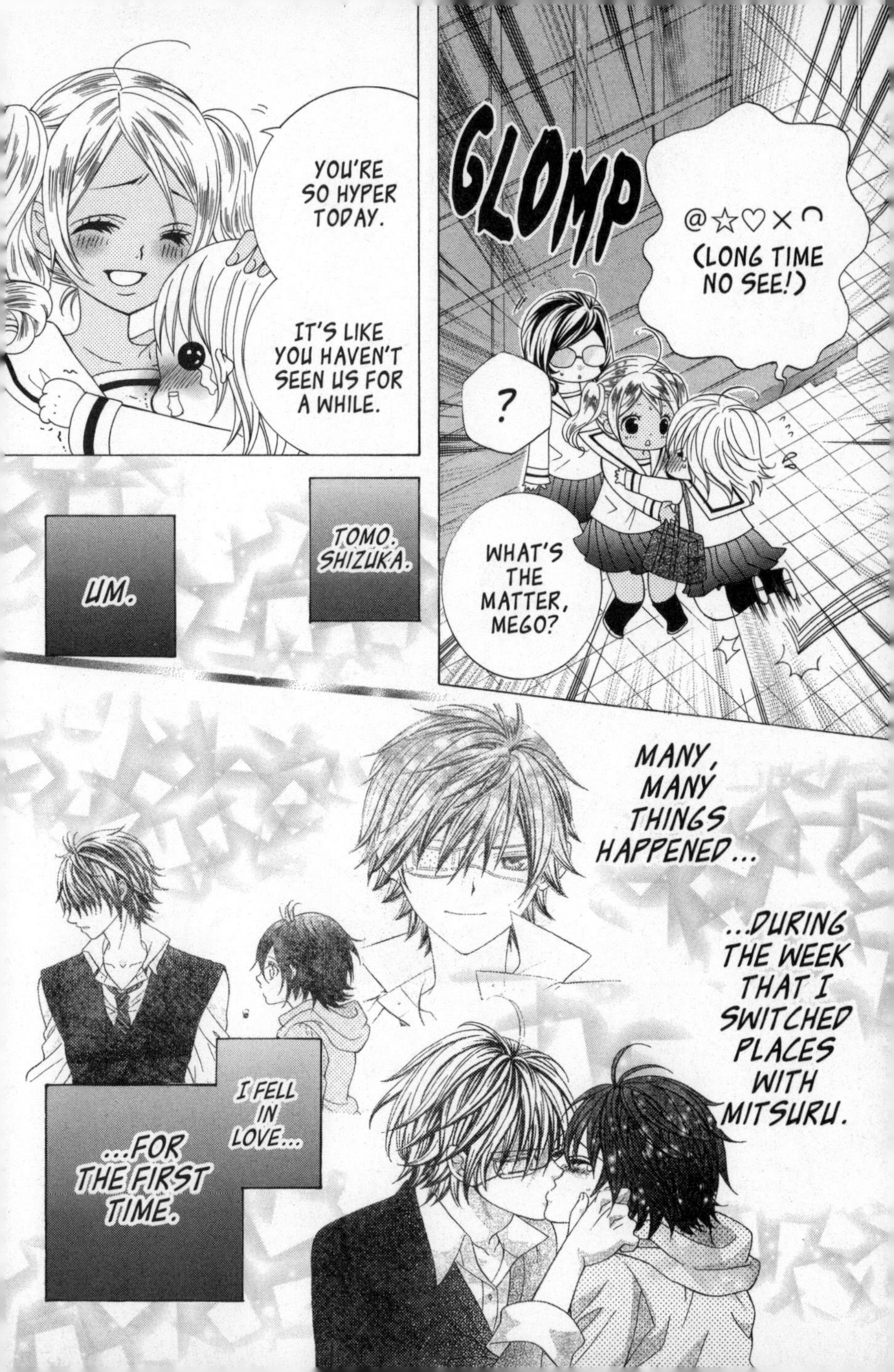
GLOMP
@☆♡×∩
(LONG TIME NO SEE!)
?
WHAT'S THE MATTER, MEGO?
YOU'RE SO HYPER TODAY.
IT'S LIKE YOU HAVEN'T SEEN US FOR A WHILE.
TOMO. SHIZUKA.
UM.
MANY, MANY THINGS HAPPENED...
...DURING THE WEEK THAT I SWITCHED PLACES WITH MITSURU.
I FELL IN LOVE...
...FOR THE FIRST TIME.

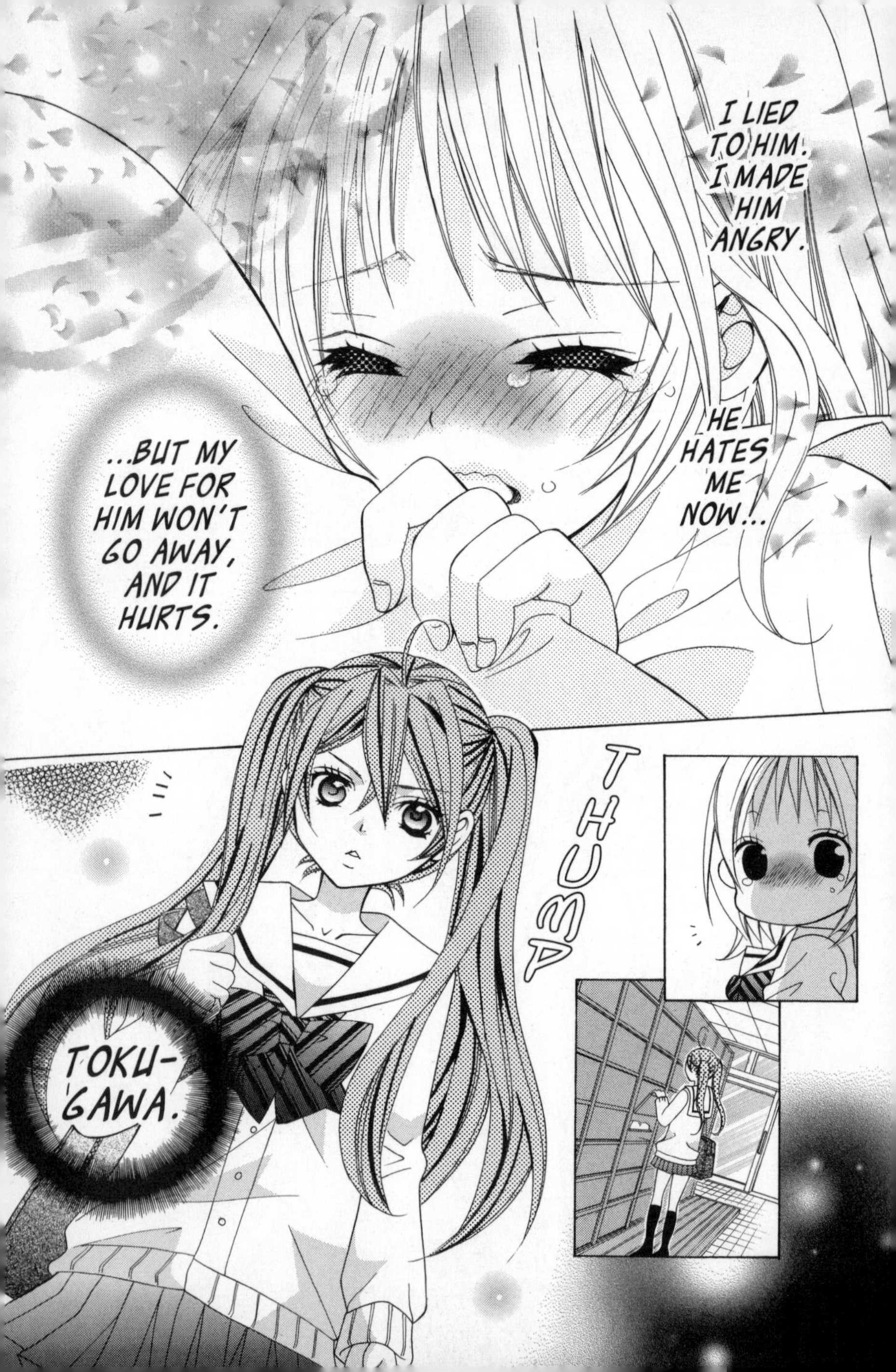
I LIED TO HIM. I MADE HIM ANGRY.
HE HATES ME NOW...
...BUT MY LOVE FOR HIM WON'T GO AWAY, AND IT HURTS.
THUMP
TOKU-GAWA.

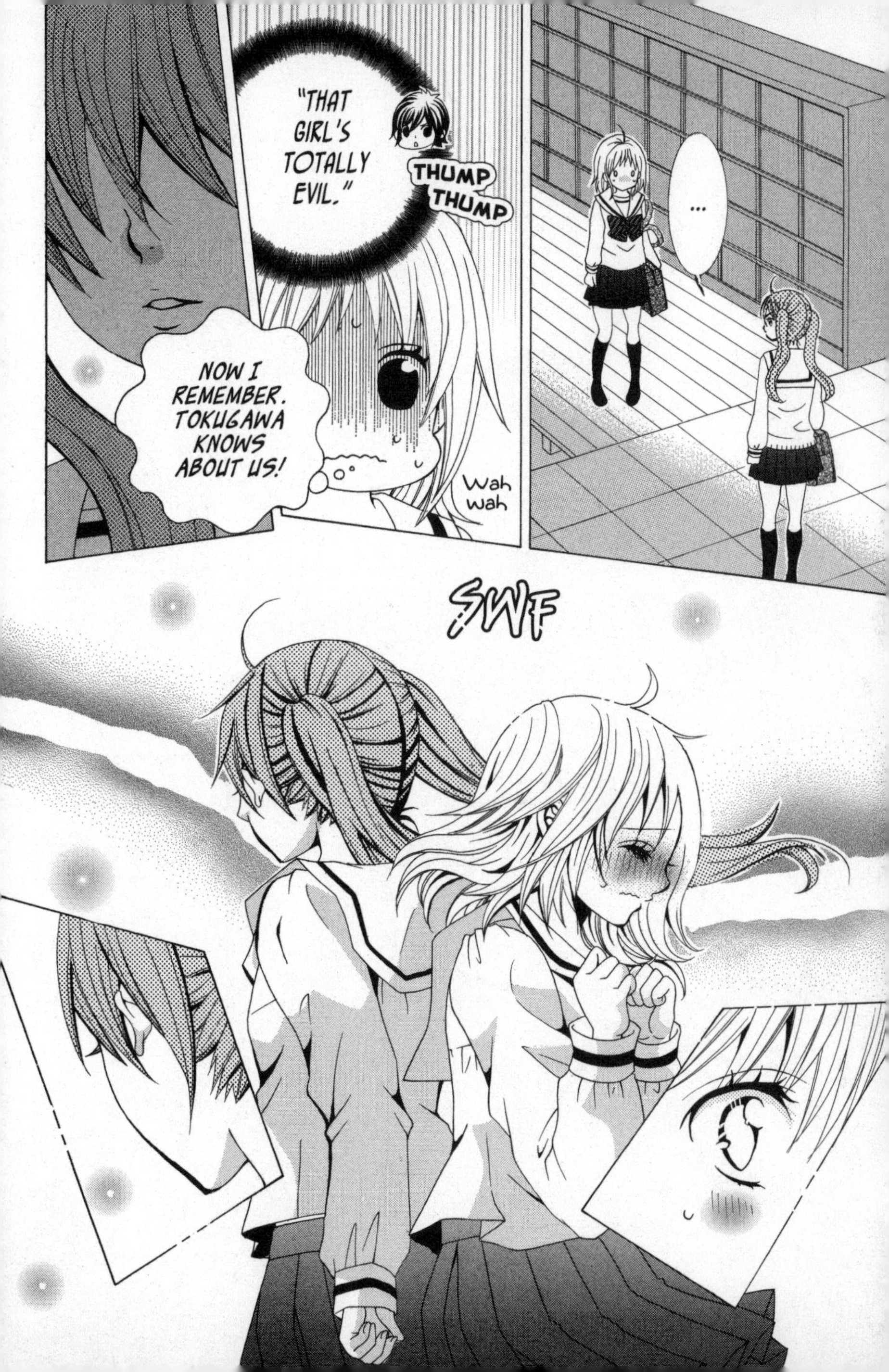
...
"THAT GIRL'S TOTALLY EVIL."
THUMP THUMP
NOW I REMEMBER. TOKUGAWA KNOWS ABOUT US!
Wah wah
SWF

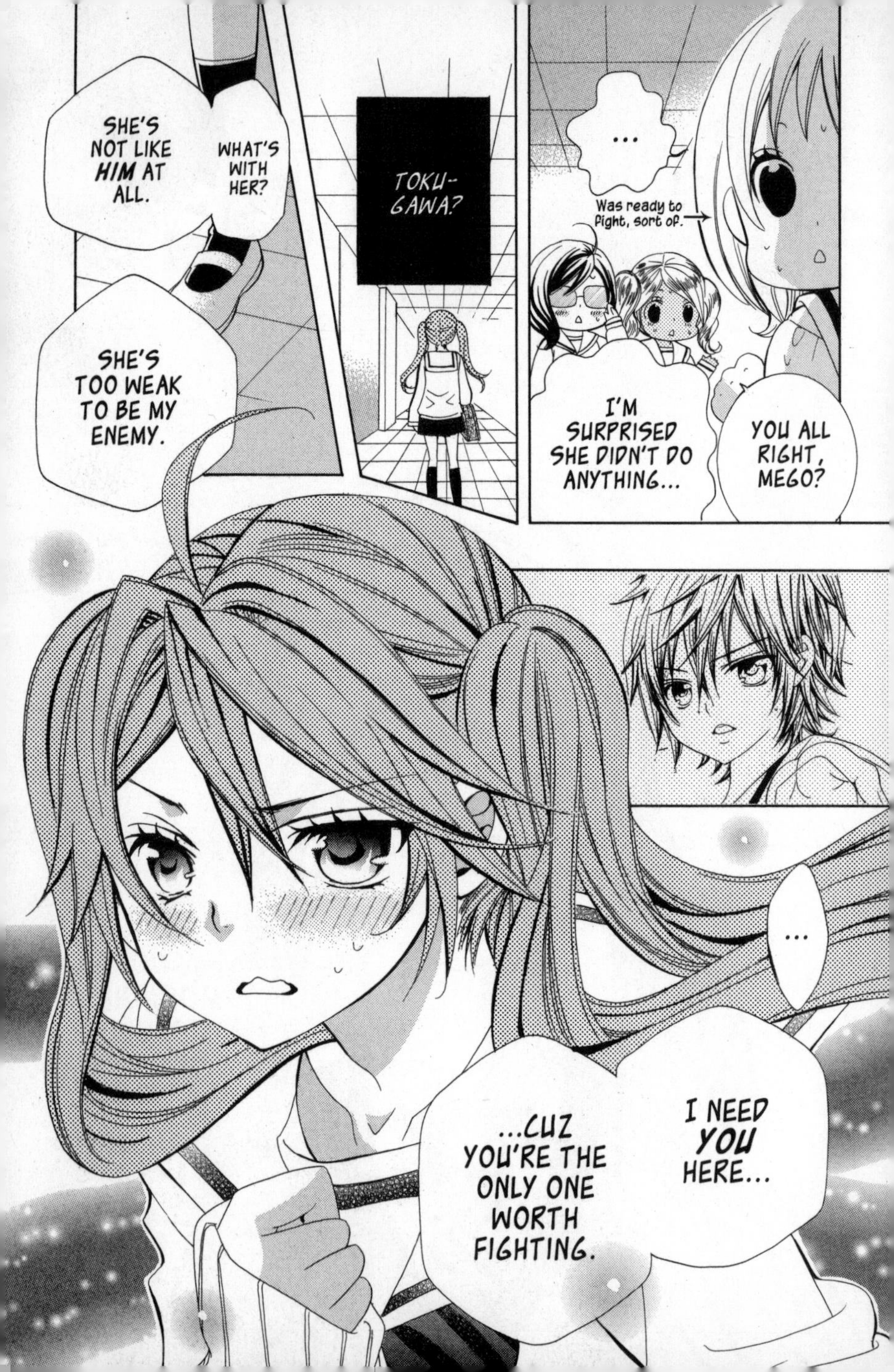
...
Was ready to fight, sort of.
YOU ALL RIGHT, MEGO?
I'M SURPRISED SHE DIDN'T DO ANYTHING...
TOKU-GAWA?
WHAT'S WITH HER?
SHE'S NOT LIKE *HIM* AT ALL.
SHE'S TOO WEAK TO BE MY ENEMY.
...
I NEED *YOU* HERE...
...CUZ YOU'RE THE ONLY ONE WORTH FIGHTING.

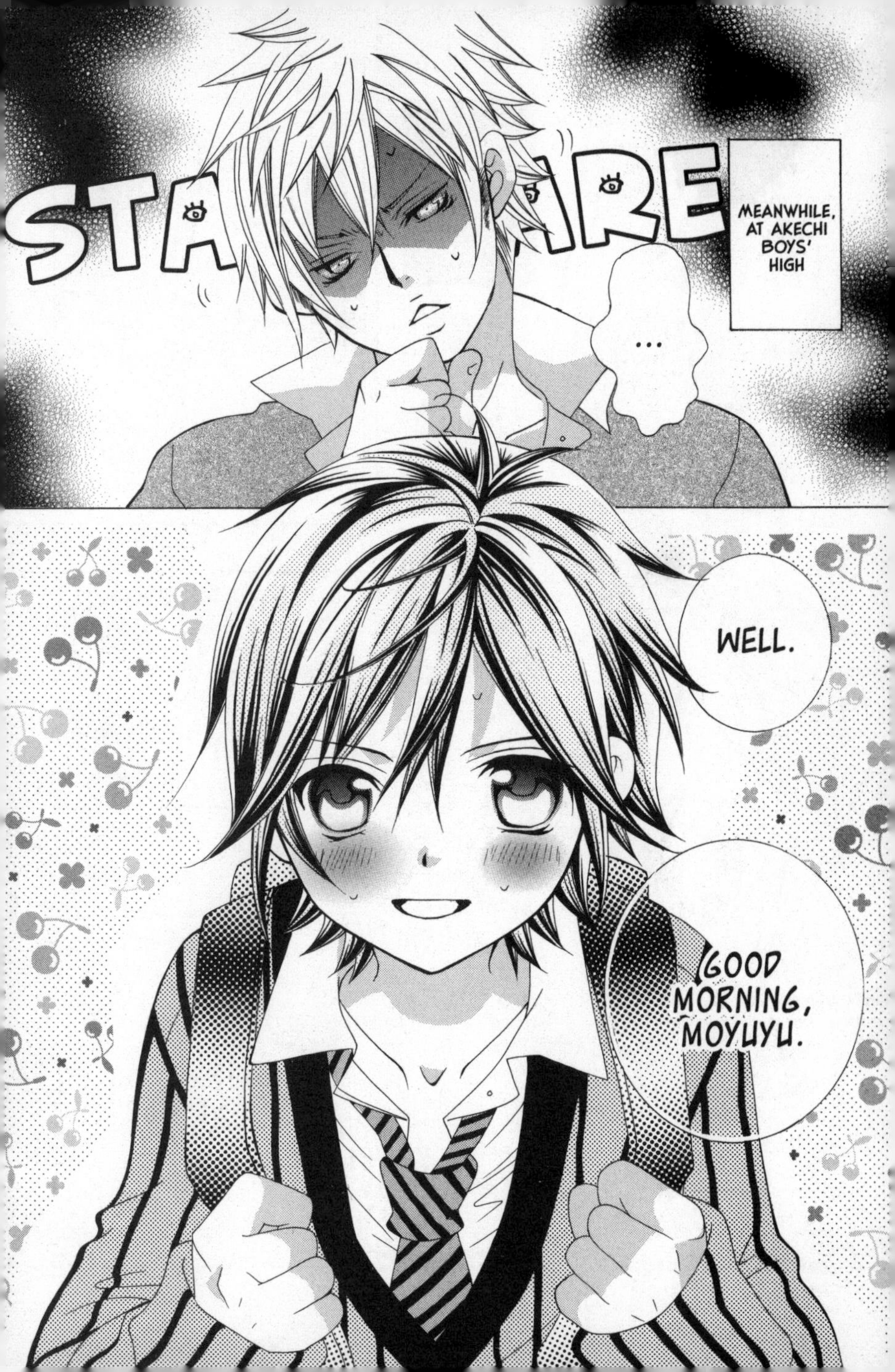
MEANWHILE, AT AKECHI BOYS' HIGH
...
STA ARE
WELL.
GOOD MORNING, MOYUYU.

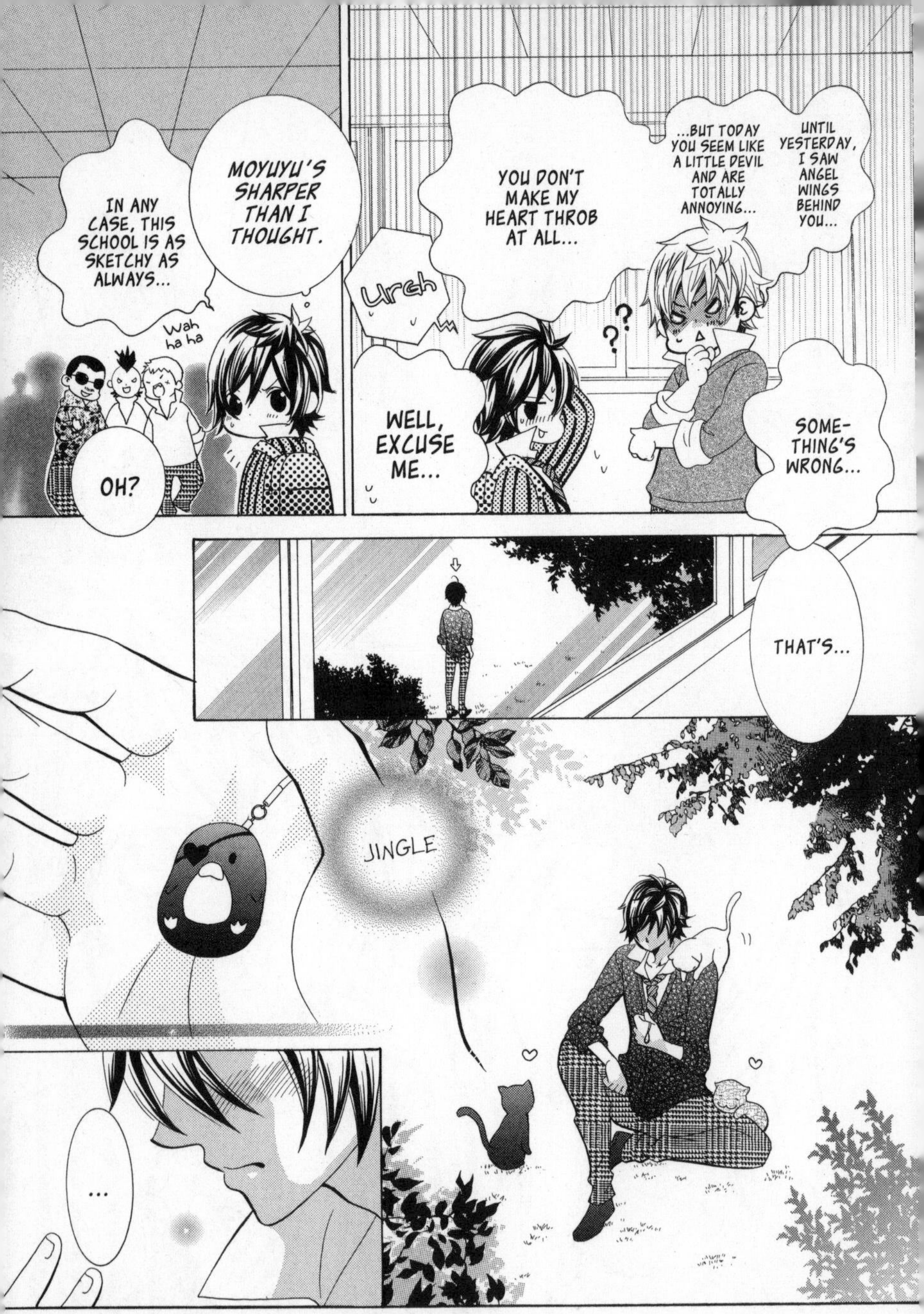
UNTIL YESTERDAY, I SAW ANGEL WINGS BEHIND YOU...
...BUT TODAY YOU SEEM LIKE A LITTLE DEVIL AND ARE TOTALLY ANNOYING...
YOU DON'T MAKE MY HEART THROB AT ALL...
Urgh
WELL, EXCUSE ME...
SOME-THING'S WRONG...
MOYUYU'S SHARPER THAN I THOUGHT.
IN ANY CASE, THIS SCHOOL IS AS SKETCHY AS ALWAYS...
Wah ha ha
OH?
THAT'S...
JINGLE
...

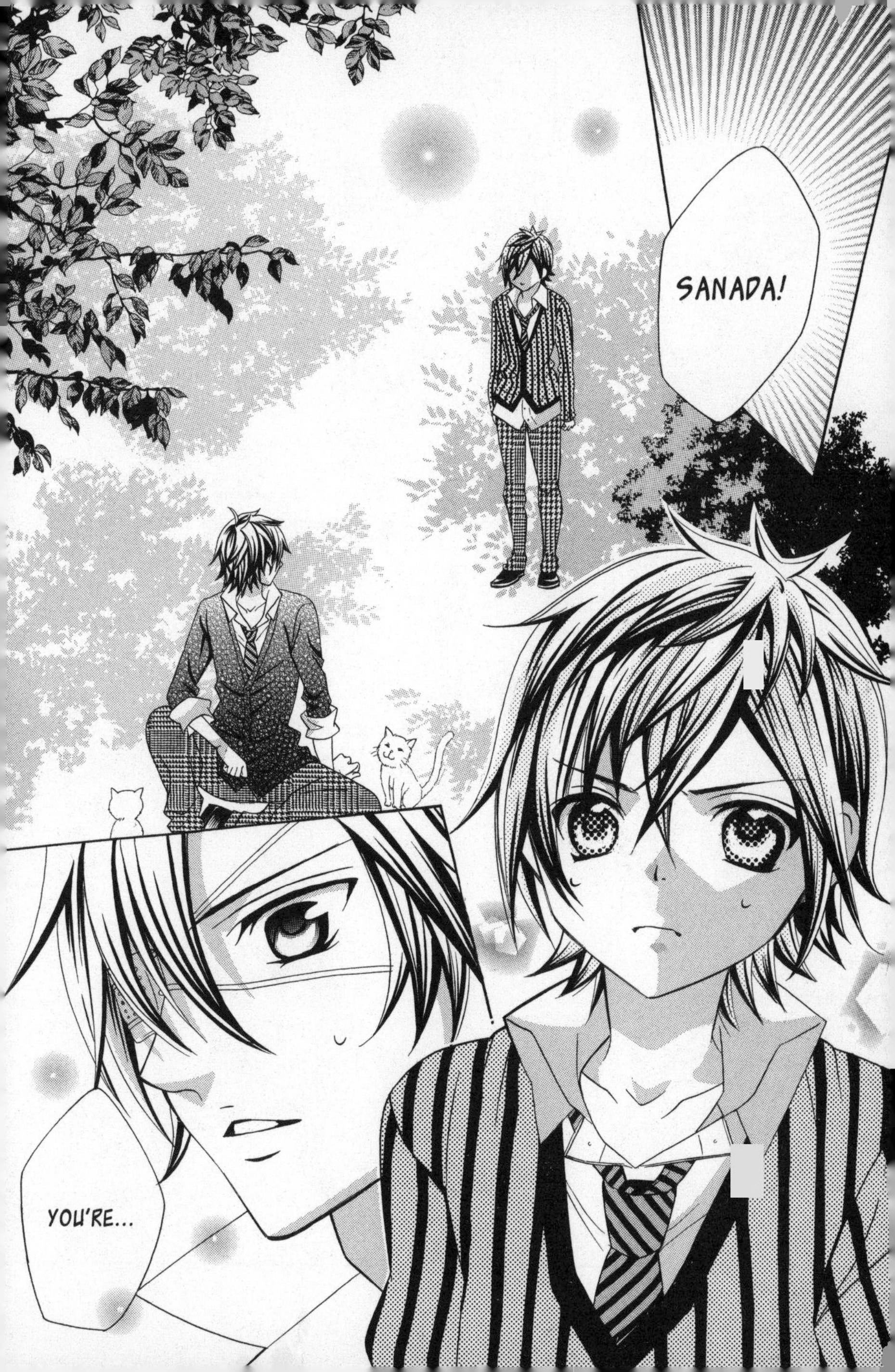
SANADA!
YOU'RE...

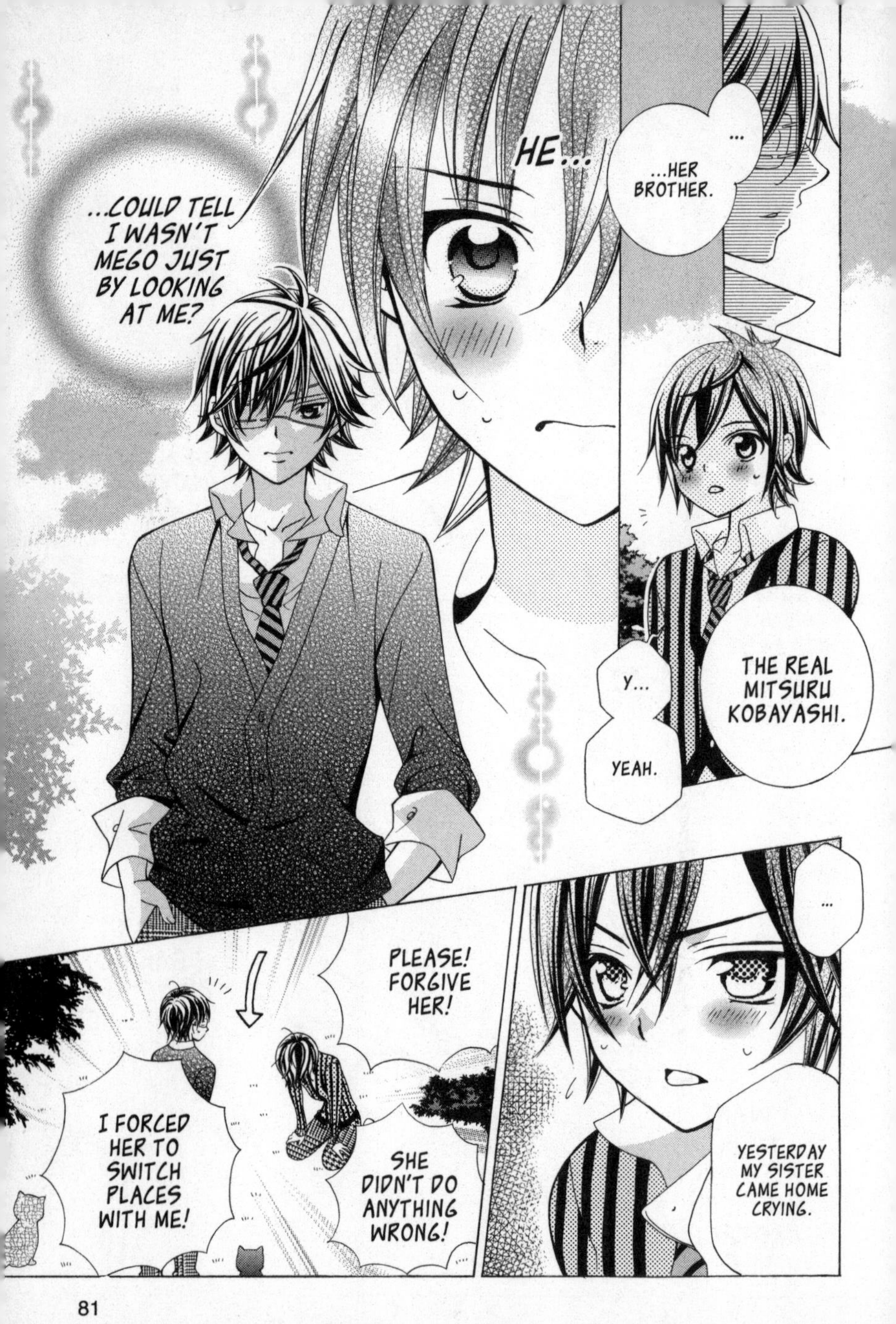
...
...HER BROTHER.
THE REAL MITSURU KOBAYASHI.
Y...
YEAH.
HE...
...COULD TELL I WASN'T MEGO JUST BY LOOKING AT ME?
...
YESTERDAY MY SISTER CAME HOME CRYING.
PLEASE! FORGIVE HER!
SHE DIDN'T DO ANYTHING WRONG!
I FORCED HER TO SWITCH PLACES WITH ME!

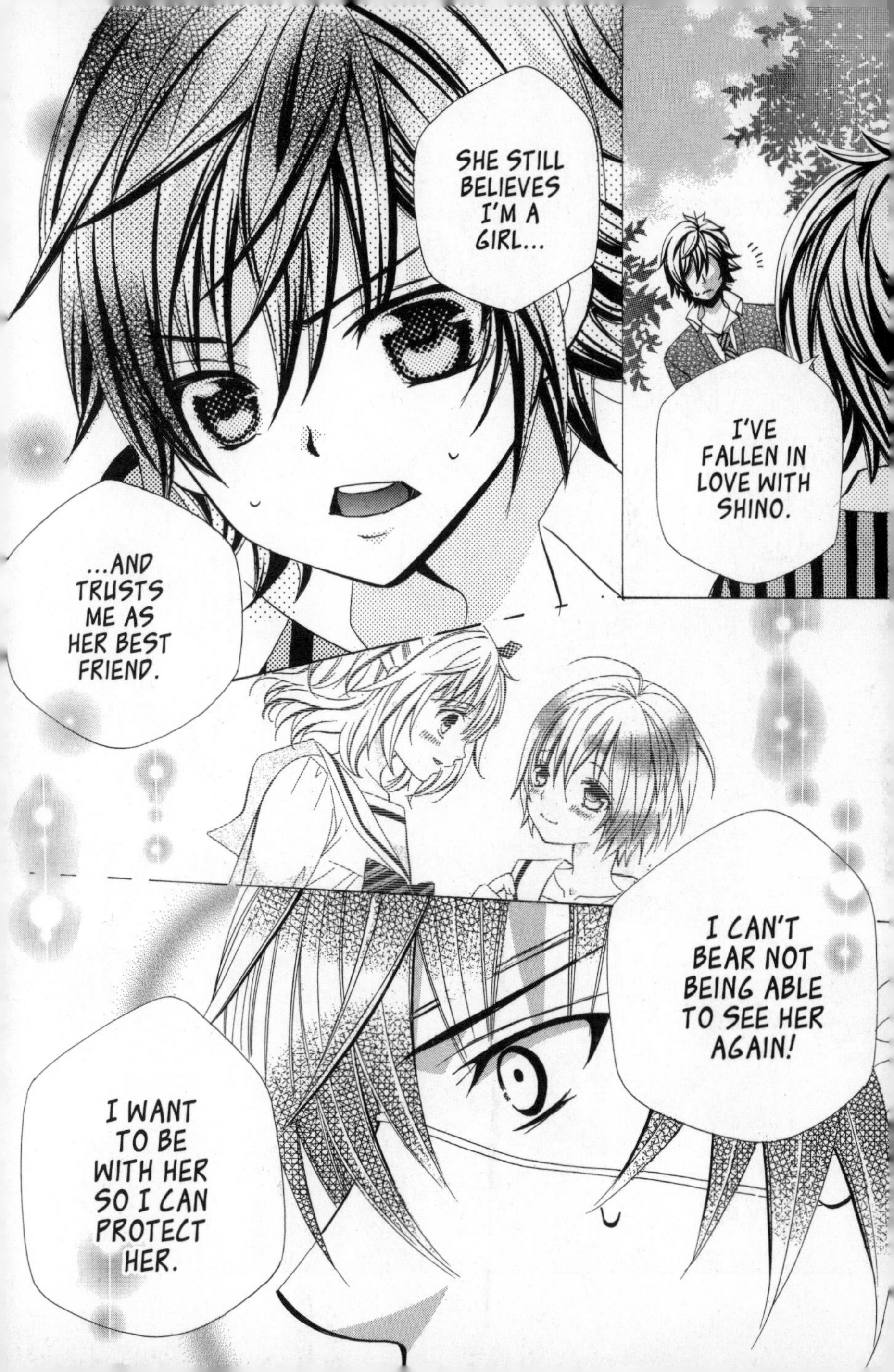
I'VE FALLEN IN LOVE WITH SHINO.
SHE STILL BELIEVES I'M A GIRL...
...AND TRUSTS ME AS HER BEST FRIEND.
I CAN'T BEAR NOT BEING ABLE TO SEE HER AGAIN!
I WANT TO BE WITH HER SO I CAN PROTECT HER.

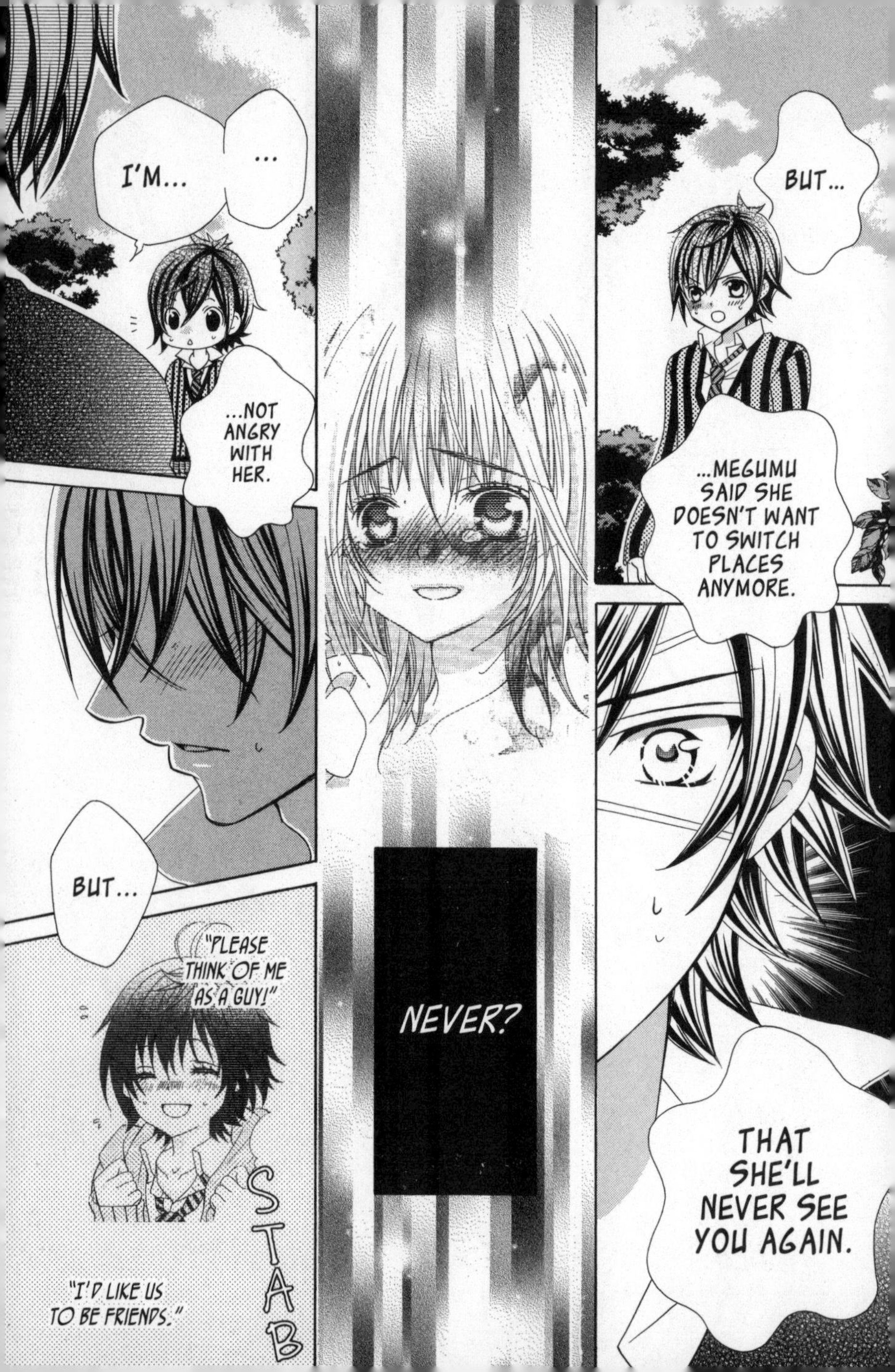
BUT...
...MEGUMU SAID SHE DOESN'T WANT TO SWITCH PLACES ANYMORE.
THAT SHE'LL NEVER SEE YOU AGAIN.
NEVER?
...
I'M...
...NOT ANGRY WITH HER.
BUT...
"PLEASE THINK OF ME AS A GUY!"
STAB
"I'D LIKE US TO BE FRIENDS."

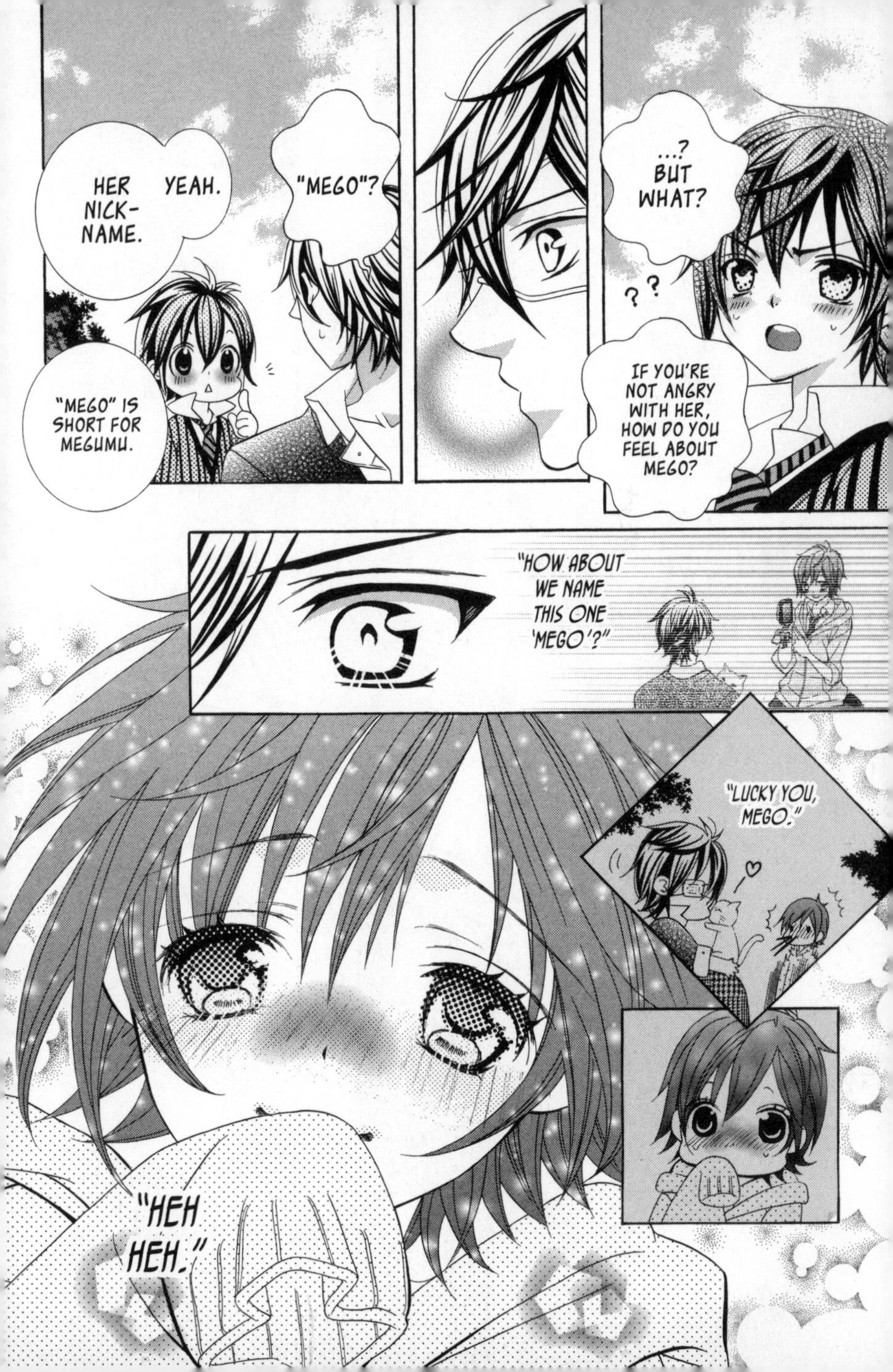
...? BUT WHAT?
IF YOU'RE NOT ANGRY WITH HER, HOW DO YOU FEEL ABOUT MEGO?
"MEGO"?
YEAH.
HER NICK-NAME.
"MEGO" IS SHORT FOR MEGUMU.
"HOW ABOUT WE NAME THIS ONE 'MEGO'?"
"LUCKY YOU, MEGO."
"HEH HEH."

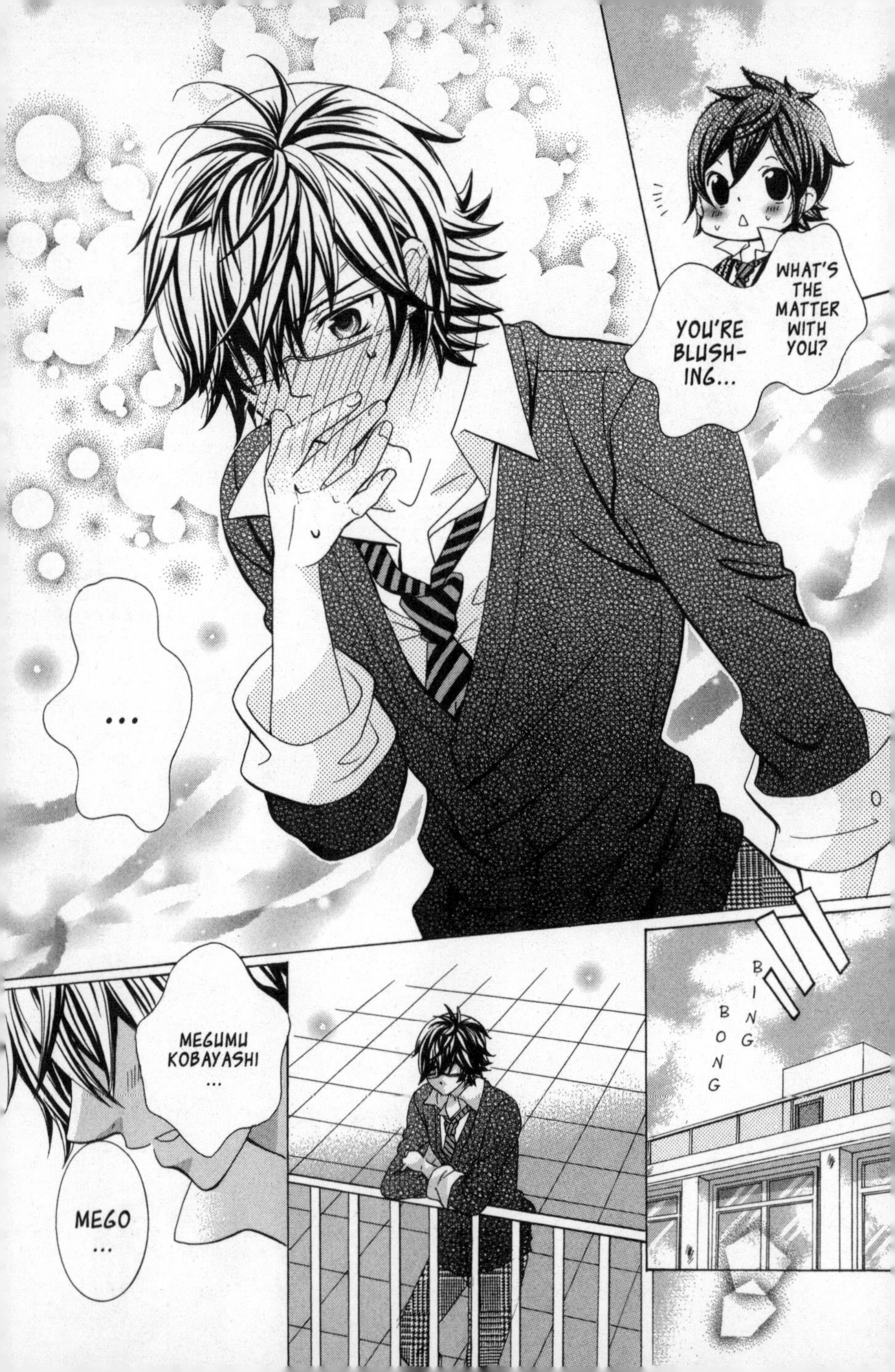
WHAT'S THE MATTER WITH YOU?
YOU'RE BLUSH-ING...
...
BING BONG
MEGUMU KOBAYASHI ...
MEGO ...

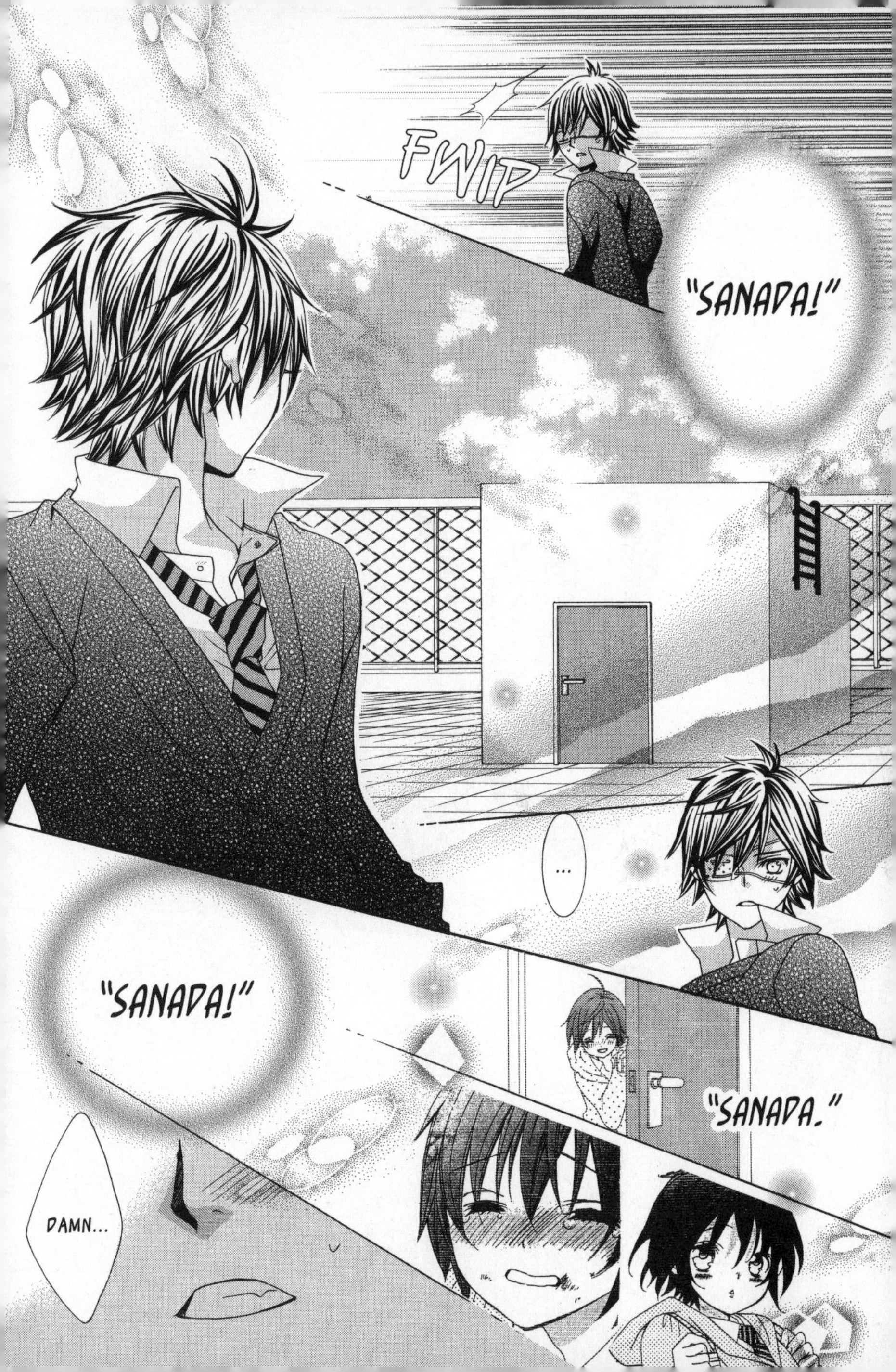
"SANADA!"
FWIP
...
"SANADA!"
"SANADA."
DAMN...

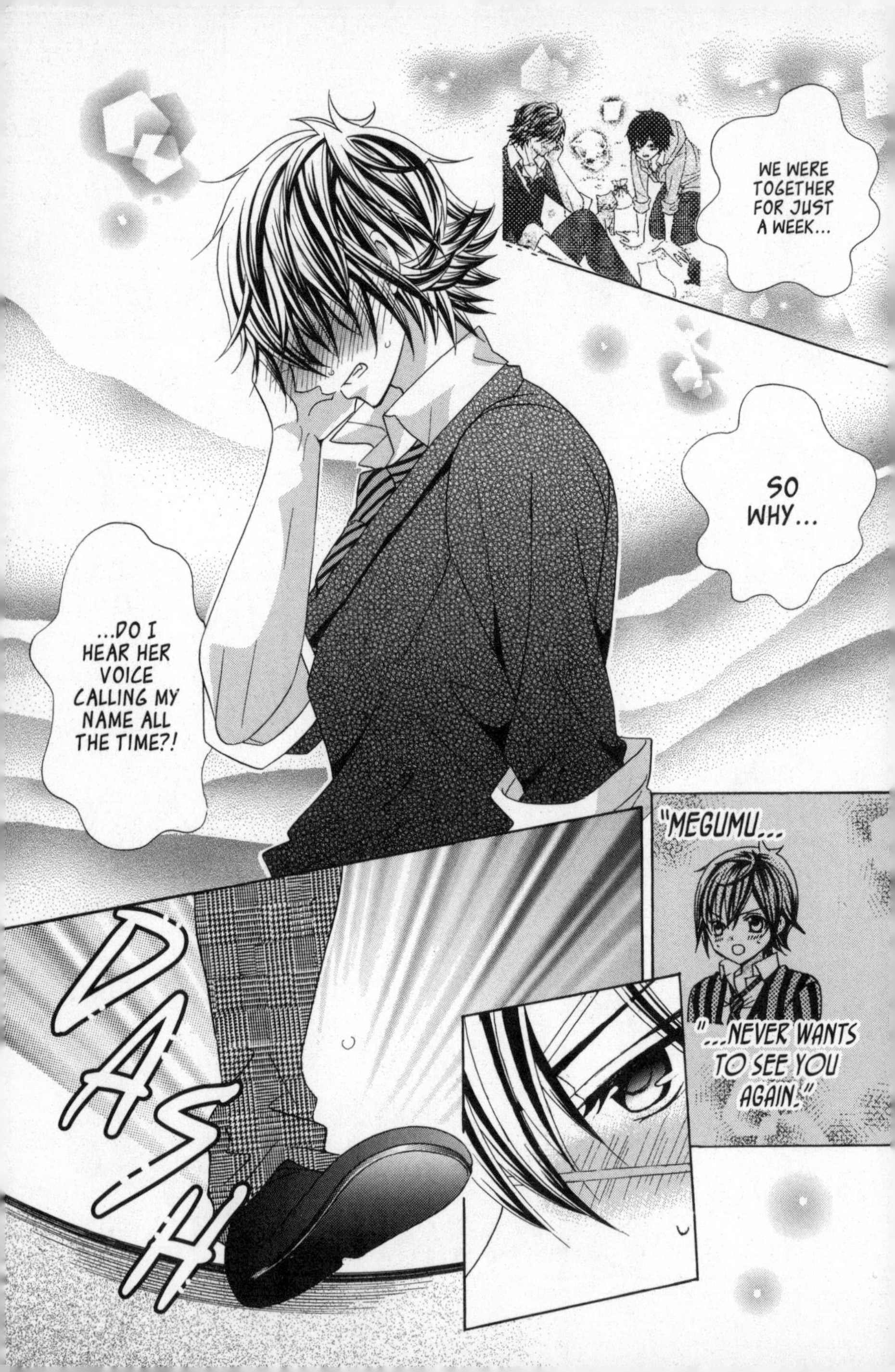
WE WERE TOGETHER FOR JUST A WEEK...
SO WHY...
...DO I HEAR HER VOICE CALLING MY NAME ALL THE TIME?!
"MEGUMU...
"...NEVER WANTS TO SEE YOU AGAIN."
DASH

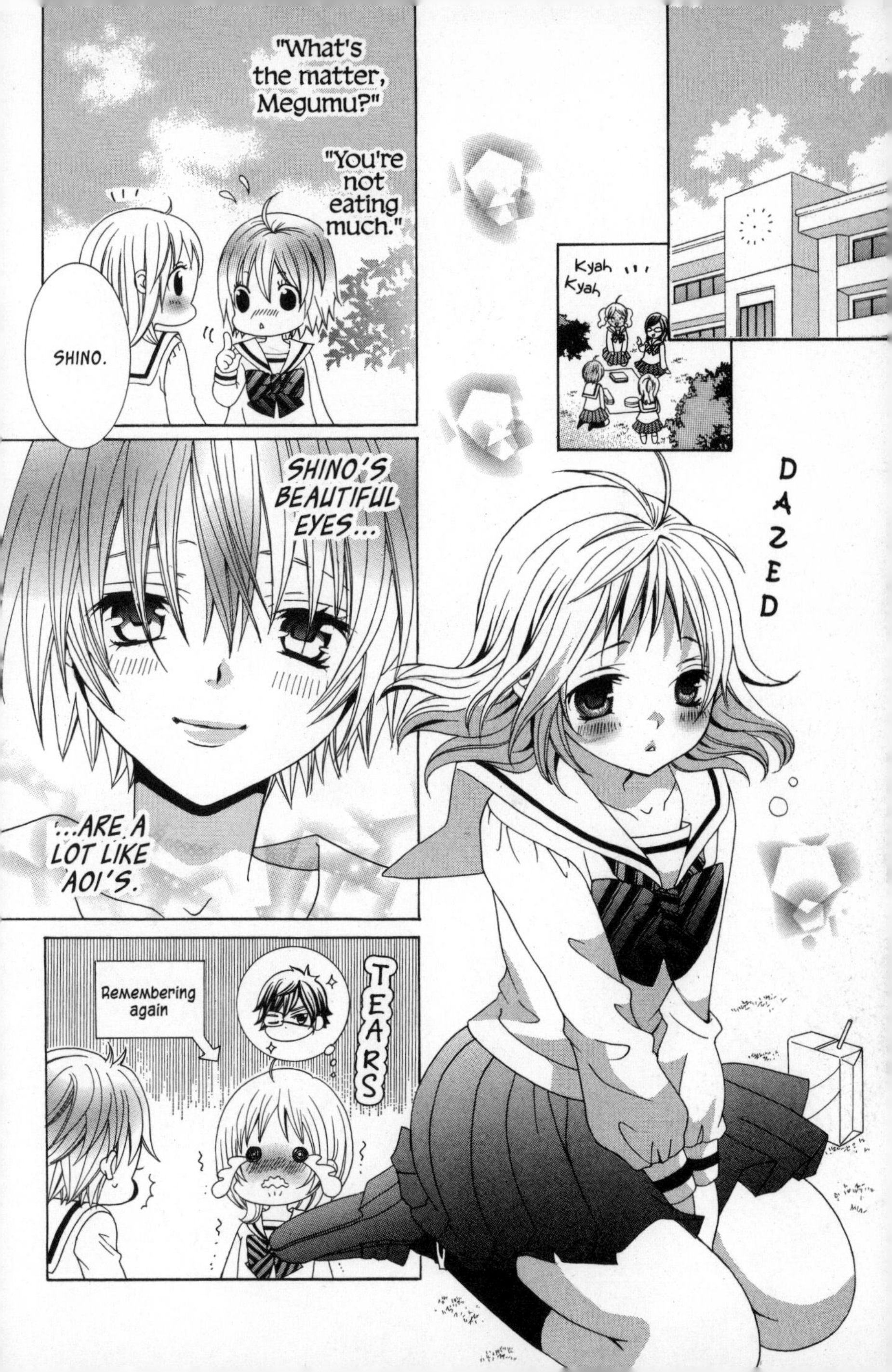
Kyah Kyah
DAZED
"What's the matter, Megumu?"
"You're not eating much."
SHINO.
SHINO'S BEAUTIFUL EYES...
...ARE A LOT LIKE AOI'S.
TEARS
Remembering again

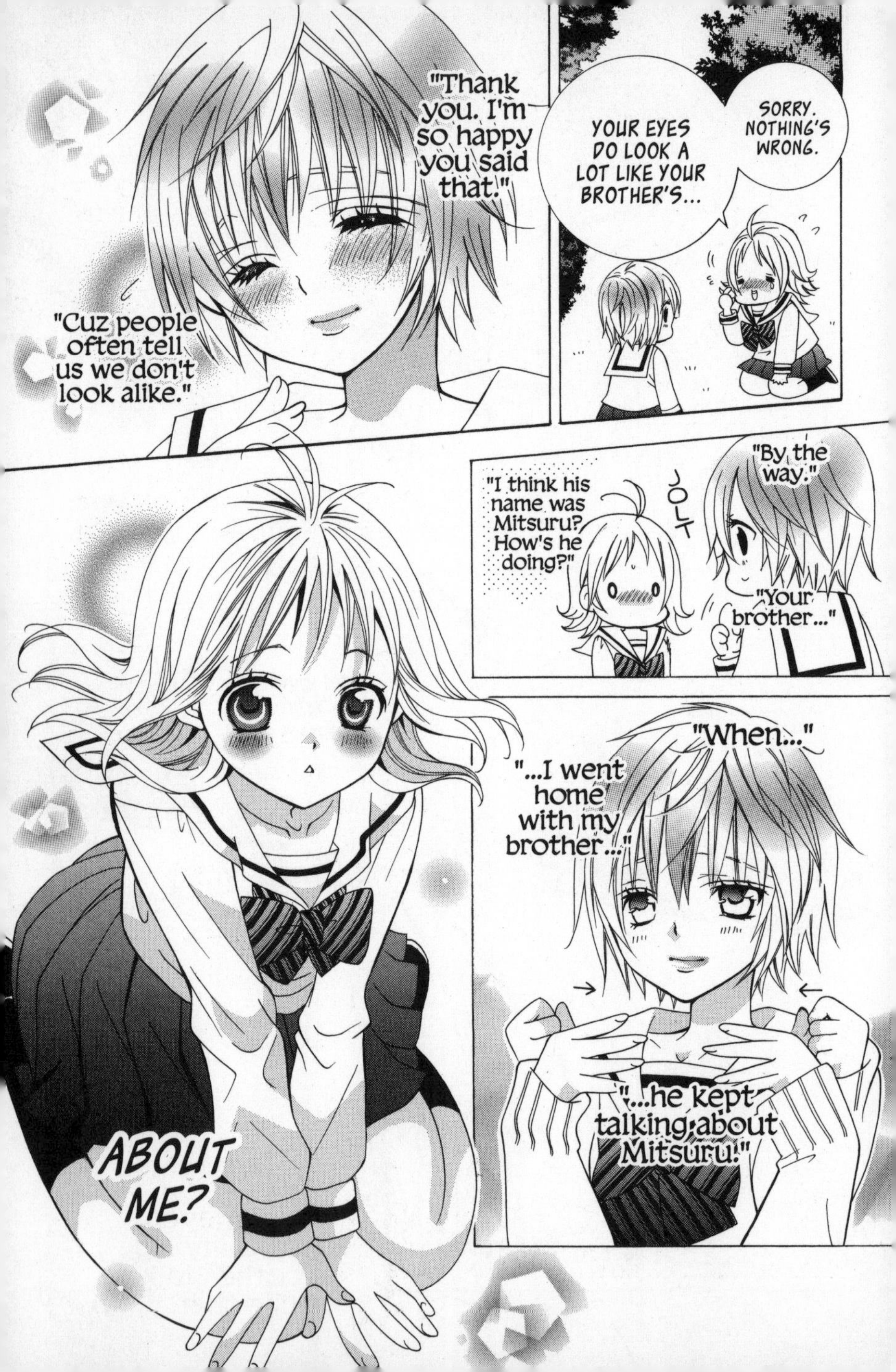
SORRY. NOTHING'S WRONG.
YOUR EYES DO LOOK A LOT LIKE YOUR BROTHER'S...
"Thank you. I'm so happy you said that."
"Cuz people often tell us we don't look alike."
"By the way."
"Your brother..."
JOLT
"I think his name was Mitsuru? How's he doing?"
"When..."
"...I went home with my brother..."
"...he kept talking about Mitsuru."
ABOUT ME?

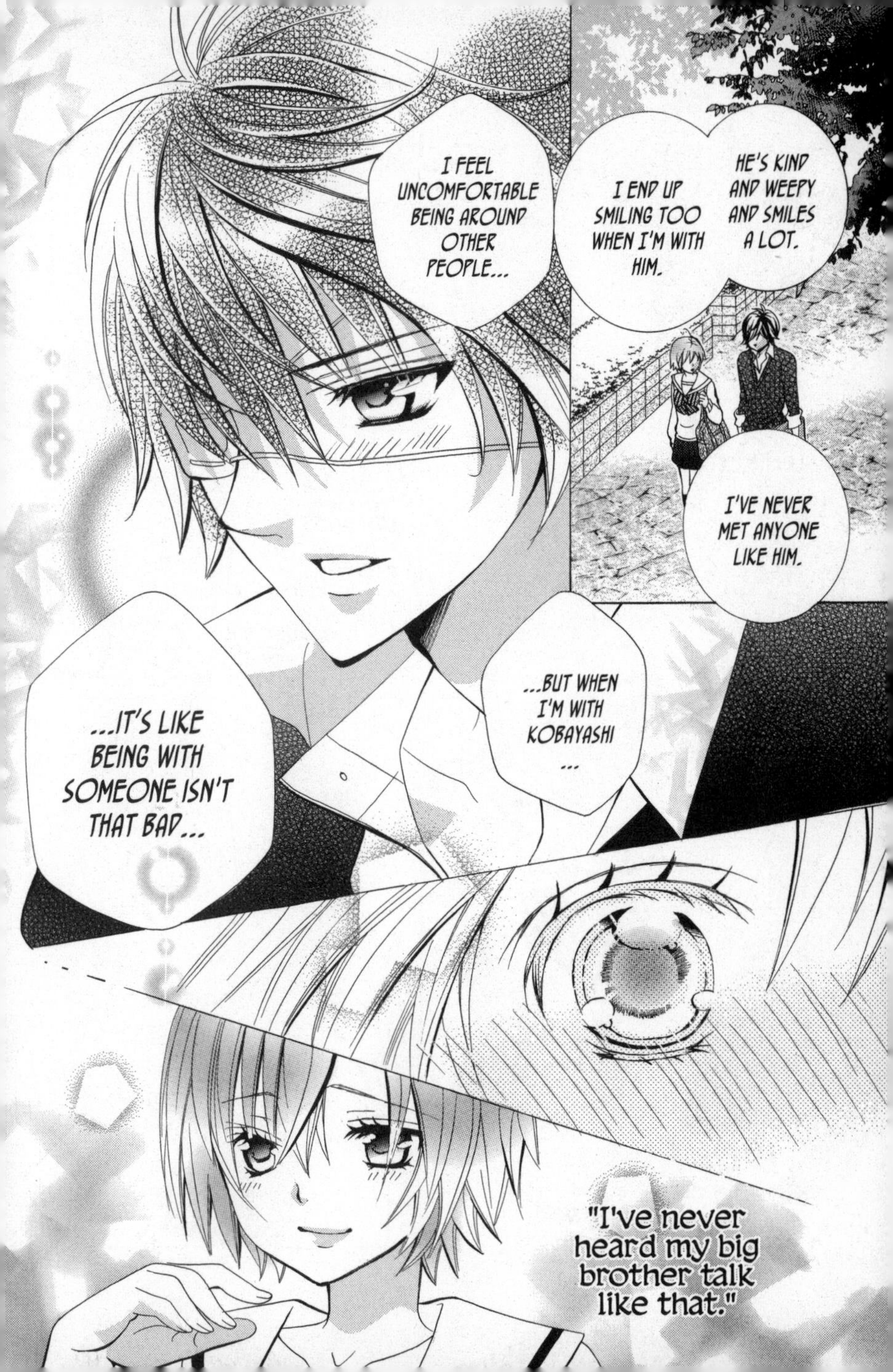
HE'S KIND AND WEEPY AND SMILES A LOT.
I END UP SMILING TOO WHEN I'M WITH HIM.
I'VE NEVER MET ANYONE LIKE HIM.
I FEEL UNCOMFORTABLE BEING AROUND OTHER PEOPLE...
...BUT WHEN I'M WITH KOBAYASHI ...
...IT'S LIKE BEING WITH SOMEONE ISN'T THAT BAD...
"I've never heard my big brother talk like that."

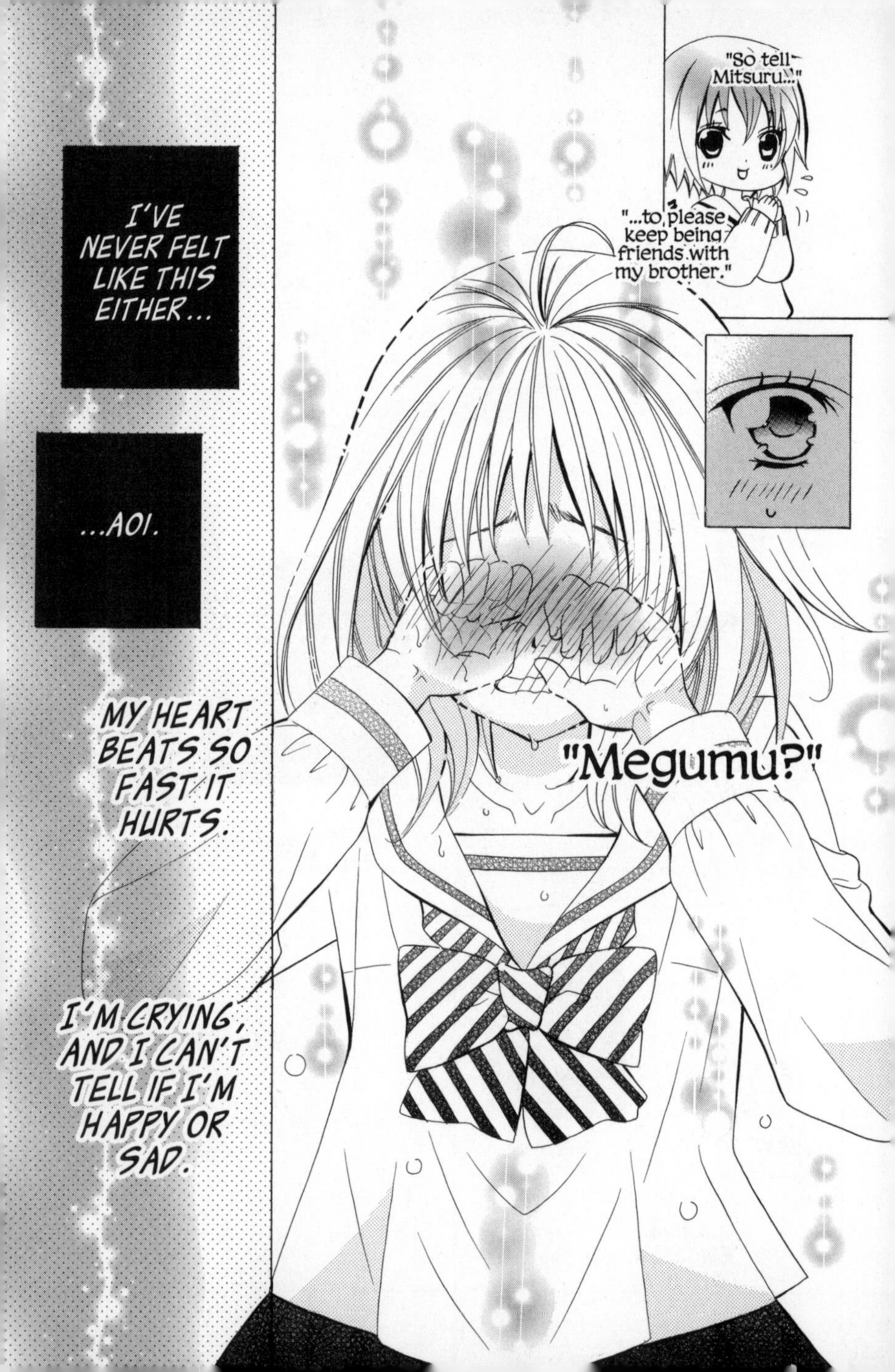
"So tell Mitsuru..."
"...to please keep being friends with my brother."
"Megumu?"
I'VE NEVER FELT LIKE THIS EITHER...
...AOI.
MY HEART BEATS SO FAST IT HURTS.
I'M CRYING, AND I CAN'T TELL IF I'M HAPPY OR SAD.

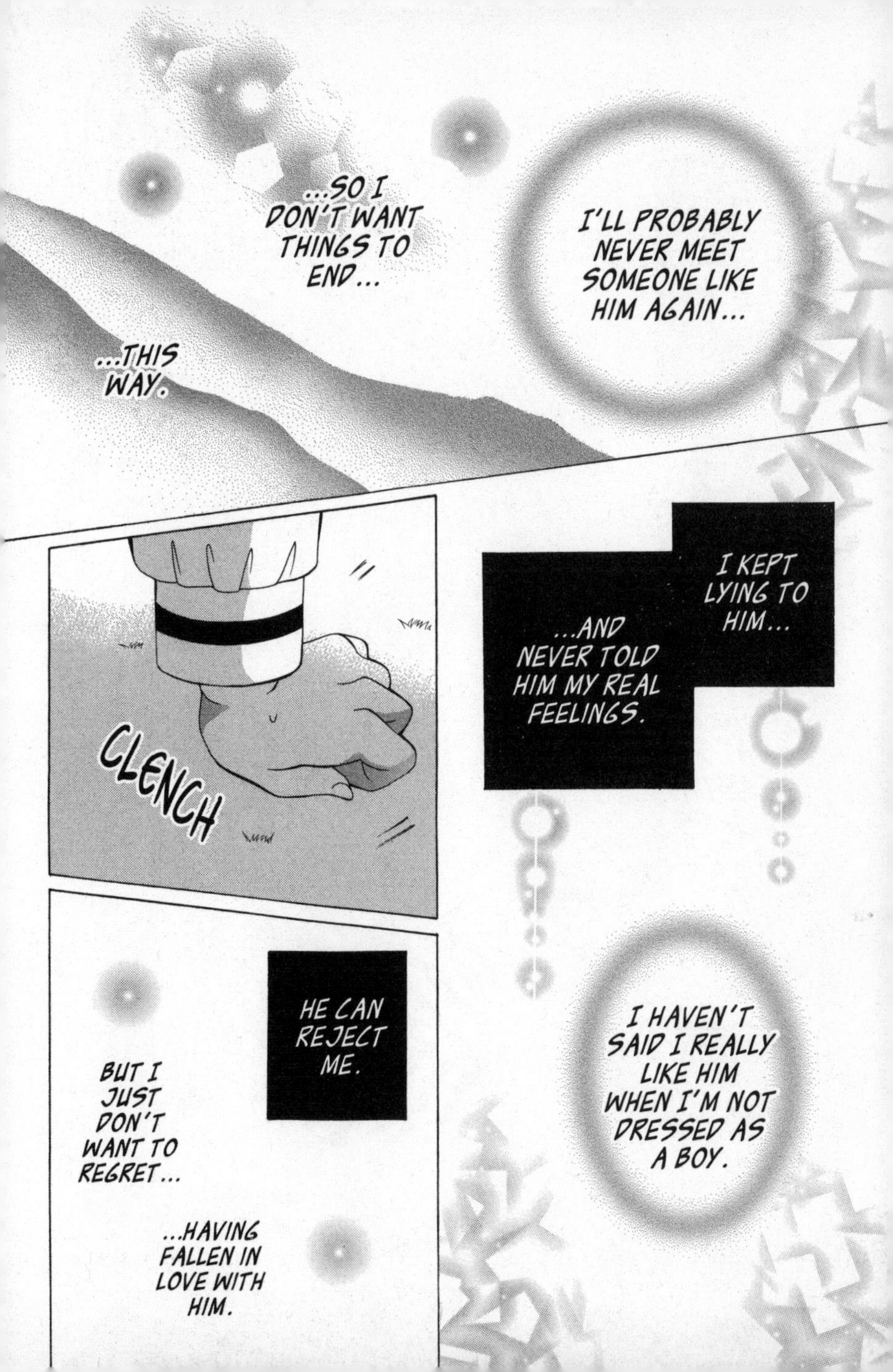
I'LL PROBABLY NEVER MEET SOMEONE LIKE HIM AGAIN...
...SO I DON'T WANT THINGS TO END...
...THIS WAY.
I KEPT LYING TO HIM...
...AND NEVER TOLD HIM MY REAL FEELINGS.
CLENCH
I HAVEN'T SAID I REALLY LIKE HIM WHEN I'M NOT DRESSED AS A BOY.
HE CAN REJECT ME.
BUT I JUST DON'T WANT TO REGRET...
...HAVING FALLEN IN LOVE WITH HIM.

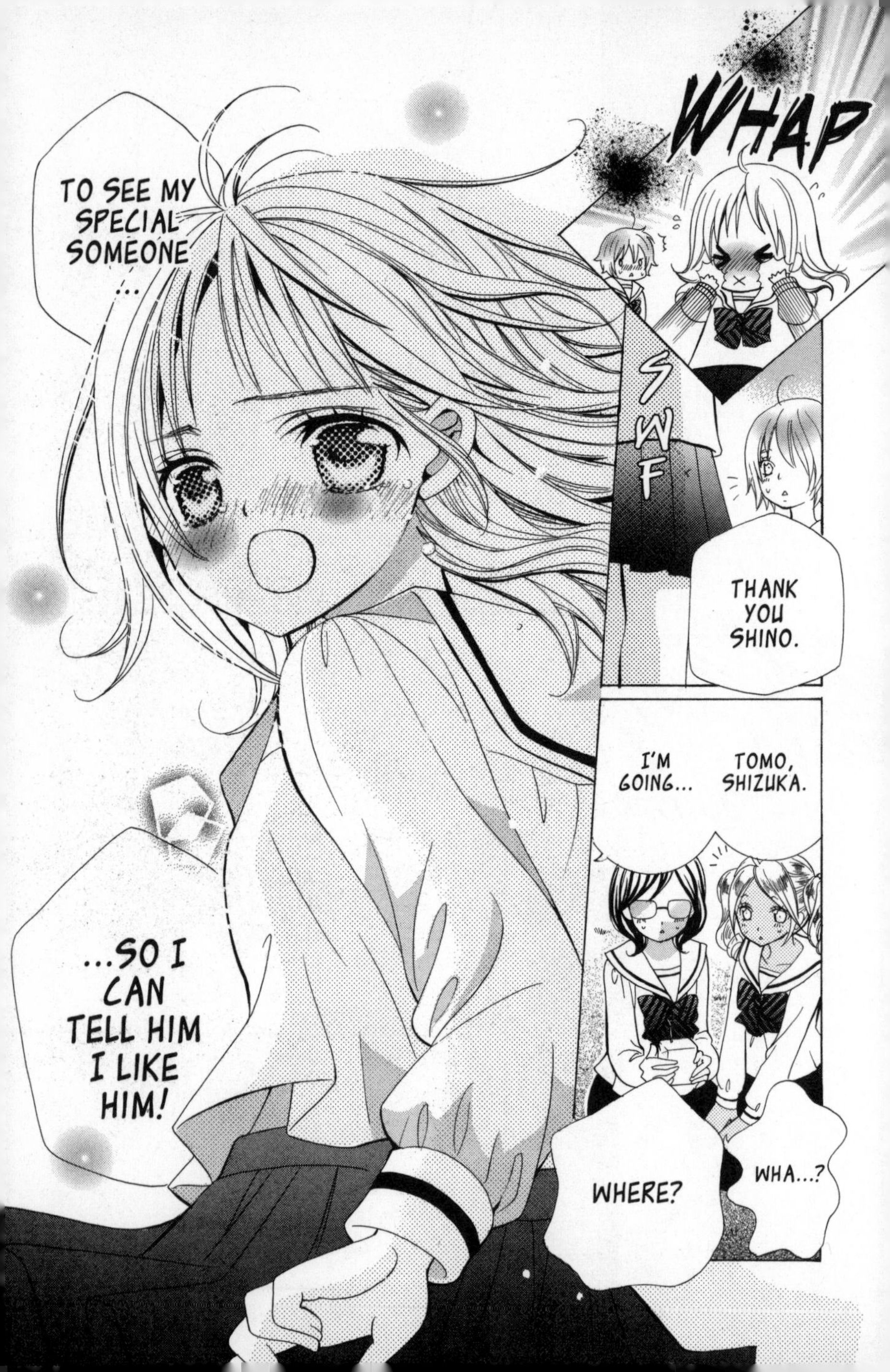
WHAP
SWF
THANK YOU SHINO.
I'M GOING... TOMO, SHIZUKA.
WHA...?
WHERE?
TO SEE MY SPECIAL SOMEONE...
...SO I CAN TELL HIM I LIKE HIM!

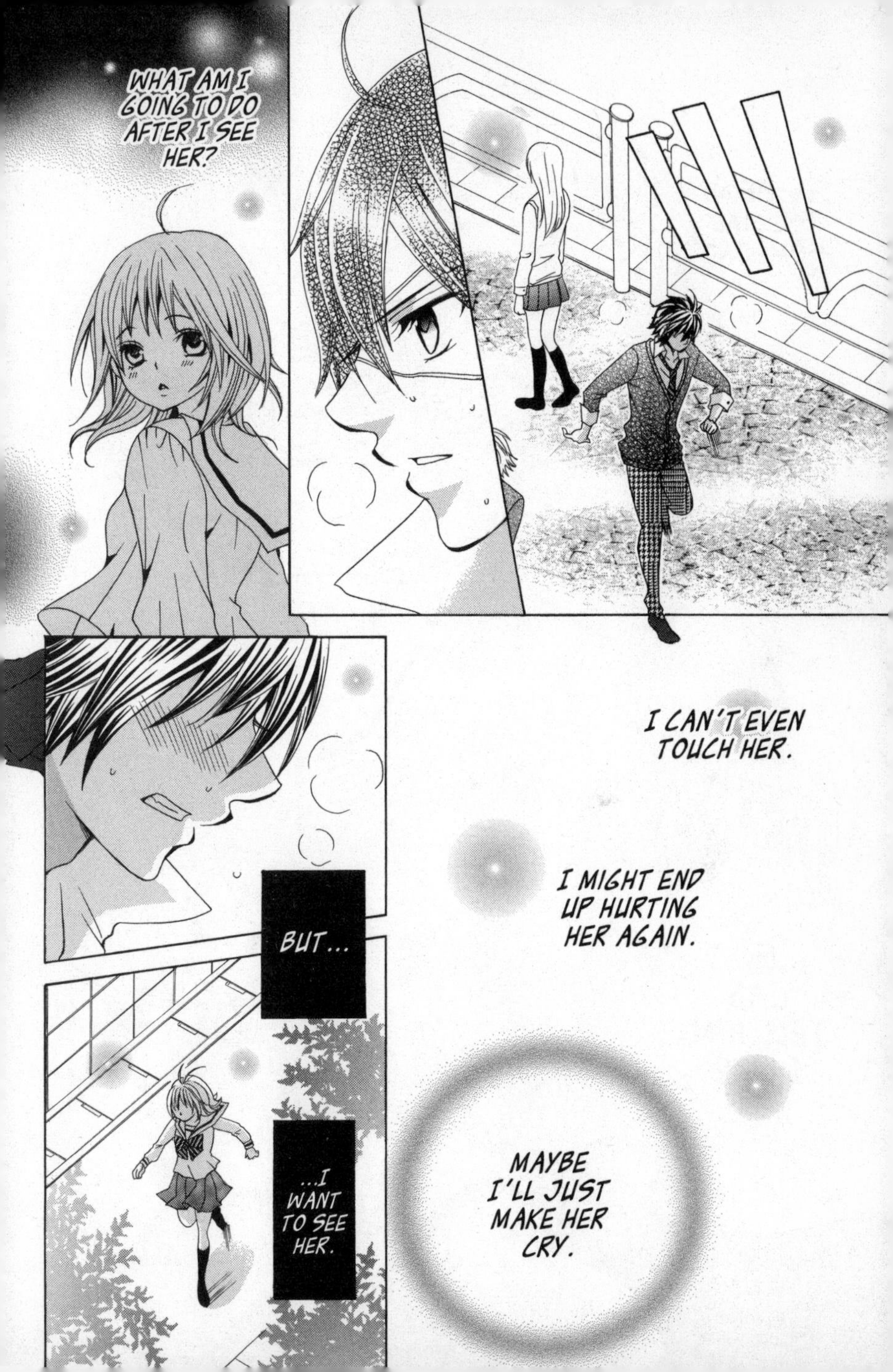
WHAT AM I GOING TO DO AFTER I SEE HER?
I CAN'T EVEN TOUCH HER.
I MIGHT END UP HURTING HER AGAIN.
MAYBE I'LL JUST MAKE HER CRY.
BUT...
...I WANT TO SEE HER.

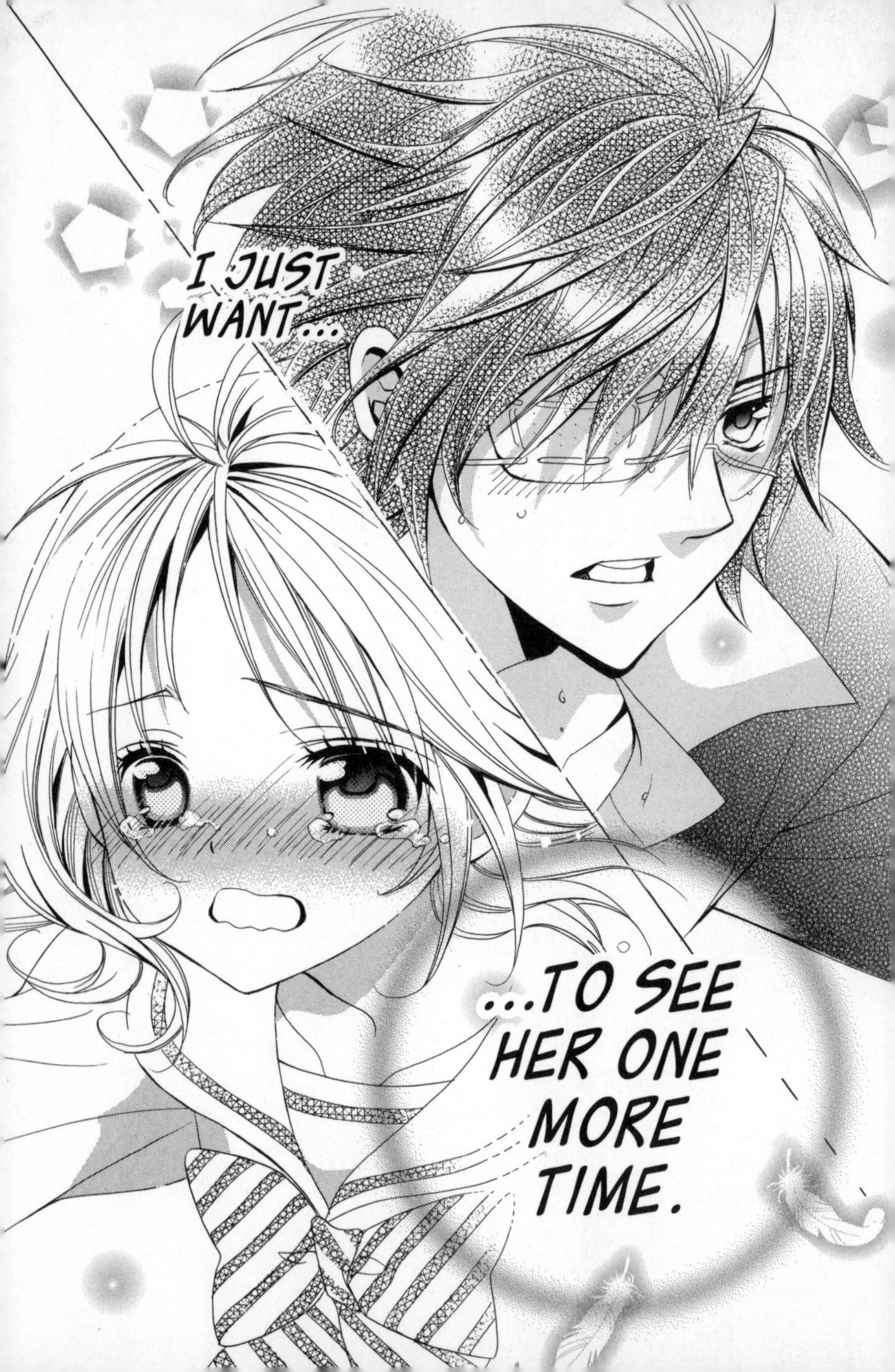
I JUST WANT...
...TO SEE HER ONE MORE TIME.

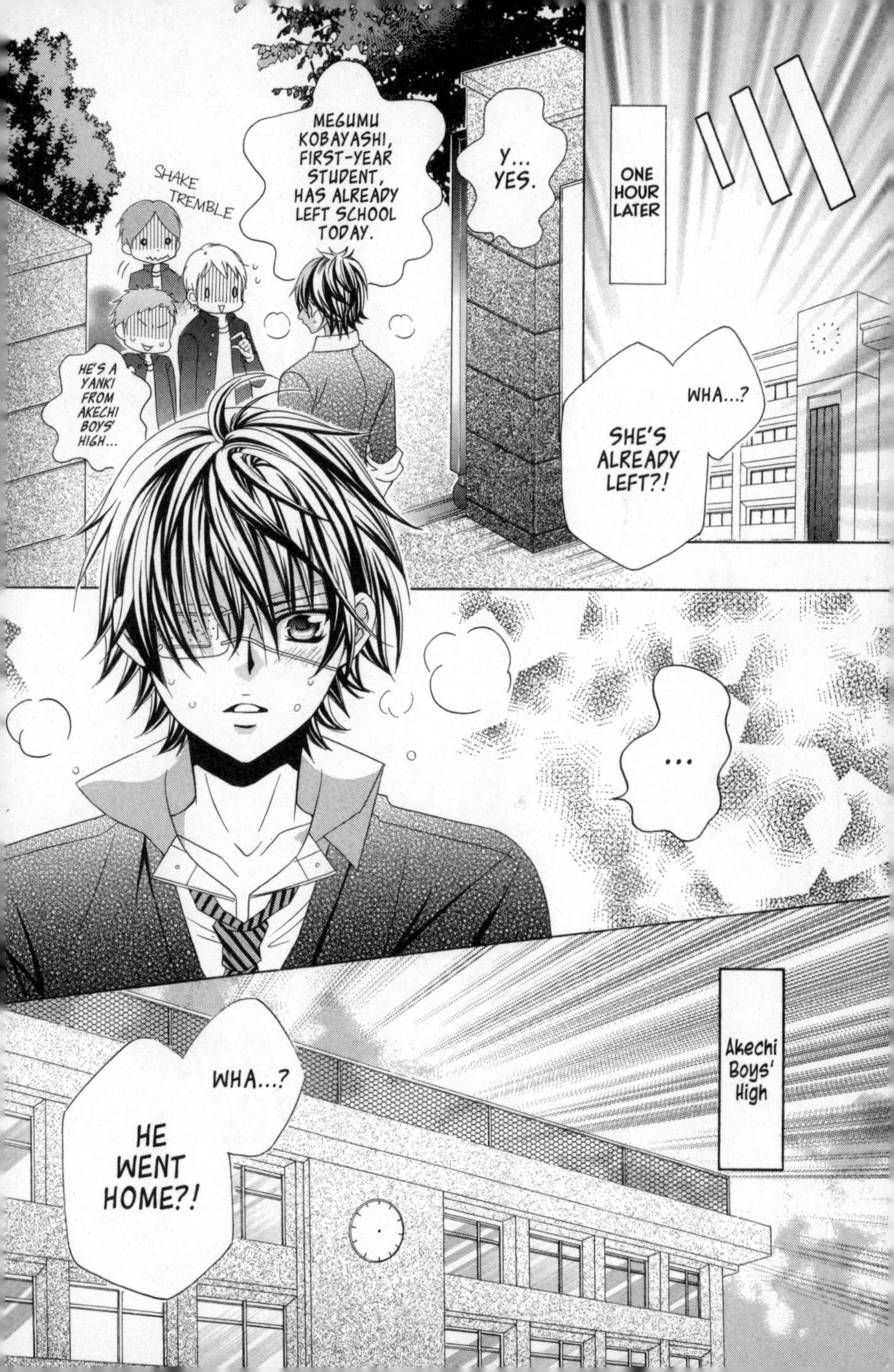
ONE HOUR LATER
WHA...? SHE'S ALREADY LEFT?!
Y... YES.
MEGUMU KOBAYASHI, FIRST-YEAR STUDENT, HAS ALREADY LEFT SCHOOL TODAY.
SHAKE TREMBLE
HE'S A YANKI FROM AKECHI BOYS' HIGH...
...
Akechi Boys' High
WHA...? HE WENT HOME?!

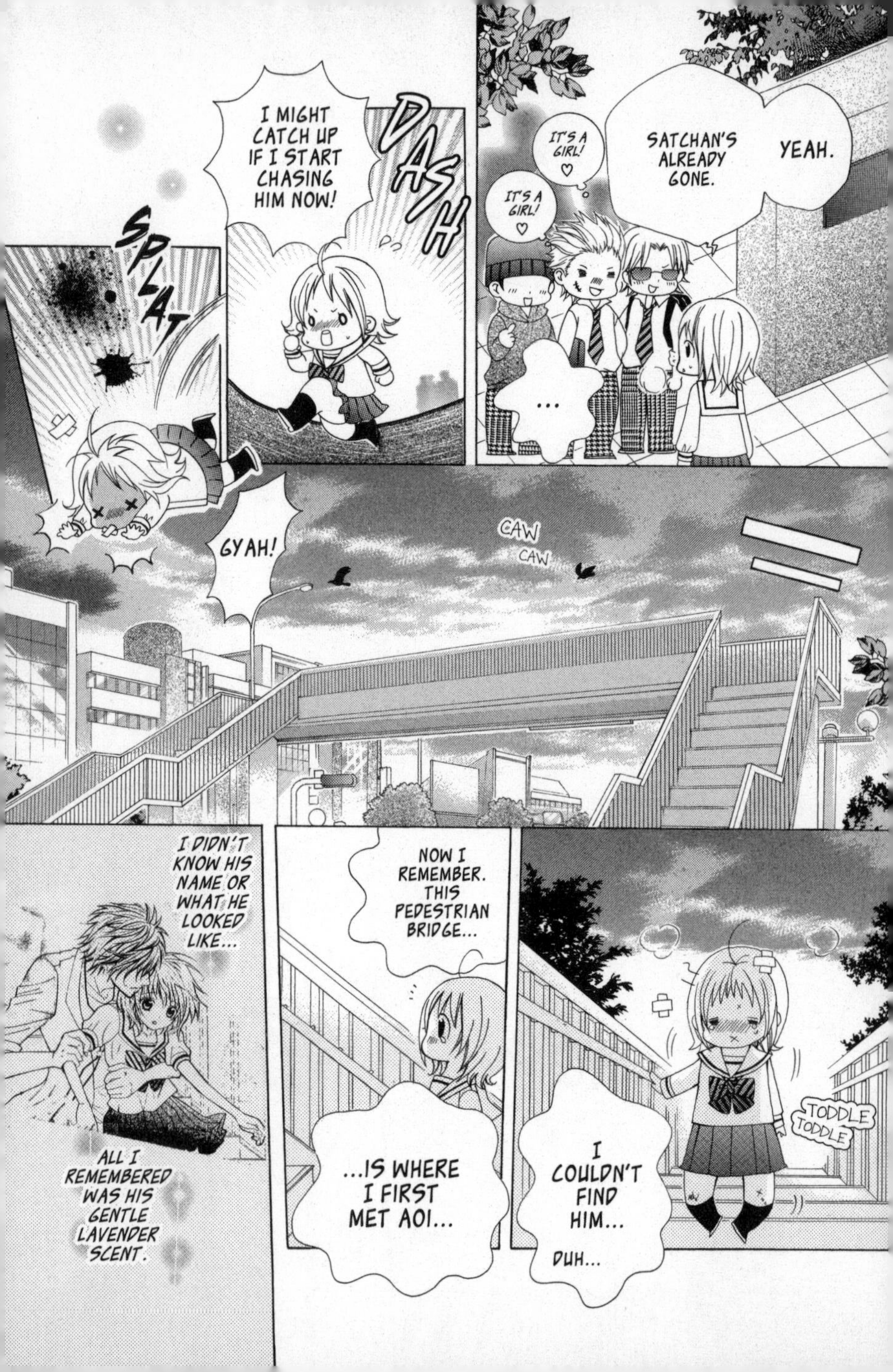
YEAH.
SATCHAN'S ALREADY GONE.
IT'S A GIRL! ♡
IT'S A GIRL! ♡
...
I MIGHT CATCH UP IF I START CHASING HIM NOW!
DASH
SPLAT
GYAH!
CAW
CAW
TODDLE TODDLE
I COULDN'T FIND HIM...
DUH...
NOW I REMEMBER. THIS PEDESTRIAN BRIDGE...
...IS WHERE I FIRST MET AOI...
I DIDN'T KNOW HIS NAME OR WHAT HE LOOKED LIKE...
ALL I REMEMBERED WAS HIS GENTLE LAVENDER SCENT.

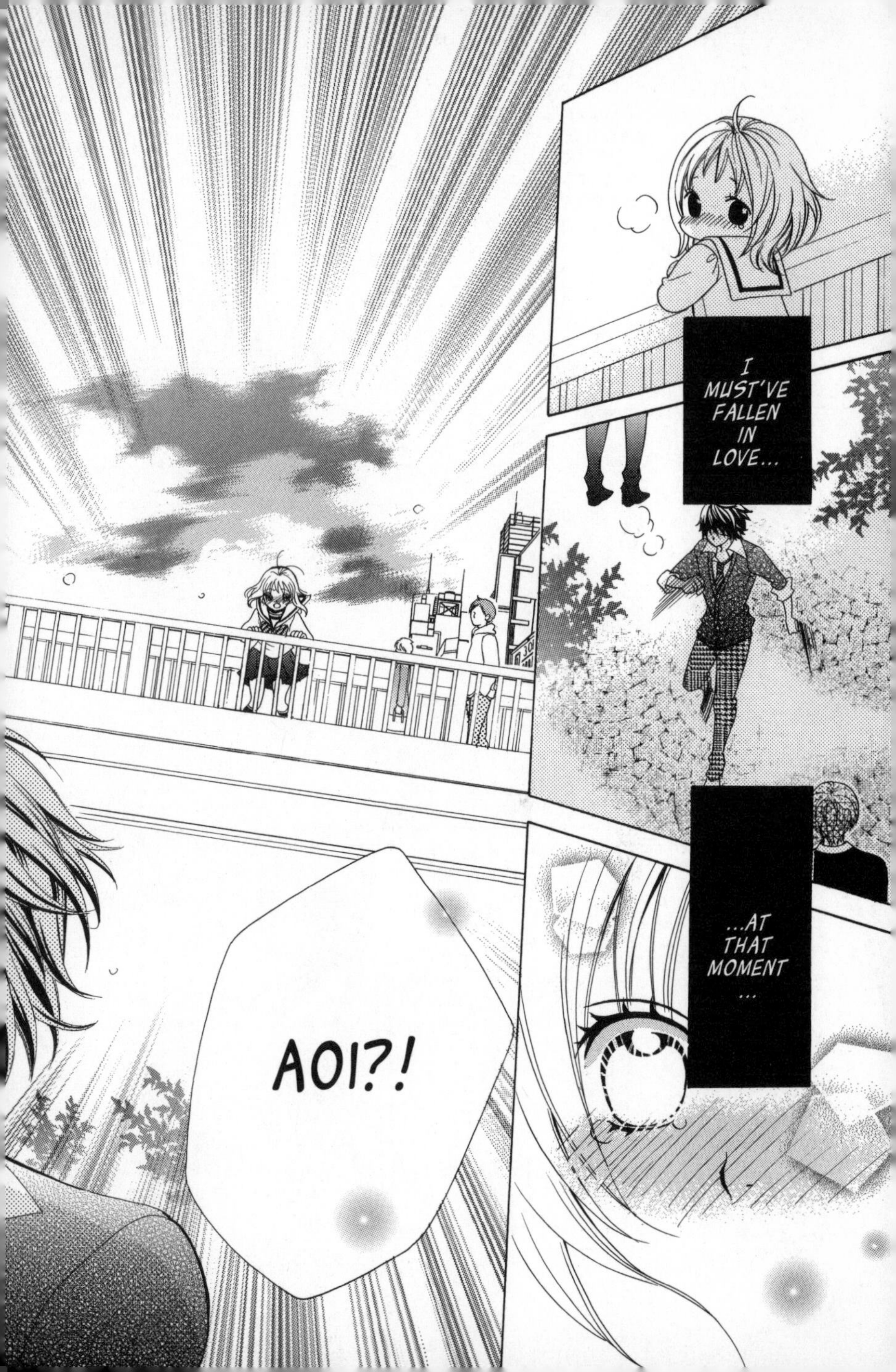
I MUST'VE FALLEN IN LOVE...
...AT THAT MOMENT...
AOI?!

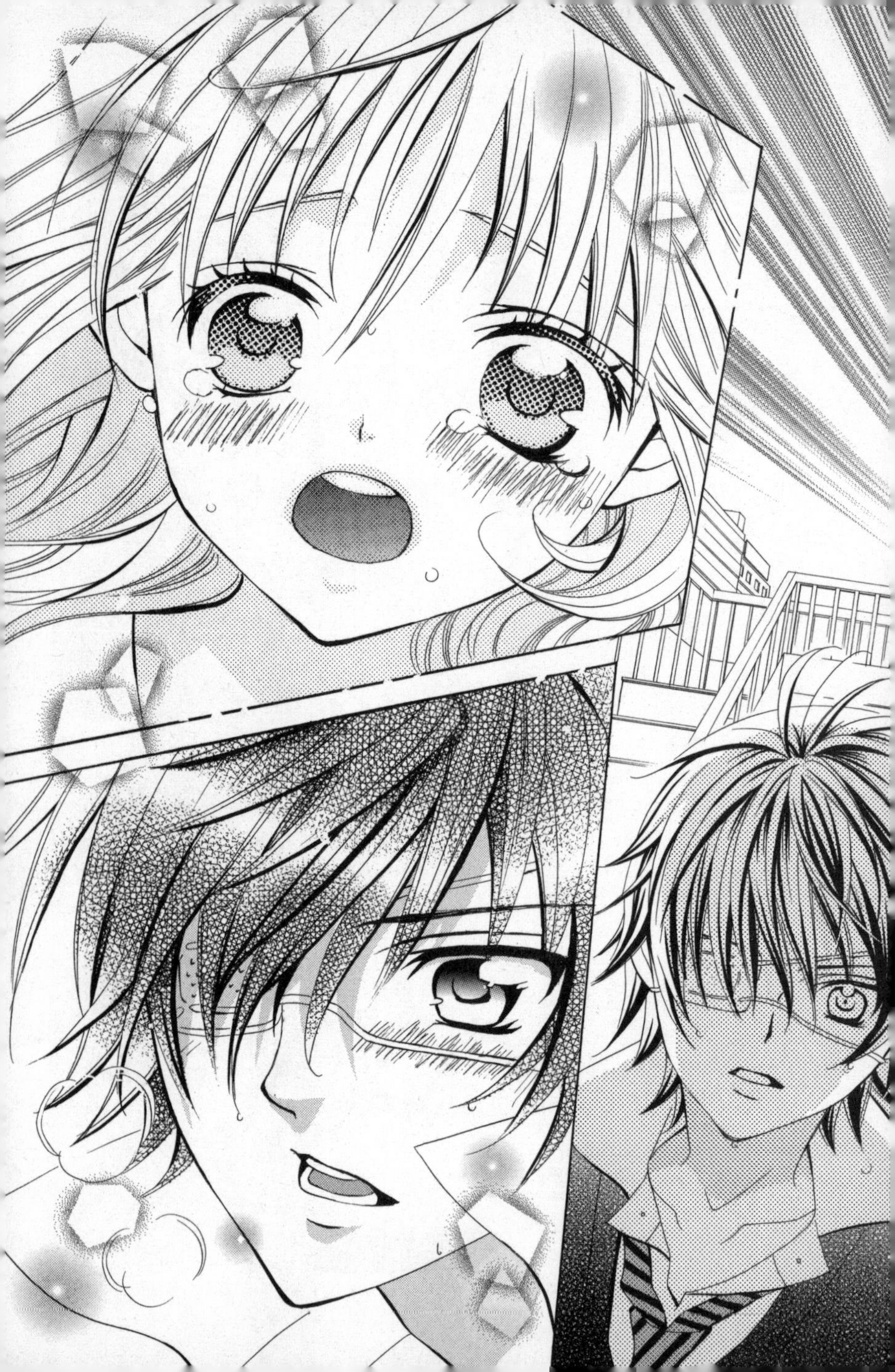

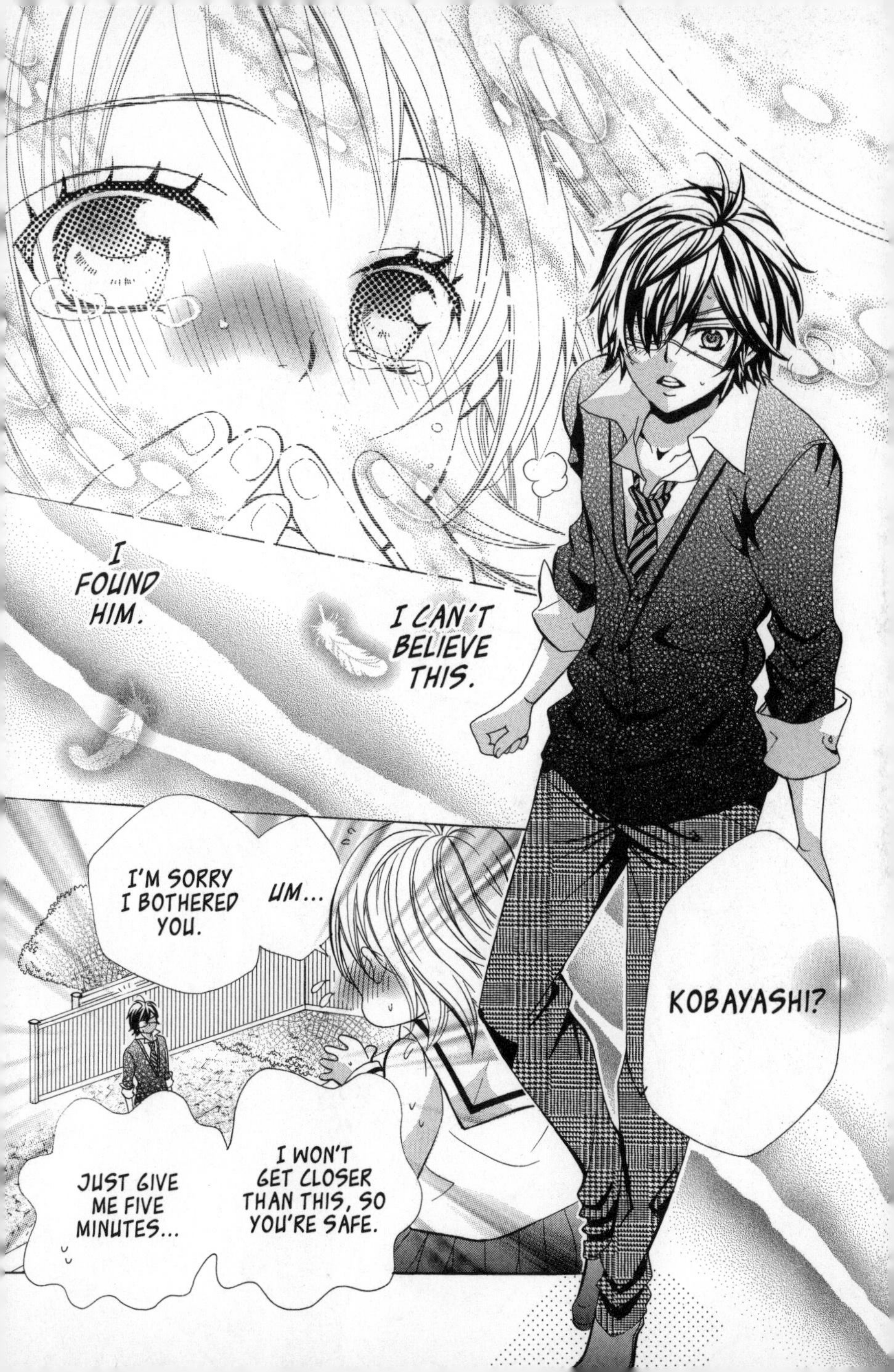
I FOUND HIM.
I CAN'T BELIEVE THIS.
KOBAYASHI?
UM...
I'M SORRY I BOTHERED YOU.
I WON'T GET CLOSER THAN THIS, SO YOU'RE SAFE.
JUST GIVE ME FIVE MINUTES...

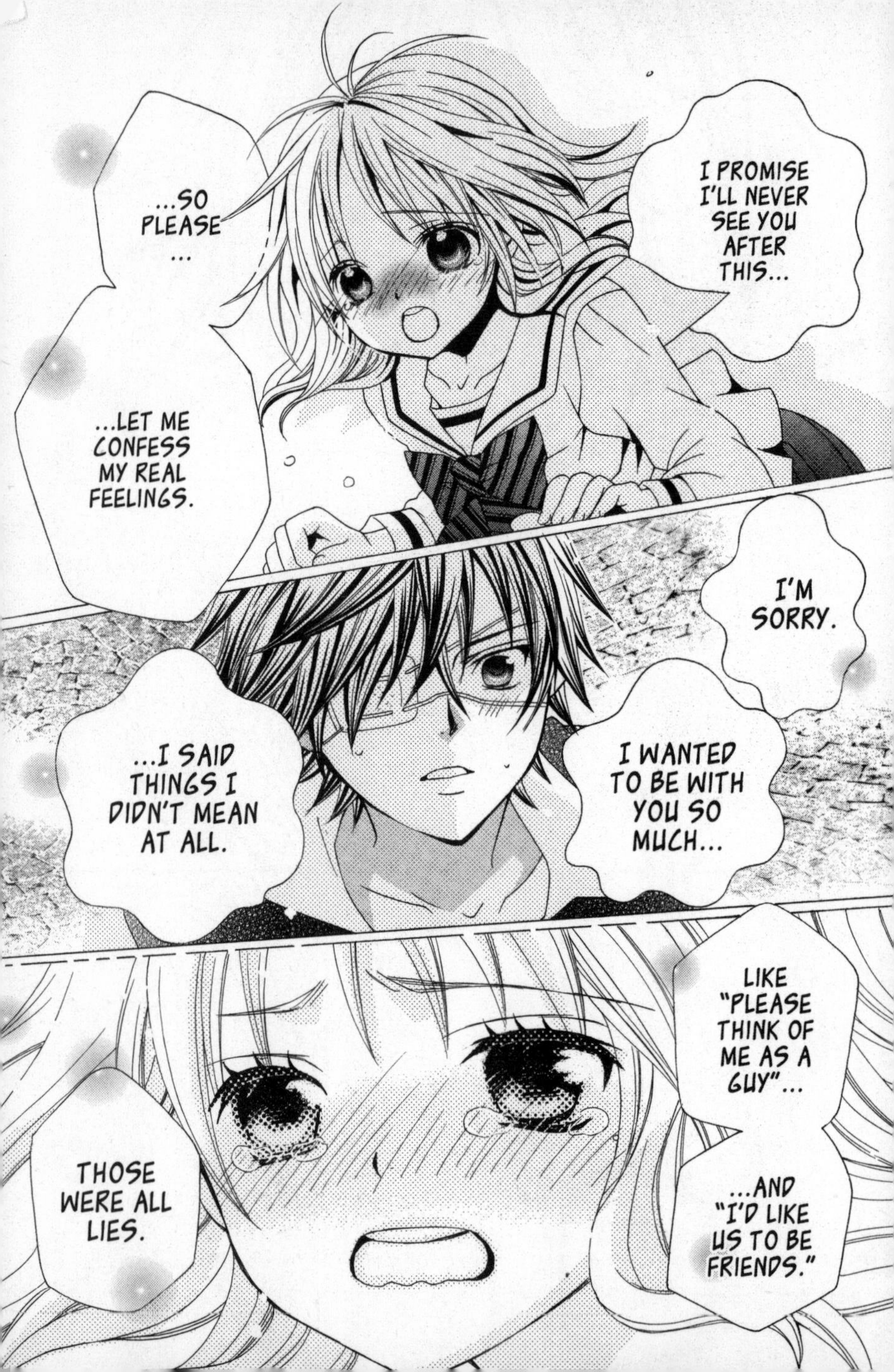
I PROMISE I'LL NEVER SEE YOU AFTER THIS...
...SO PLEASE ...
...LET ME CONFESS MY REAL FEELINGS.
I'M SORRY.
I WANTED TO BE WITH YOU SO MUCH...
...I SAID THINGS I DIDN'T MEAN AT ALL.
LIKE "PLEASE THINK OF ME AS A GUY"...
...AND "I'D LIKE US TO BE FRIENDS."
THOSE WERE ALL LIES.

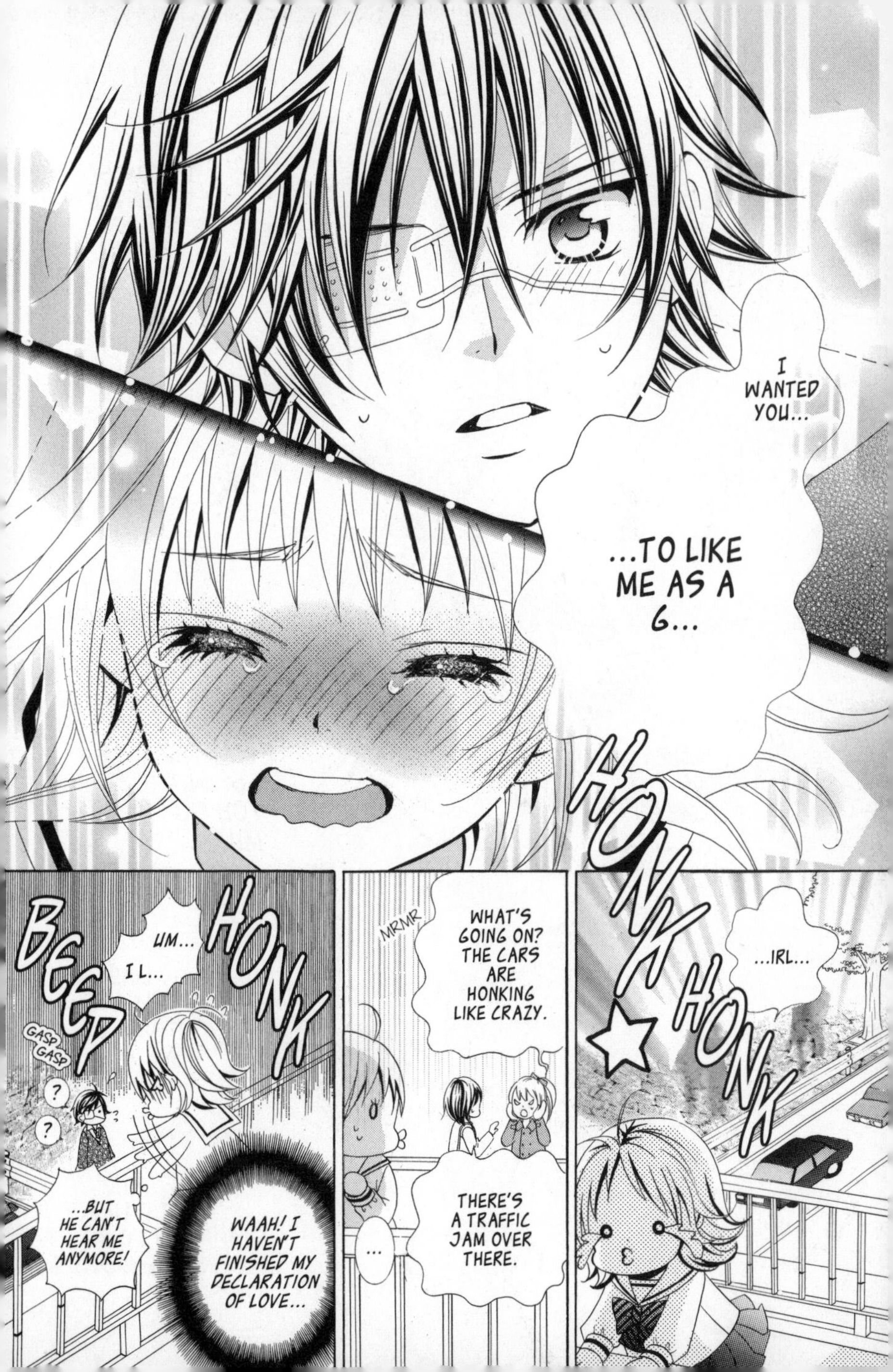

I WANTED YOU...
...TO LIKE ME AS A G...
HONK
HONK HONK
...IRL...
WHAT'S GOING ON? THE CARS ARE HONKING LIKE CRAZY.
MRMR
THERE'S A TRAFFIC JAM OVER THERE.
...
HONK
UM... I L...
BEEP
GASP GASP
?
?
WAAH! I HAVEN'T FINISHED MY DECLARATION OF LOVE...
...BUT HE CAN'T HEAR ME ANYMORE!

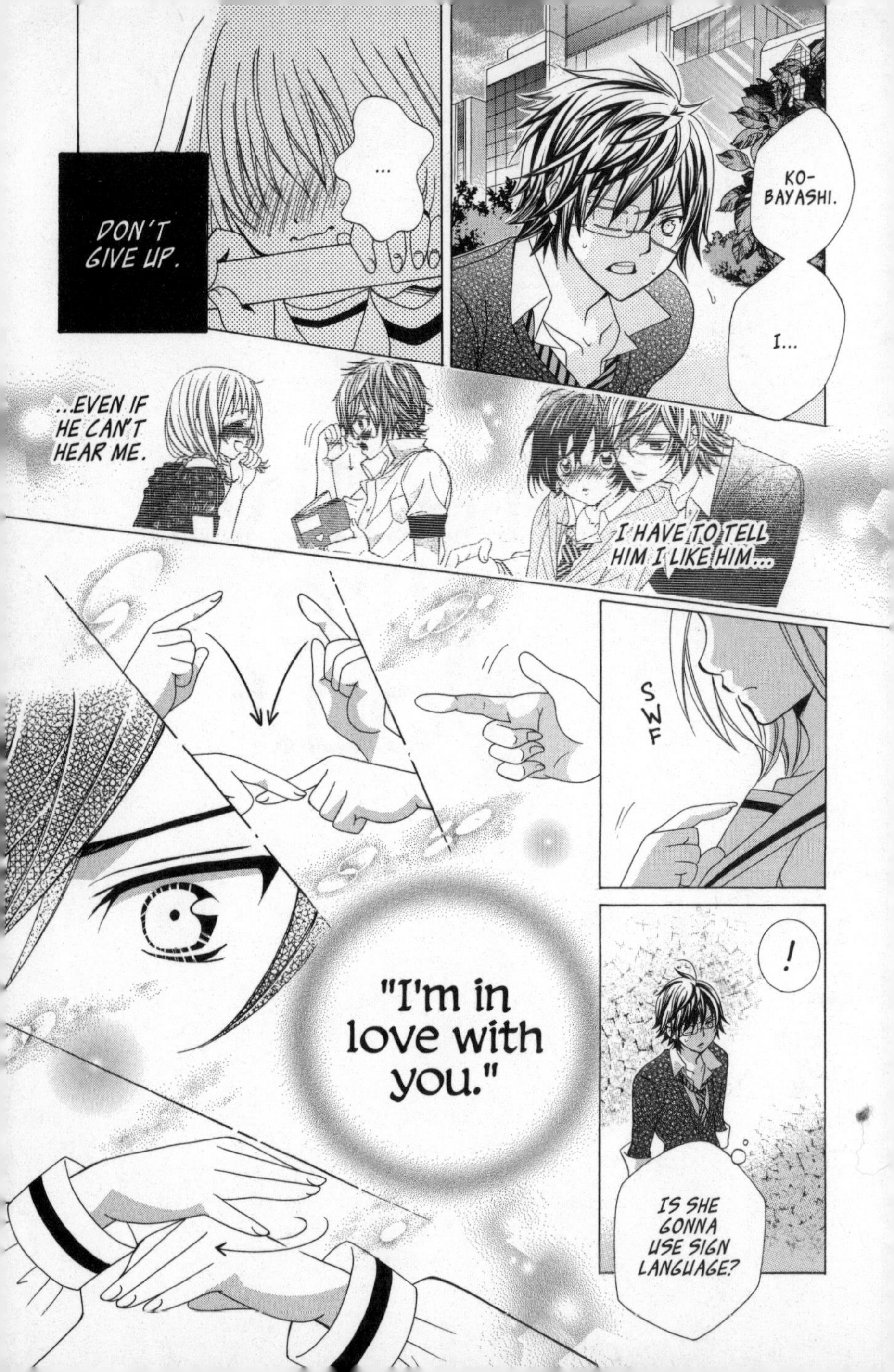
KO-BAYASHI.
I...
...
DON'T GIVE UP.
I HAVE TO TELL HIM I LIKE HIM...
...EVEN IF HE CAN'T HEAR ME.
SWF
!
IS SHE GONNA USE SIGN LANGUAGE?
"I'm in love with you."

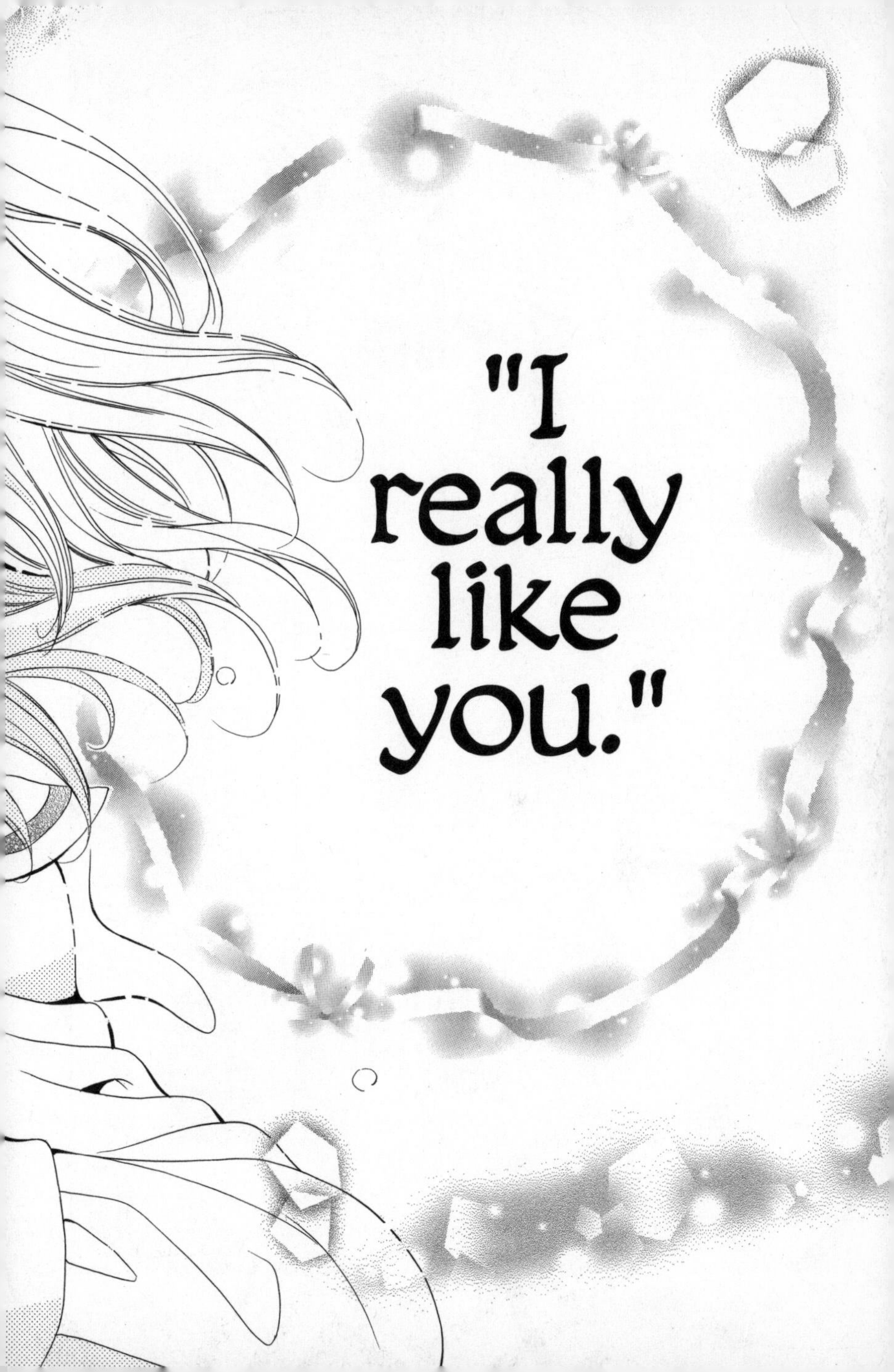
"I really like you."

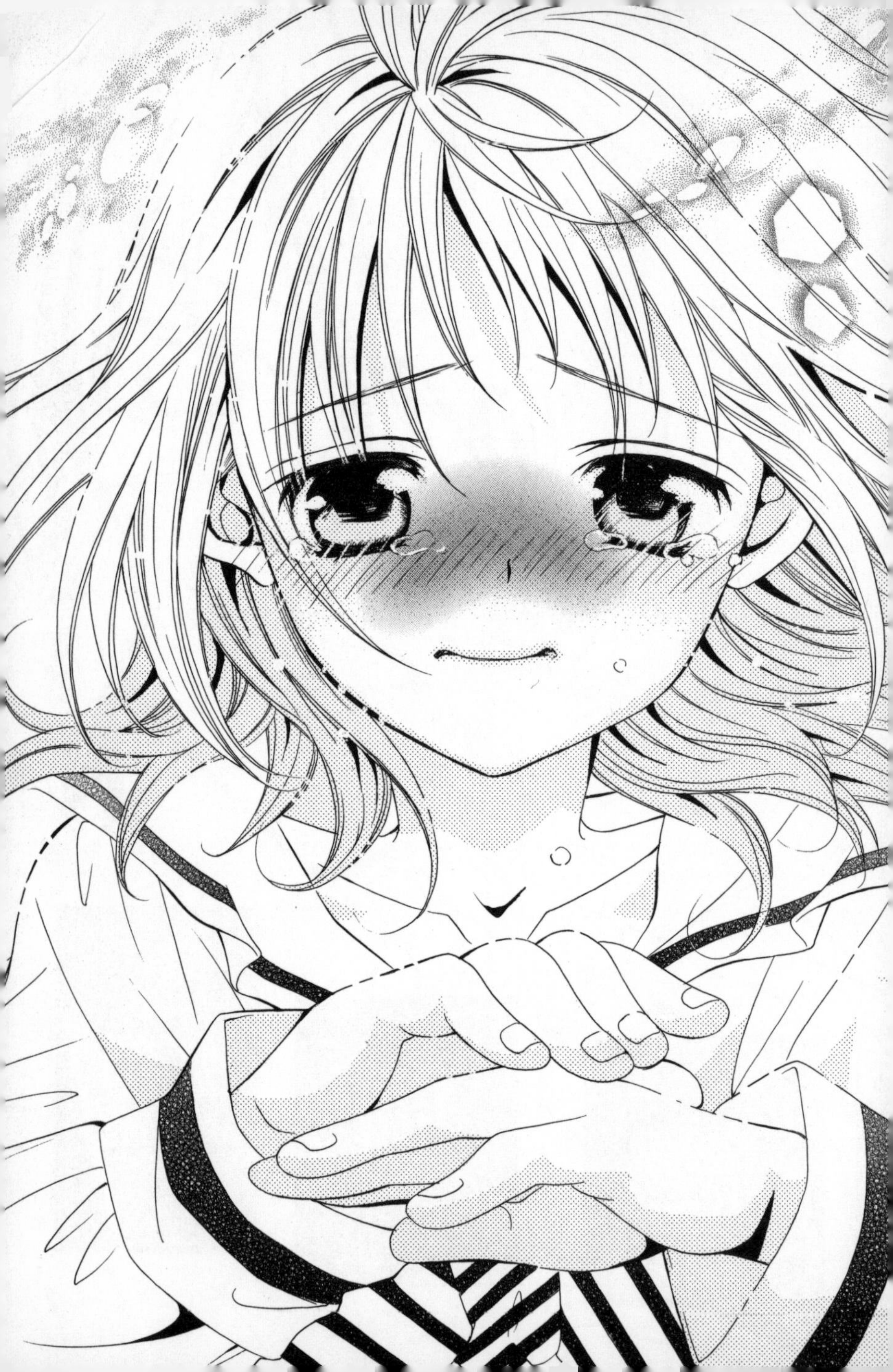

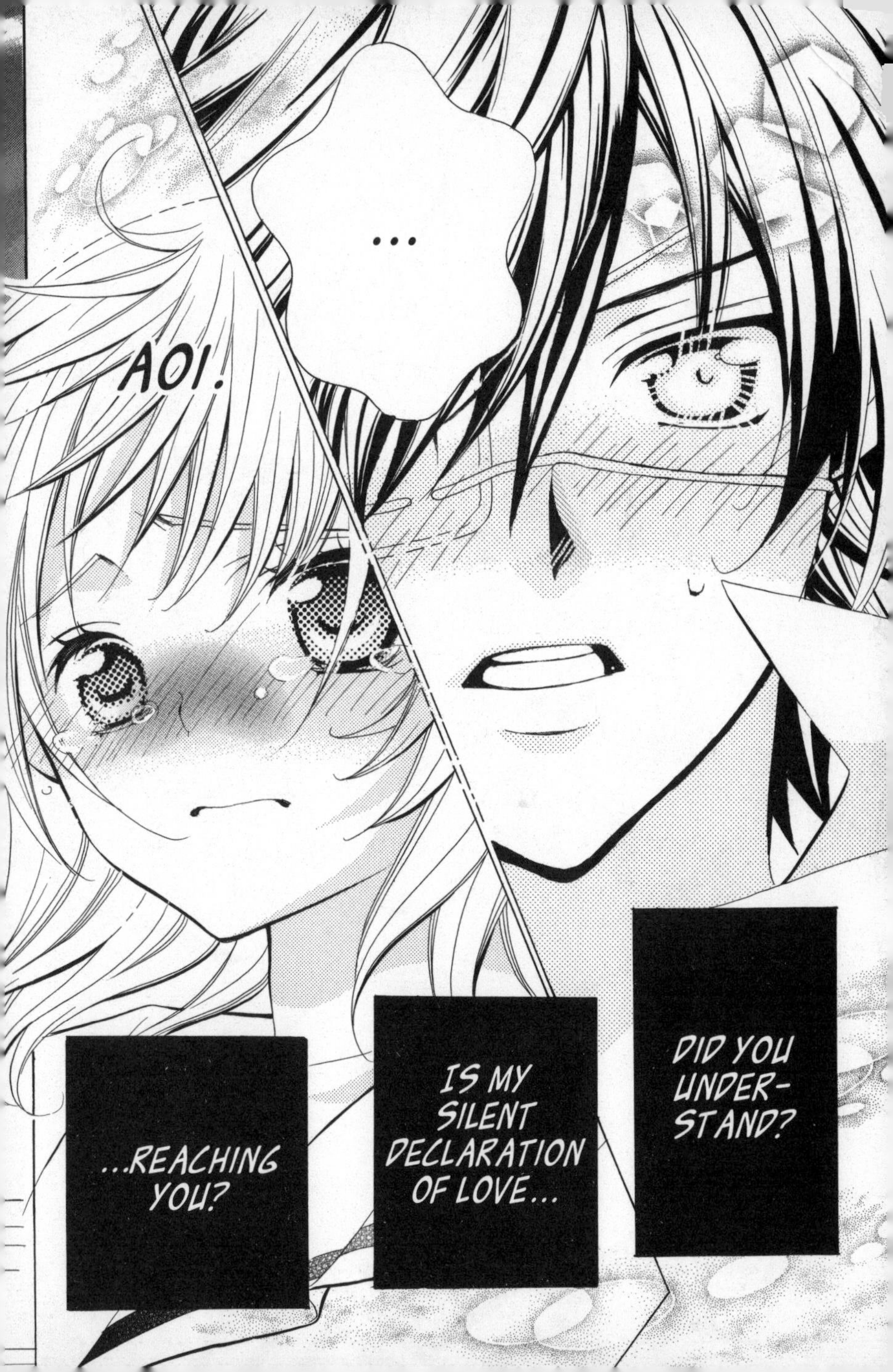
...
AOI.
DID YOU UNDER-STAND?
IS MY SILENT DECLARATION OF LOVE...
...REACHING YOU?

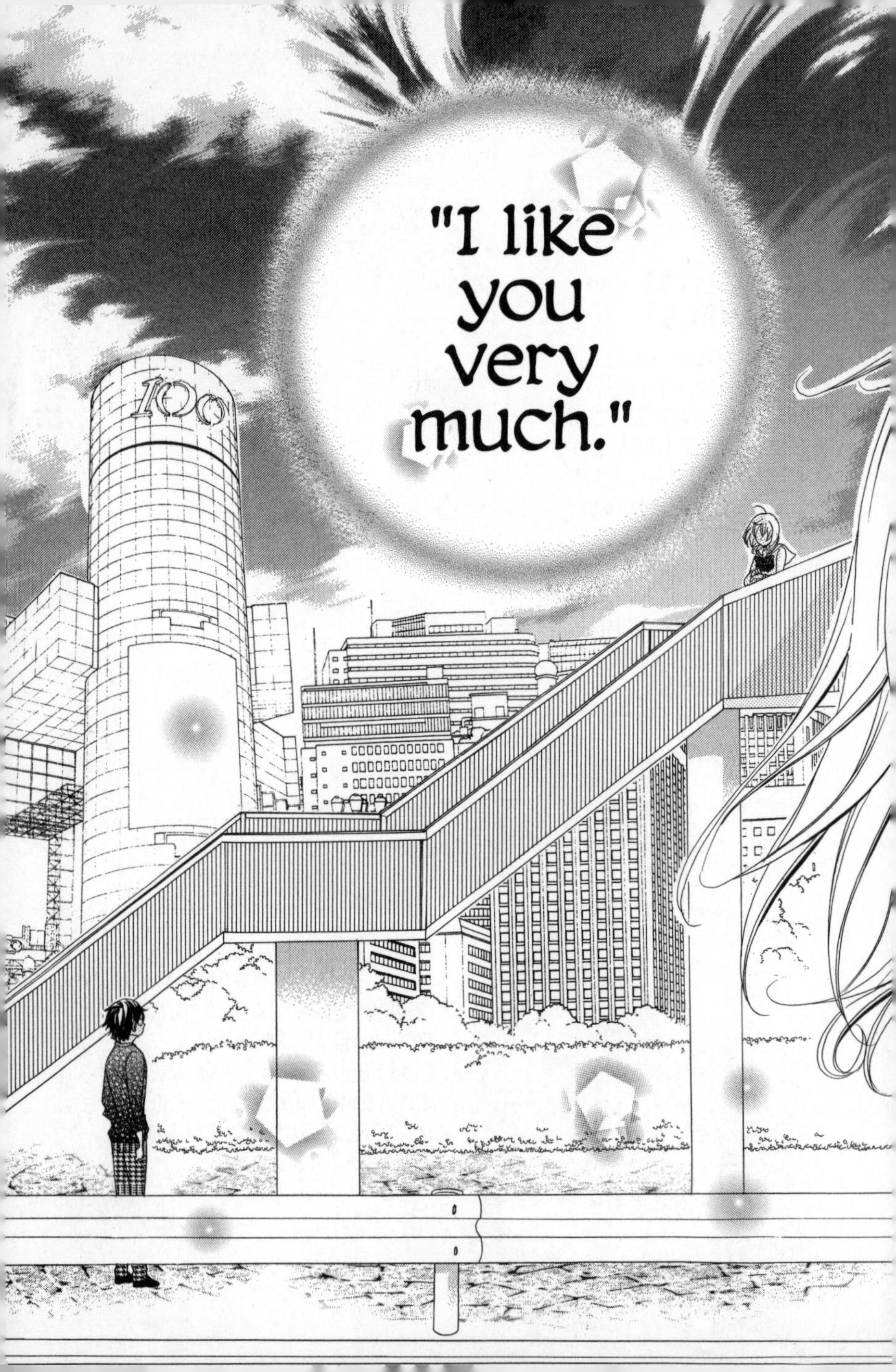
"I like you very much."
100

SO CUTE! NOVELS!

TWO *SO CUTE!* NOVELS HAVE BEEN PUBLISHED, ONE FROM SHOGAKUKAN JUNIOR BOOKS AND ONE FROM LULULU BOOKS! (^0^) IN *AFTER SCHOOL IS SO WILD IT'S DANGEROUS!* (JUNIOR BOOKS), MEGO AND MITSURU BECOME INVOLVED IN A CERTAIN INCIDENT AND...?! IT'S A HEARTWARMING COMEDY THAT'LL MAKE YOUR HEART POUND IN SUSPENSE.♡♡

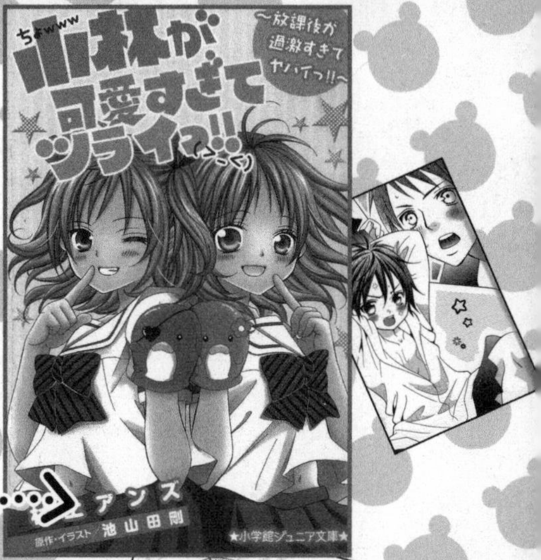
ちょwww
小林が可愛すぎてツライっ!!
～放課後が過激すぎてヤバイっ!!～
原作・イラスト 池山田剛
★小学館ジュニア文庫★

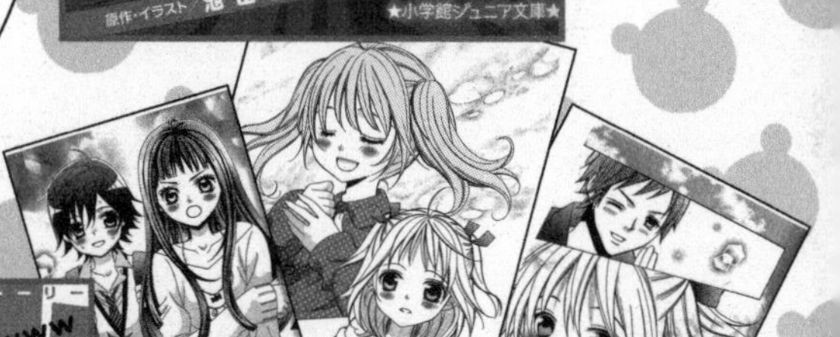

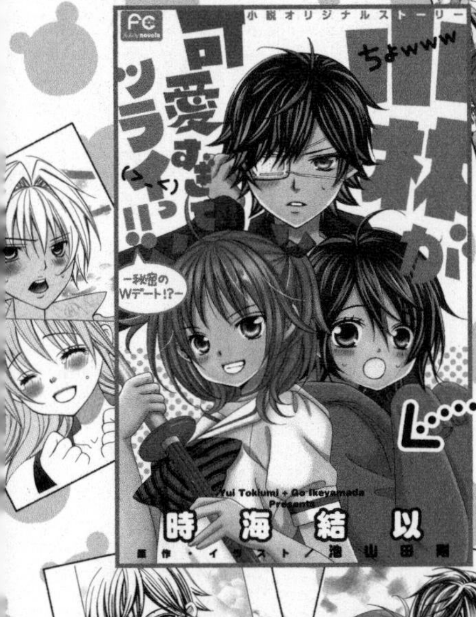
小説オリジナルストーリー
ちょwww
小林が可愛すぎてツライっ!!
ー秘密のWデート!?ー
Yui Tokiumi + Go Ikeyamada Presents
時海結以
原作・イラスト／池山田剛

IN *SECRET DOUBLE DATE?!* (LULULU BOOKS), CHISA AND REO, FROM MY PREVIOUS SERIES *SUKI DESU SUZUKI KUN!!*, MAKE AN APPEARANCE.♡ CHISA HONDA, A NEW SINGER, MEETS MITSURU AND MEGO ONE DAY AND...?! ENJOY THE *SO CUTE!* X *SUZUKI-KUN* CHARACTER COLLAB!

♪♪

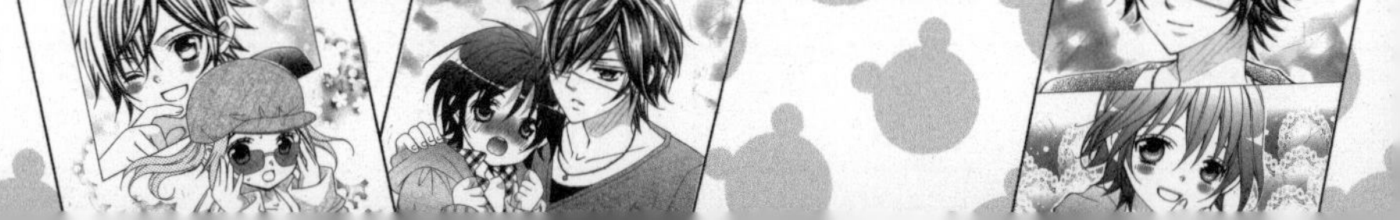

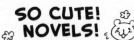

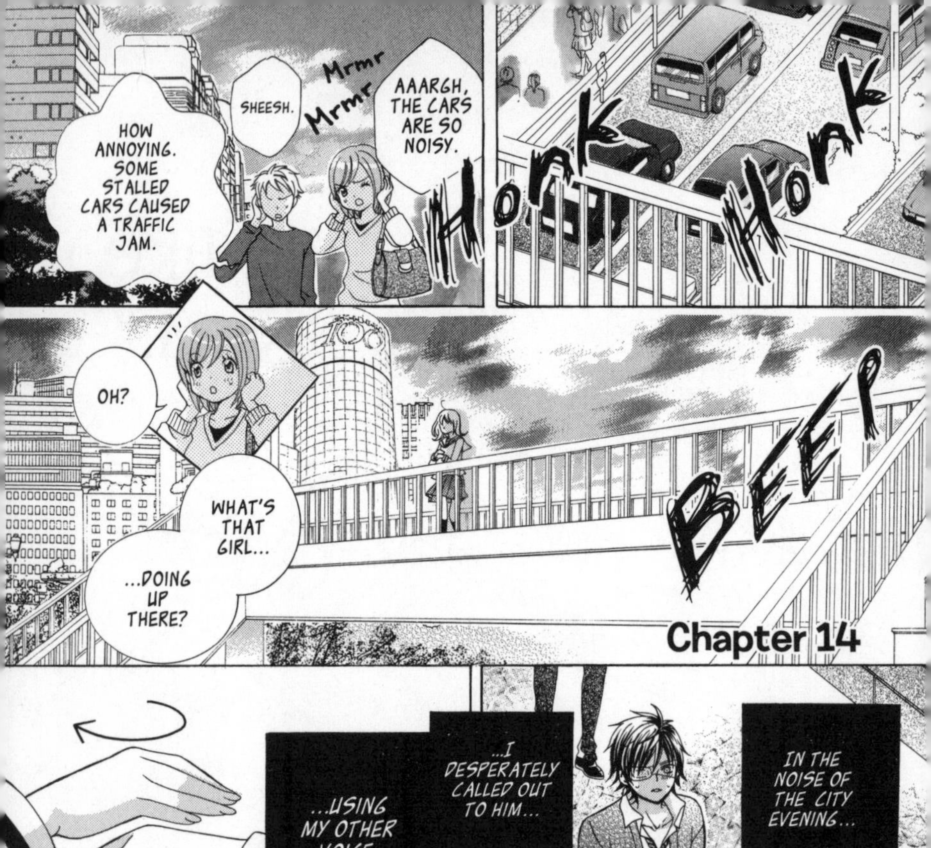
Honk
Honk
AAARGH, THE CARS ARE SO NOISY.
Mrmr
Mrmr
SHEESH.
HOW ANNOYING. SOME STALLED CARS CAUSED A TRAFFIC JAM.
BEEP
OH?
WHAT'S THAT GIRL...
...DOING UP THERE?
Chapter 14
IN THE NOISE OF THE CITY EVENING...
...I DESPERATELY CALLED OUT TO HIM...
...USING MY OTHER VOICE.

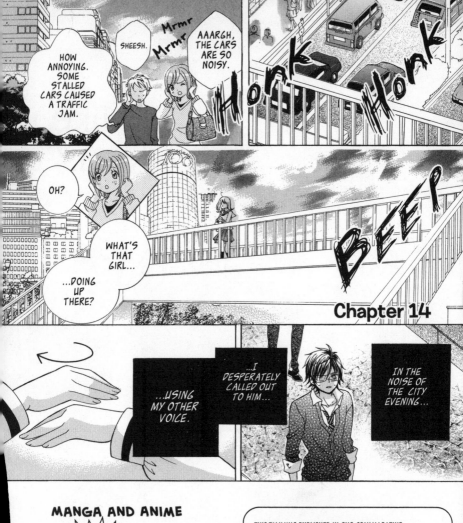

MANGA AND ANIME

I HAD MY FIRST TALK WITH YUU WATASE SENSEI, WHOSE *ARATA: THE LEGEND* MANGA IS RUNNING IN *SHONEN SUNDAY* MAGAZINE. ♡♡

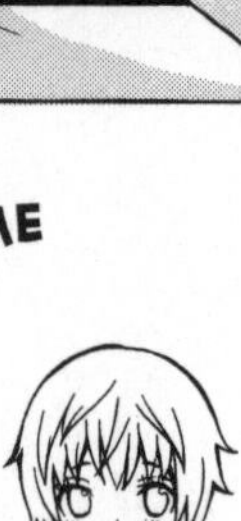

THIS TALK WAS PUBLISHED IN *SHO-COMI* MAGAZINE TO CELEBRATE THE *ARATA* ANIME. ♪
WATASE SENSEI IS A VERY SENIOR *SHO-COMI* CREATOR, AND I'VE ADORED HER SINCE I WAS IN GRADE SCHOOL. SHE WAS VERY BEAUTIFUL AND SWEET, AND I FELT LIKE I WAS IN A DREAM.♡
I WAS HAPPY I WAS ABLE TO TALK ABOUT HOW MUCH I LOVE KOTOHA-CHAN AND AKACHI-SAMA. ♡

I LOVE THE NEW *INAZUMA ELEVEN GO GALAXY* ANIME TOO. ♪♪ I CRIED FOR JOY WHEN KIDOU-SAN APPEARED IN THE FIRST EPISODE WEARING HIS CLOAK. (*SMILE*) ♡♡ I HOPE KIRINO-KUN AND SAKUMA-KUN APPEAR TOO. ♪♪ THE *SENGOKU BASARA 4* GAME WILL BE ON SALE.♡ I WANT TO PLAY MASAMUNE-SAMA SOON! LOL.

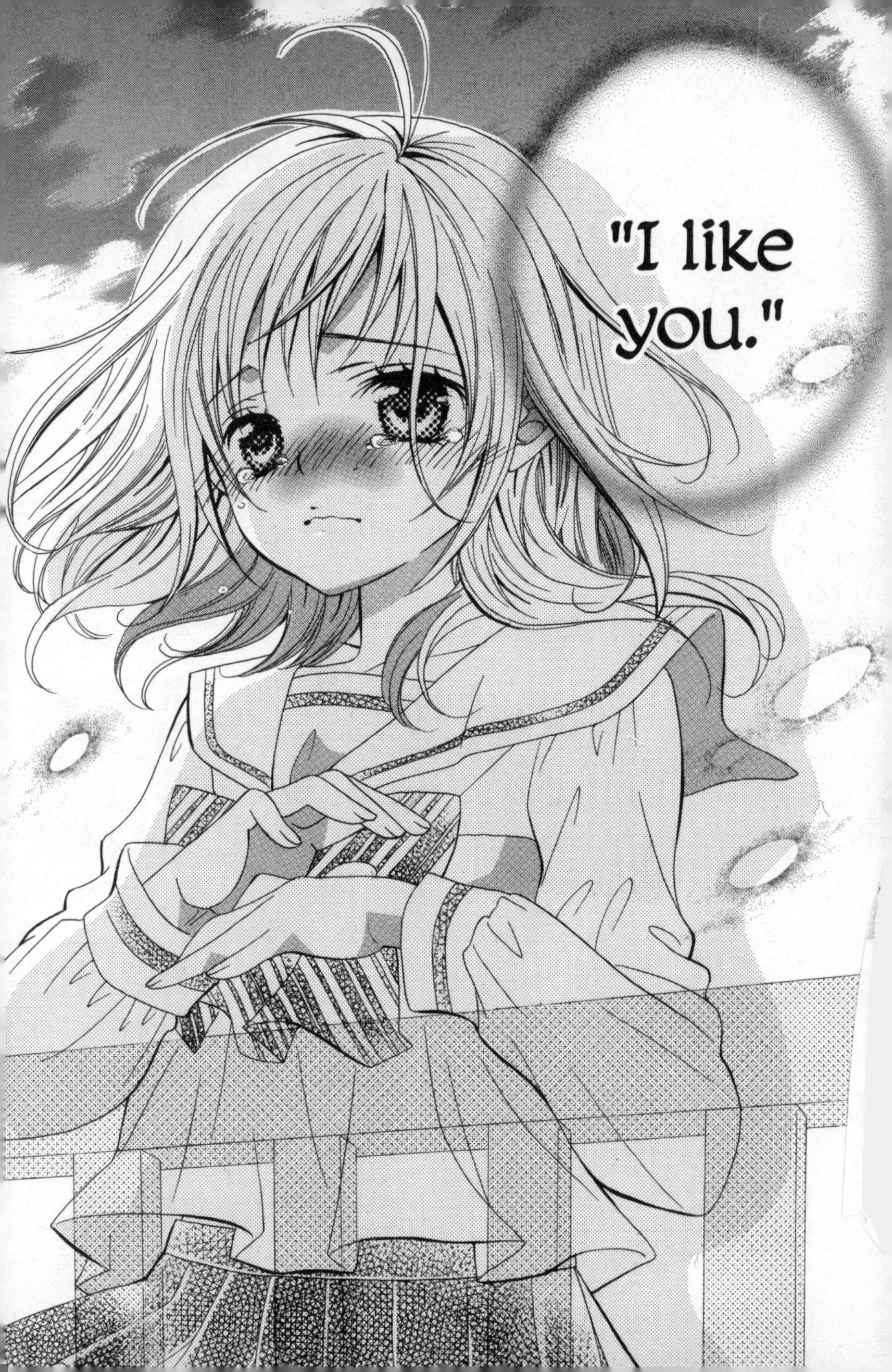
"I like you."

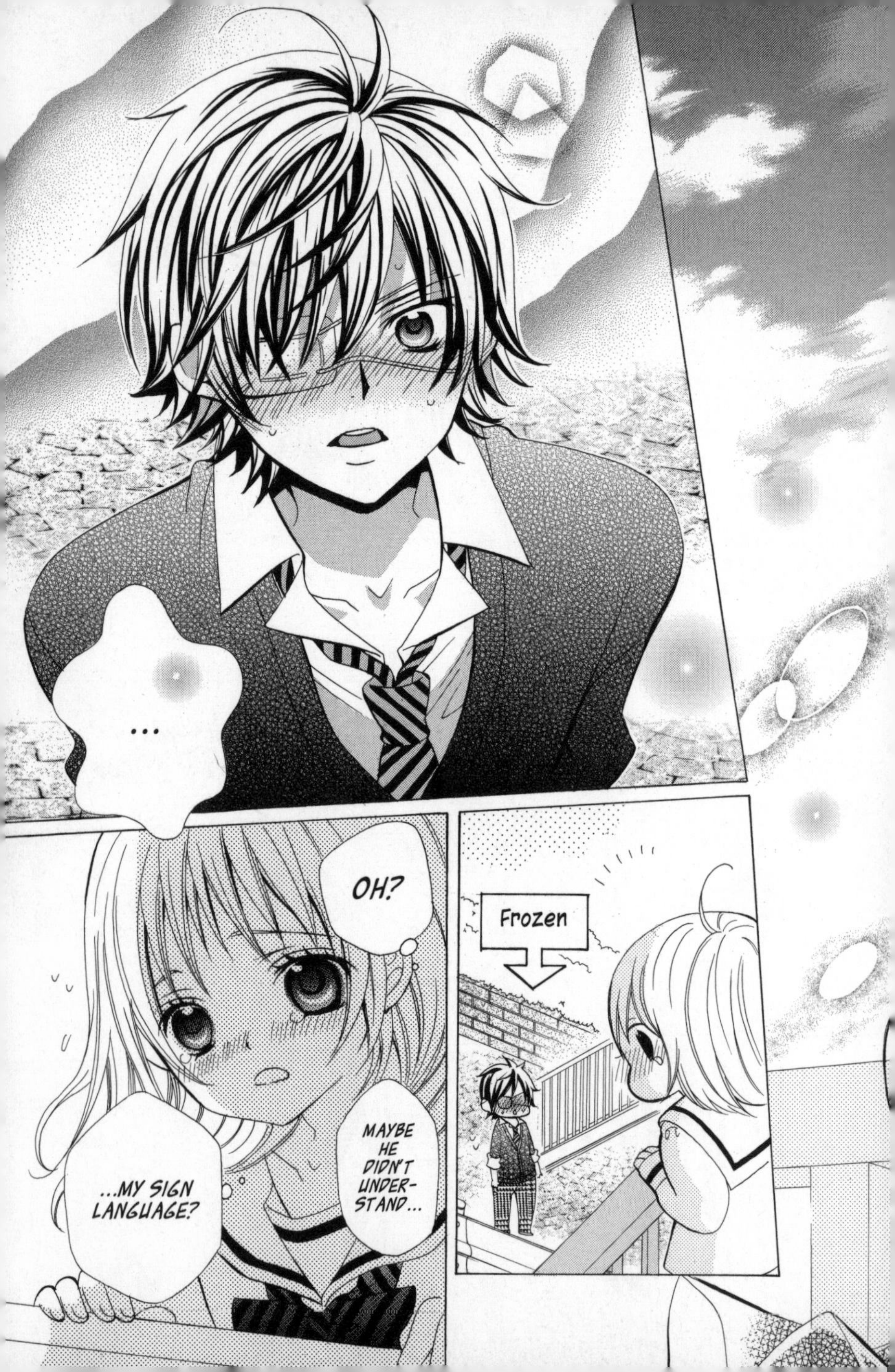
...
Frozen
OH?
MAYBE HE DIDN'T UNDER-STAND...
...MY SIGN LANGUAGE?

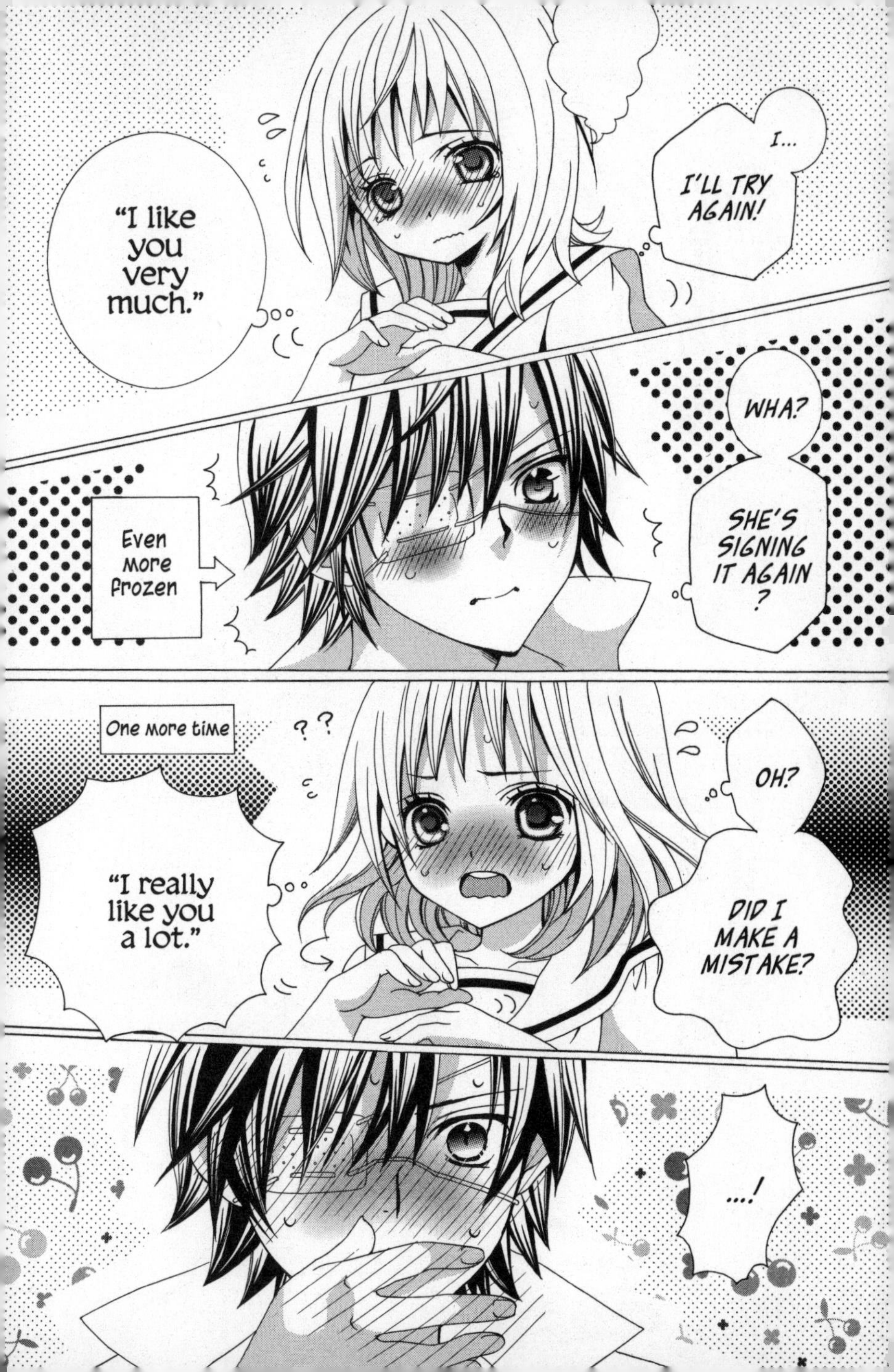
I...
I'LL TRY AGAIN!
"I like you very much."
WHA?
SHE'S SIGNING IT AGAIN?
Even more frozen
OH?
DID I MAKE A MISTAKE?
One more time
"I really like you a lot."
...!

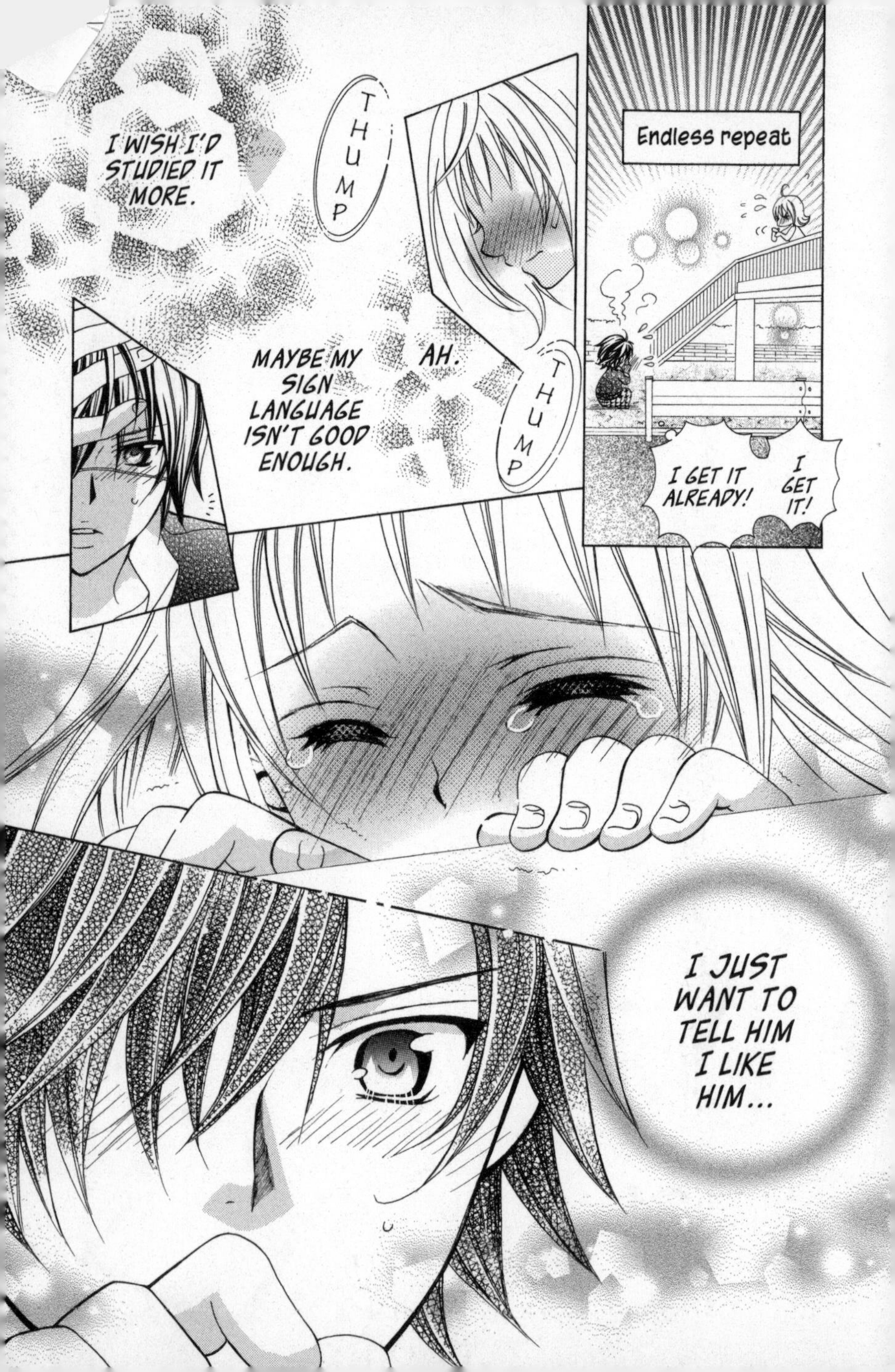
Endless repeat
I GET IT!
I GET IT ALREADY!
THUMP
THUMP
AH.
I WISH I'D STUDIED IT MORE.
MAYBE MY SIGN LANGUAGE ISN'T GOOD ENOUGH.
I JUST WANT TO TELL HIM I LIKE HIM...

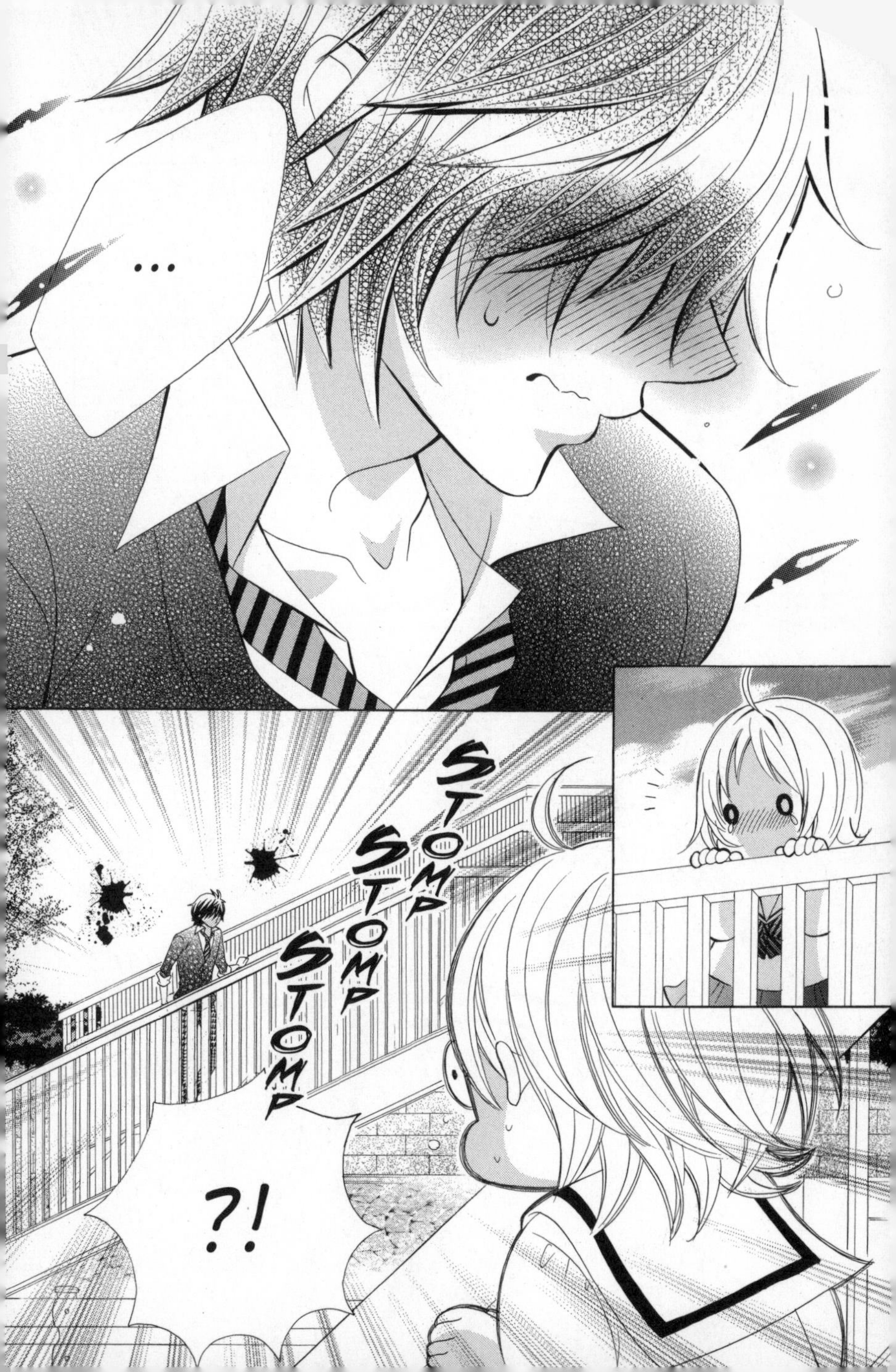
...
STOMP
STOMP
STOMP
STOMP
?!

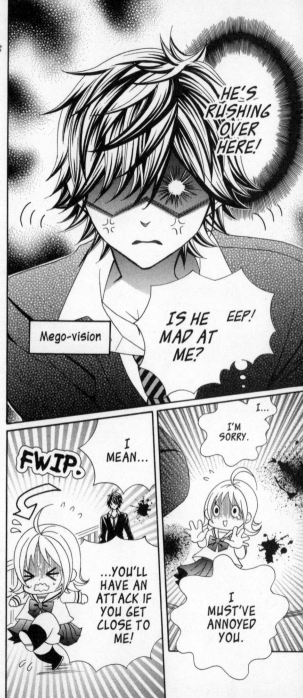

HE'S RUSHING OVER HERE!
Mego-vision
EEP!
IS HE MAD AT ME?
I...
I'M SORRY.
I MUST'VE ANNOYED YOU.
FWIP.
I MEAN...
...YOU'LL HAVE AN ATTACK IF YOU GET CLOSE TO ME!

So Cute It Hurts!!

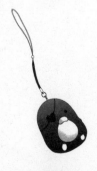

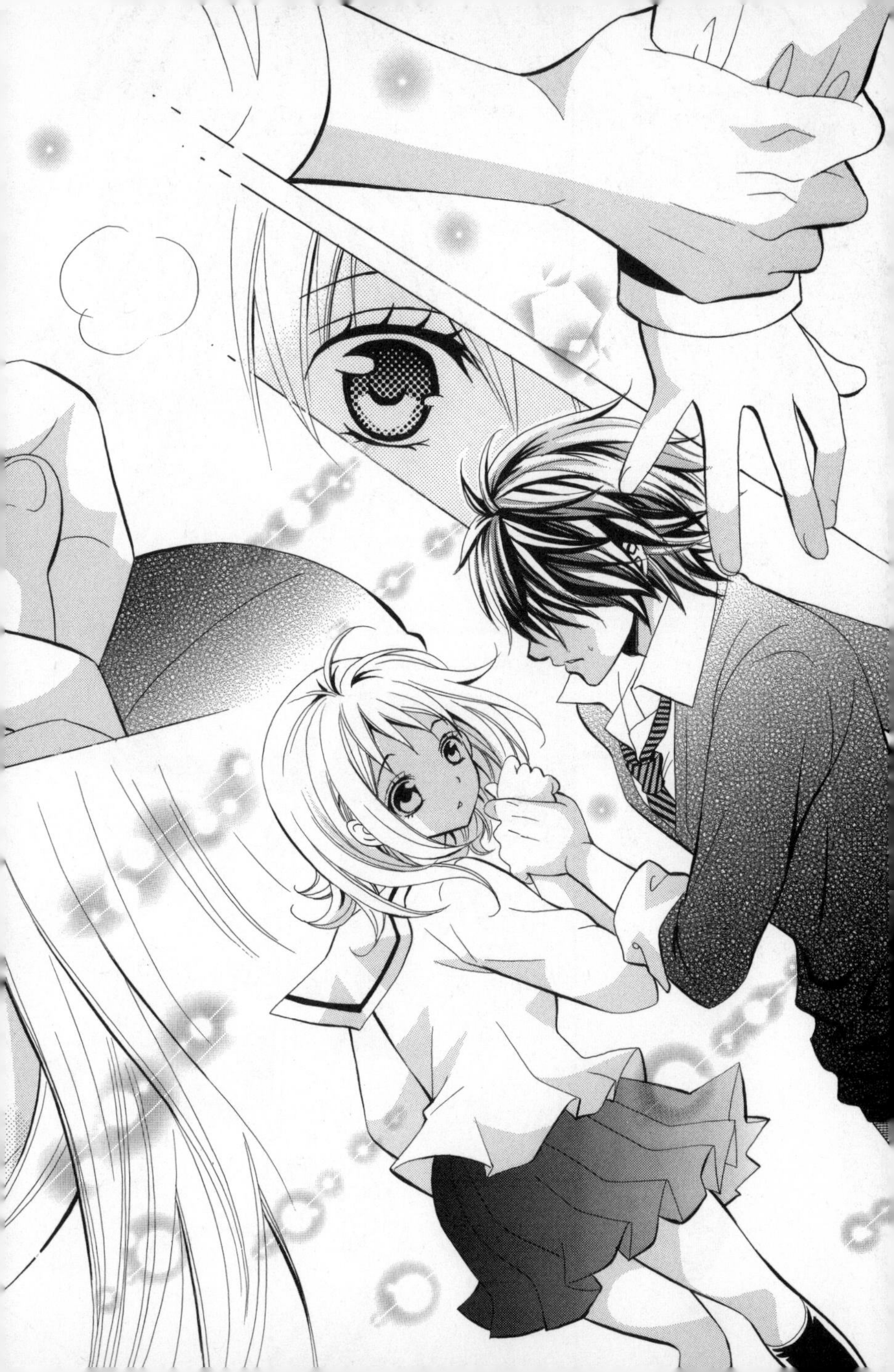

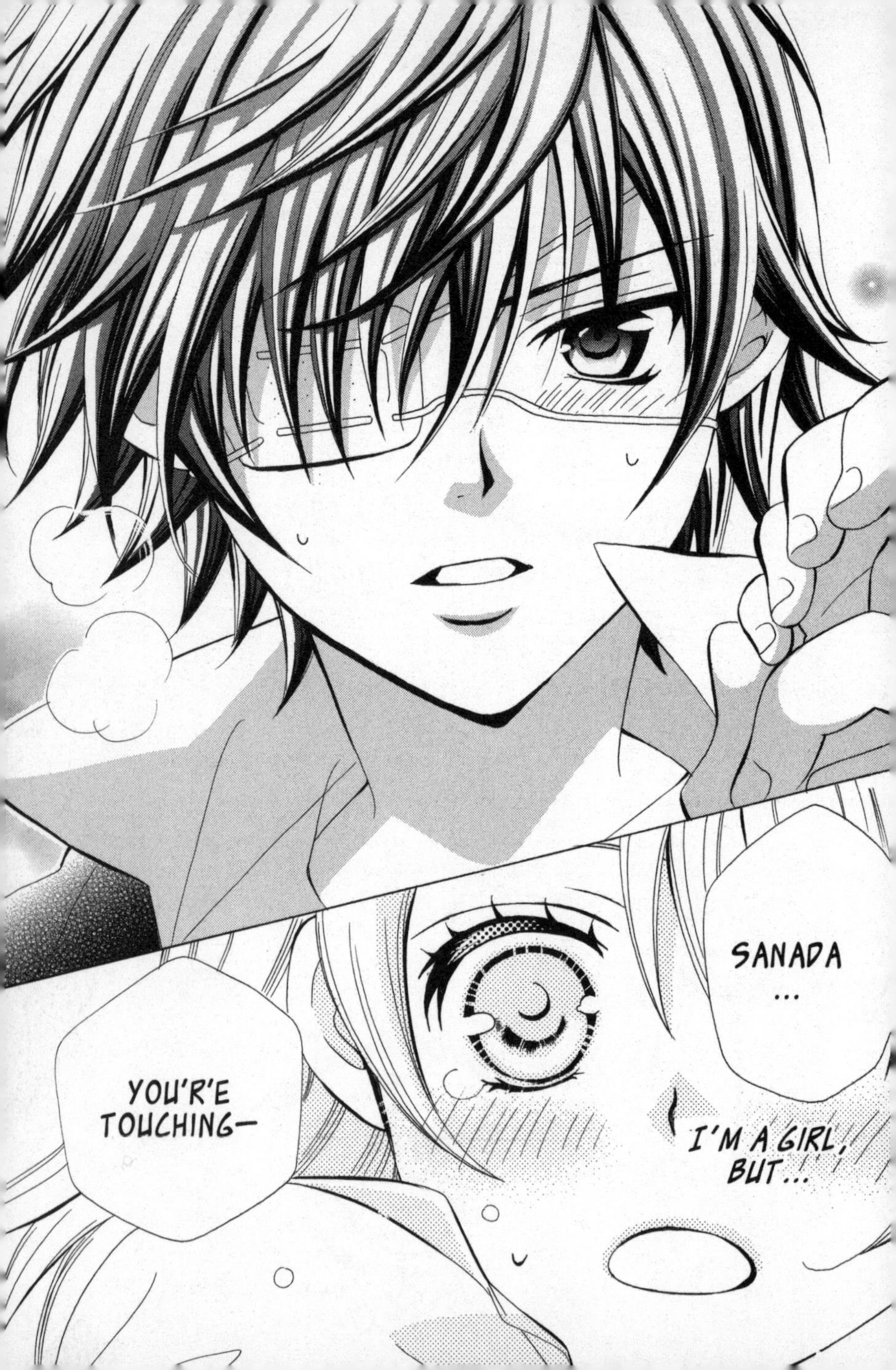
SANADA ...
YOU'R'E TOUCHING—
I'M A GIRL, BUT...

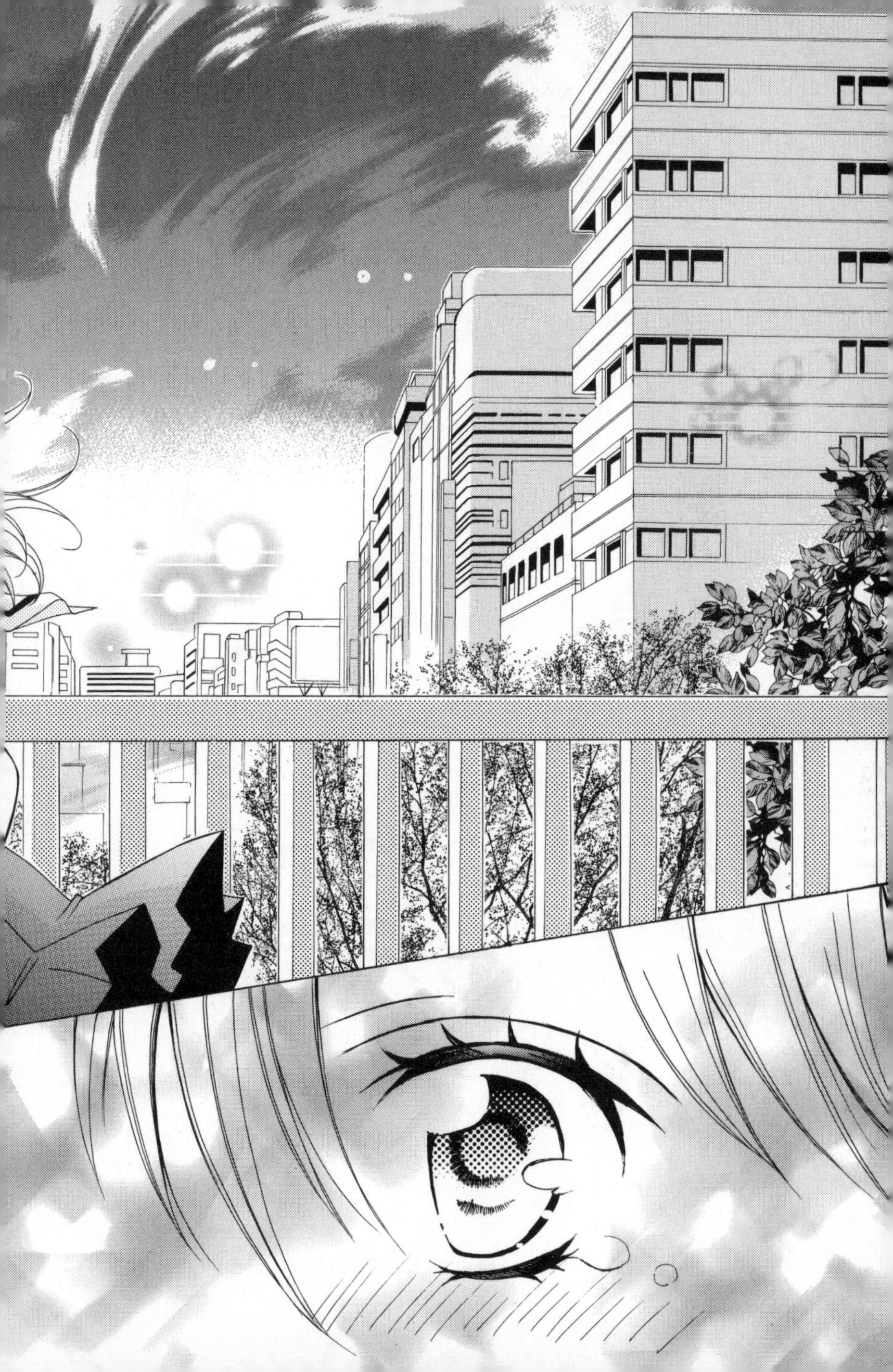

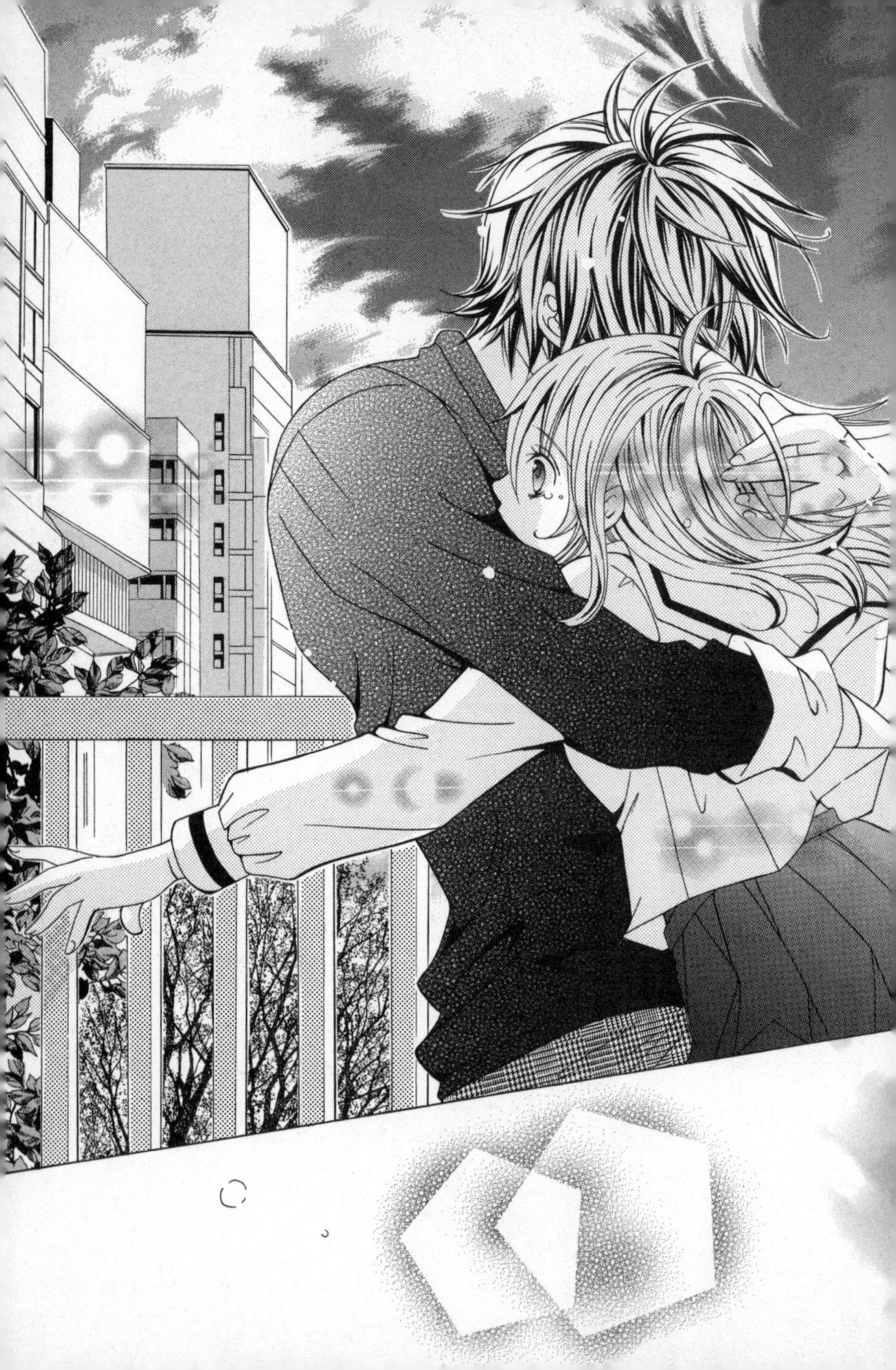

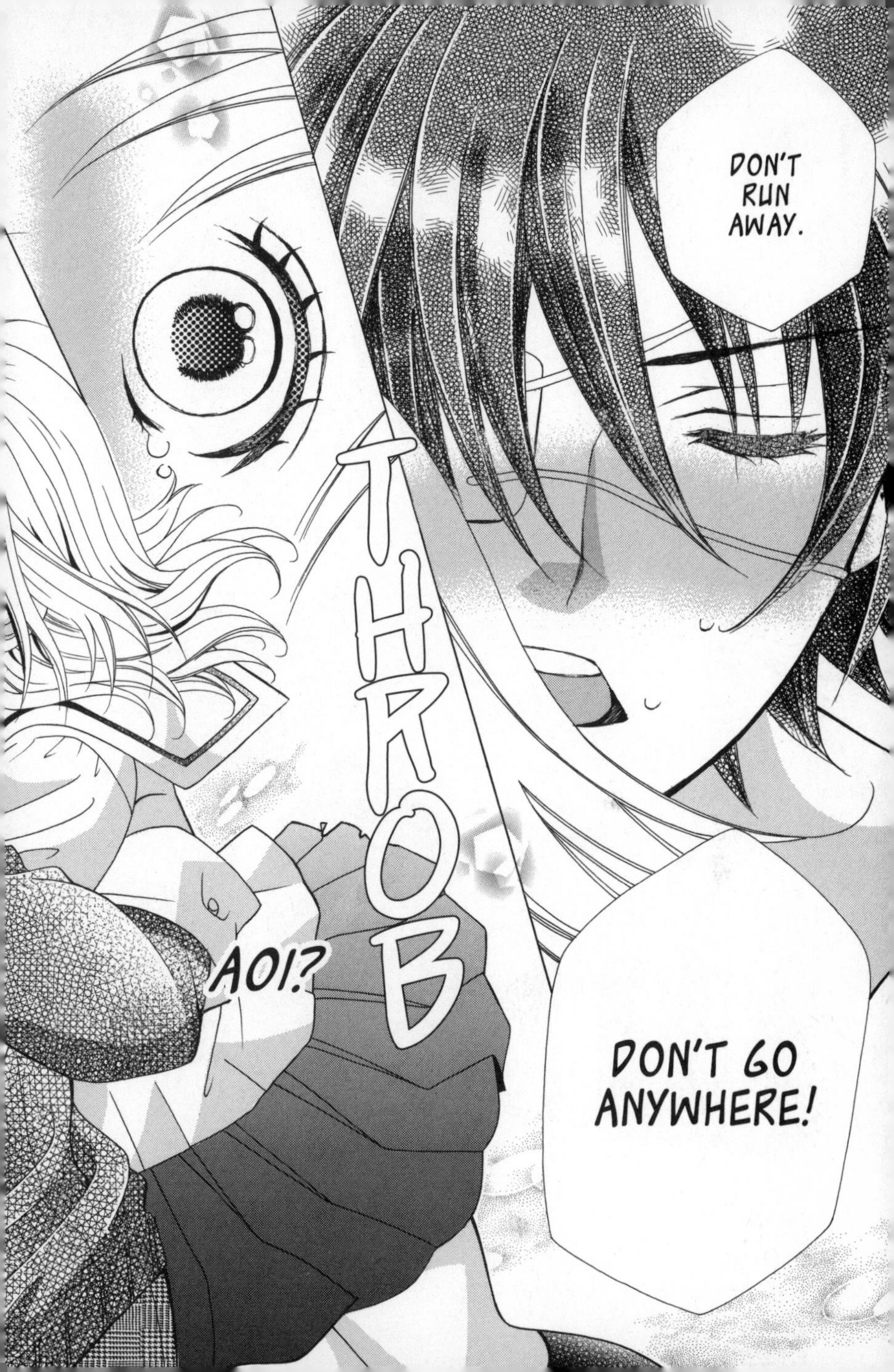
DON'T RUN AWAY.
THROB
AOI!?
DON'T GO ANYWHERE!

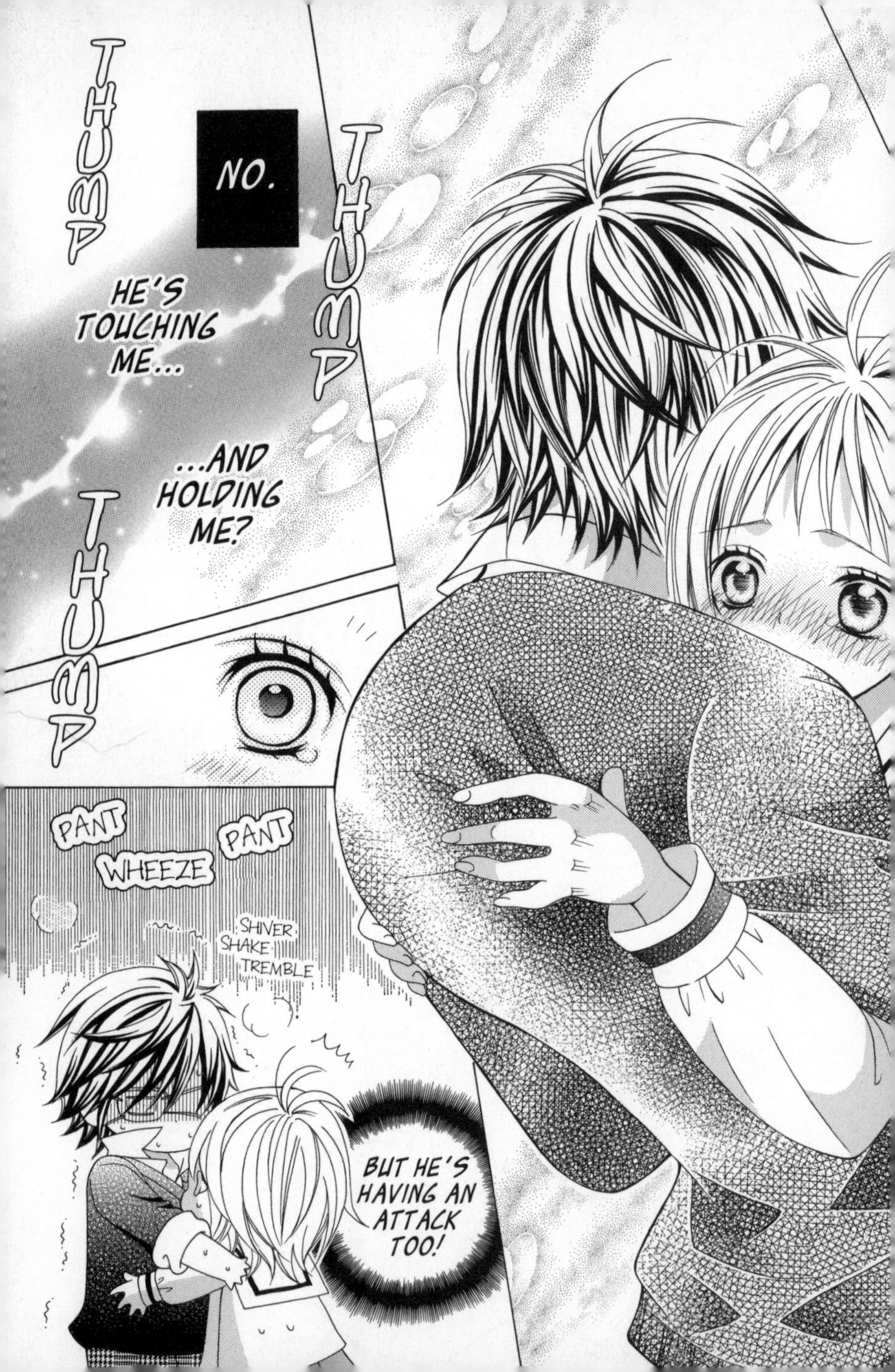
THUMP
THUMP
NO.
HE'S TOUCHING ME...
...AND HOLDING ME?
THUMP
THUMP
PANT
PANT
WHEEZE
SHIVER SHAKE TREMBLE
BUT HE'S HAVING AN ATTACK TOO!

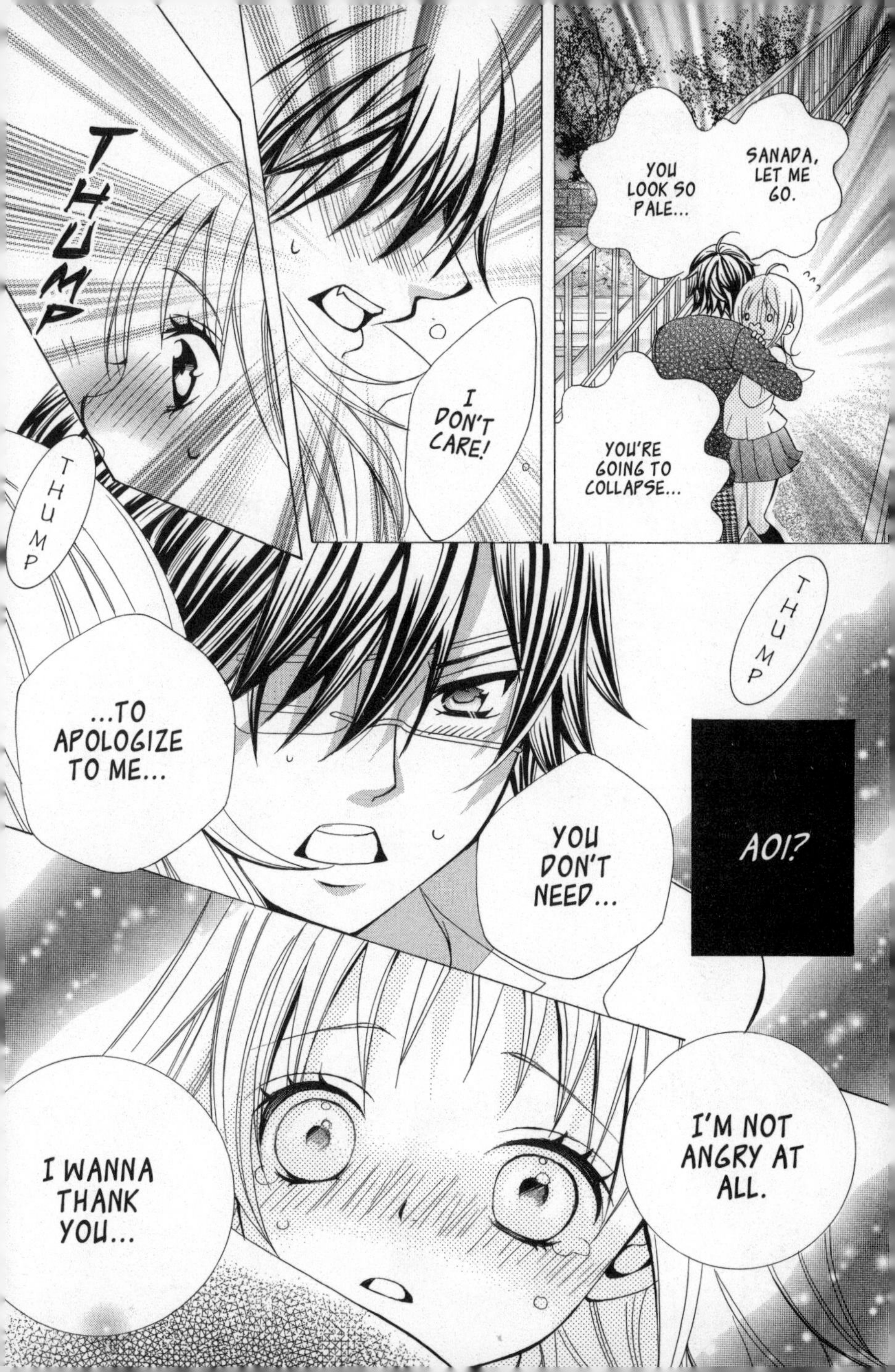
SANADA, LET ME GO.
YOU LOOK SO PALE...
YOU'RE GOING TO COLLAPSE...
I DON'T CARE!
THUMP
THUMP
THUMP
AOI?
YOU DON'T NEED...
...TO APOLOGIZE TO ME...
I'M NOT ANGRY AT ALL.
I WANNA THANK YOU...

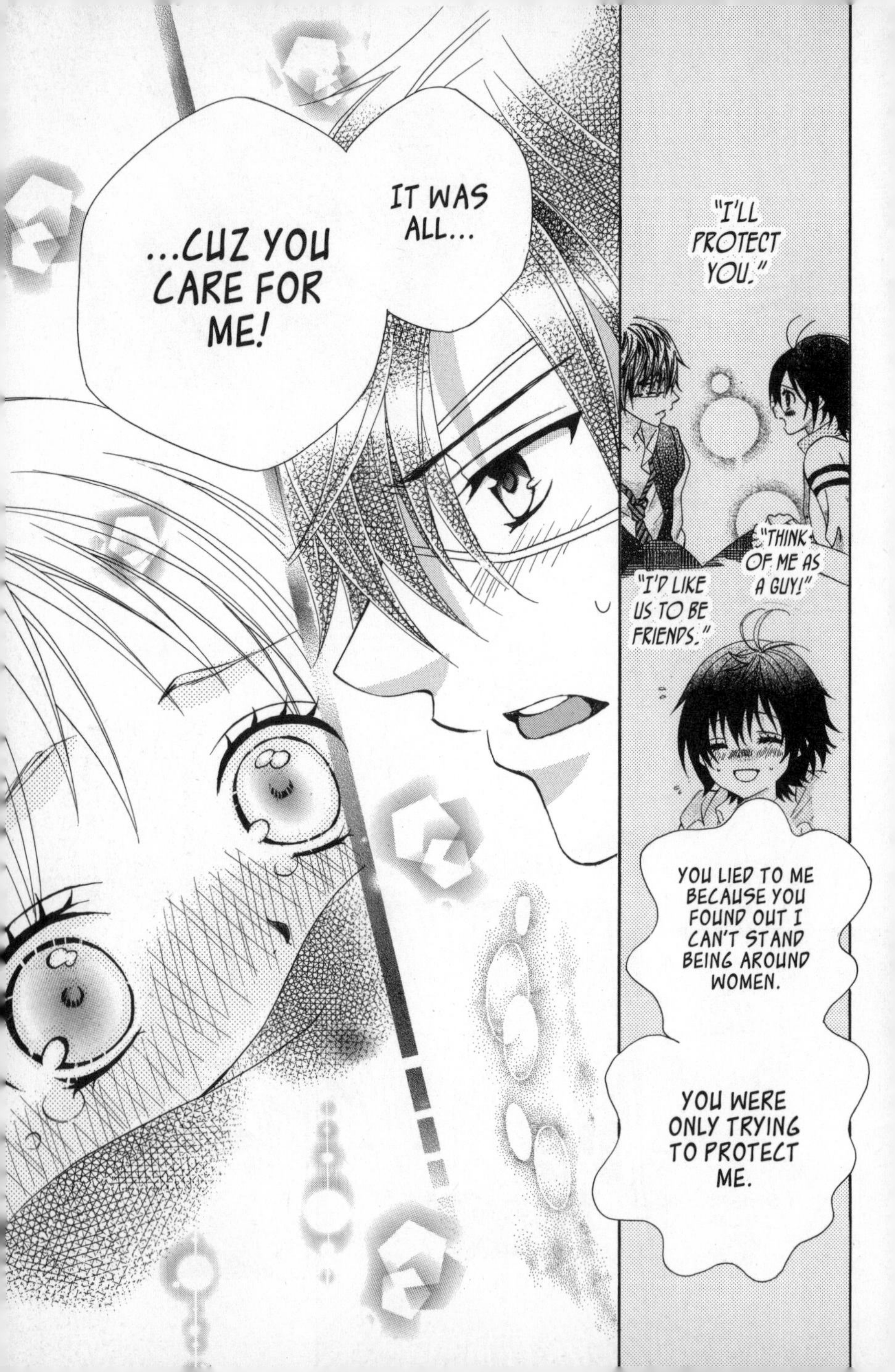
"I'LL PROTECT YOU."
"THINK OF ME AS A GUY!"
"I'D LIKE US TO BE FRIENDS."
YOU LIED TO ME BECAUSE YOU FOUND OUT I CAN'T STAND BEING AROUND WOMEN.
YOU WERE ONLY TRYING TO PROTECT ME.
IT WAS ALL...
...CUZ YOU CARE FOR ME!

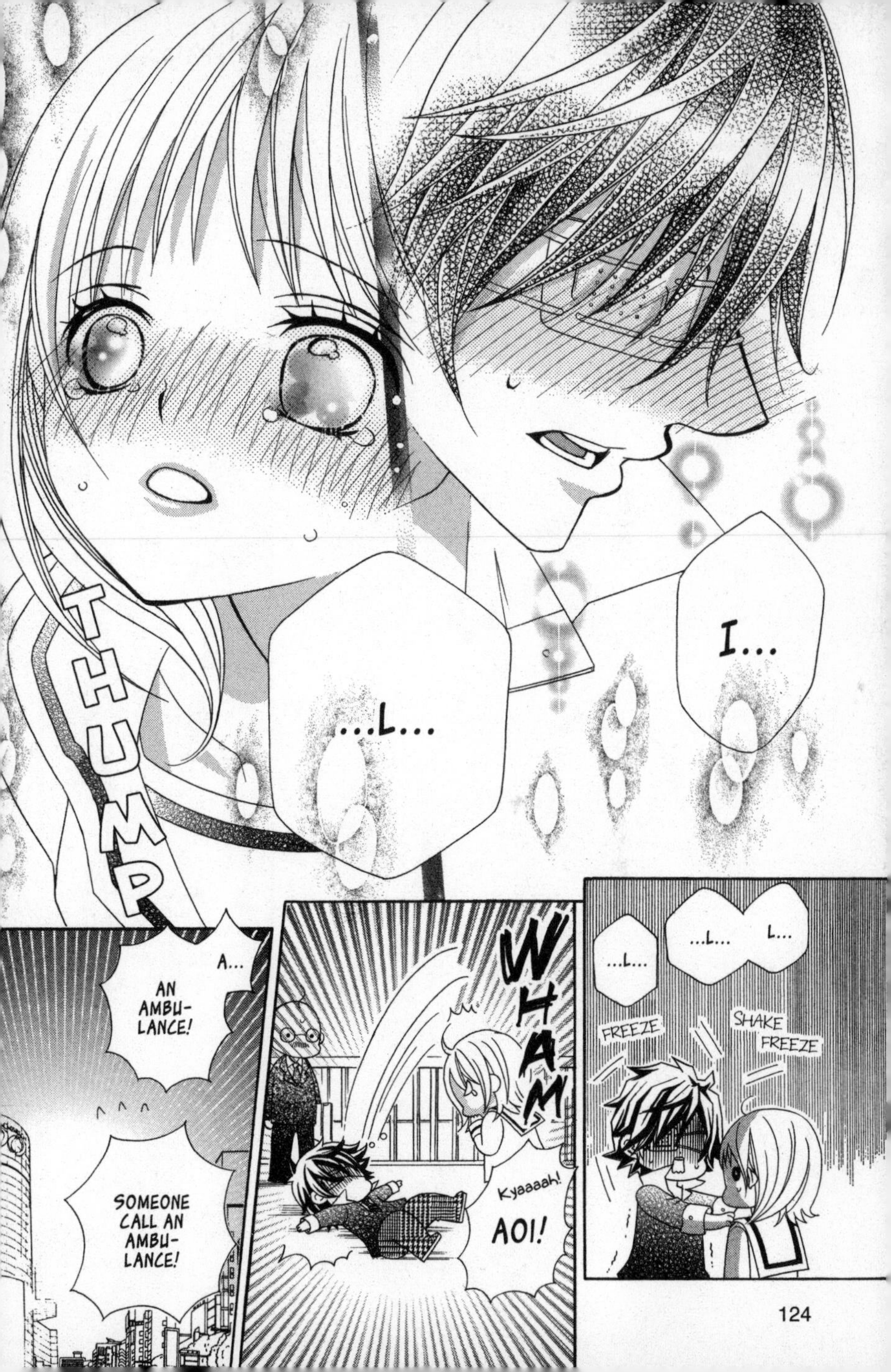
I...
...L...
THUMP
L...
...L...
...L...
SHAKE FREEZE
FREEZE
WHAM
Kyaaaah!
AOI!
A...
AN AMBULANCE!
SOMEONE CALL AN AMBULANCE!

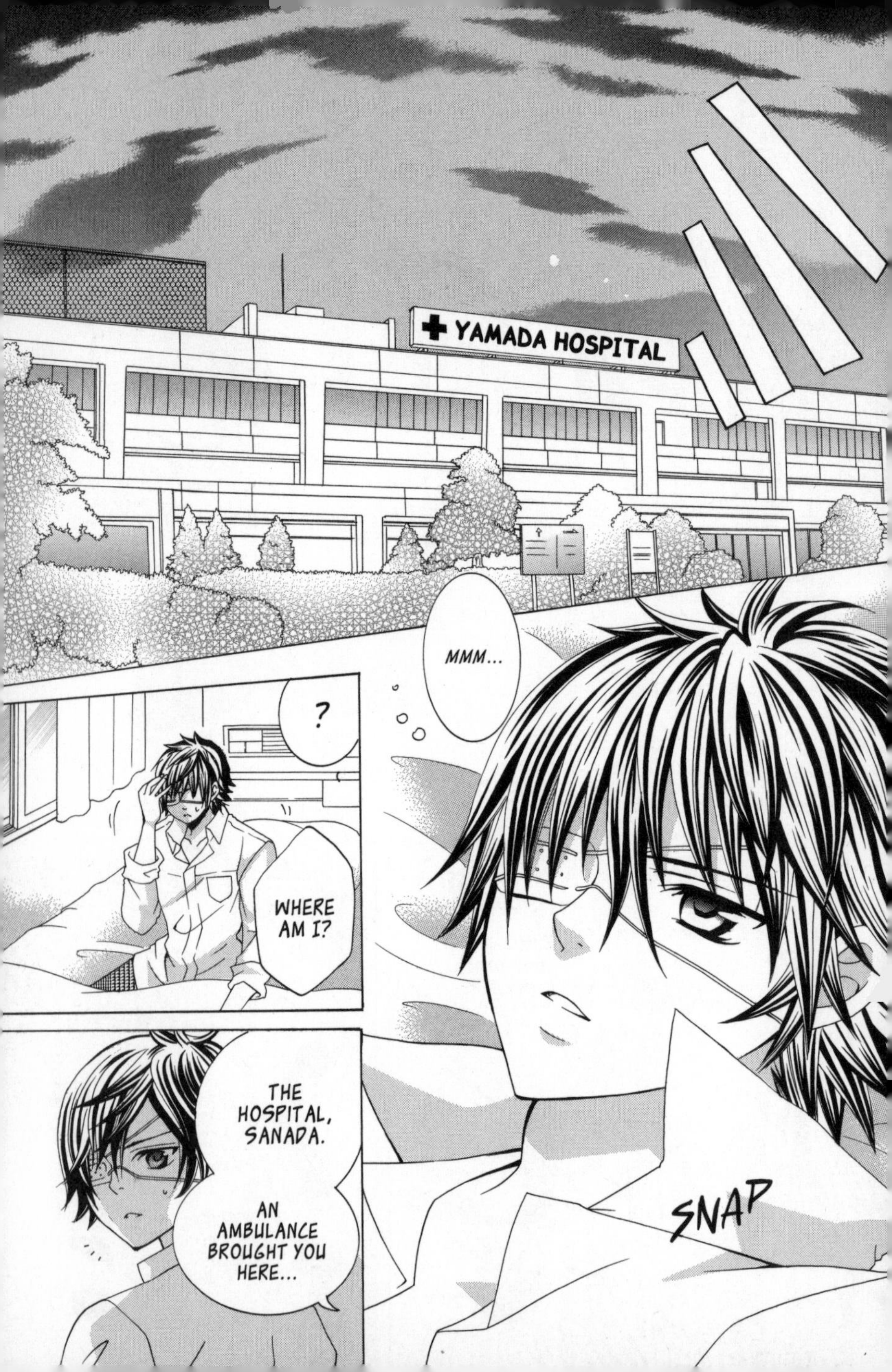
YAMADA HOSPITAL
MMM...
SNAP
?
WHERE AM I?
THE HOSPITAL, SANADA.
AN AMBULANCE BROUGHT YOU HERE...

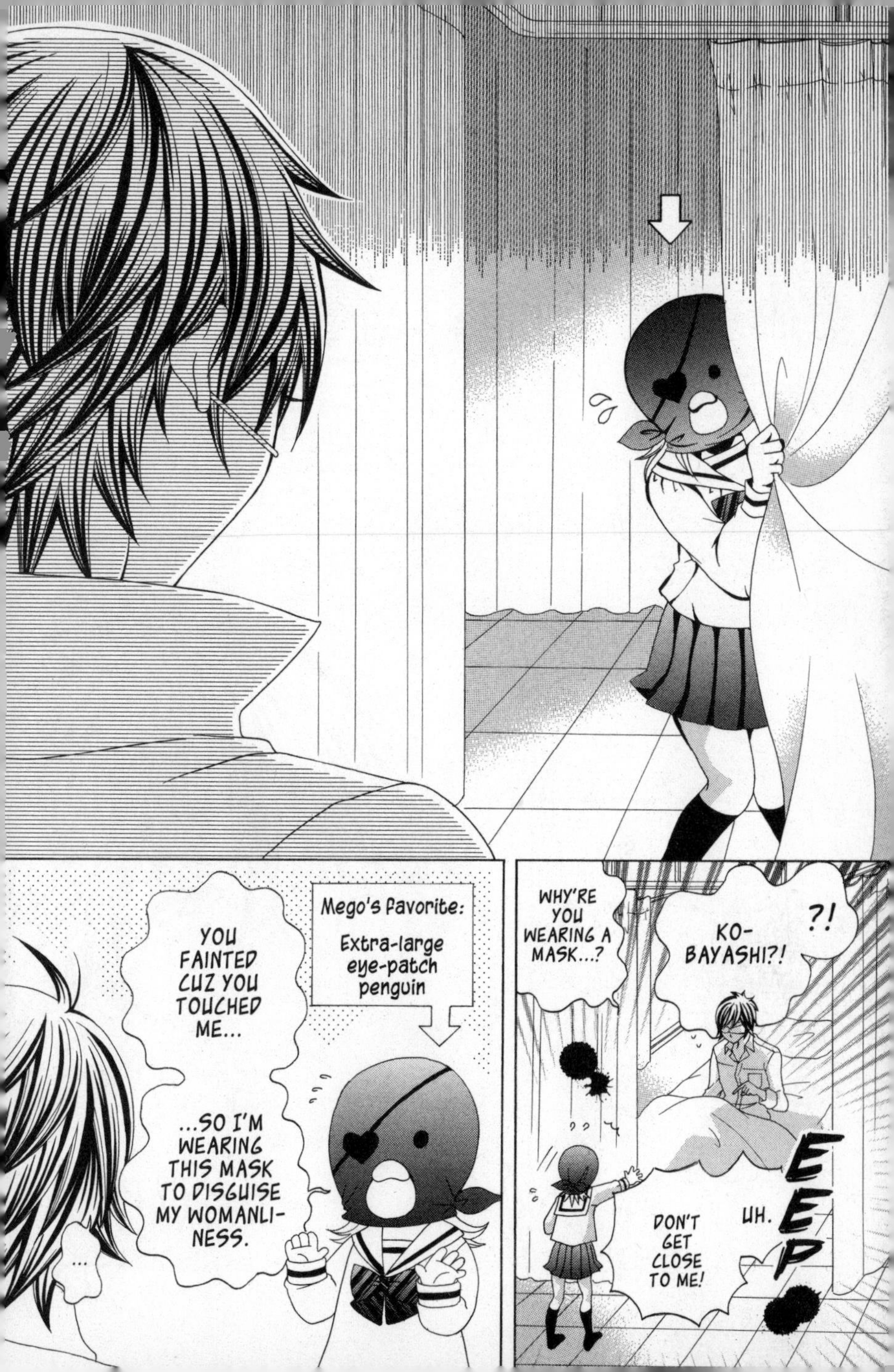
?!
KO-BAYASHI?!
WHY'RE YOU WEARING A MASK...?
EEEP
UH.
DON'T GET CLOSE TO ME!
Mego's favorite: Extra-large eye-patch penguin
YOU FAINTED CUZ YOU TOUCHED ME...
...SO I'M WEARING THIS MASK TO DISGUISE MY WOMANLINESS.
...

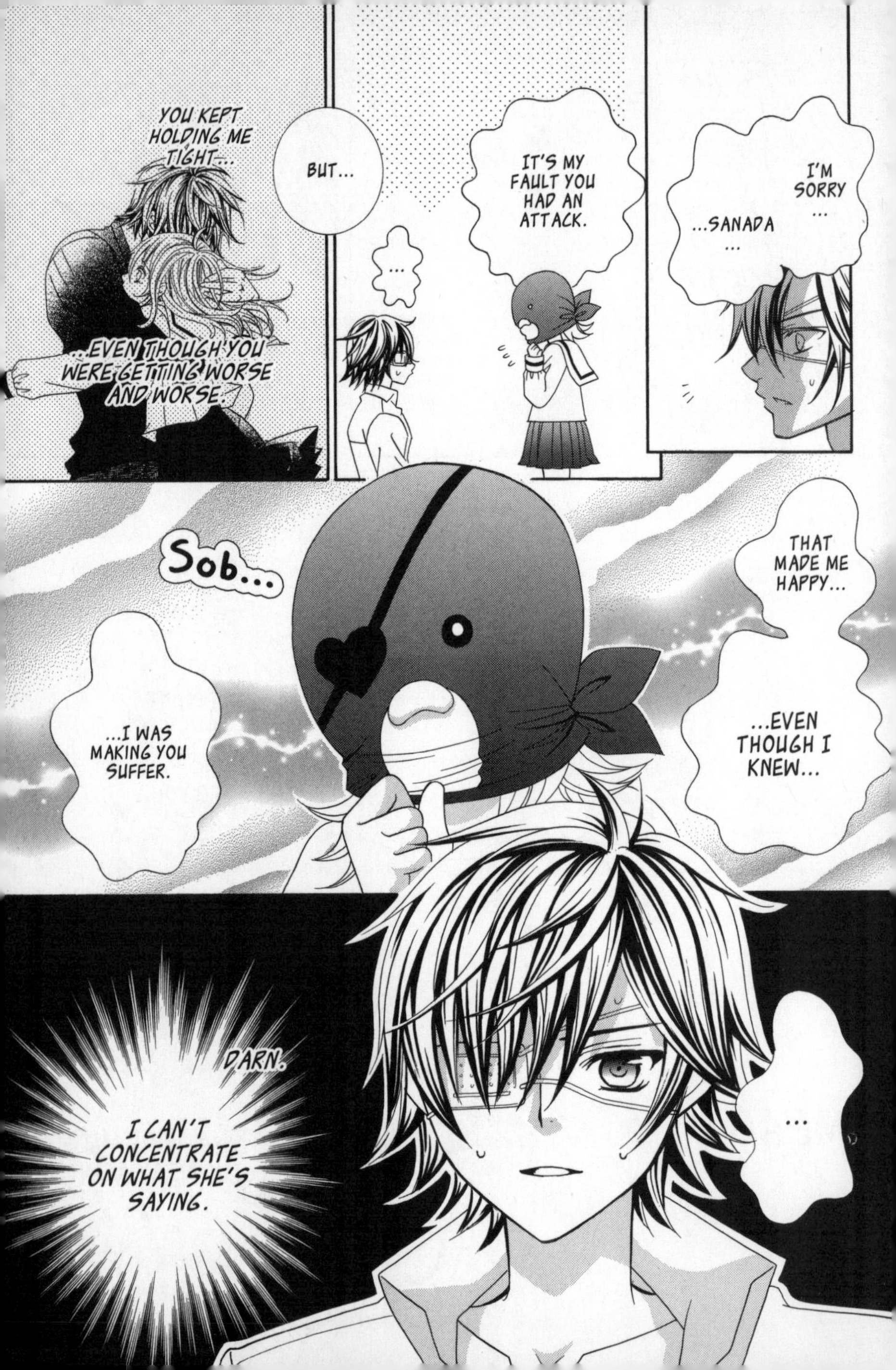
I'M SORRY...
...SANADA...
IT'S MY FAULT YOU HAD AN ATTACK.
...
BUT...
YOU KEPT HOLDING ME TIGHT...
...EVEN THOUGH YOU WERE GETTING WORSE AND WORSE.
THAT MADE ME HAPPY...
...EVEN THOUGH I KNEW...
Sob...
...I WAS MAKING YOU SUFFER.
...
DARN.
I CAN'T CONCENTRATE ON WHAT SHE'S SAYING.

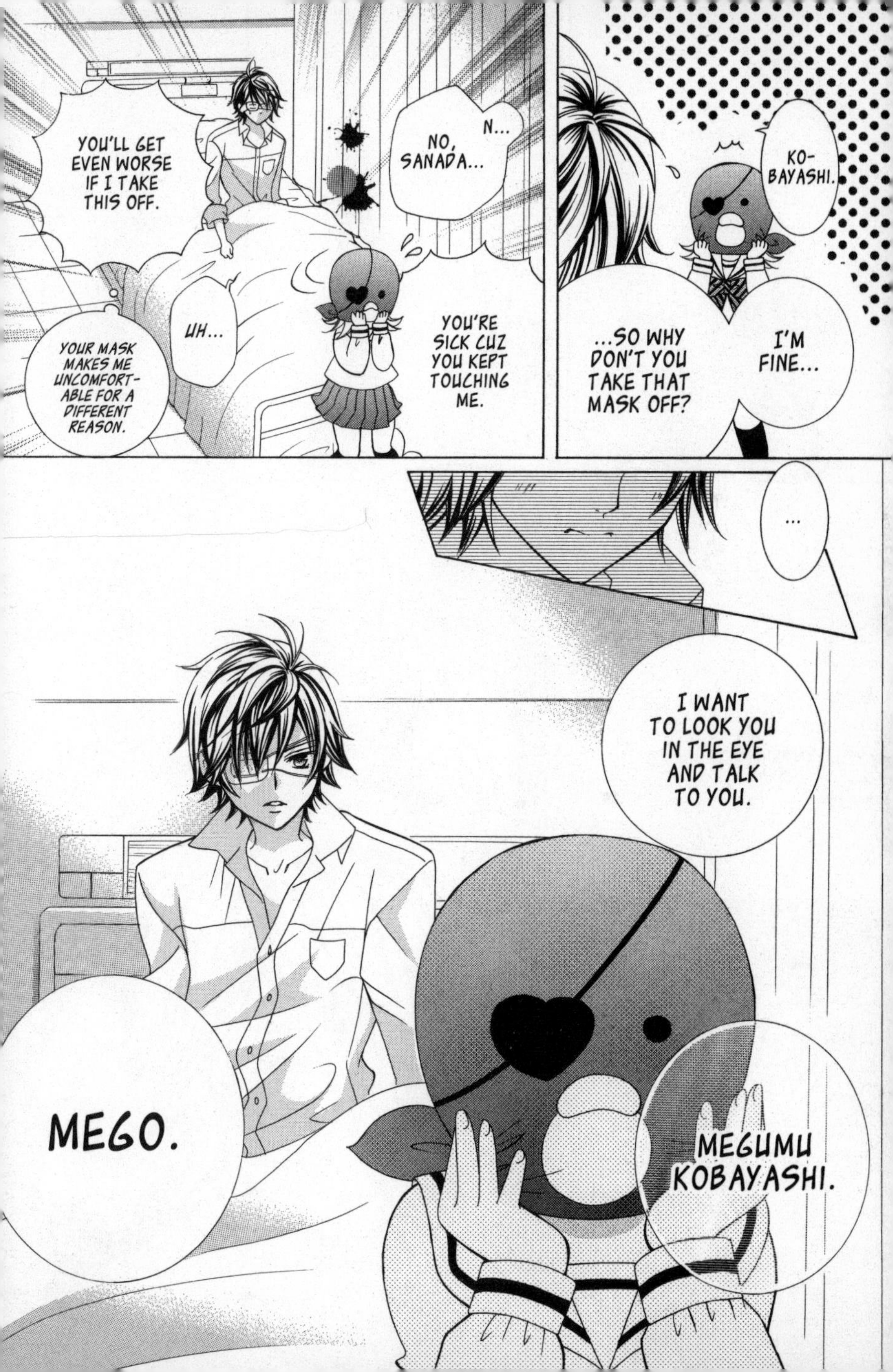
KO-BAYASHI.
I'M FINE...
...SO WHY DON'T YOU TAKE THAT MASK OFF?
N... NO, SANADA...
YOU'LL GET EVEN WORSE IF I TAKE THIS OFF.
YOU'RE SICK CUZ YOU KEPT TOUCHING ME.
UH...
YOUR MASK MAKES ME UNCOMFORT-ABLE FOR A DIFFERENT REASON.
...
I WANT TO LOOK YOU IN THE EYE AND TALK TO YOU.
MEGUMU KOBAYASHI.
MEGO.

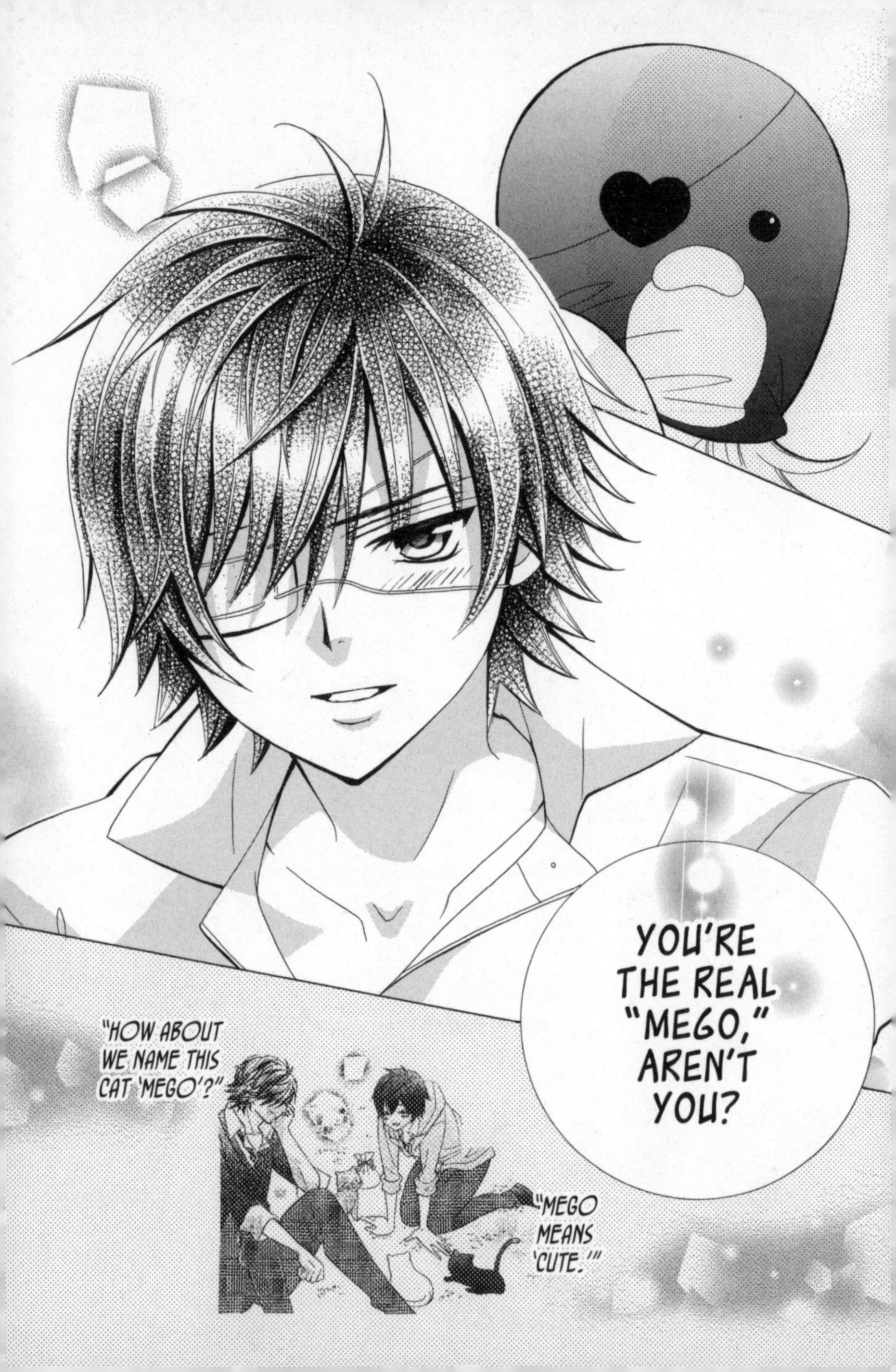
YOU'RE THE REAL "MEGO," AREN'T YOU?
"HOW ABOUT WE NAME THIS CAT 'MEGO'?"
"MEGO MEANS 'CUTE.'"

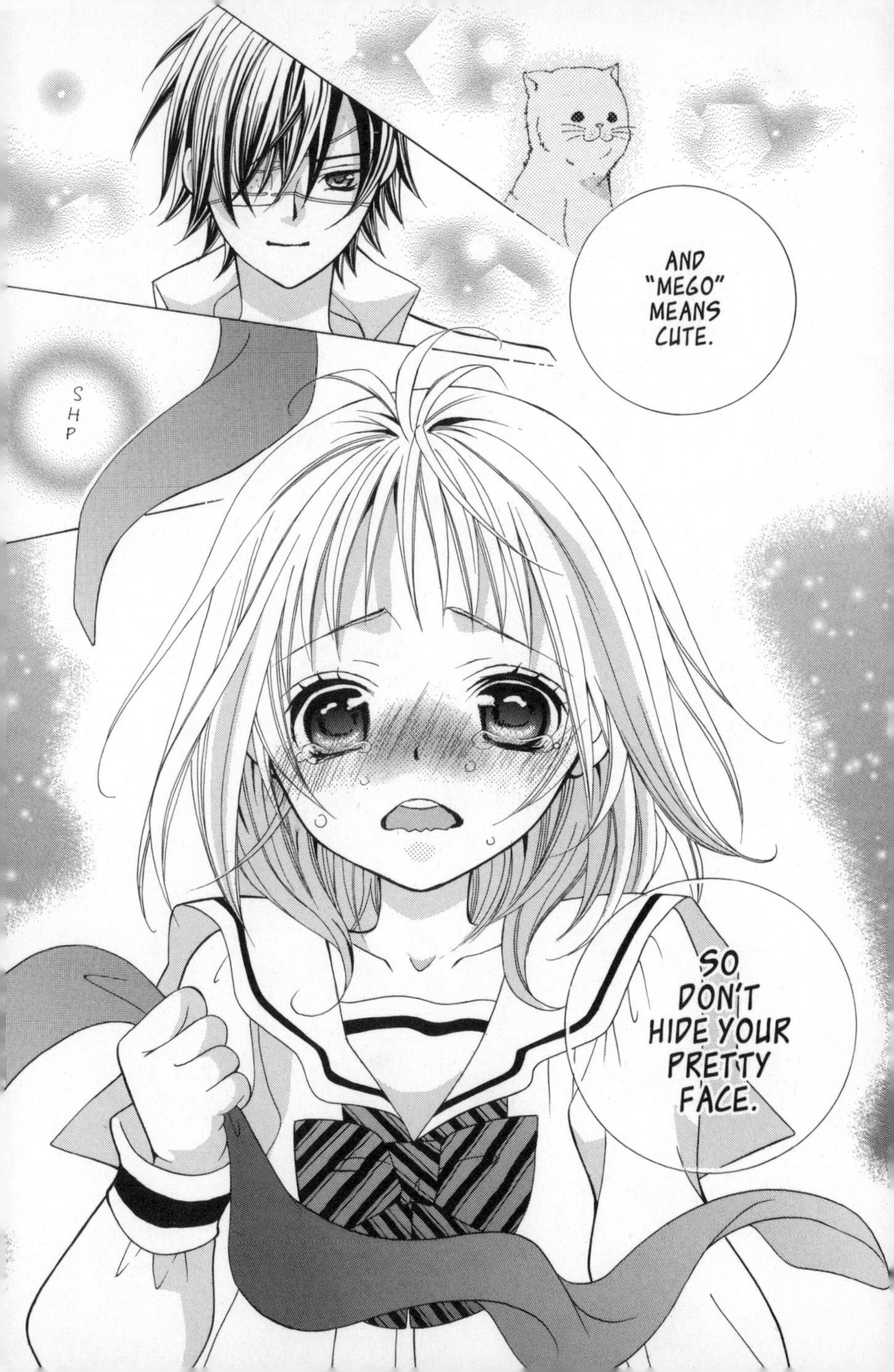
AND "MEGO" MEANS CUTE.
SHP
SO DON'T HIDE YOUR PRETTY FACE.

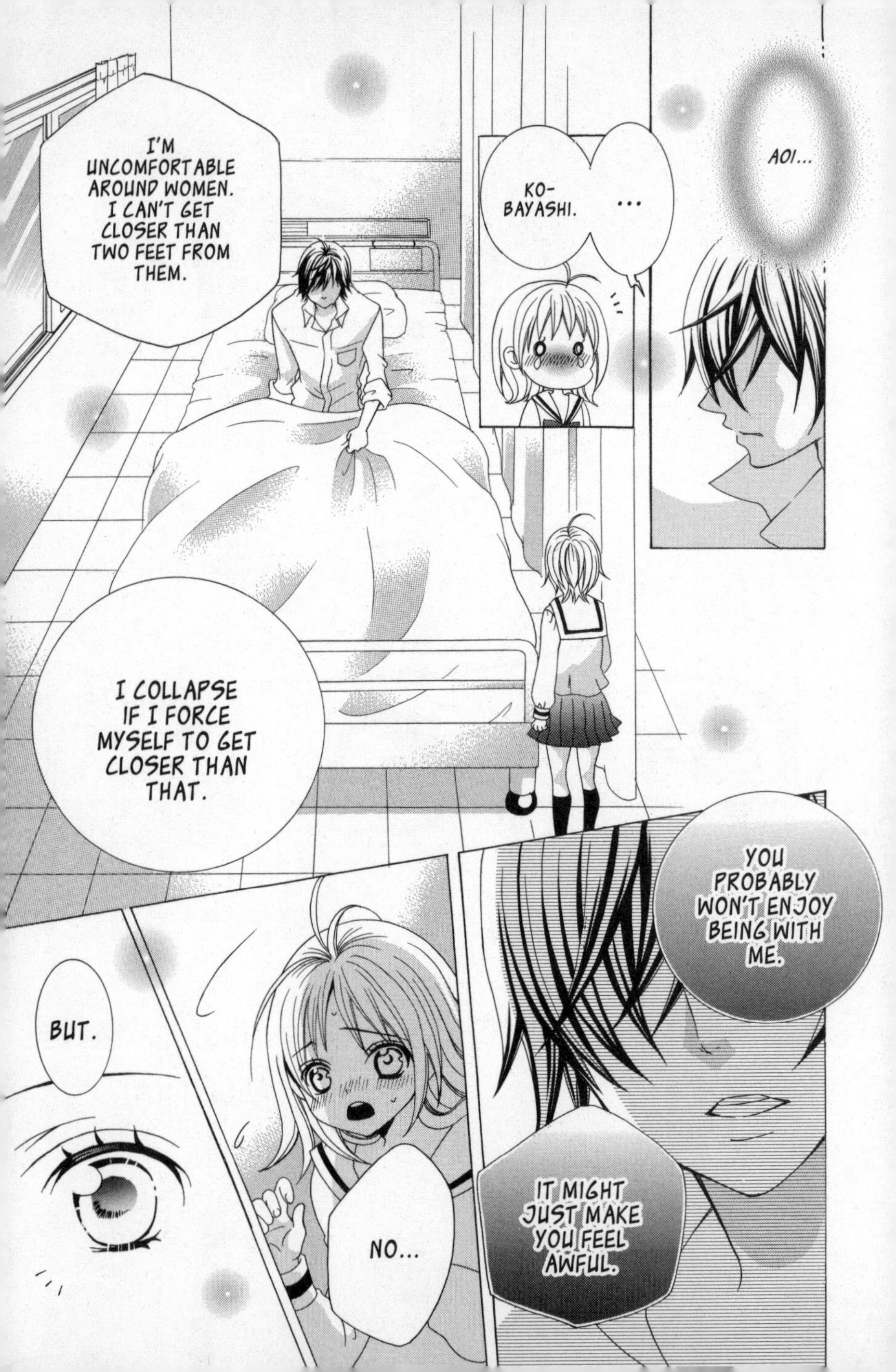
AOI...
...
KO-BAYASHI.
I'M UNCOMFORTABLE AROUND WOMEN. I CAN'T GET CLOSER THAN TWO FEET FROM THEM.
I COLLAPSE IF I FORCE MYSELF TO GET CLOSER THAN THAT.
YOU PROBABLY WON'T ENJOY BEING WITH ME.
IT MIGHT JUST MAKE YOU FEEL AWFUL.
NO...
BUT.

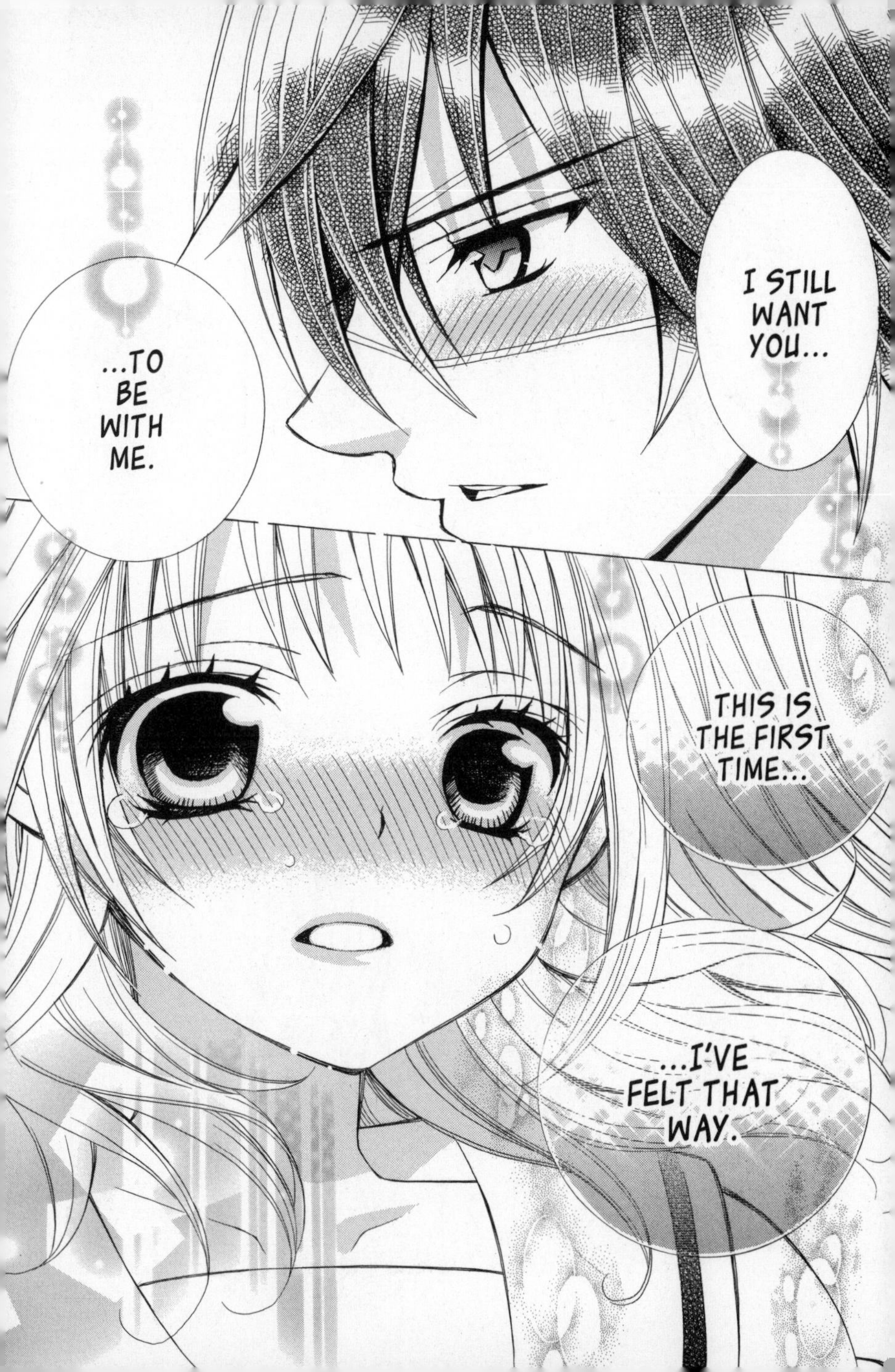
I STILL WANT YOU...
...TO BE WITH ME.
THIS IS THE FIRST TIME...
...I'VE FELT THAT WAY.

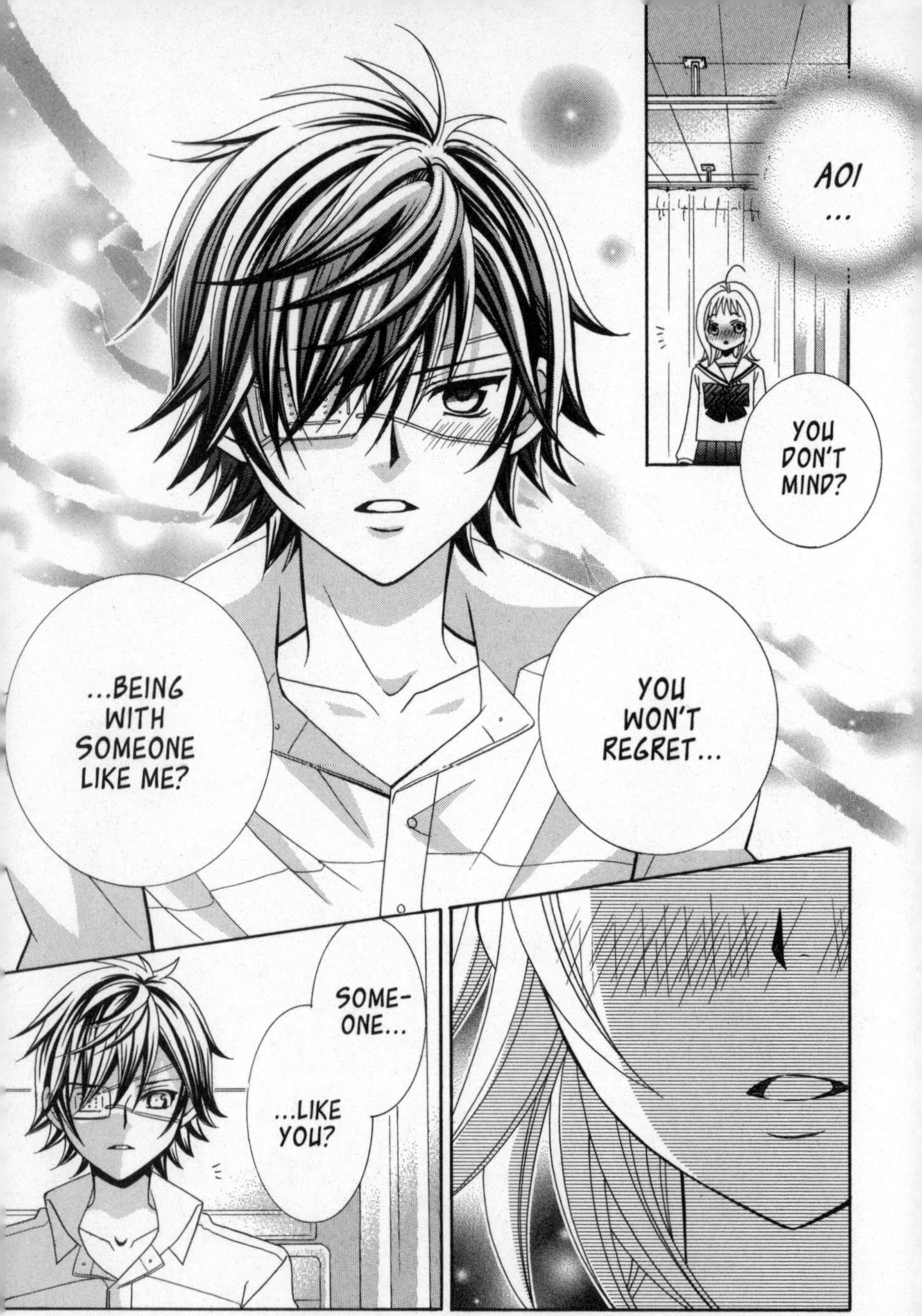
AOI ...
YOU DON'T MIND?
YOU WON'T REGRET...
...BEING WITH SOMEONE LIKE ME?
SOME-ONE...
...LIKE YOU?

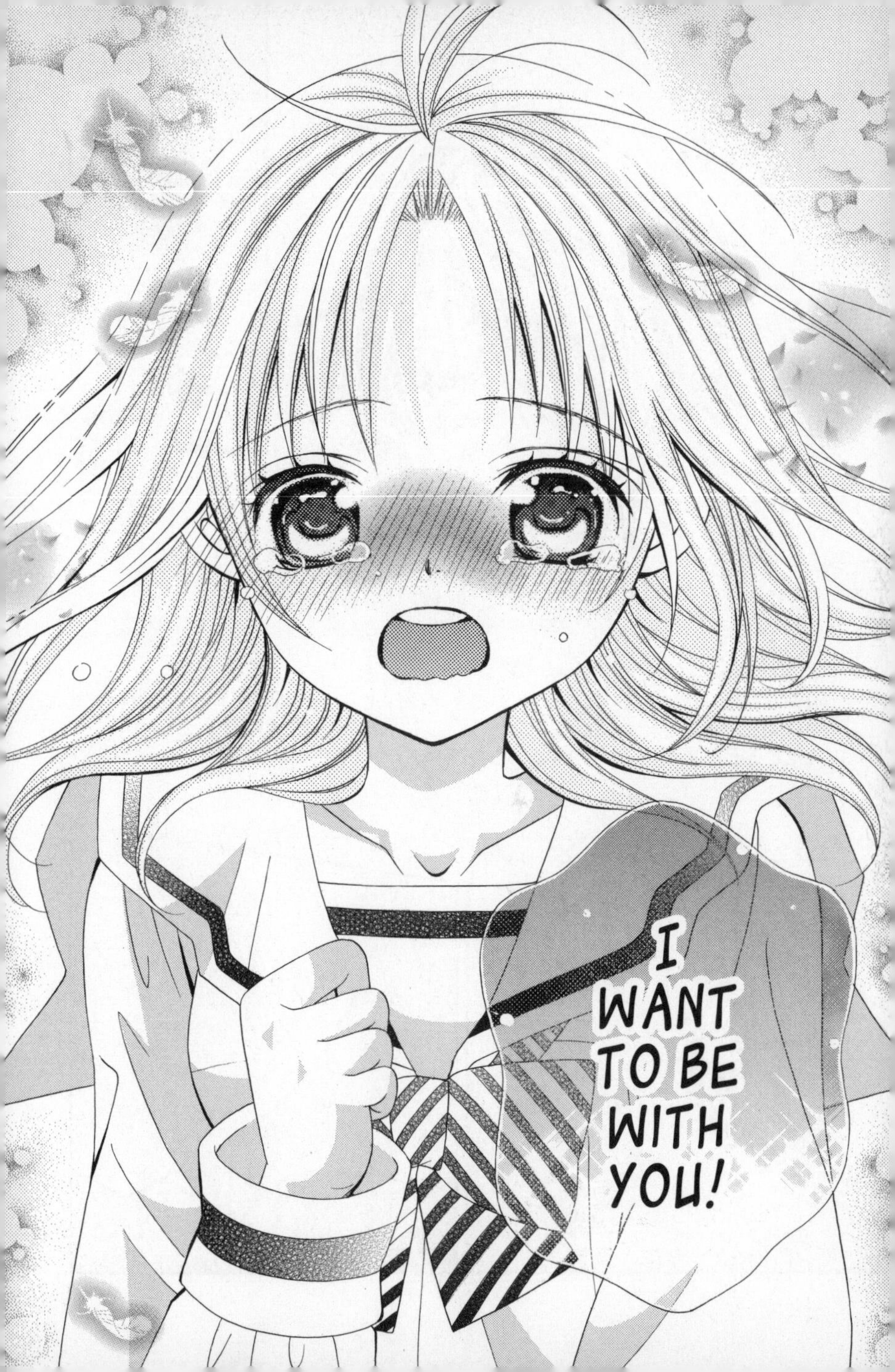
I WANT TO BE WITH YOU!

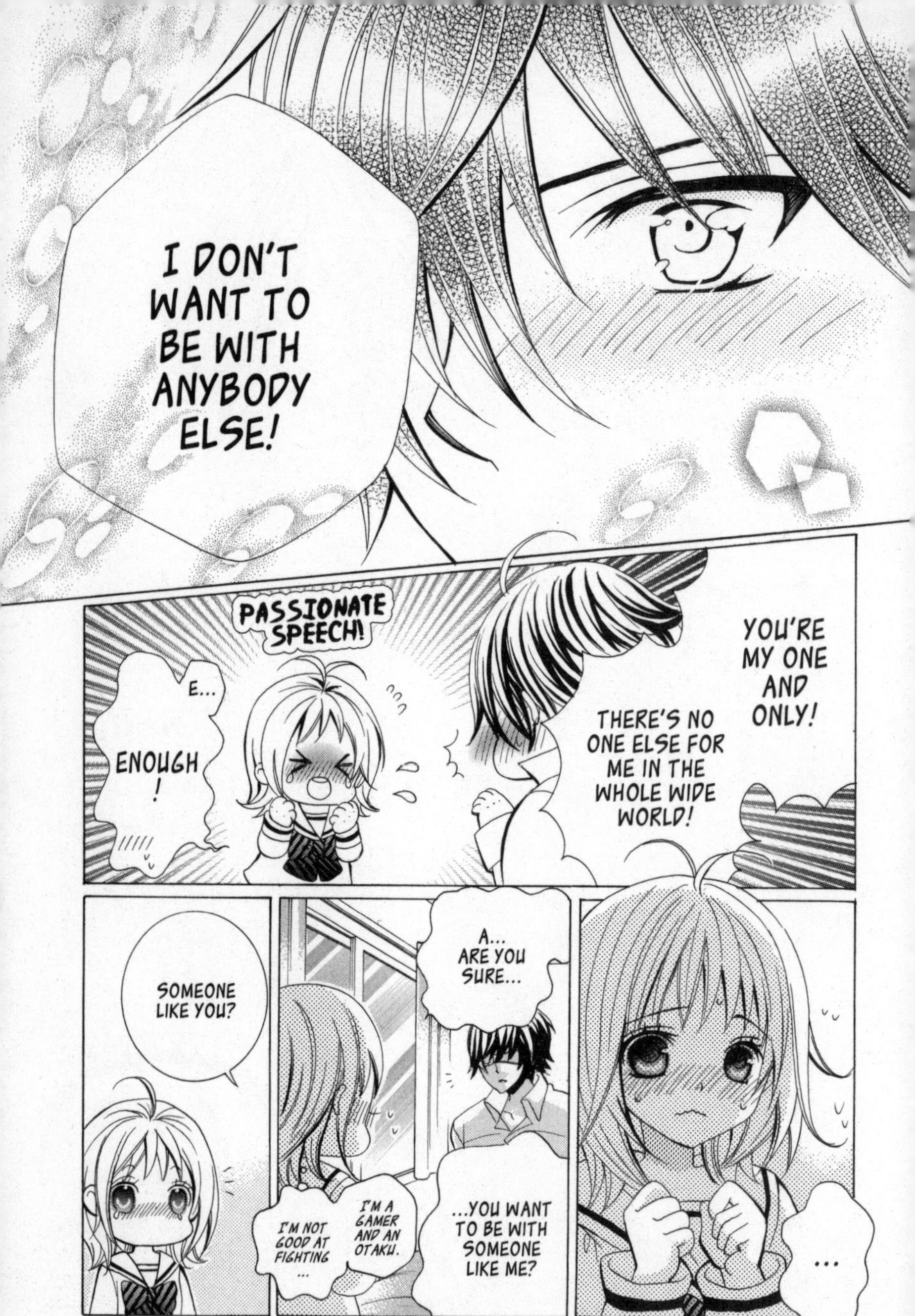
I DON'T WANT TO BE WITH ANYBODY ELSE!
YOU'RE MY ONE AND ONLY!
THERE'S NO ONE ELSE FOR ME IN THE WHOLE WIDE WORLD!
PASSIONATE SPEECH!
E... ENOUGH!
...
A... ARE YOU SURE...
...YOU WANT TO BE WITH SOMEONE LIKE ME?
I'M A GAMER AND AN OTAKU.
I'M NOT GOOD AT FIGHTING...
SOMEONE LIKE YOU?

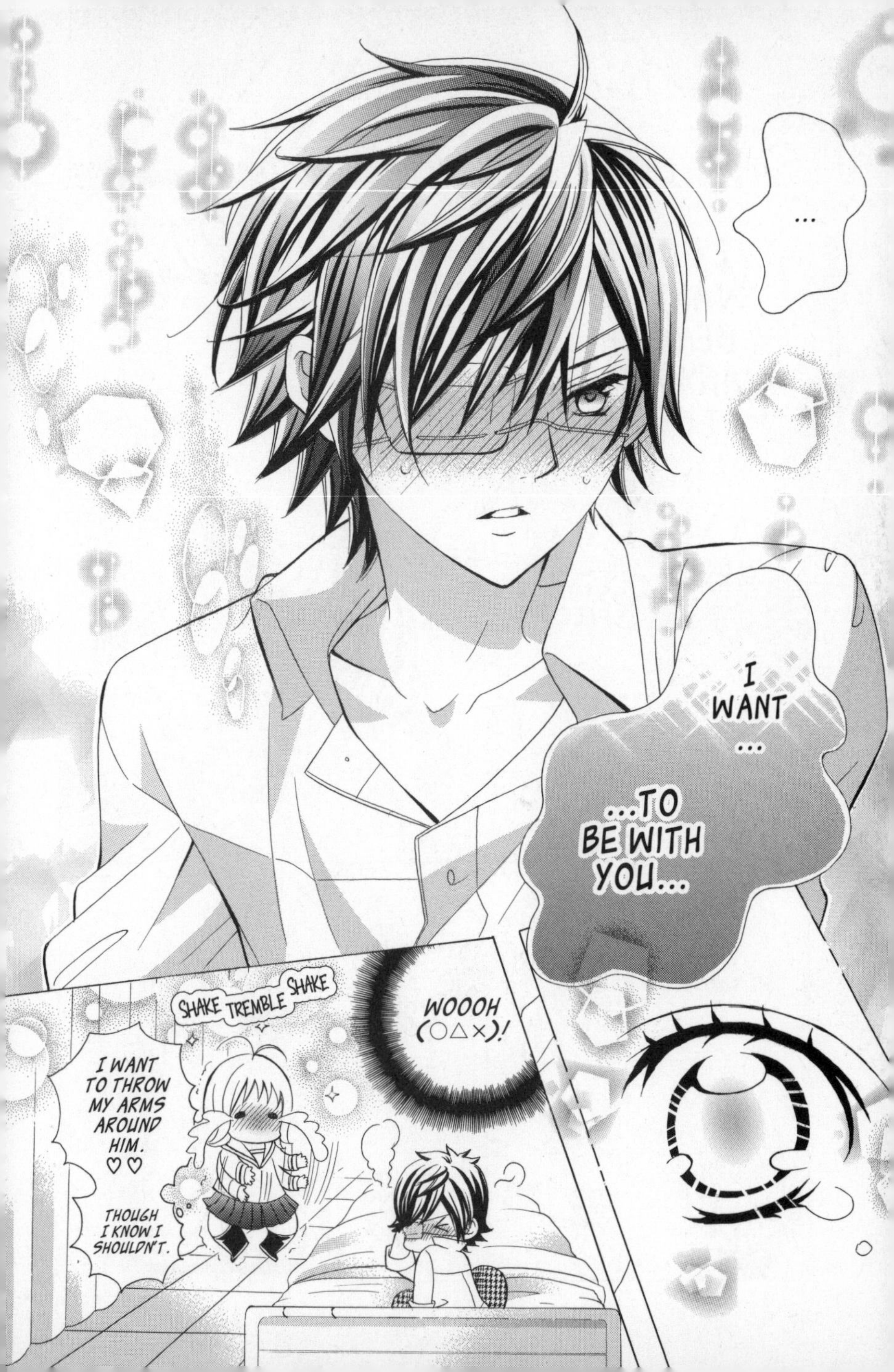
...
I WANT ...
...TO BE WITH YOU...
WOOOH (○△×)!
SHAKE TREMBLE SHAKE
I WANT TO THROW MY ARMS AROUND HIM. ♡♡
THOUGH I KNOW I SHOULDN'T.

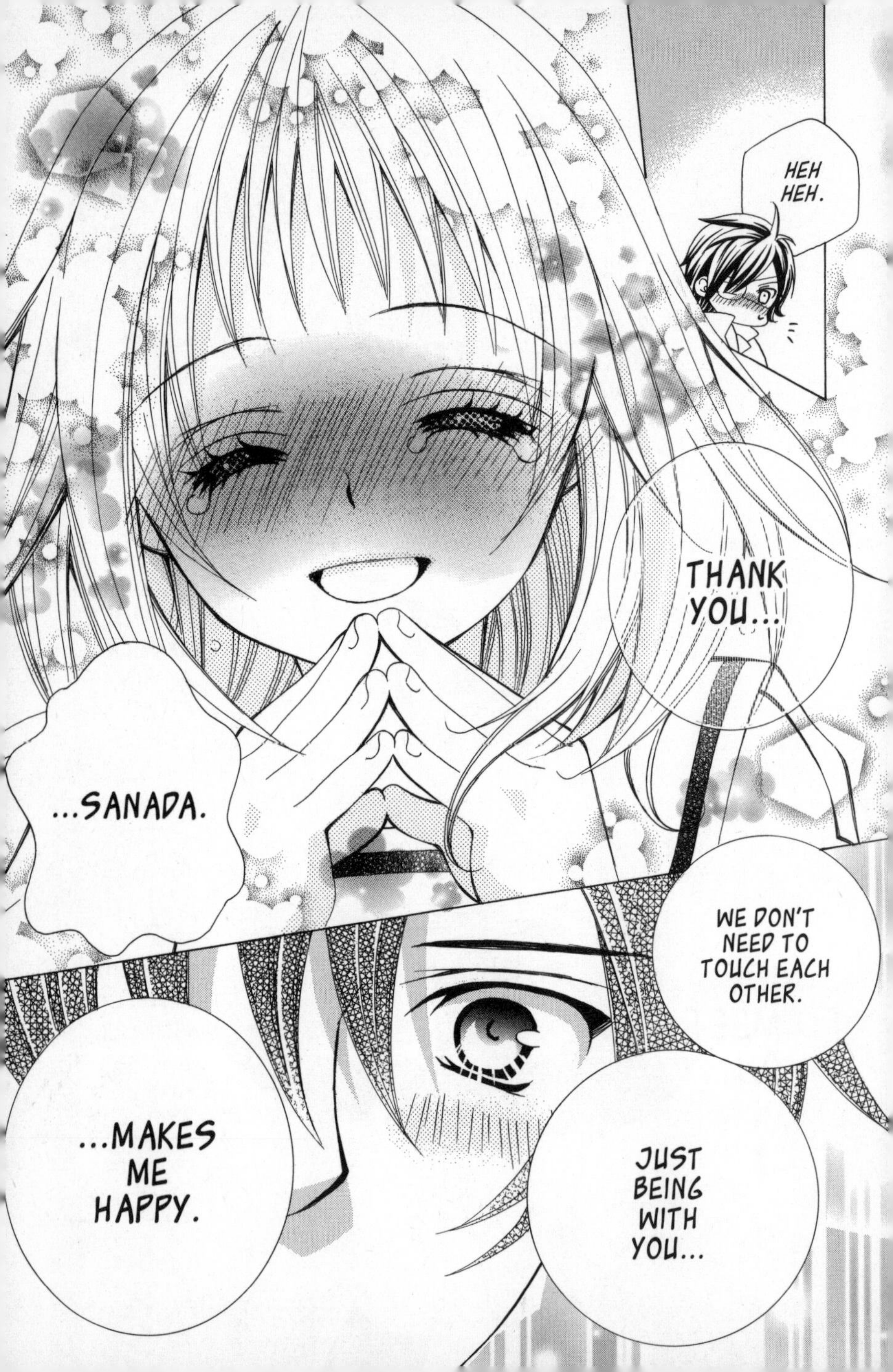
HEH HEH.
THANK YOU...
...SANADA.
WE DON'T NEED TO TOUCH EACH OTHER.
JUST BEING WITH YOU...
...MAKES ME HAPPY.

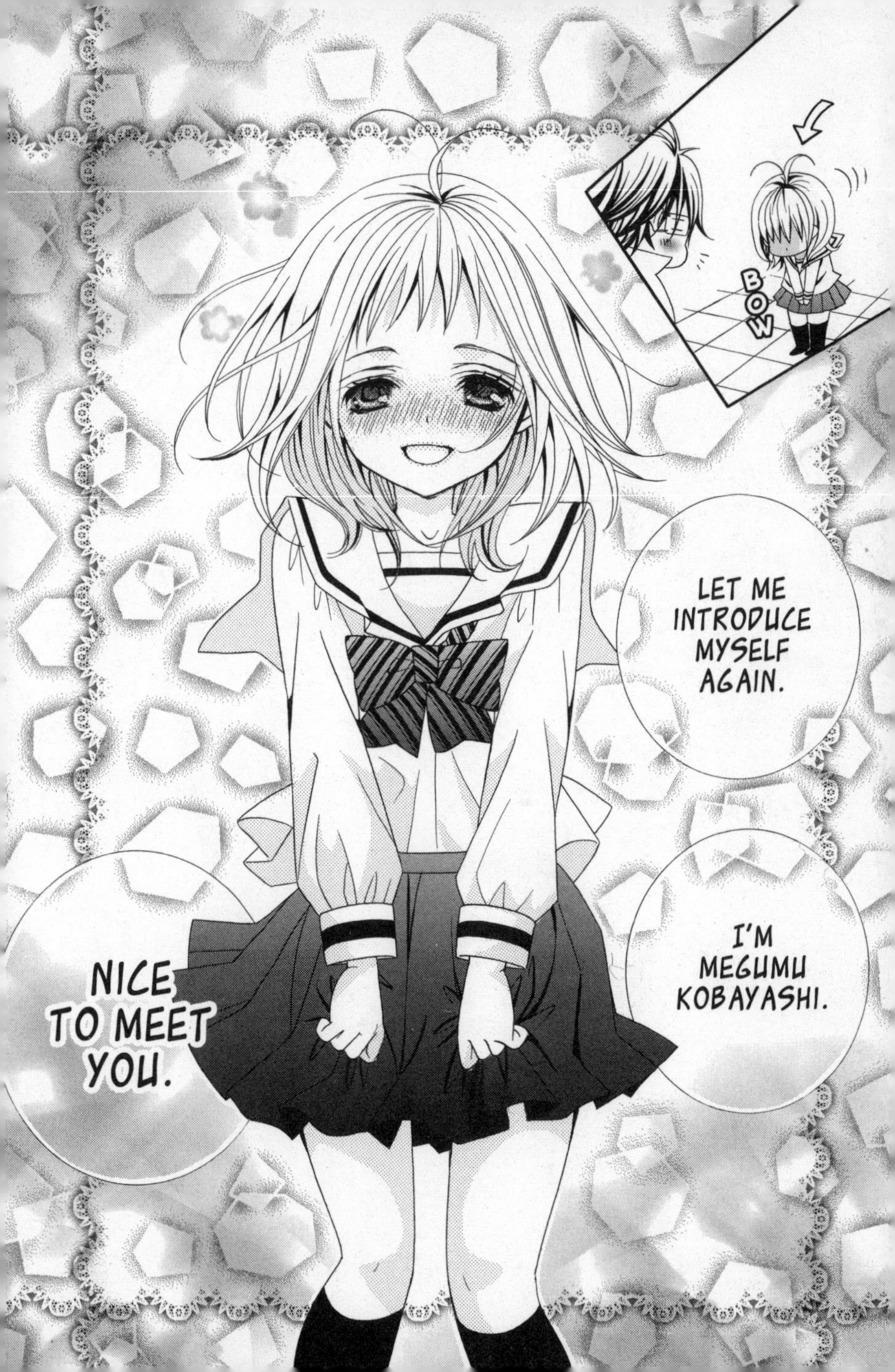
BOW
LET ME INTRODUCE MYSELF AGAIN.
I'M MEGUMU KOBAYASHI.
NICE TO MEET YOU.

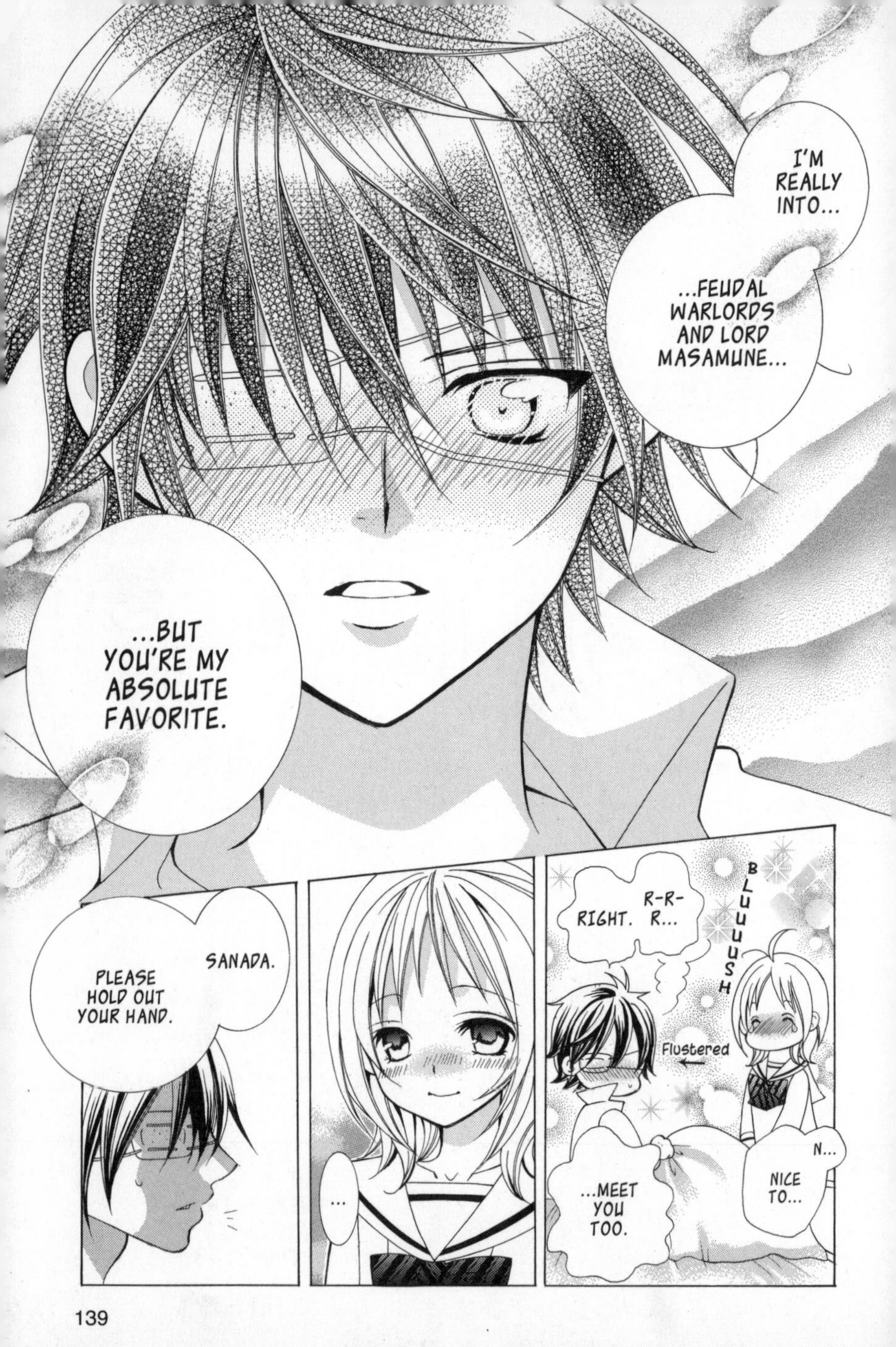
I'M REALLY INTO...
...FEUDAL WARLORDS AND LORD MASAMUNE...
...BUT YOU'RE MY ABSOLUTE FAVORITE.
R-R-R... RIGHT.
BLUUUUSH
Flustered
N... NICE TO...
...MEET YOU TOO.
...
SANADA.
PLEASE HOLD OUT YOUR HAND.

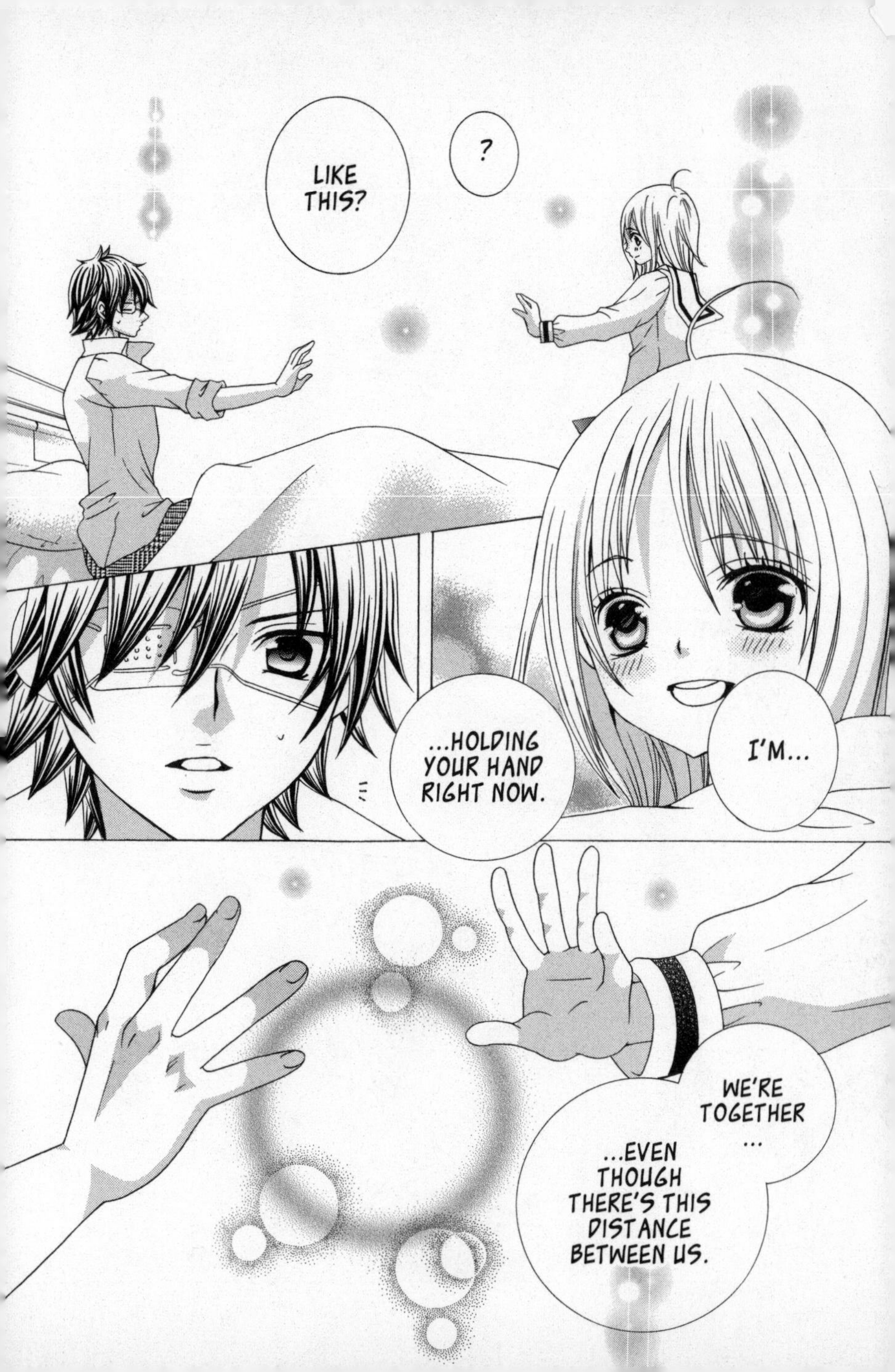
?
LIKE THIS?
I'M...
...HOLDING YOUR HAND RIGHT NOW.
WE'RE TOGETHER ...
...EVEN THOUGH THERE'S THIS DISTANCE BETWEEN US.

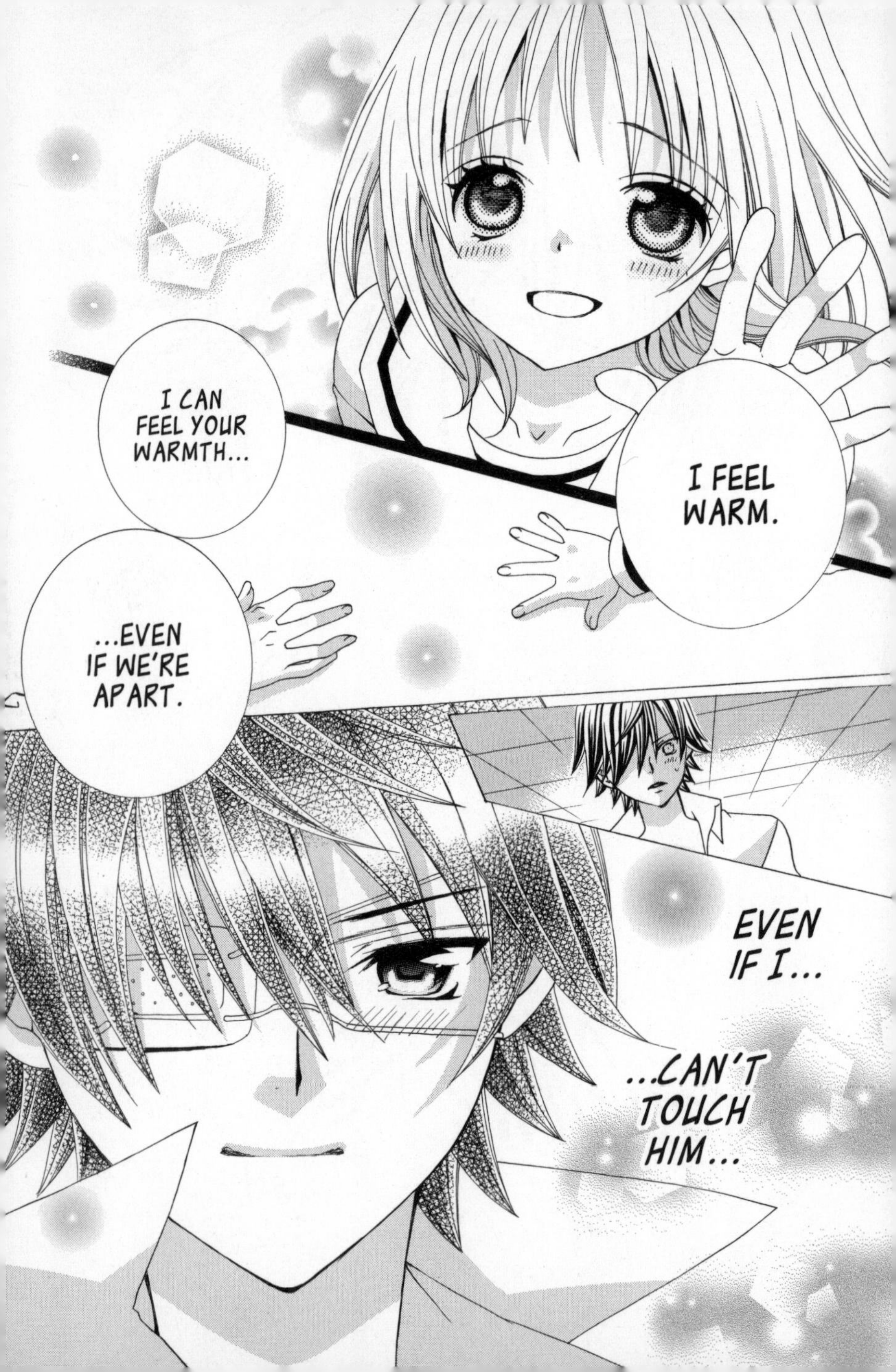
I FEEL WARM.
I CAN FEEL YOUR WARMTH...
...EVEN IF WE'RE APART.
EVEN IF I...
...CAN'T TOUCH HIM...

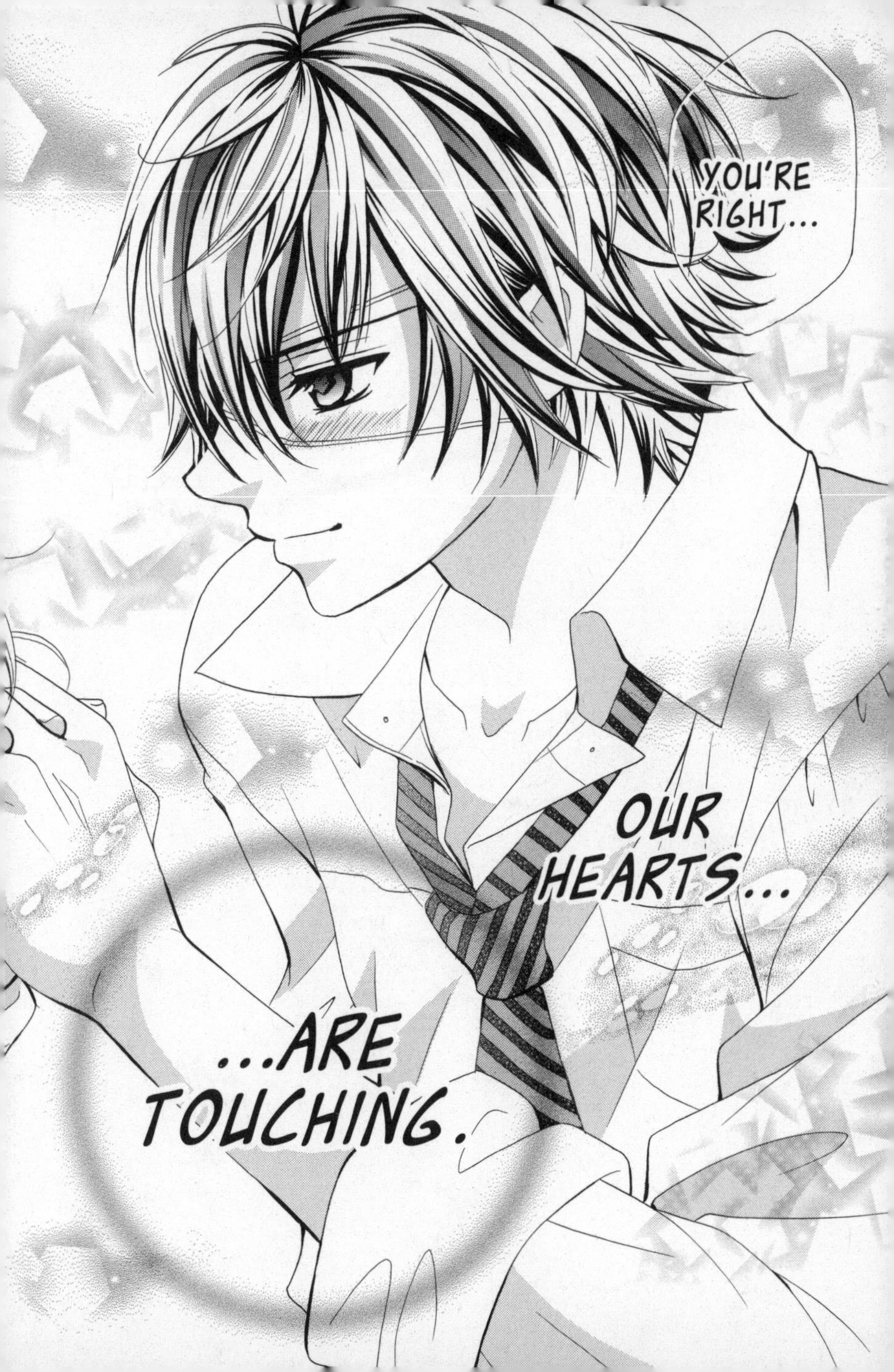
YOU'RE RIGHT...
OUR HEARTS...
...ARE TOUCHING.

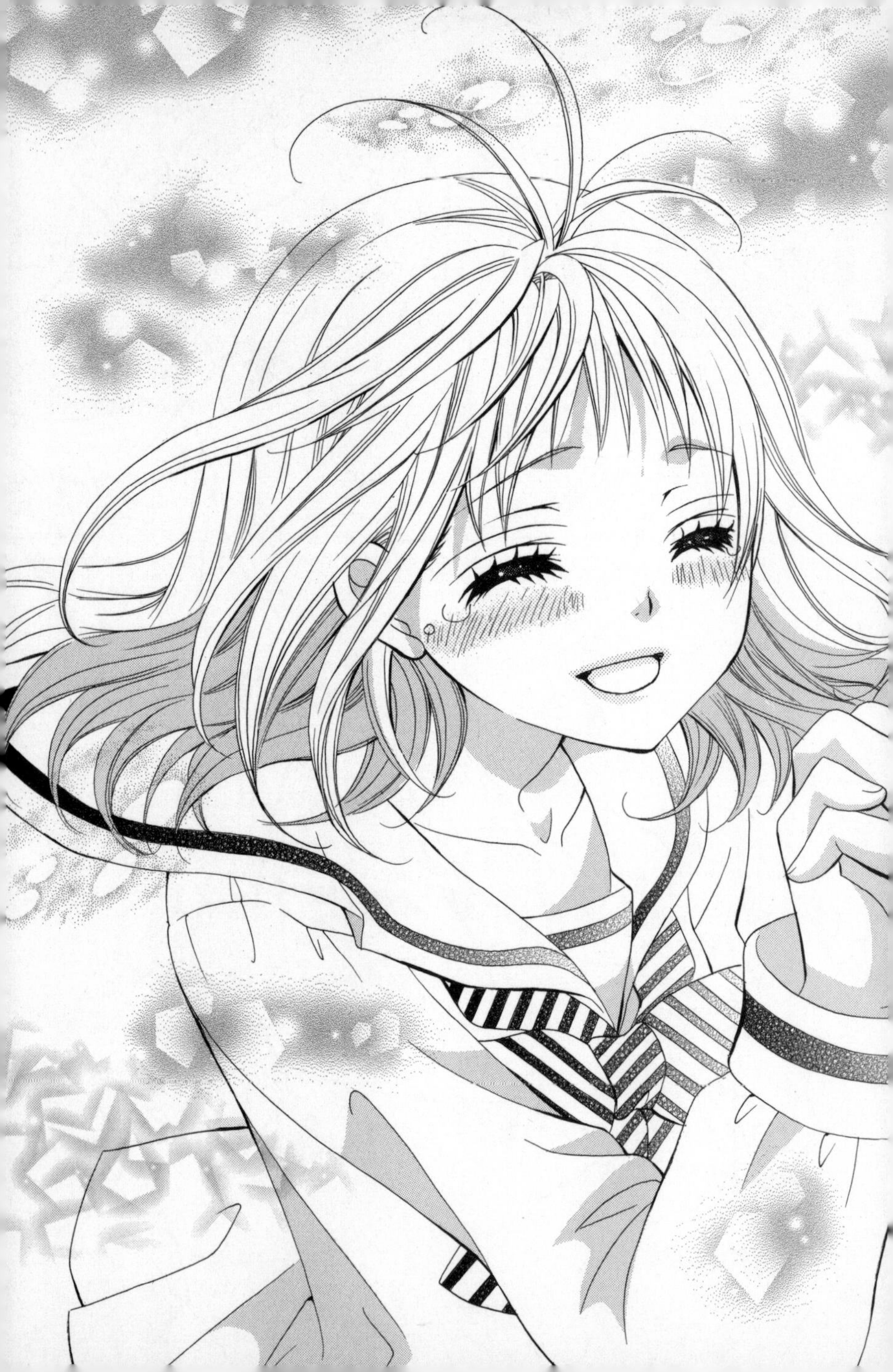

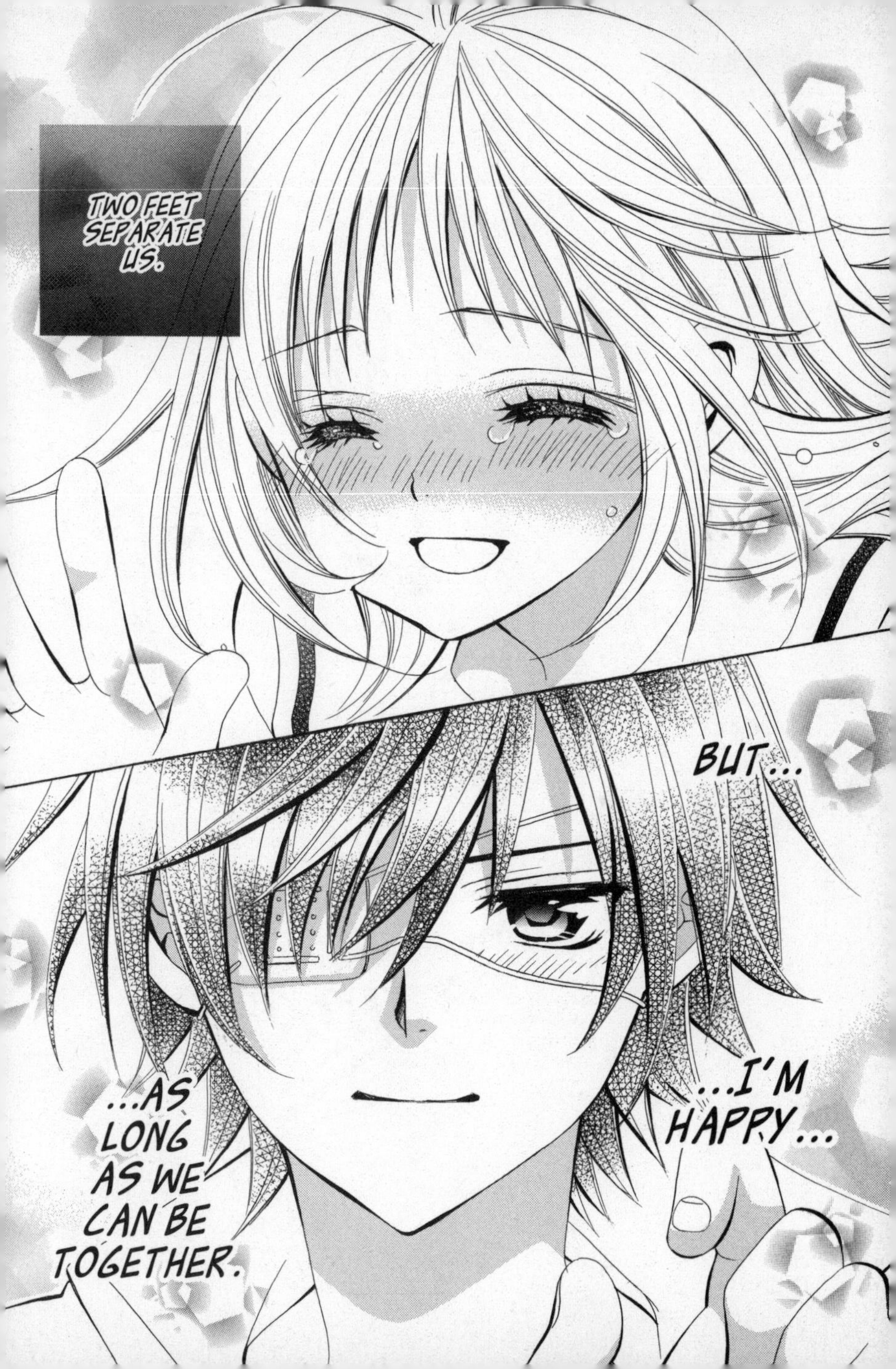
TWO FEET SEPARATE US.
BUT...
...I'M HAPPY...
...AS LONG AS WE CAN BE TOGETHER.

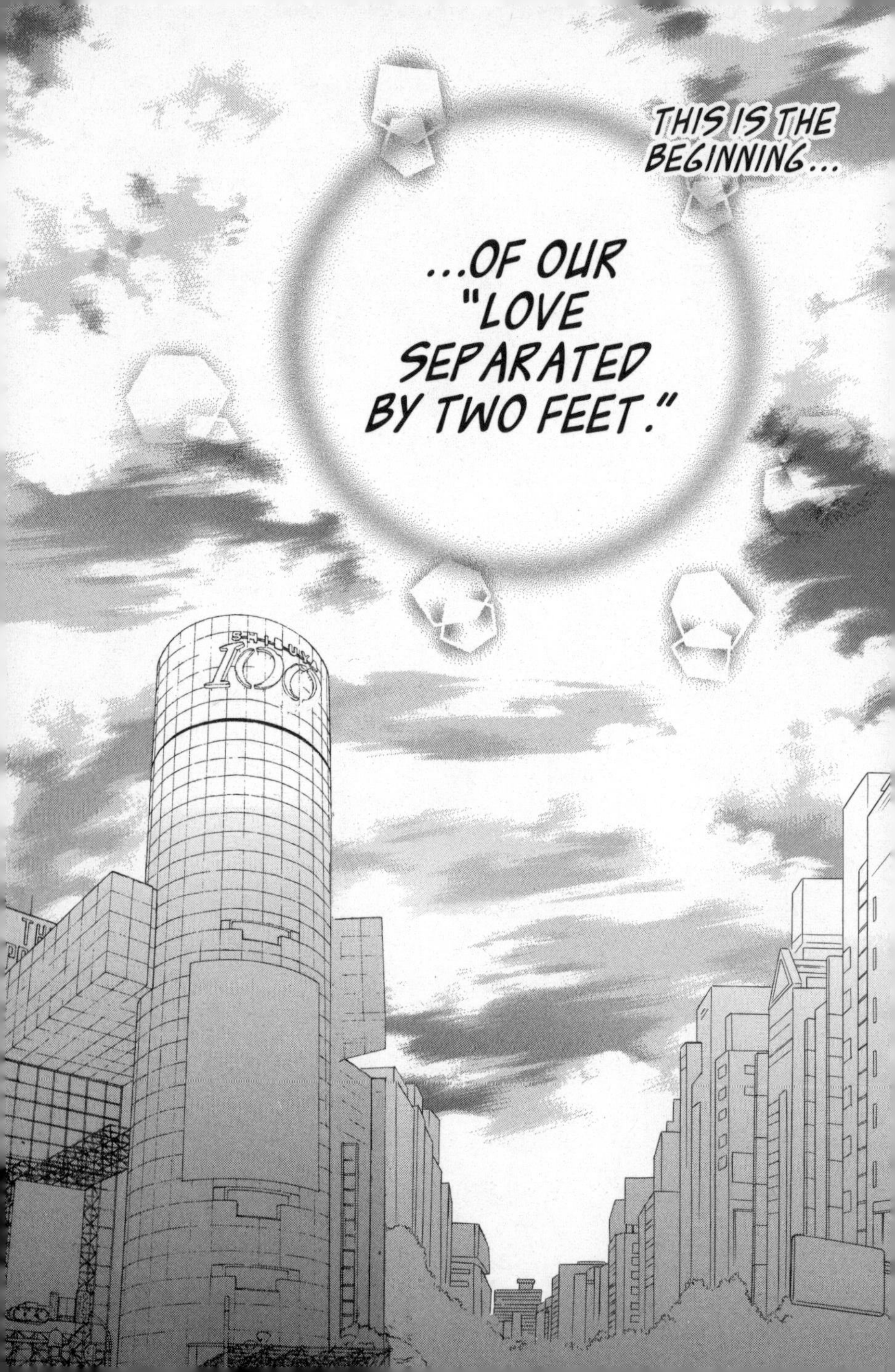
THIS IS THE BEGINNING...
...OF OUR "LOVE SEPARATED BY TWO FEET."

Chapter 15

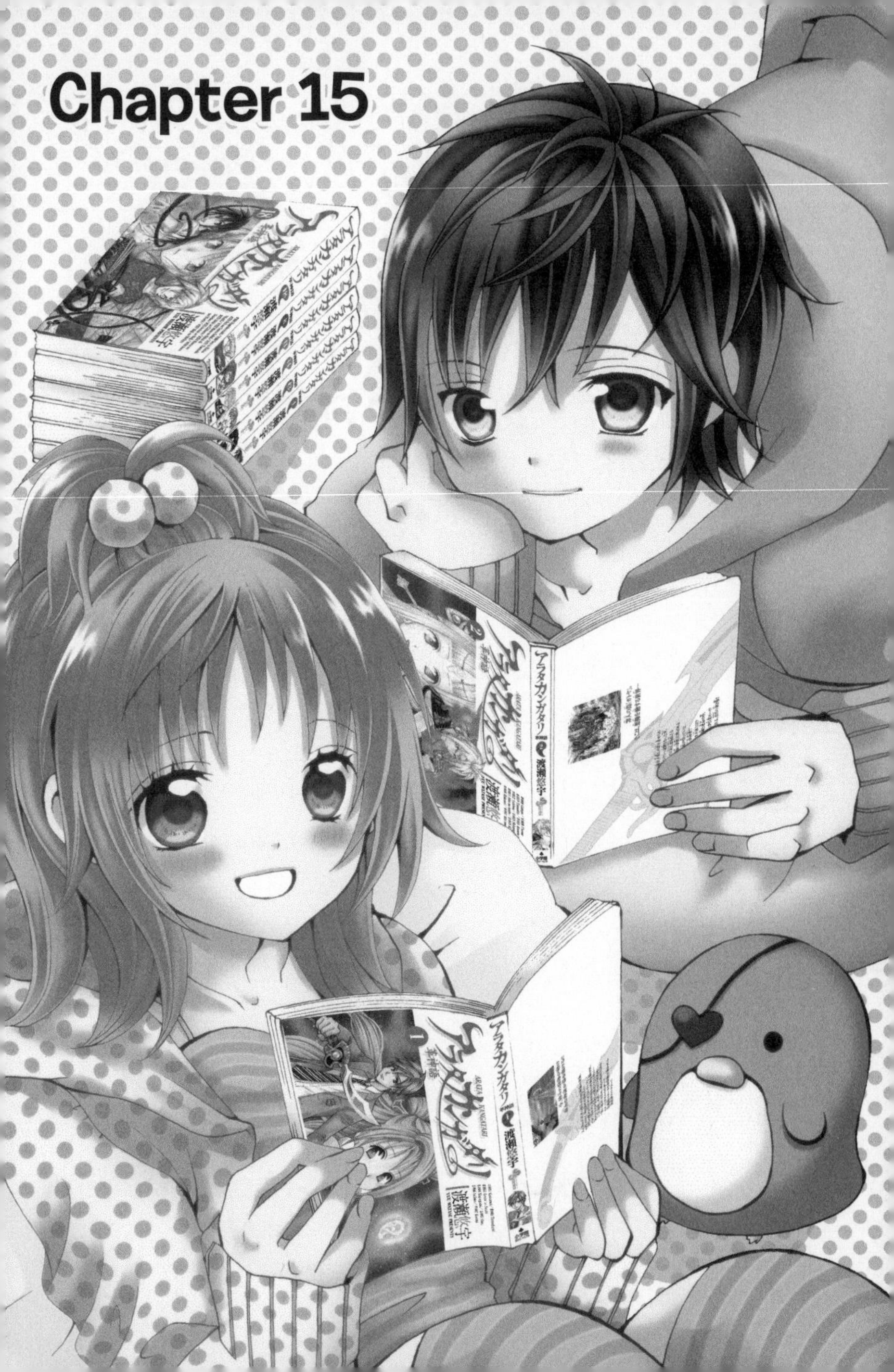
アラタカンガタリ
渡瀬悠宇

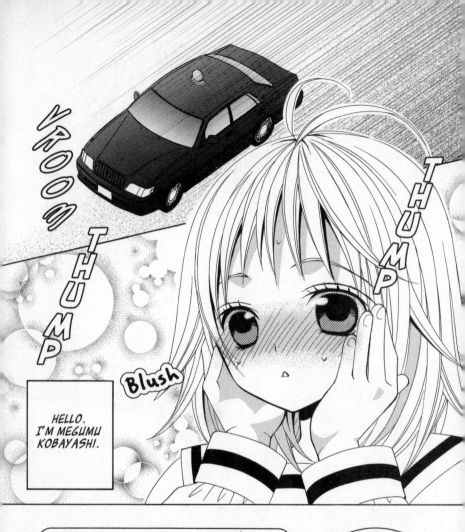

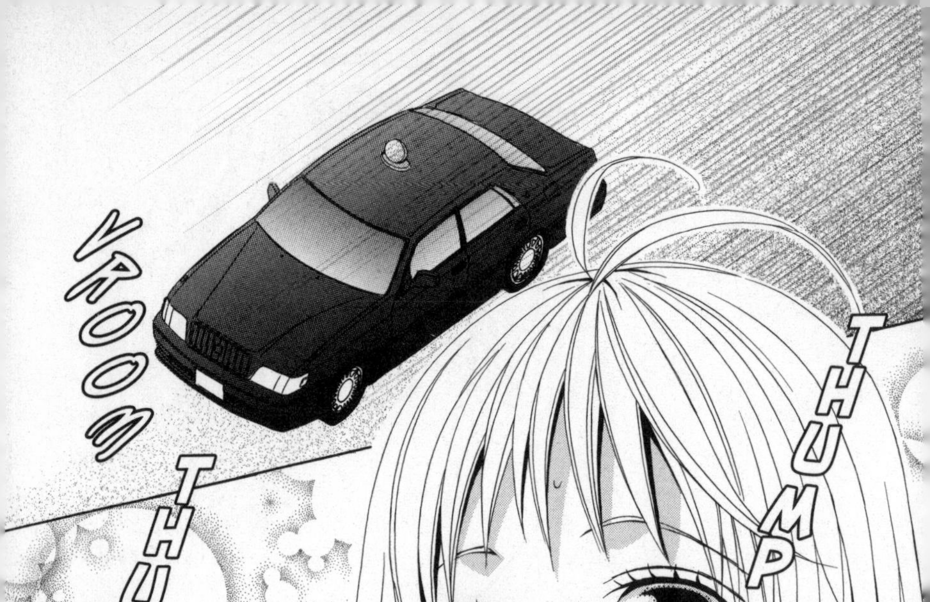
VROOM
THUMP
THUMP
Blush
HELLO. I'M MEGUMU KOBAYASHI.

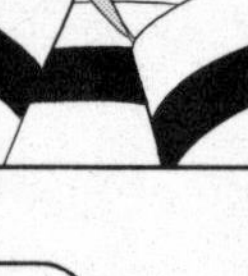

I'M HAPPY I'M GETTING MORE DRAWINGS OF AZUSA IN MY FAN LETTERS ♡ (READERS SEEM TO LOVE HER WEIRD FACES IN CHAPTER 11)... (*SMILE*)

VOLUME 4 WILL INCLUDE A BONUS CHAPTER, **"AOI IS SO CUTE IT HURTS!!"** SO PLEASE LOOK FORWARD TO IT! ♡♡

THE AFTERWORD IS ACTUALLY RIGHT HERE, BECAUSE OF SPACE ISSUES. THANK YOU FOR READING VOLUME 3 OF *SO CUTE!* I WAS FINALLY ABLE TO DRAW THE DECLARATION OF LOVE SCENE USING SIGN LANGUAGE, WHICH I'VE WANTED TO DRAW SINCE THE SERIES BEGAN. AND THE **"LOVE SEPARATED BY TWO FEET,"** A TAGLINE FOR THE SERIES, IS STARTING NOW.
HOW DEEPLY CAN YOU LOVE SOMEONE WHEN YOU CAN'T TOUCH THEM, OR WHEN YOU CAN'T COMMUNICATE WELL USING JUST WORDS? I'LL BE HAPPY IF YOU KEEP WATCHING OVER THE TWINS' LOVE STORIES.
I HOPE WE'LL MEET AGAIN IN VOLUME 4! ♡

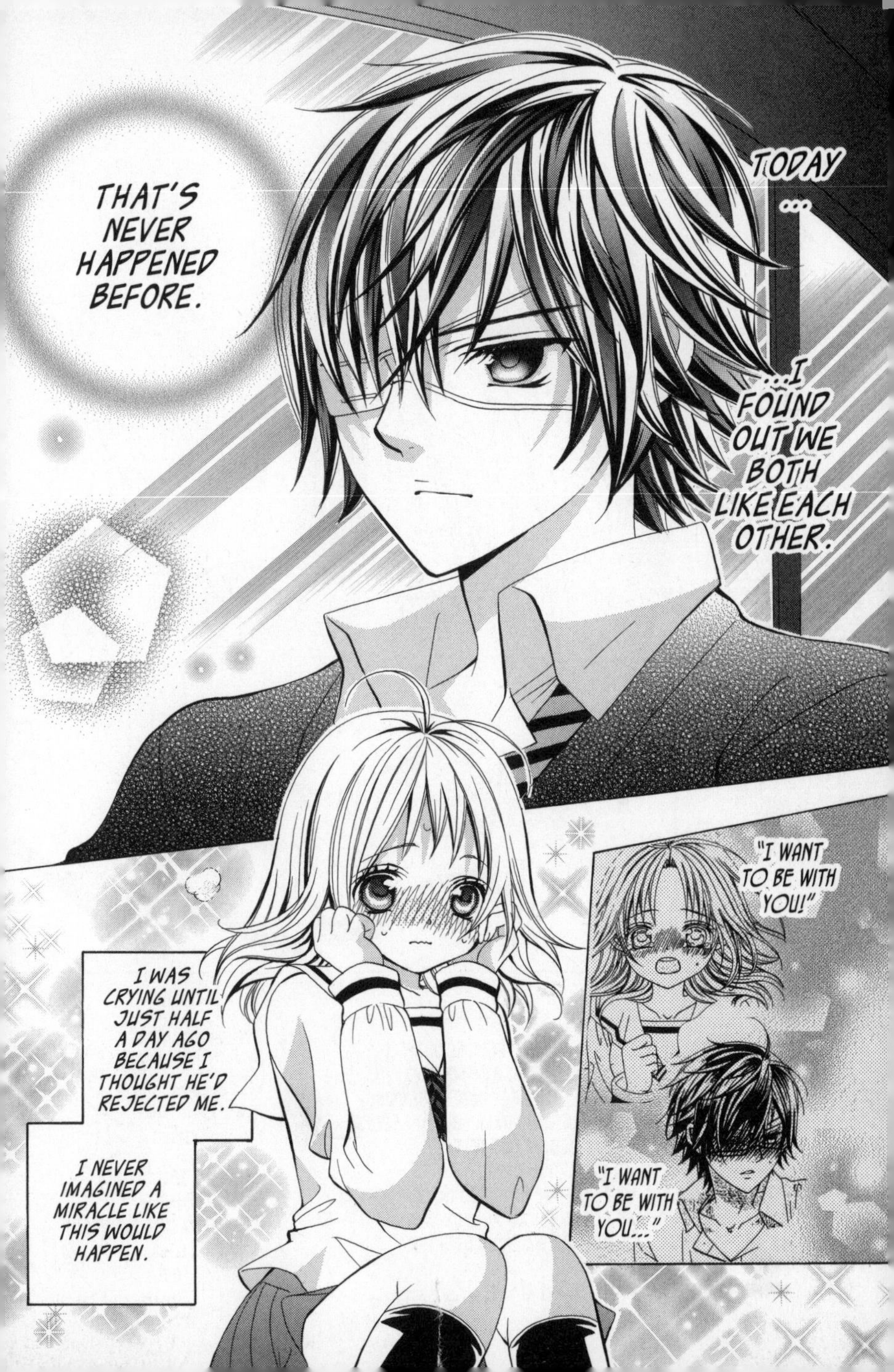
TODAY...
...I FOUND OUT WE BOTH LIKE EACH OTHER.
THAT'S NEVER HAPPENED BEFORE.
"I WANT TO BE WITH YOU!"
"I WANT TO BE WITH YOU..."
I WAS CRYING UNTIL JUST HALF A DAY AGO BECAUSE I THOUGHT HE'D REJECTED ME.
I NEVER IMAGINED A MIRACLE LIKE THIS WOULD HAPPEN.

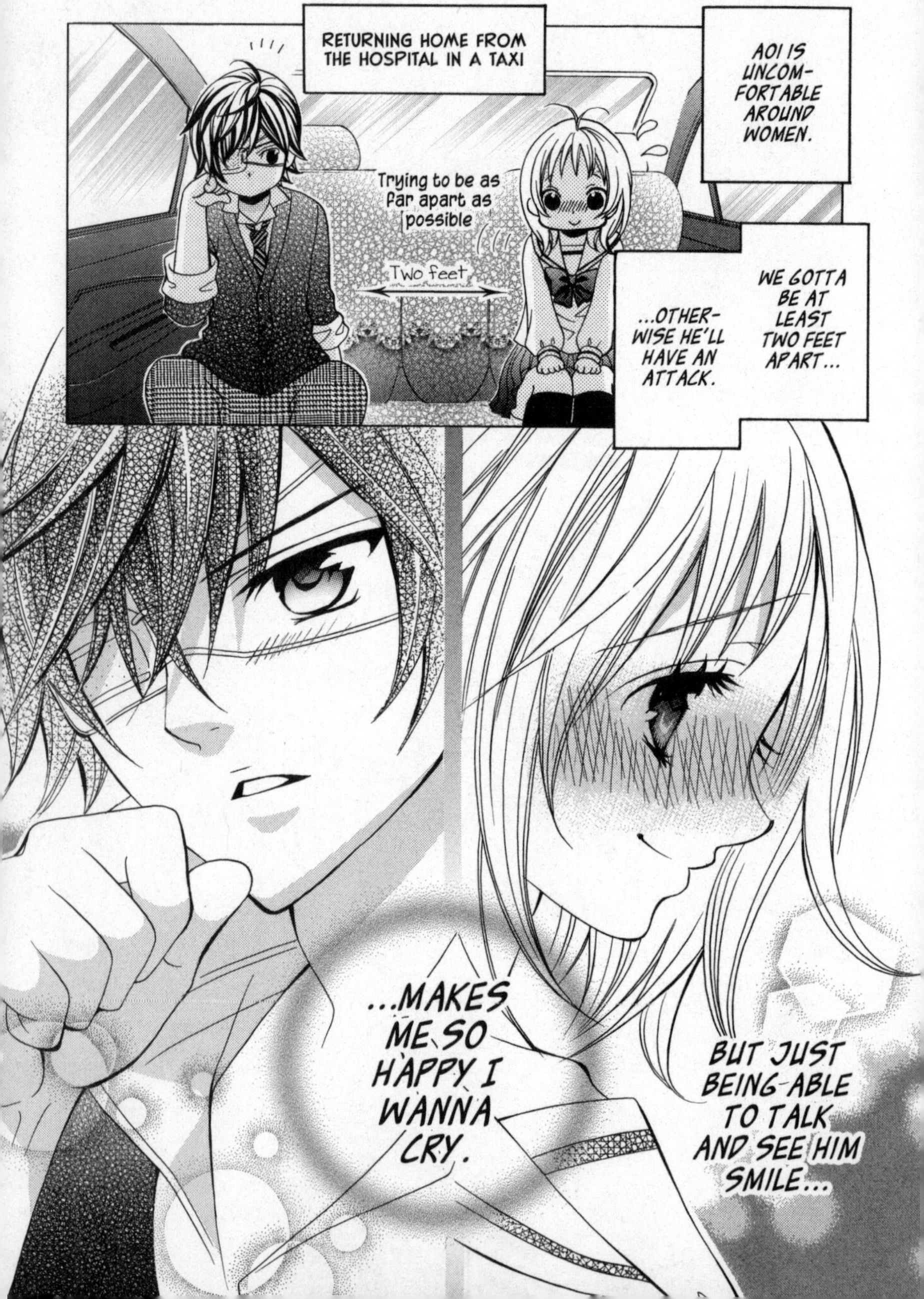
RETURNING HOME FROM THE HOSPITAL IN A TAXI
AOI IS UNCOMFORTABLE AROUND WOMEN.
WE GOTTA BE AT LEAST TWO FEET APART...
...OTHERWISE HE'LL HAVE AN ATTACK.
Trying to be as far apart as possible
Two feet
BUT JUST BEING ABLE TO TALK AND SEE HIM SMILE...
...MAKES ME SO HAPPY I WANNA CRY.

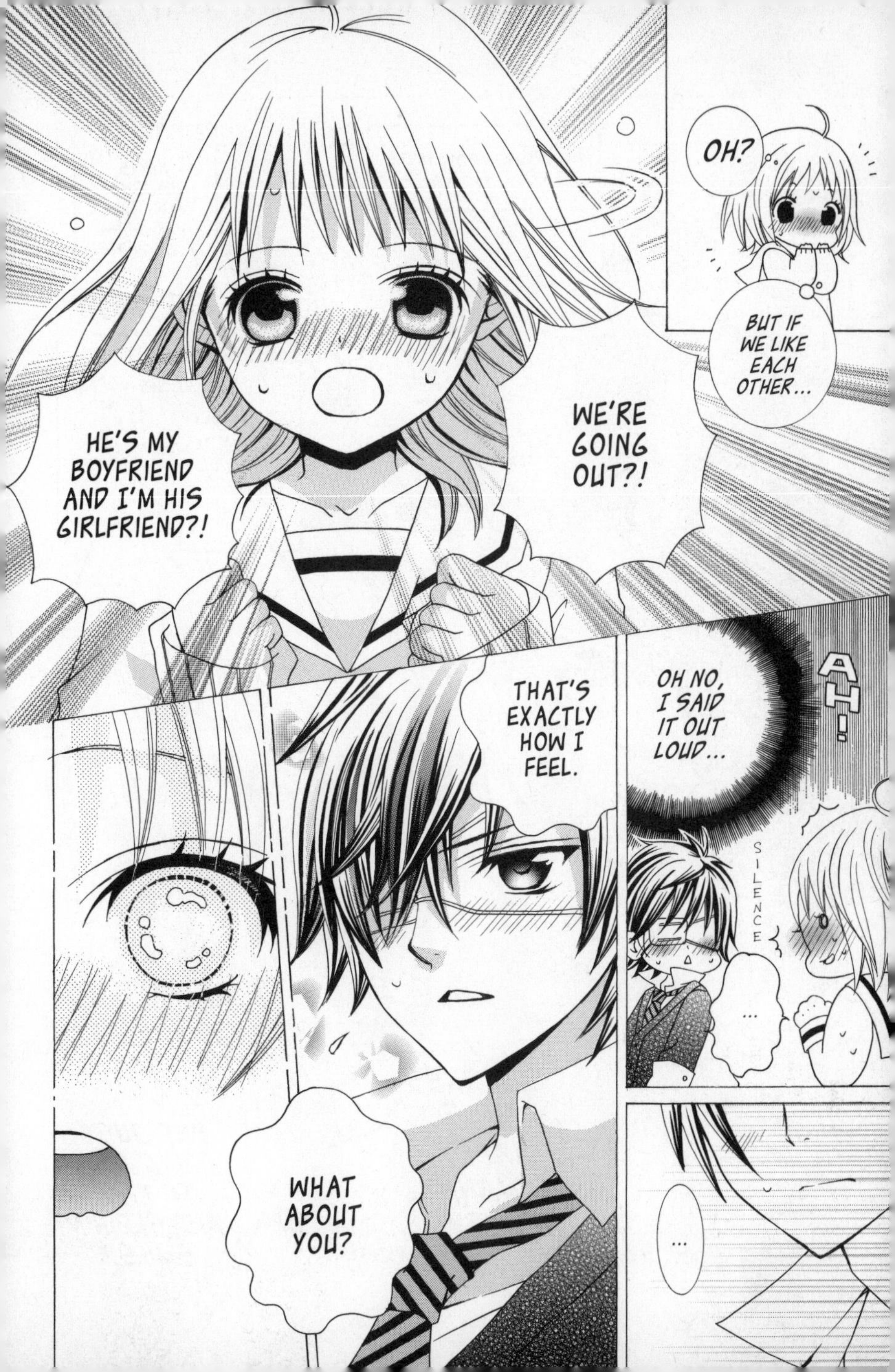
OH?
BUT IF WE LIKE EACH OTHER...
WE'RE GOING OUT?!
HE'S MY BOYFRIEND AND I'M HIS GIRLFRIEND?!
AH!
OH NO, I SAID IT OUT LOUD...
SILENCE
...
...
THAT'S EXACTLY HOW I FEEL.
WHAT ABOUT YOU?

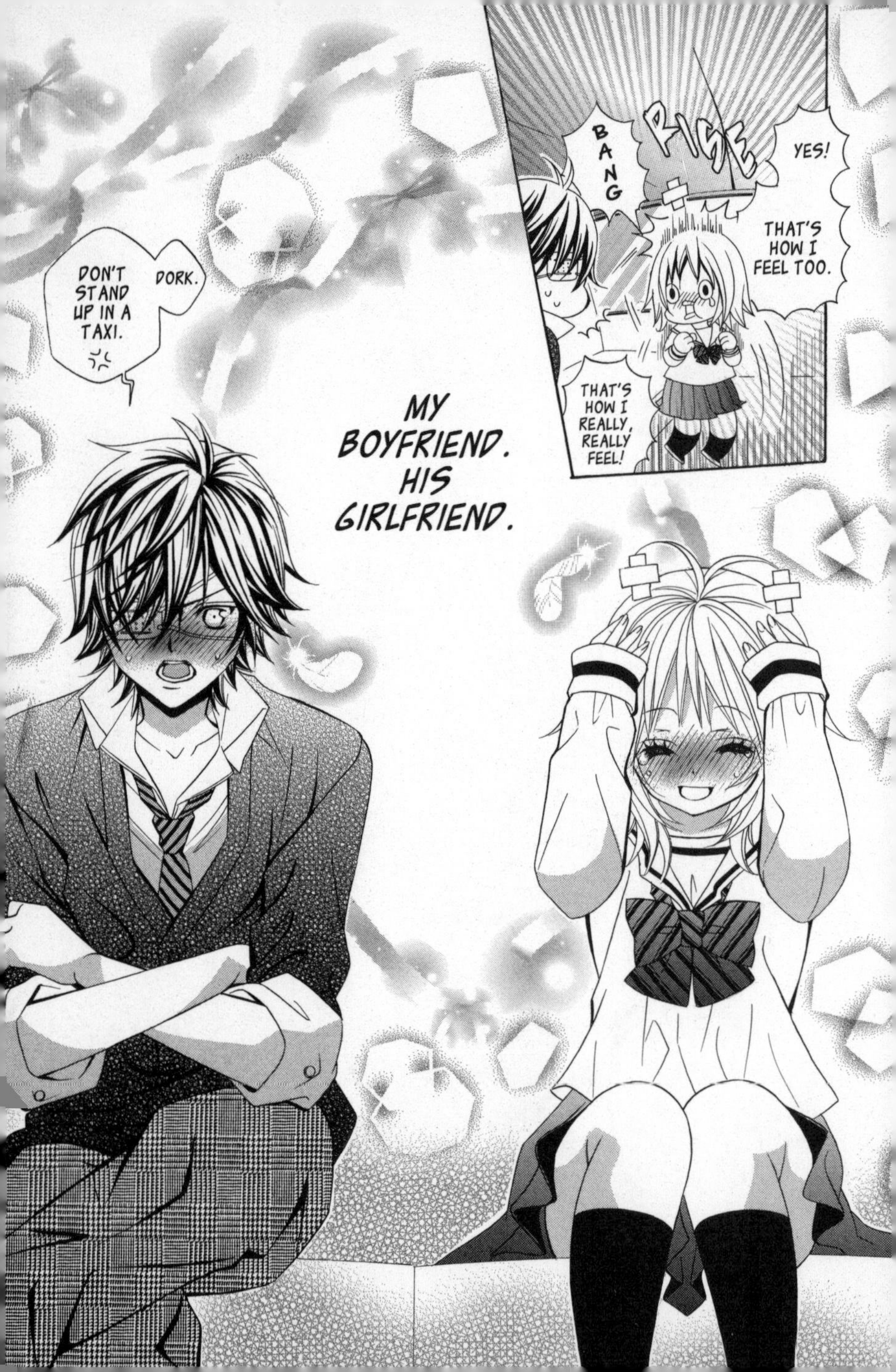
YES!
RISE
BANG
THAT'S HOW I FEEL TOO.
THAT'S HOW I REALLY, REALLY FEEL!
MY BOYFRIEND. HIS GIRLFRIEND.
DORK.
DON'T STAND UP IN A TAXI.

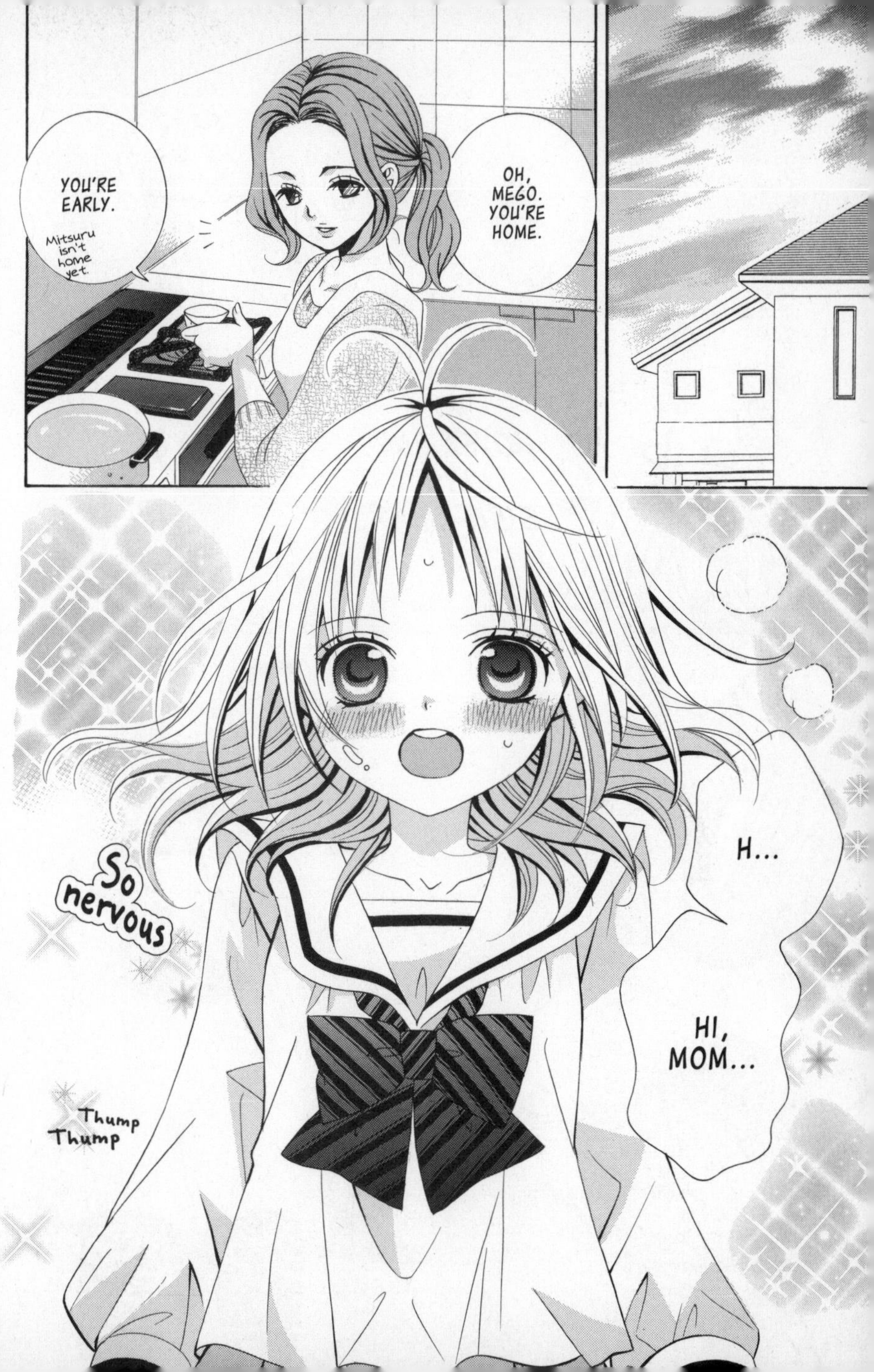
OH, MEGO. YOU'RE HOME.
YOU'RE EARLY.
Mitsuru isn't home yet.
H...
So nervous
HI, MOM...
Thump Thump

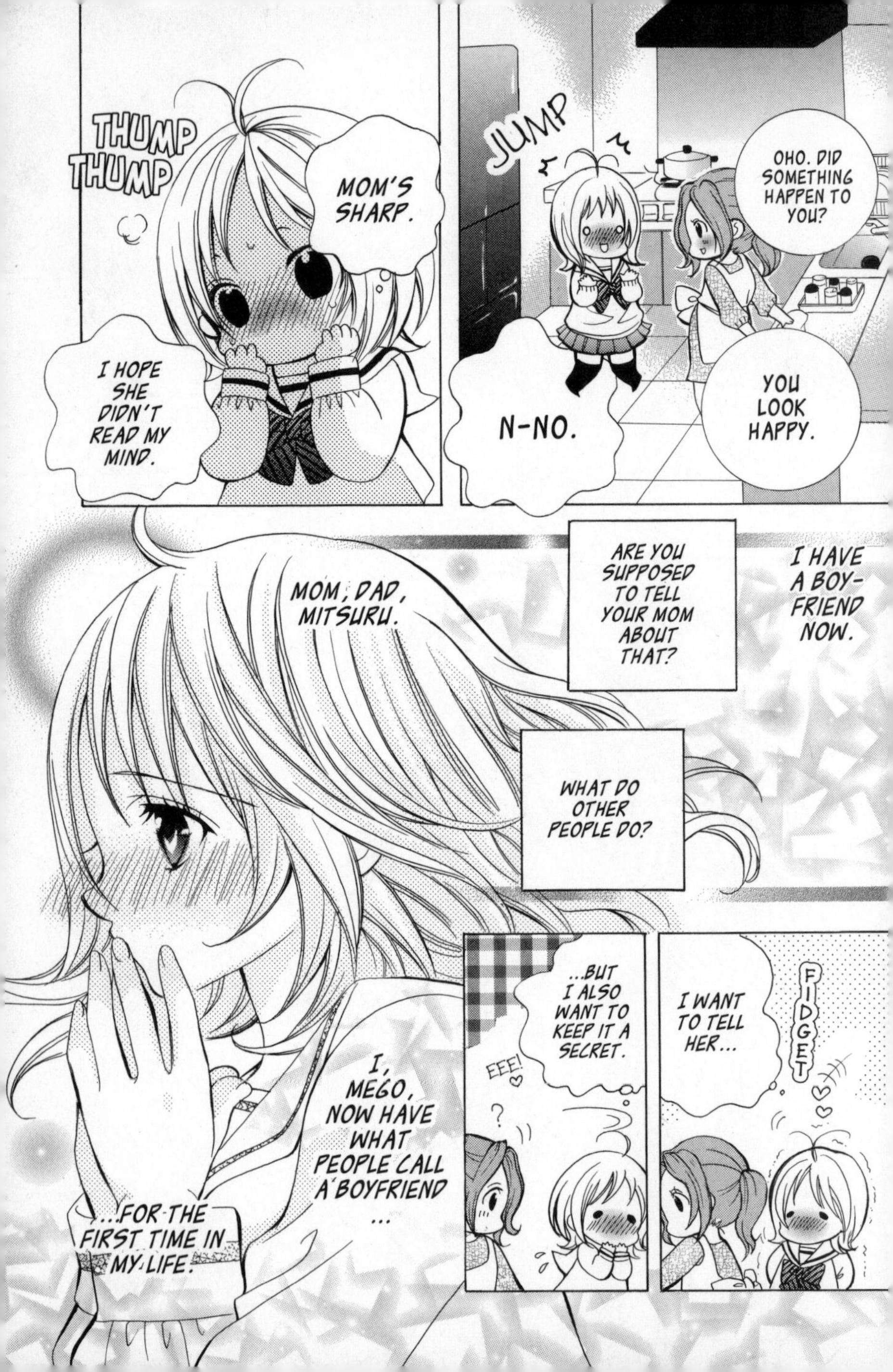
OHO. DID SOMETHING HAPPEN TO YOU?
YOU LOOK HAPPY.
JUMP
N-NO.
THUMP THUMP
MOM'S SHARP.
I HOPE SHE DIDN'T READ MY MIND.
I HAVE A BOY-FRIEND NOW.
ARE YOU SUPPOSED TO TELL YOUR MOM ABOUT THAT?
WHAT DO OTHER PEOPLE DO?
FIDGET
I WANT TO TELL HER...
...BUT I ALSO WANT TO KEEP IT A SECRET.
EEE!
MOM, DAD, MITSURU.
I, MEGO, NOW HAVE WHAT PEOPLE CALL A BOYFRIEND...
...FOR THE FIRST TIME IN MY LIFE.

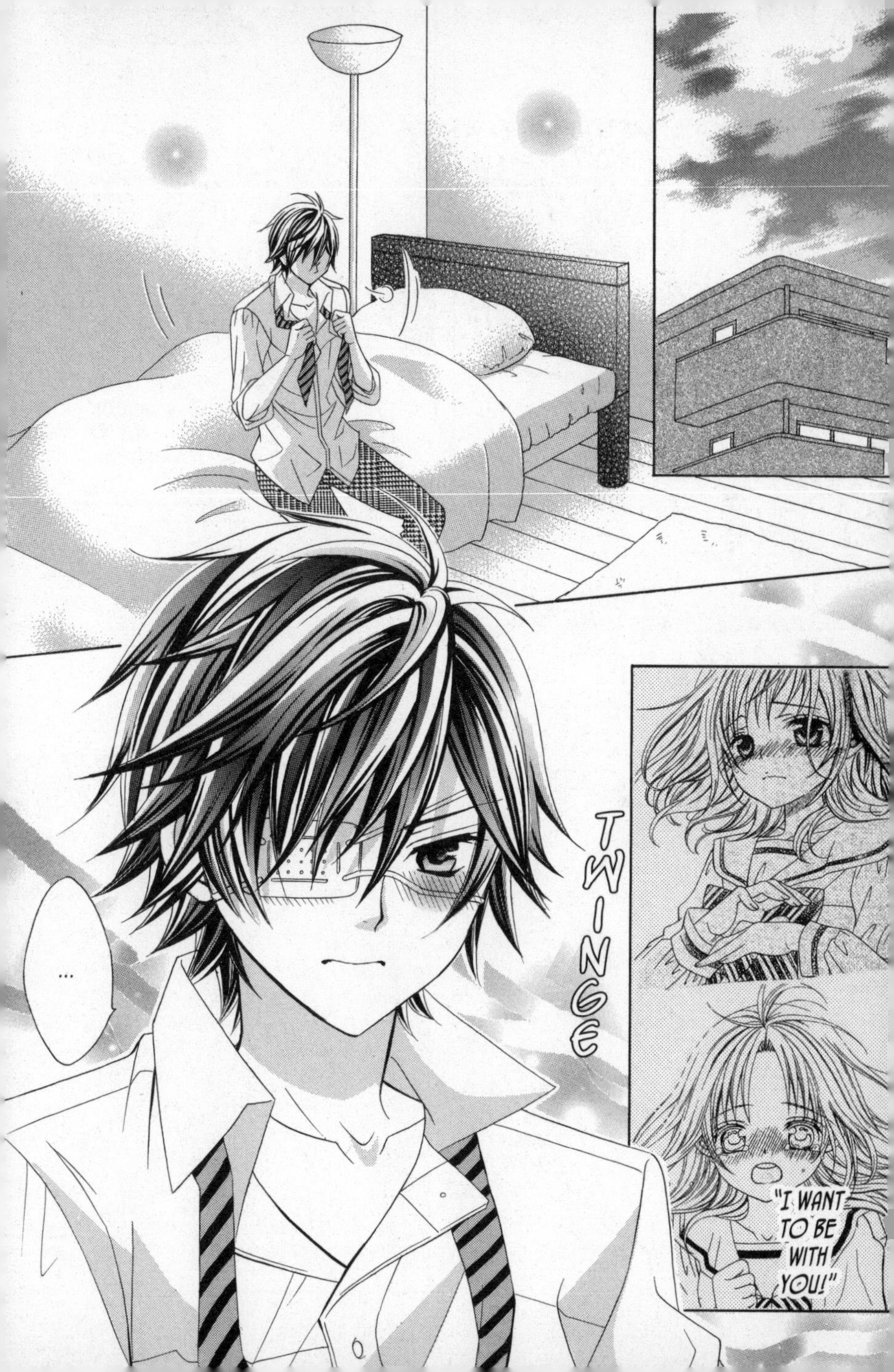
"I WANT TO BE WITH YOU!"
TWINGE
...

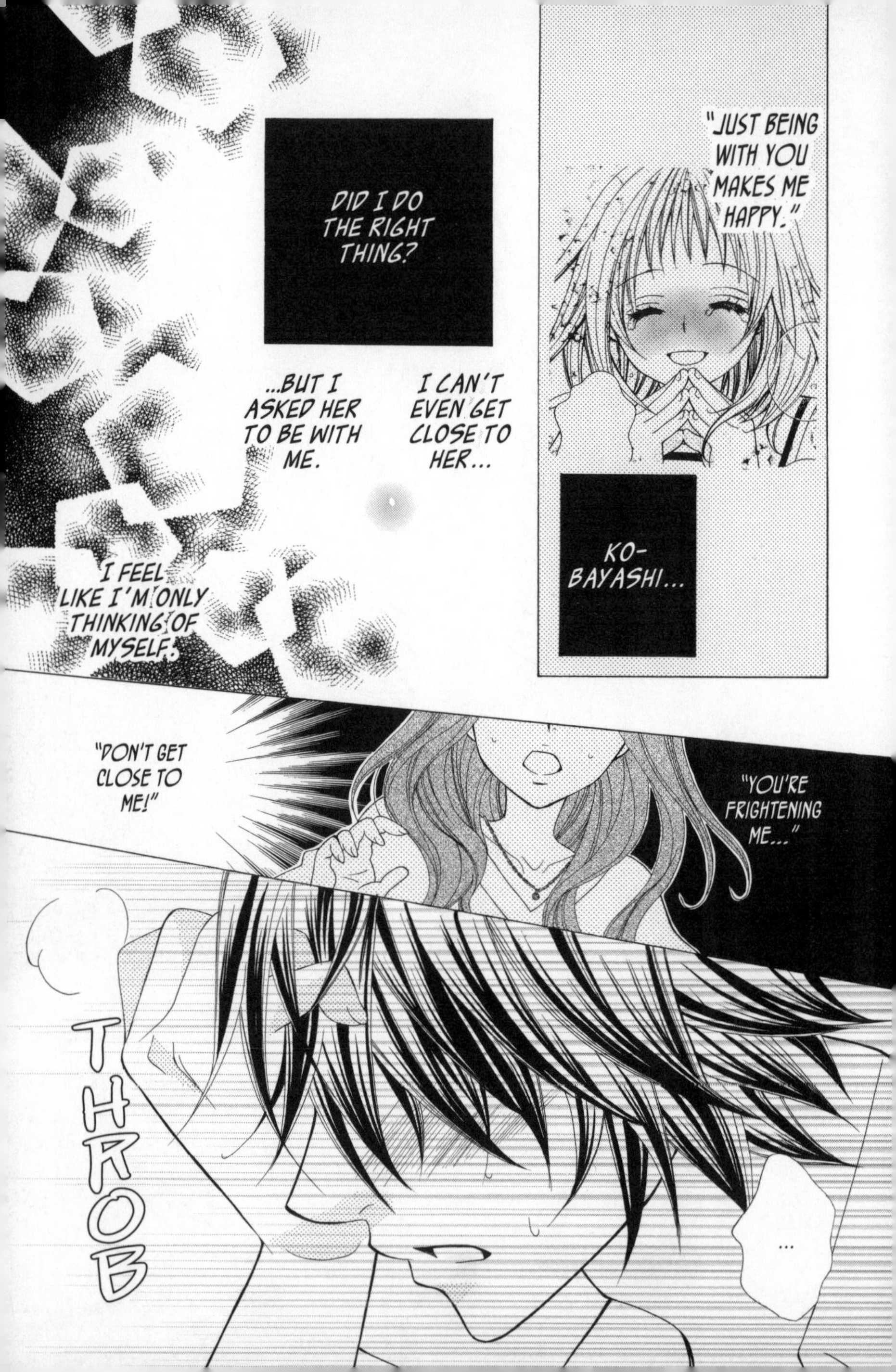
"JUST BEING WITH YOU MAKES ME HAPPY."
KO-BAYASHI...
DID I DO THE RIGHT THING?
I CAN'T EVEN GET CLOSE TO HER...
...BUT I ASKED HER TO BE WITH ME.
I FEEL LIKE I'M ONLY THINKING OF MYSELF.
"YOU'RE FRIGHTENING ME..."
"DON'T GET CLOSE TO ME!"
...
THROB

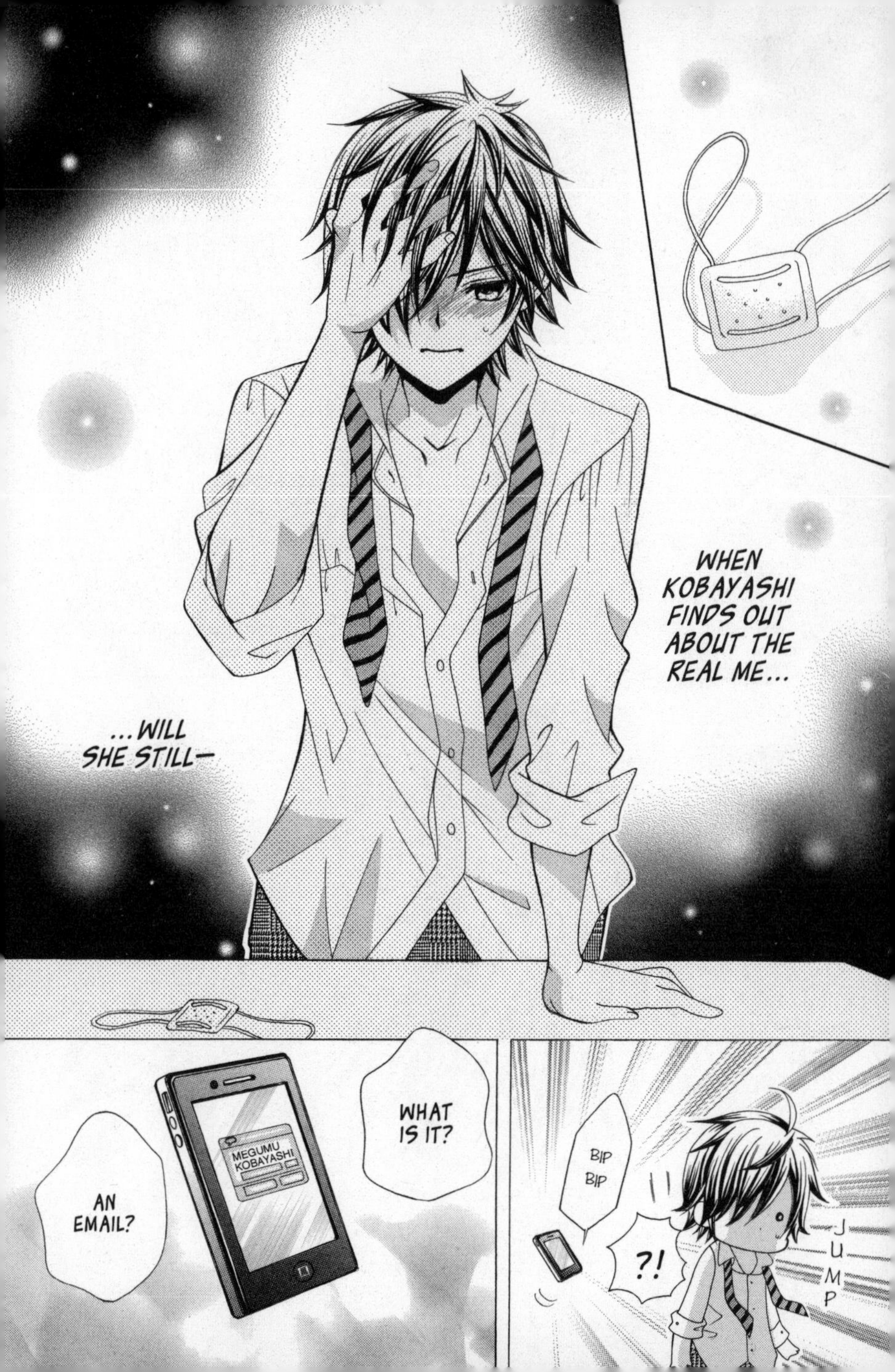
WHEN KOBAYASHI FINDS OUT ABOUT THE REAL ME...
...WILL SHE STILL—
BIP BIP
?!
JUMP
WHAT IS IT?
MEGUMU KOBAYASHI
AN EMAIL?

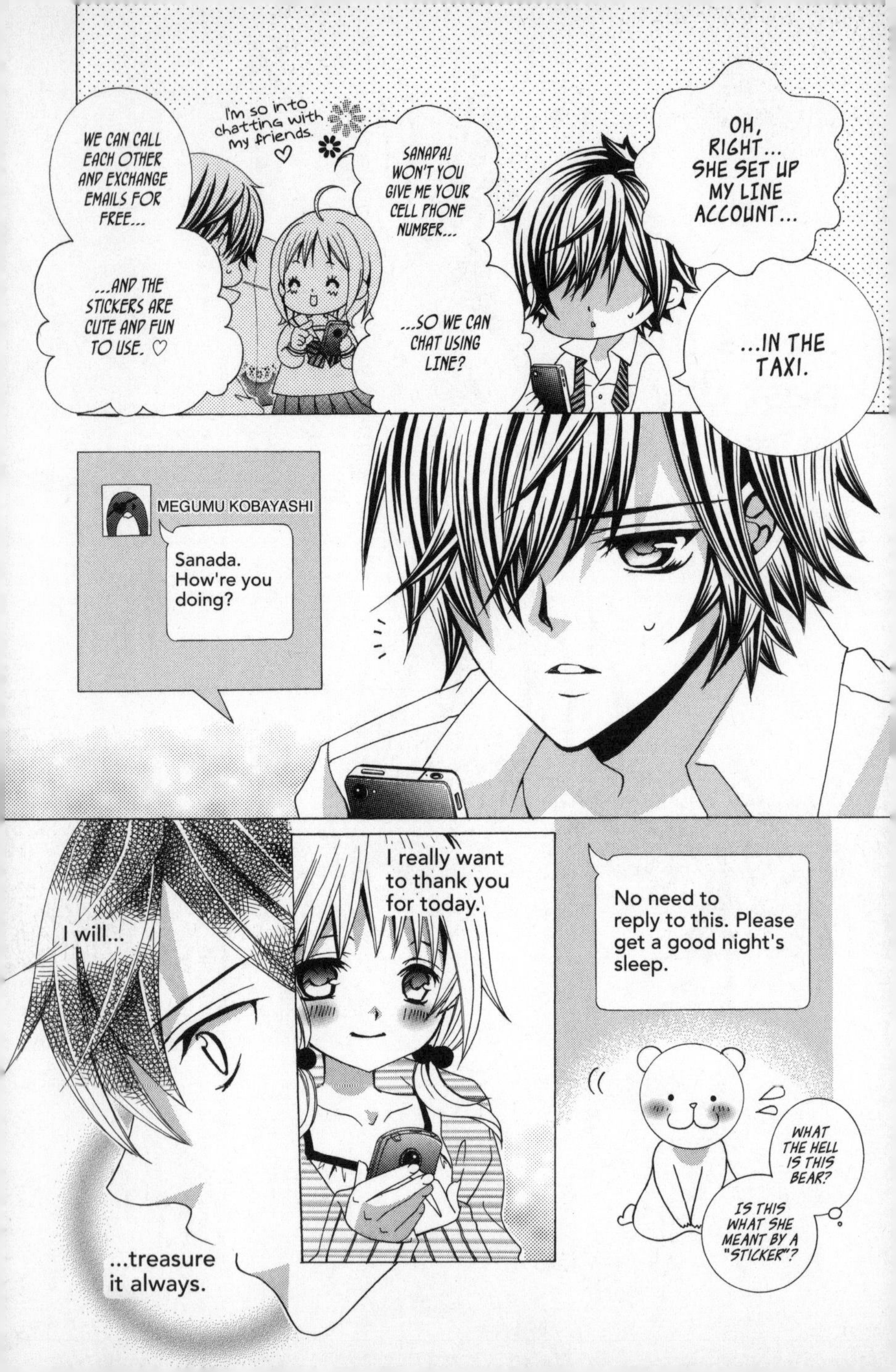
OH, RIGHT... SHE SET UP MY LINE ACCOUNT...
...IN THE TAXI.
SANADA! WON'T YOU GIVE ME YOUR CELL PHONE NUMBER...
...SO WE CAN CHAT USING LINE?
I'm so into chatting with my friends. ♡
WE CAN CALL EACH OTHER AND EXCHANGE EMAILS FOR FREE...
...AND THE STICKERS ARE CUTE AND FUN TO USE. ♡
MEGUMU KOBAYASHI
Sanada. How're you doing?
No need to reply to this. Please get a good night's sleep.
WHAT THE HELL IS THIS BEAR?
IS THIS WHAT SHE MEANT BY A "STICKER"?
I really want to thank you for today.
I will...
...treasure it always.

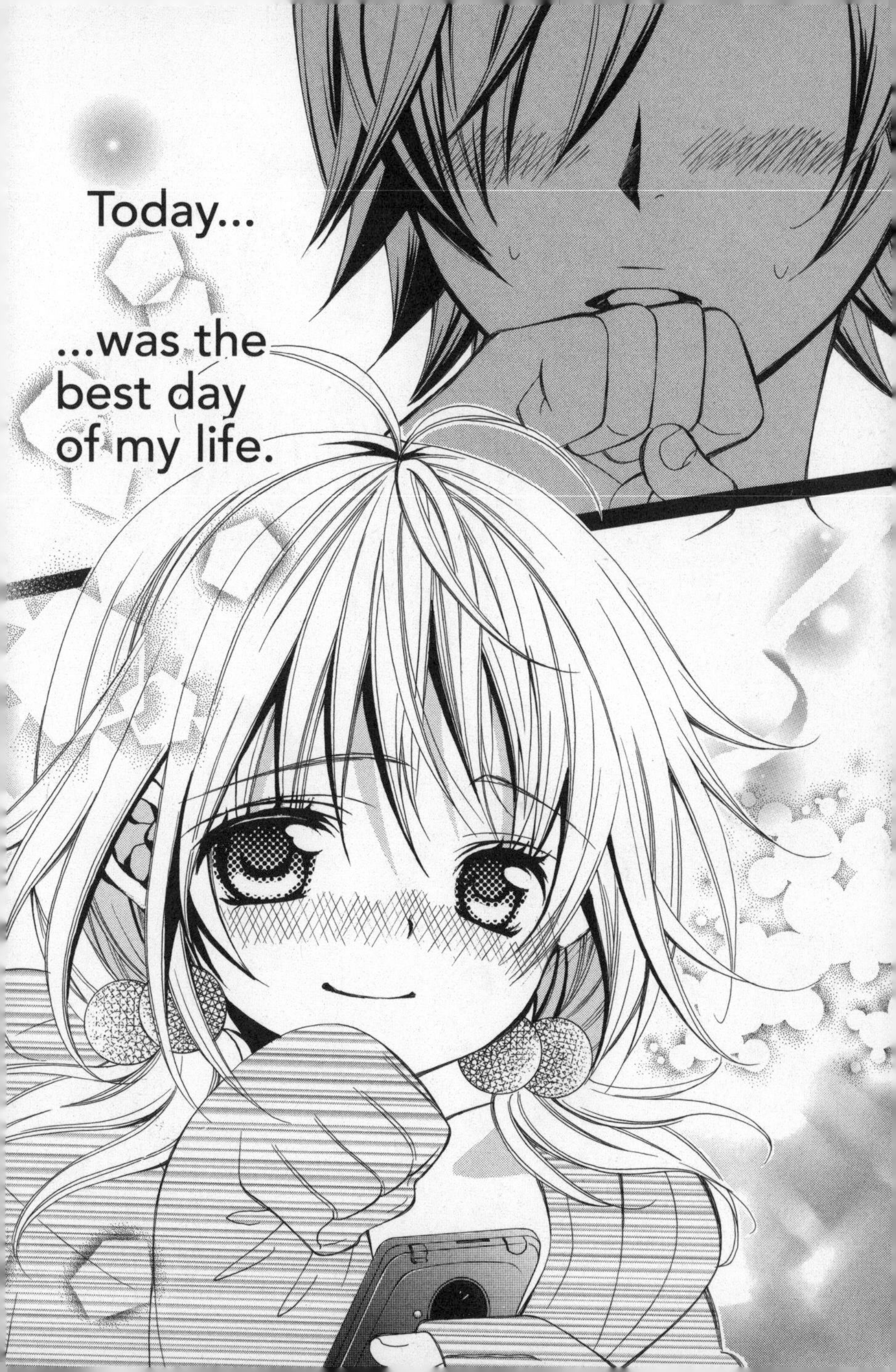
Today...
...was the best day of my life.

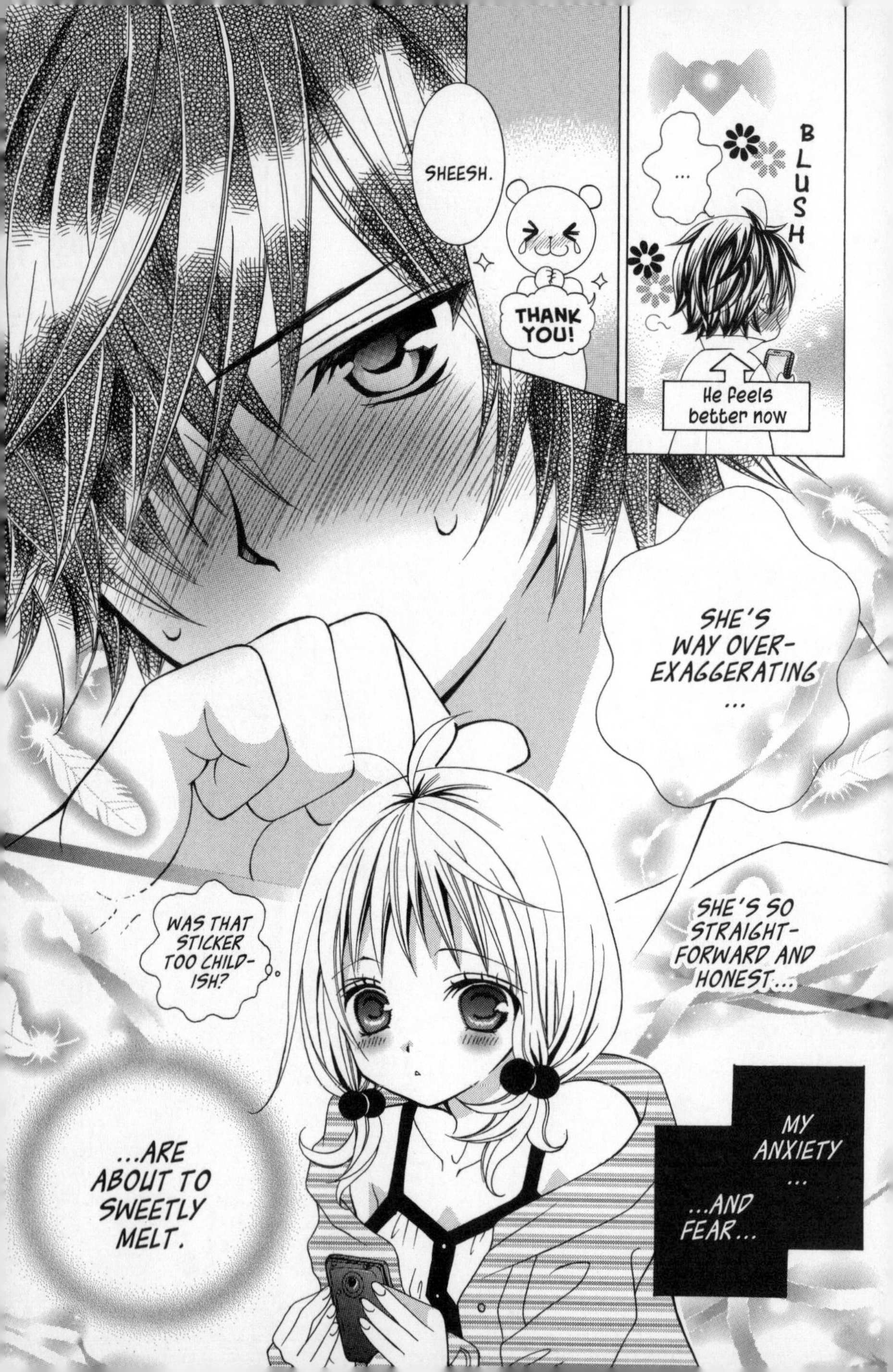
...
BLUSH
He feels better now
SHEESH.
THANK YOU!
SHE'S WAY OVER-EXAGGERATING...
SHE'S SO STRAIGHT-FORWARD AND HONEST...
WAS THAT STICKER TOO CHILD-ISH?
MY ANXIETY...
...AND FEAR...
...ARE ABOUT TO SWEETLY MELT.

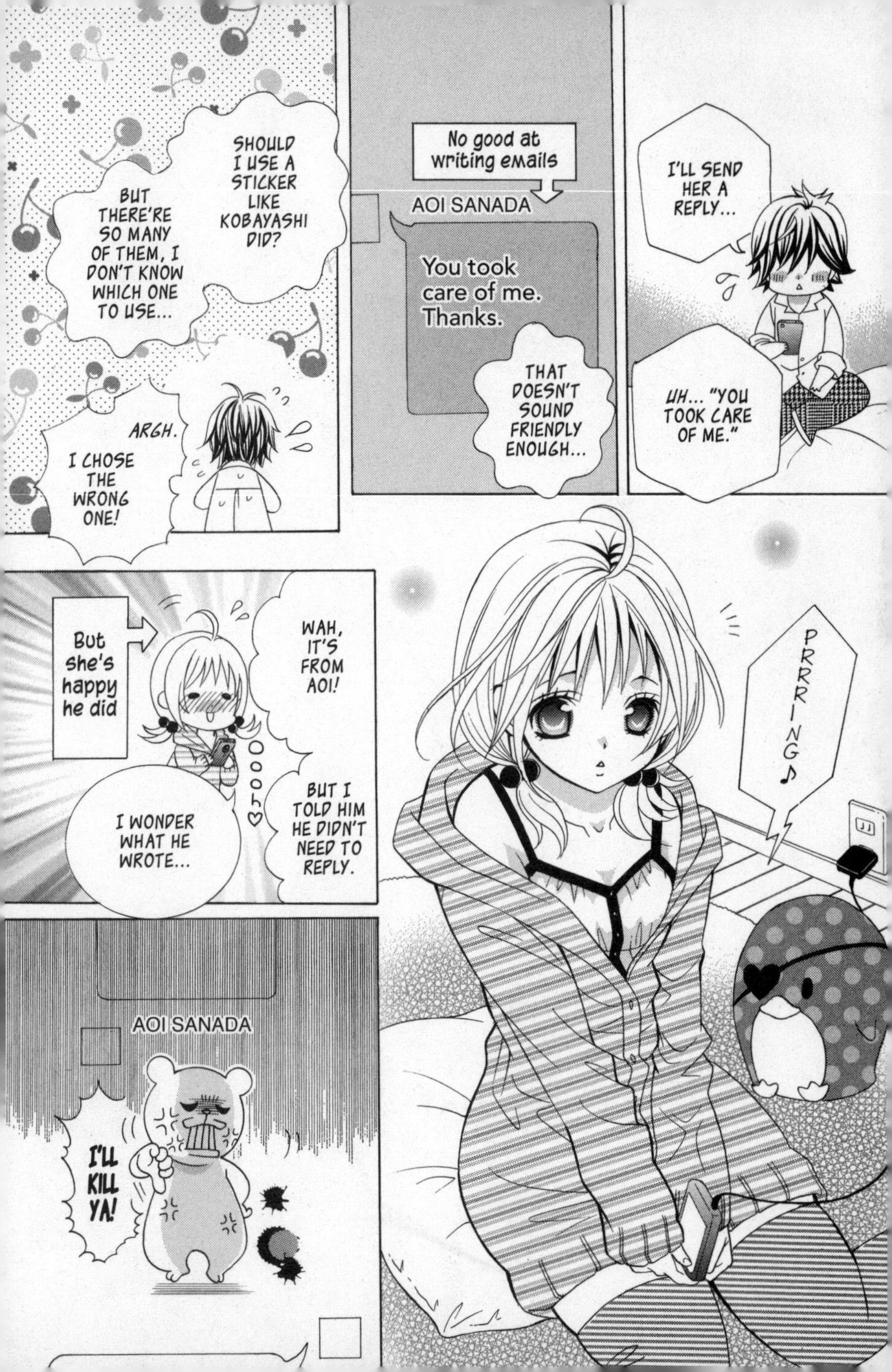
I'LL SEND HER A REPLY...
UH... "YOU TOOK CARE OF ME."
No good at writing emails
AOI SANADA
You took care of me. Thanks.
THAT DOESN'T SOUND FRIENDLY ENOUGH...
SHOULD I USE A STICKER LIKE KOBAYASHI DID?
BUT THERE'RE SO MANY OF THEM, I DON'T KNOW WHICH ONE TO USE...
ARGH.
I CHOSE THE WRONG ONE!
PRRRING♪
WAH, IT'S FROM AOI!
BUT I TOLD HIM HE DIDN'T NEED TO REPLY.
But she's happy he did
I WONDER WHAT HE WROTE...
Oooh♡
AOI SANADA
I'LL KILL YA!

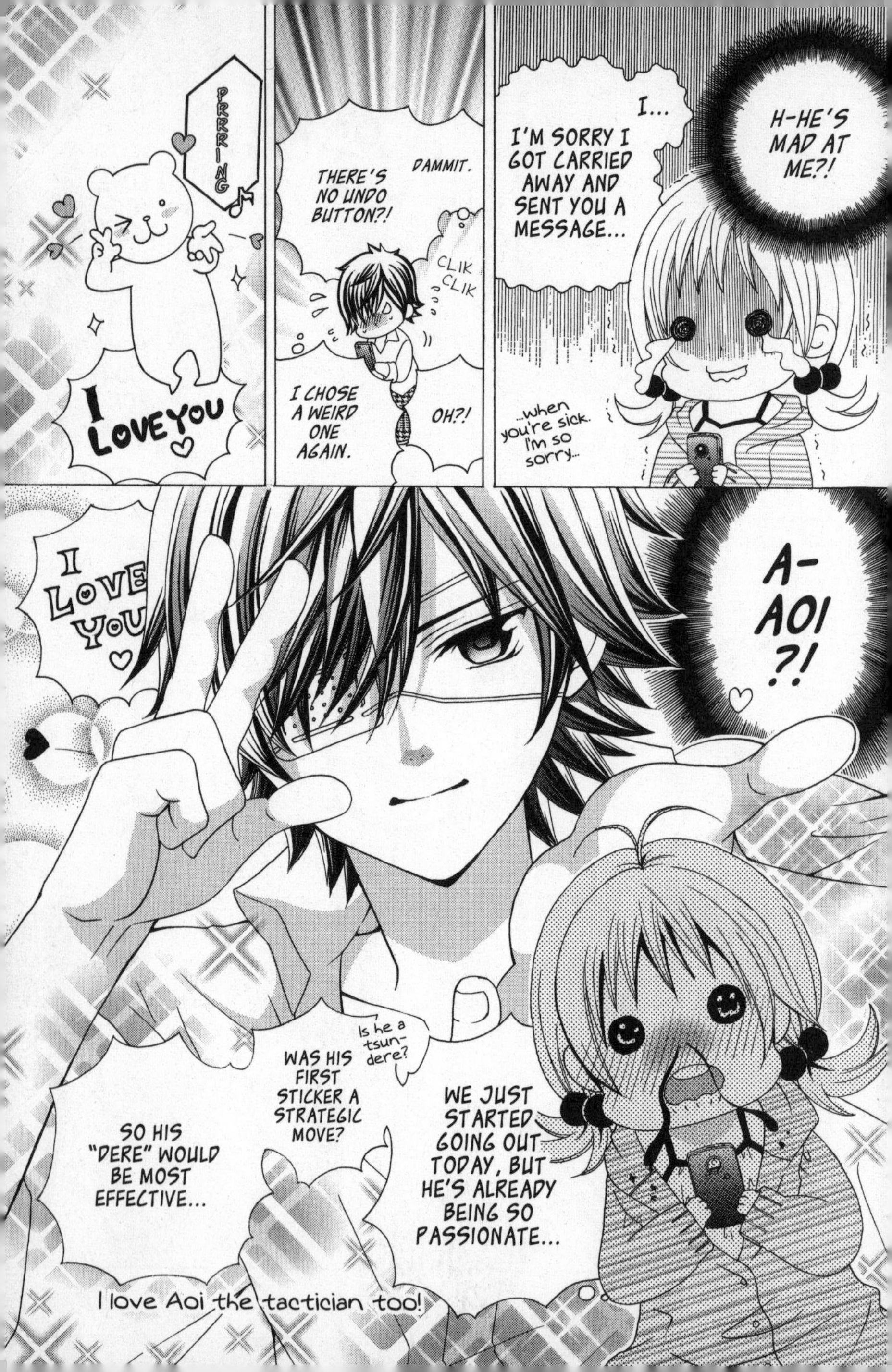
H-HE'S MAD AT ME?!
I...
I'M SORRY I GOT CARRIED AWAY AND SENT YOU A MESSAGE...
...when you're sick. I'm so sorry...
DAMMIT.
THERE'S NO UNDO BUTTON?!
CLIK CLIK
OH?!
I CHOSE A WEIRD ONE AGAIN.
PRRRING
I LOVE YOU
A-AOI?!
I LOVE YOU
WE JUST STARTED GOING OUT TODAY, BUT HE'S ALREADY BEING SO PASSIONATE...
Is he a tsundere?
WAS HIS FIRST STICKER A STRATEGIC MOVE?
SO HIS "DERE" WOULD BE MOST EFFECTIVE...
I love Aoi the tactician too!

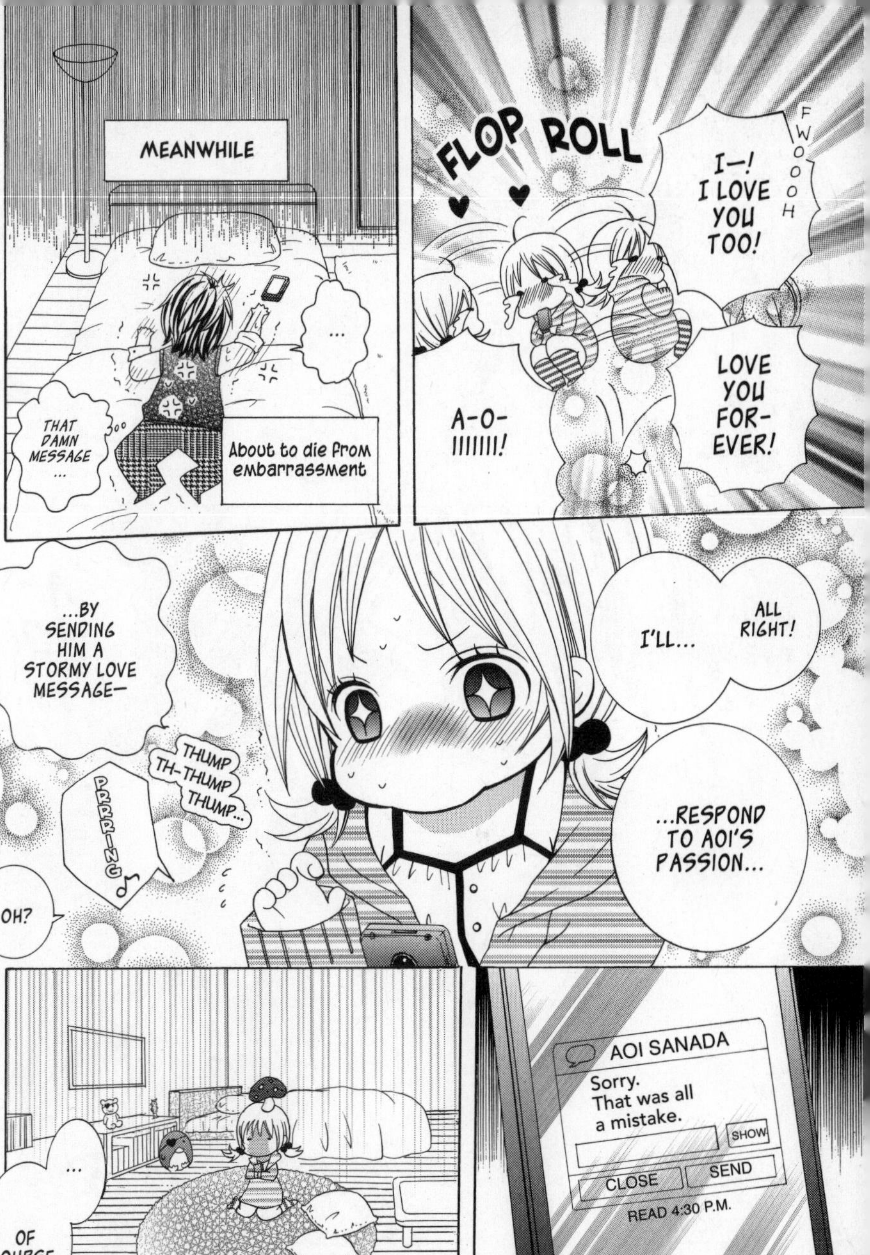
FLOP ROLL
FWOOOH
I—! I LOVE YOU TOO!
LOVE YOU FOR-EVER!
A-O-IIIIIII!
MEANWHILE
...
About to die from embarrassment
THAT DAMN MESSAGE ...
ALL RIGHT!
I'LL...
...RESPOND TO AOI'S PASSION...
...BY SENDING HIM A STORMY LOVE MESSAGE—
THUMP TH-THUMP THUMP...
PRRRING
OH?
AOI SANADA
Sorry. That was all a mistake.
SHOW
CLOSE
SEND
READ 4:30 P.M.
...
OF COURSE.

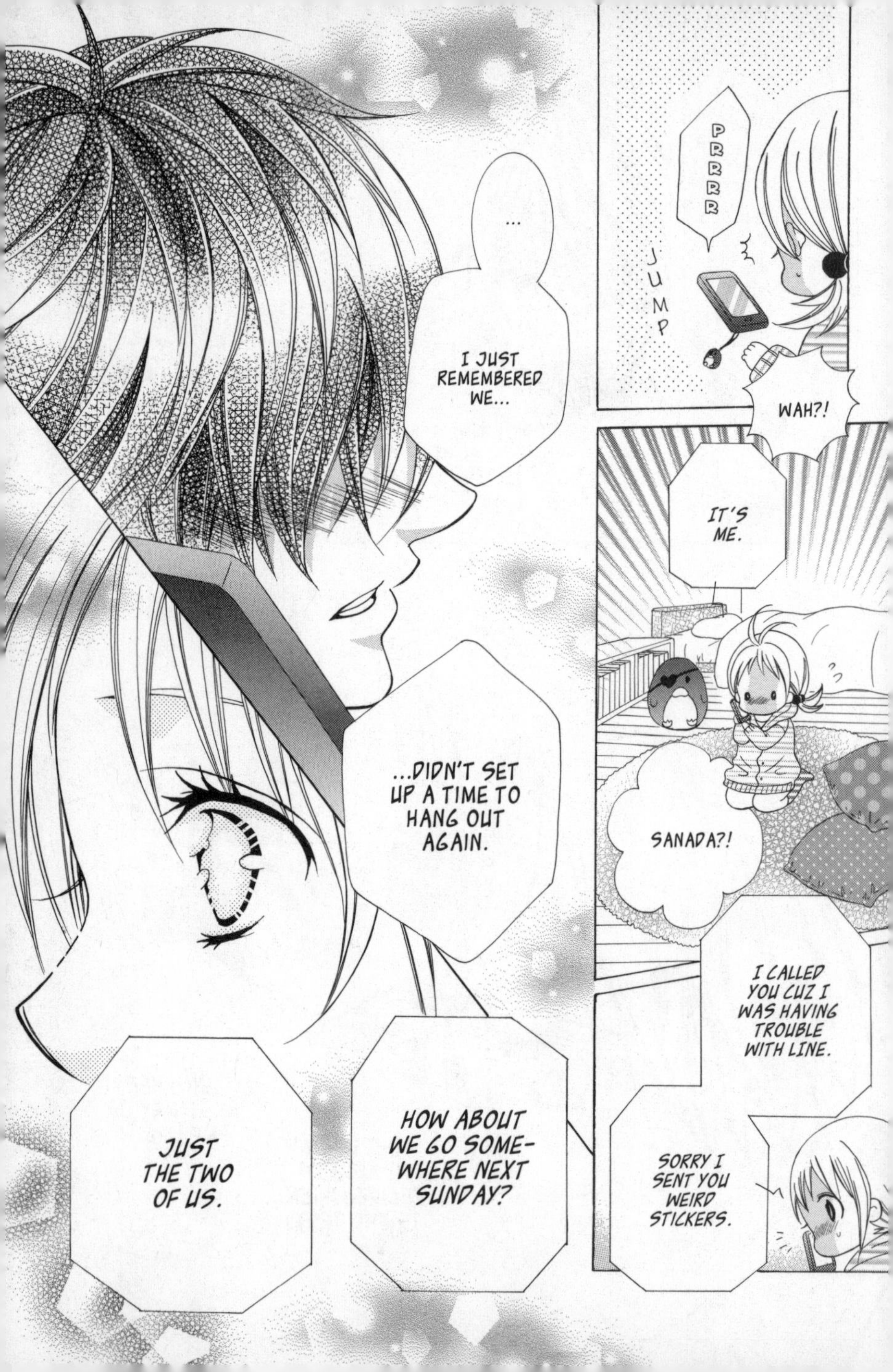
PRRRR
JUMP
WAH?!
IT'S ME.
SANADA?!
I CALLED YOU CUZ I WAS HAVING TROUBLE WITH LINE.
SORRY I SENT YOU WEIRD STICKERS.
...
I JUST REMEMBERED WE...
...DIDN'T SET UP A TIME TO HANG OUT AGAIN.
HOW ABOUT WE GO SOME-WHERE NEXT SUNDAY?
JUST THE TWO OF US.

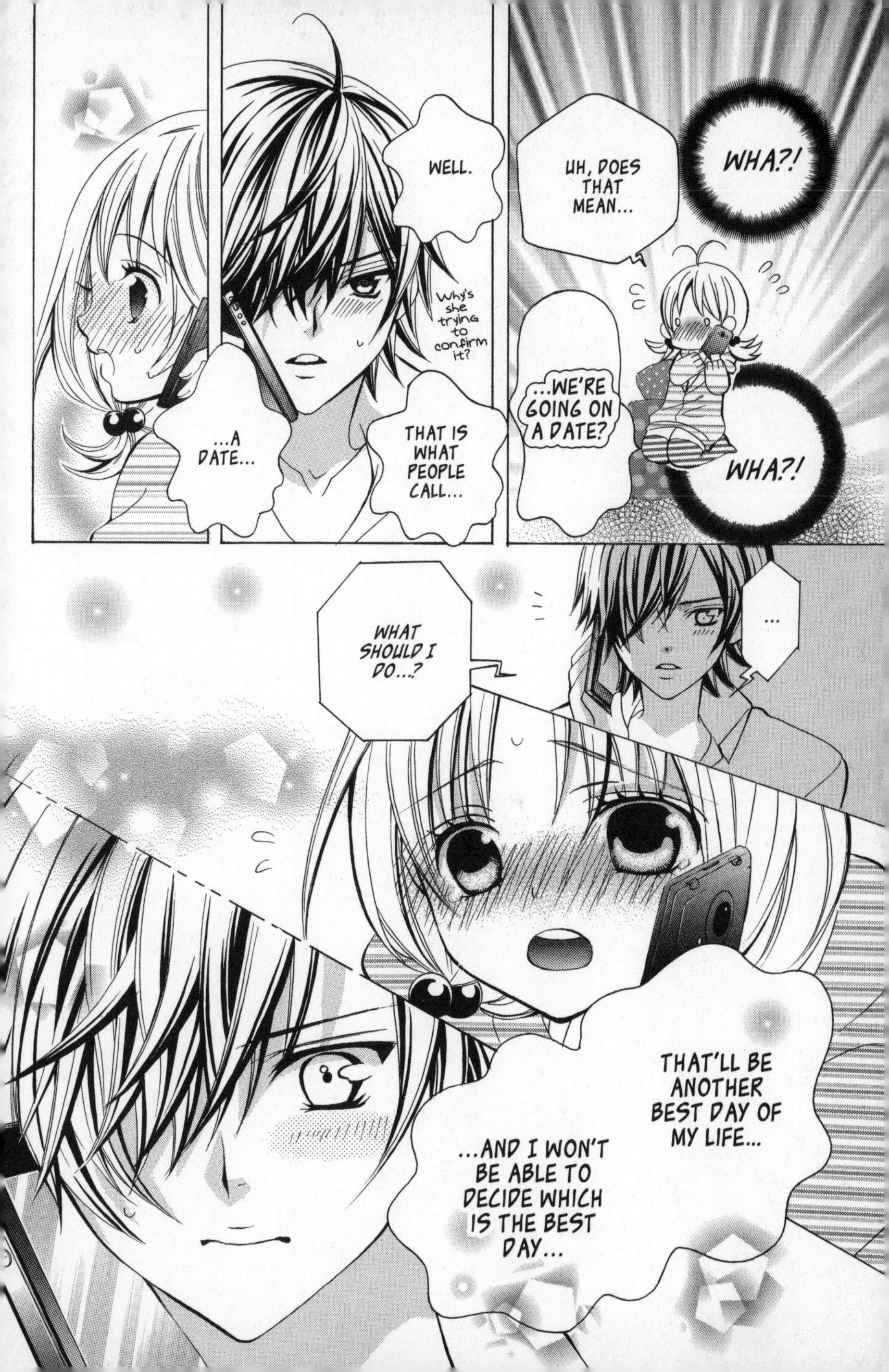
WHA?!
UH, DOES THAT MEAN...
WHA?!
...WE'RE GOING ON A DATE?
WELL.
Why's she trying to confirm it?
THAT IS WHAT PEOPLE CALL...
...A DATE...
...
WHAT SHOULD I DO...?
THAT'LL BE ANOTHER BEST DAY OF MY LIFE...
...AND I WON'T BE ABLE TO DECIDE WHICH IS THE BEST DAY...

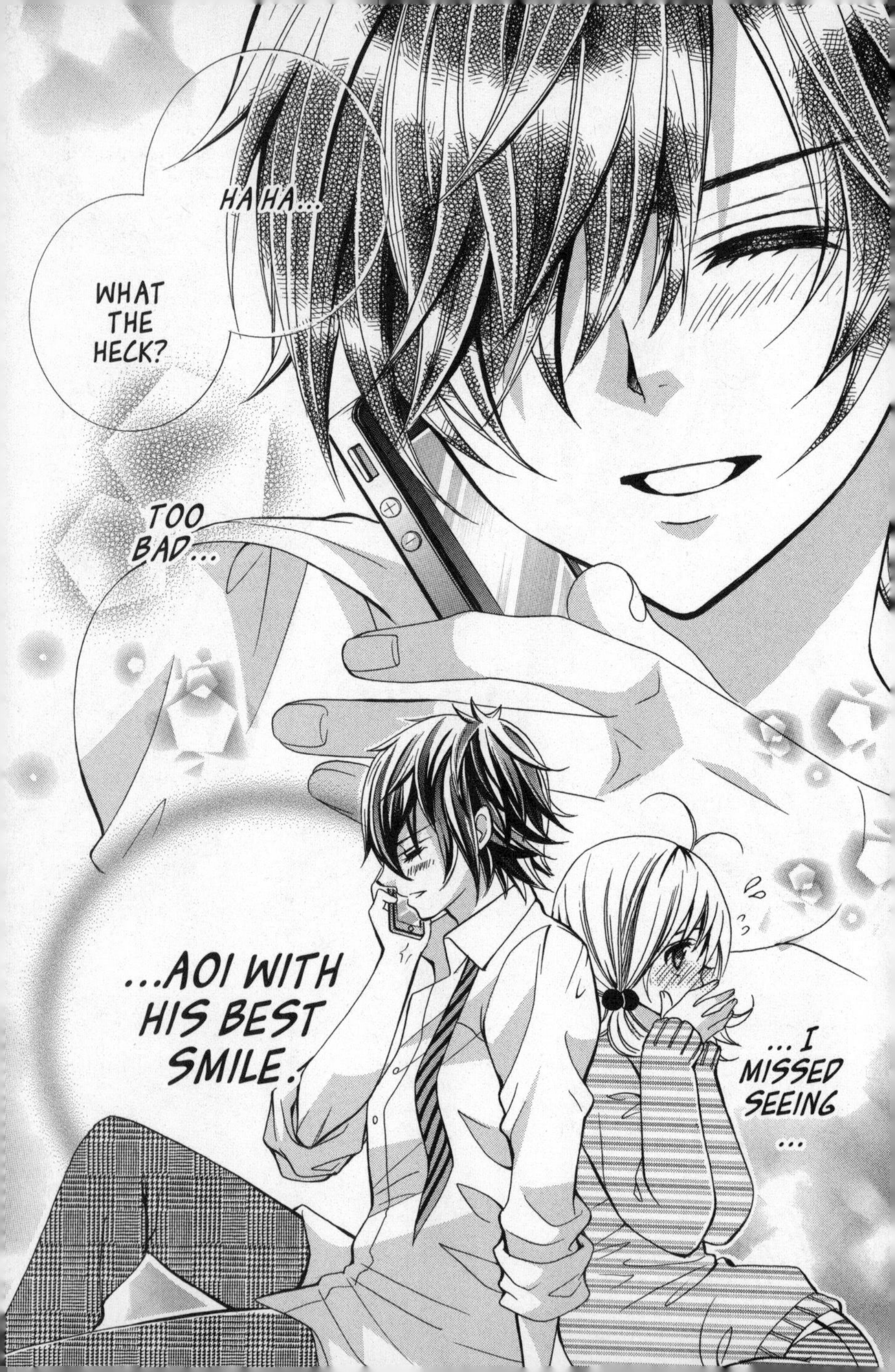
HA HA...
WHAT THE HECK?
TOO BAD...
...I MISSED SEEING...
...AOI WITH HIS BEST SMILE.

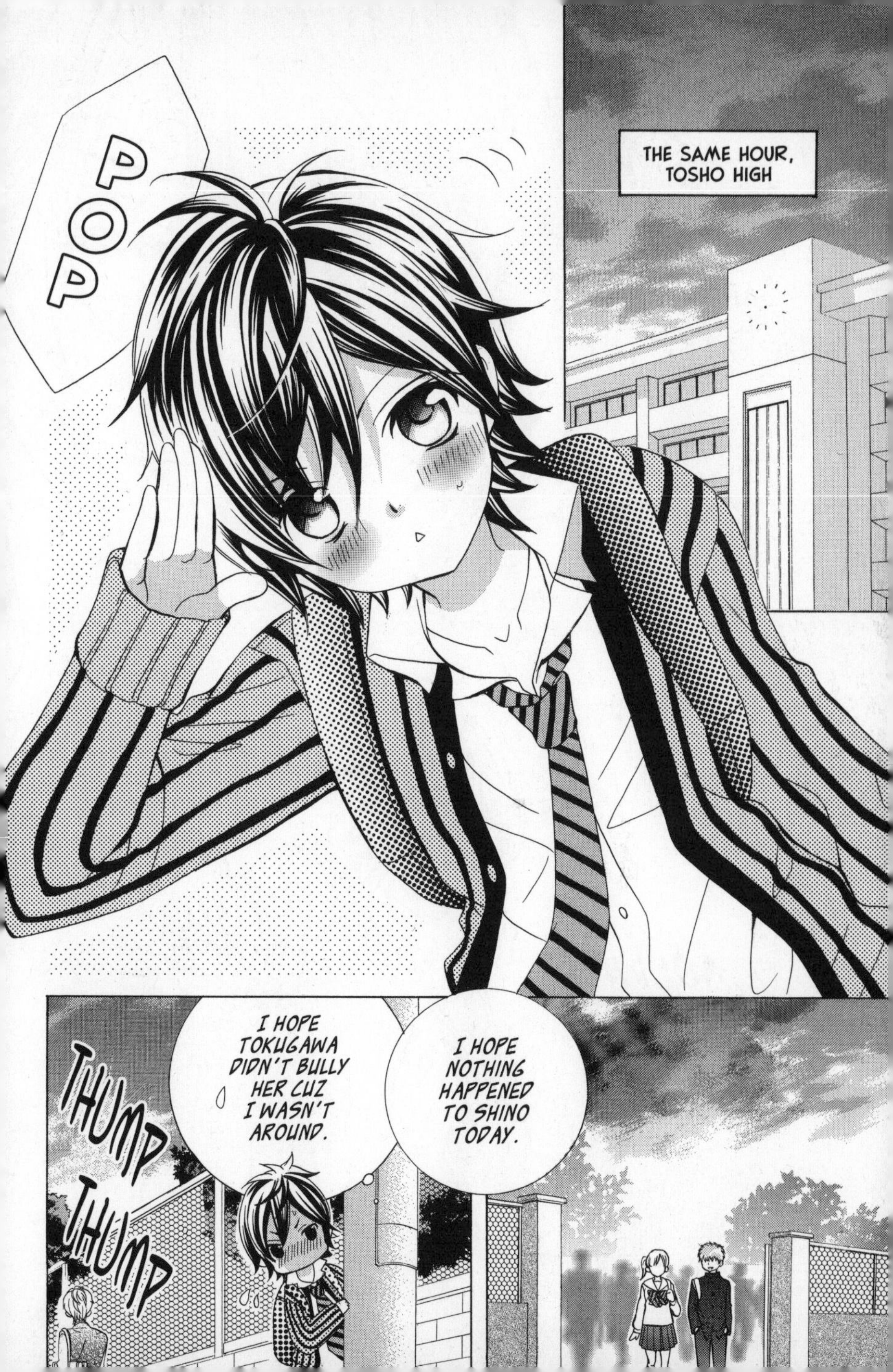
THE SAME HOUR, TOSHO HIGH
POP
I HOPE NOTHING HAPPENED TO SHINO TODAY.
I HOPE TOKUGAWA DIDN'T BULLY HER CUZ I WASN'T AROUND.
THUMP THUMP

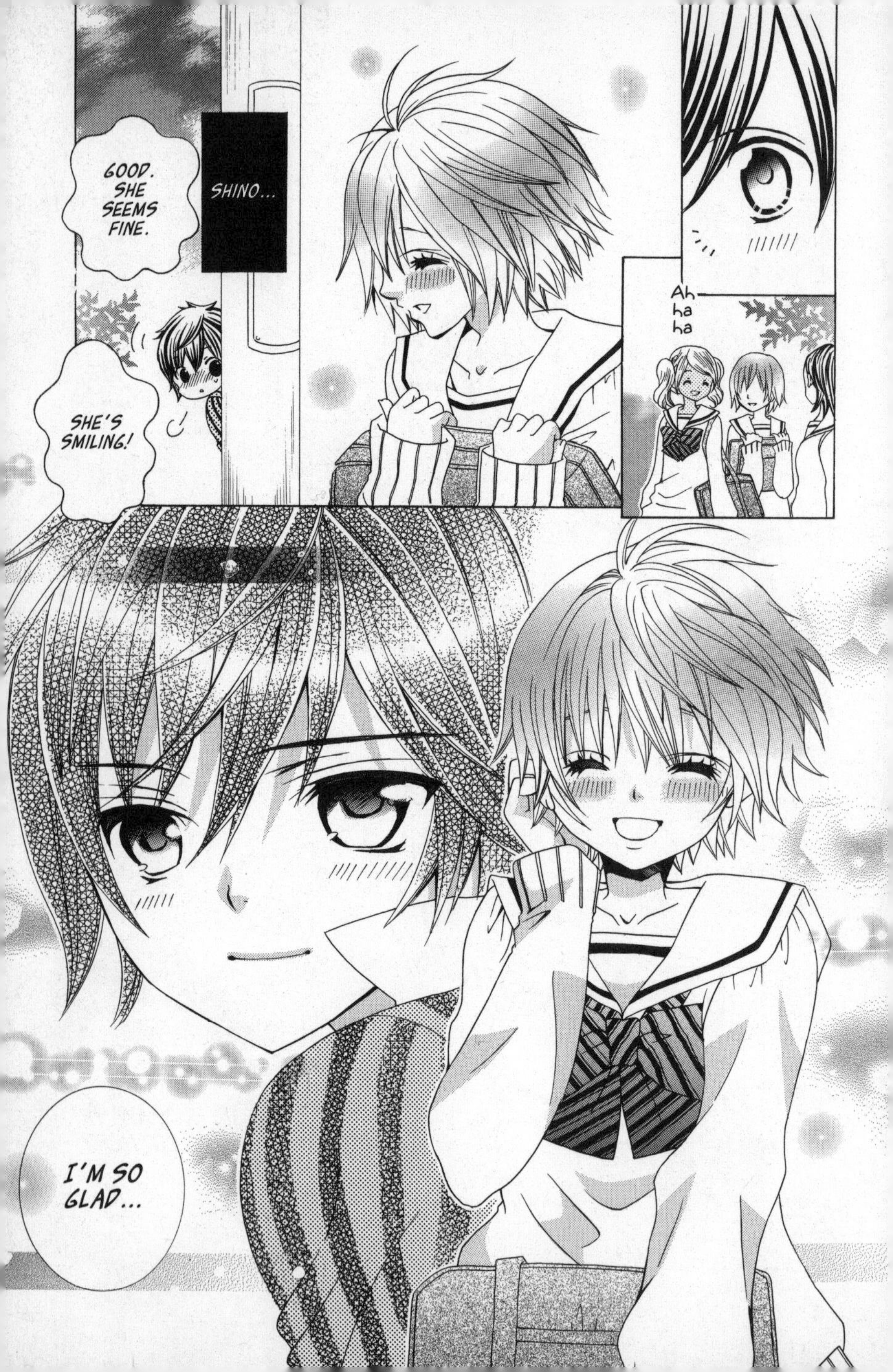

Ah ha ha
SHINO...
GOOD. SHE SEEMS FINE.
SHE'S SMILING!
I'M SO GLAD...

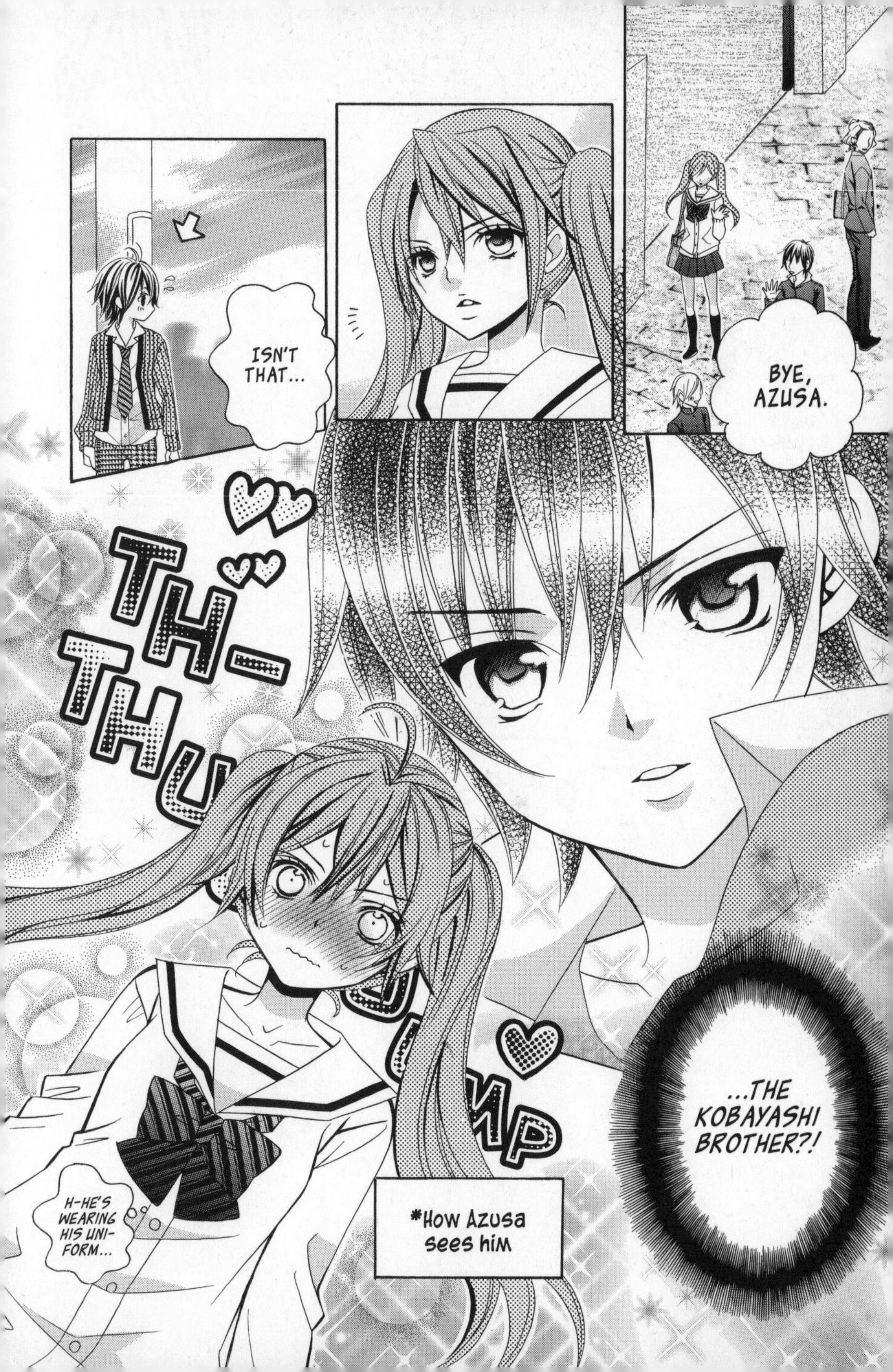
BYE, AZUSA.
ISN'T THAT...
...THE KOBAYASHI BROTHER?!
TH-THU
MP
*How Azusa sees him
H-HE'S WEARING HIS UNI-FORM...

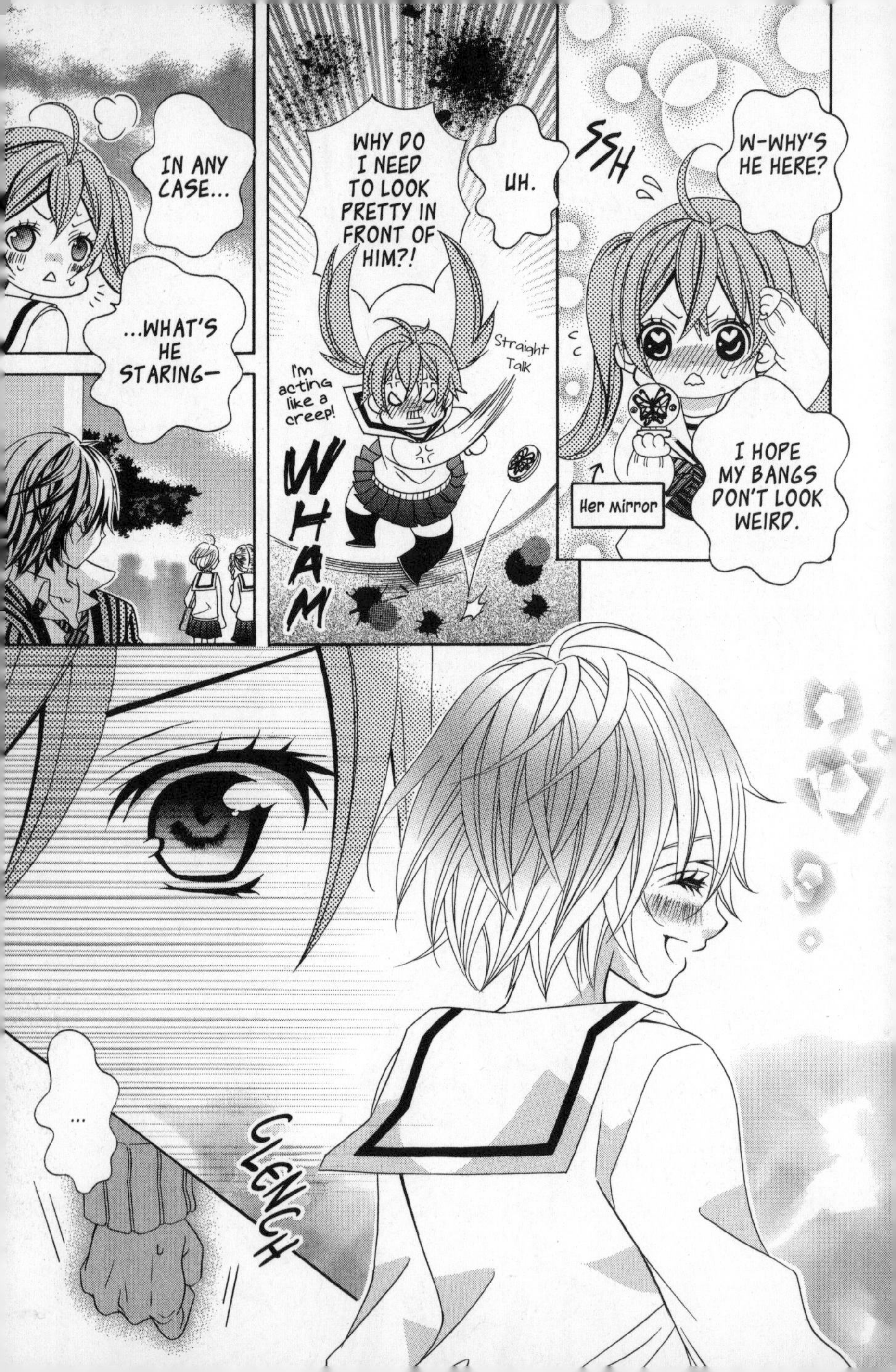
W-WHY'S HE HERE?
SSH
I HOPE MY BANGS DON'T LOOK WEIRD.
Her mirror
UH.
WHY DO I NEED TO LOOK PRETTY IN FRONT OF HIM?!
Straight Talk
I'm acting like a creep!
WHAM
IN ANY CASE...
...WHAT'S HE STARING—
...
CLENCH

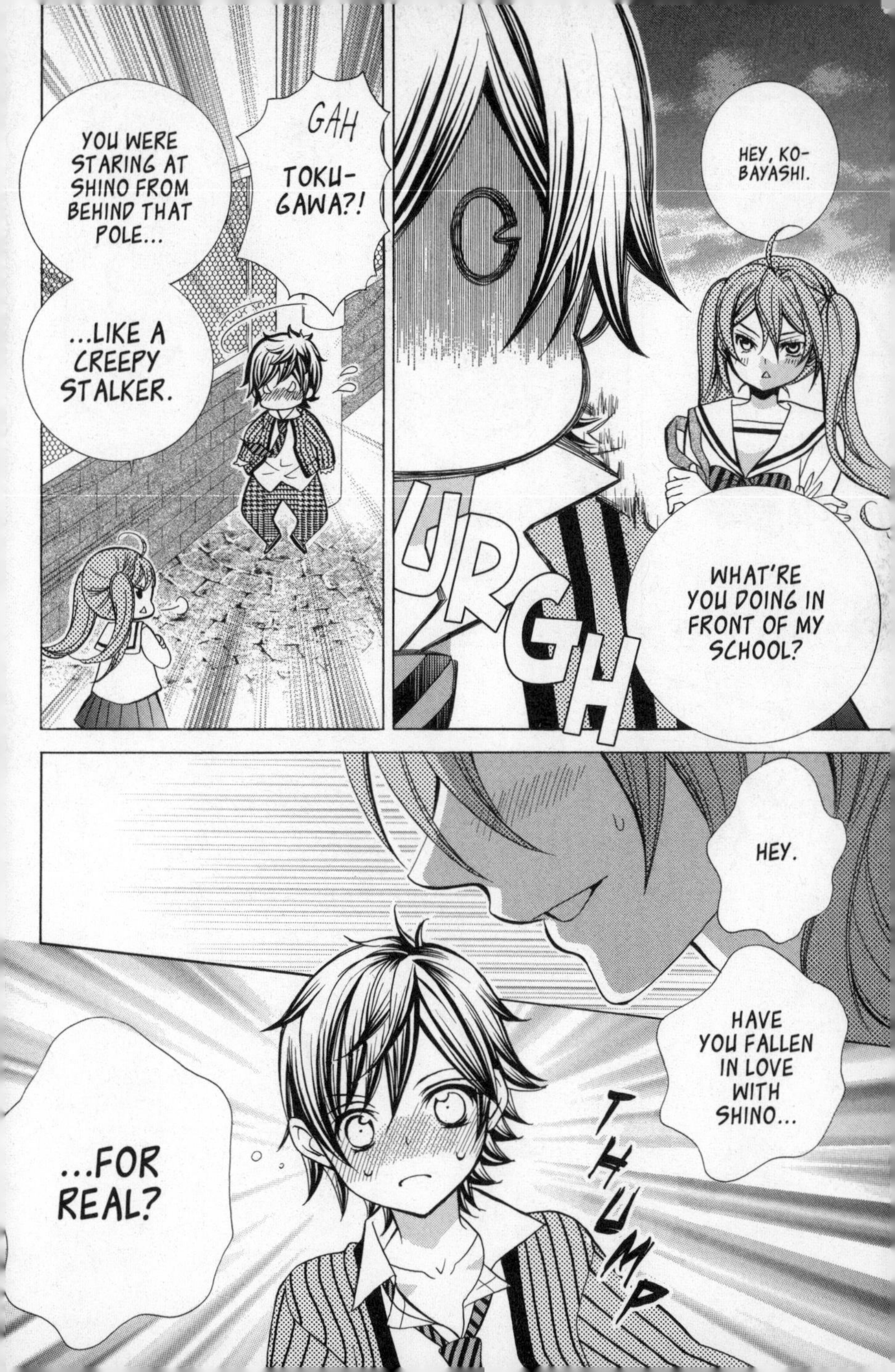
HEY, KO-BAYASHI.
WHAT'RE YOU DOING IN FRONT OF MY SCHOOL?
URGH
GAH
TOKU-GAWA?!
YOU WERE STARING AT SHINO FROM BEHIND THAT POLE...
...LIKE A CREEPY STALKER.
HEY.
HAVE YOU FALLEN IN LOVE WITH SHINO...
THUMP
...FOR REAL?

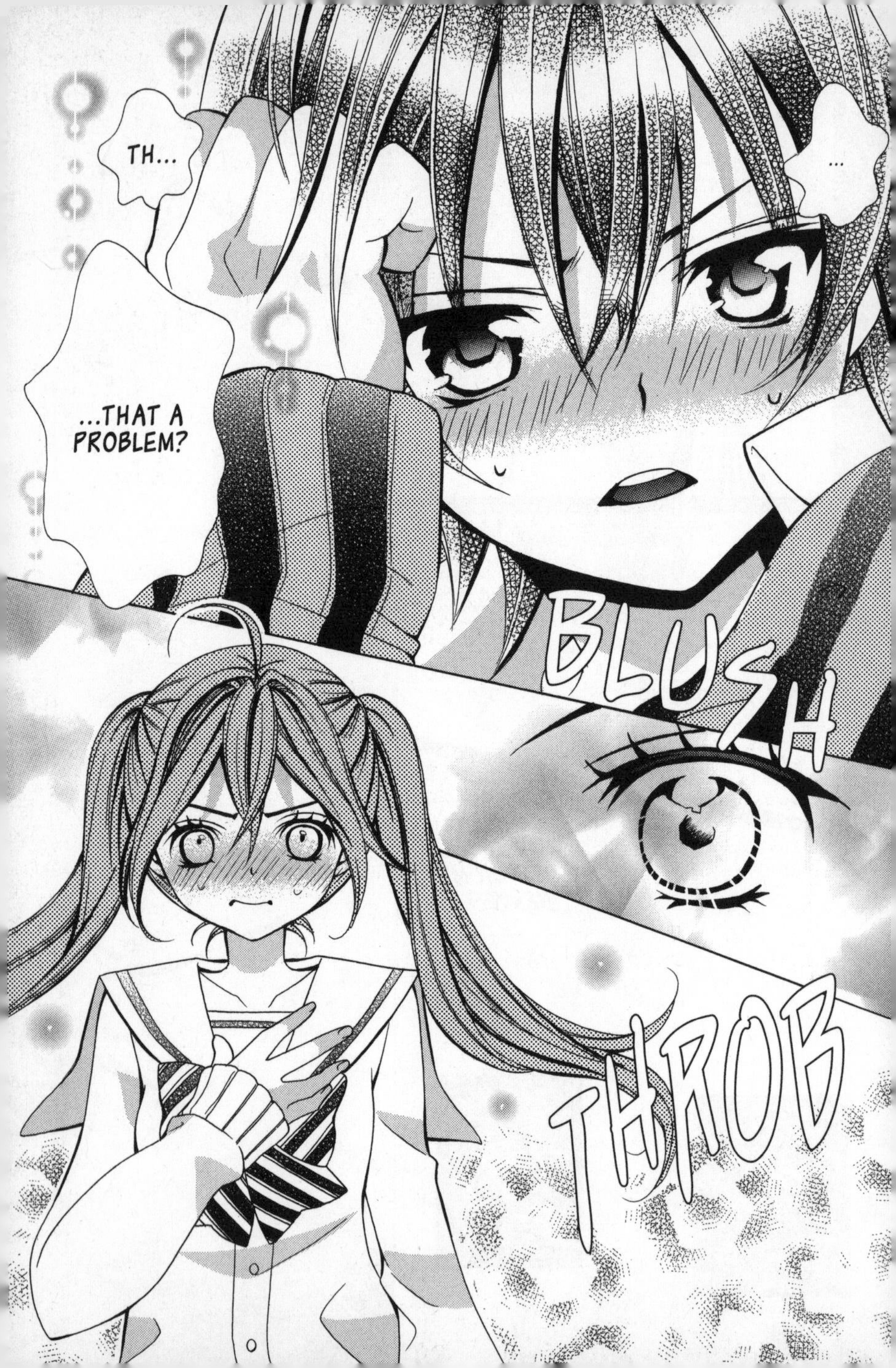
...
TH...
...THAT A PROBLEM?
BLUSH
THROB

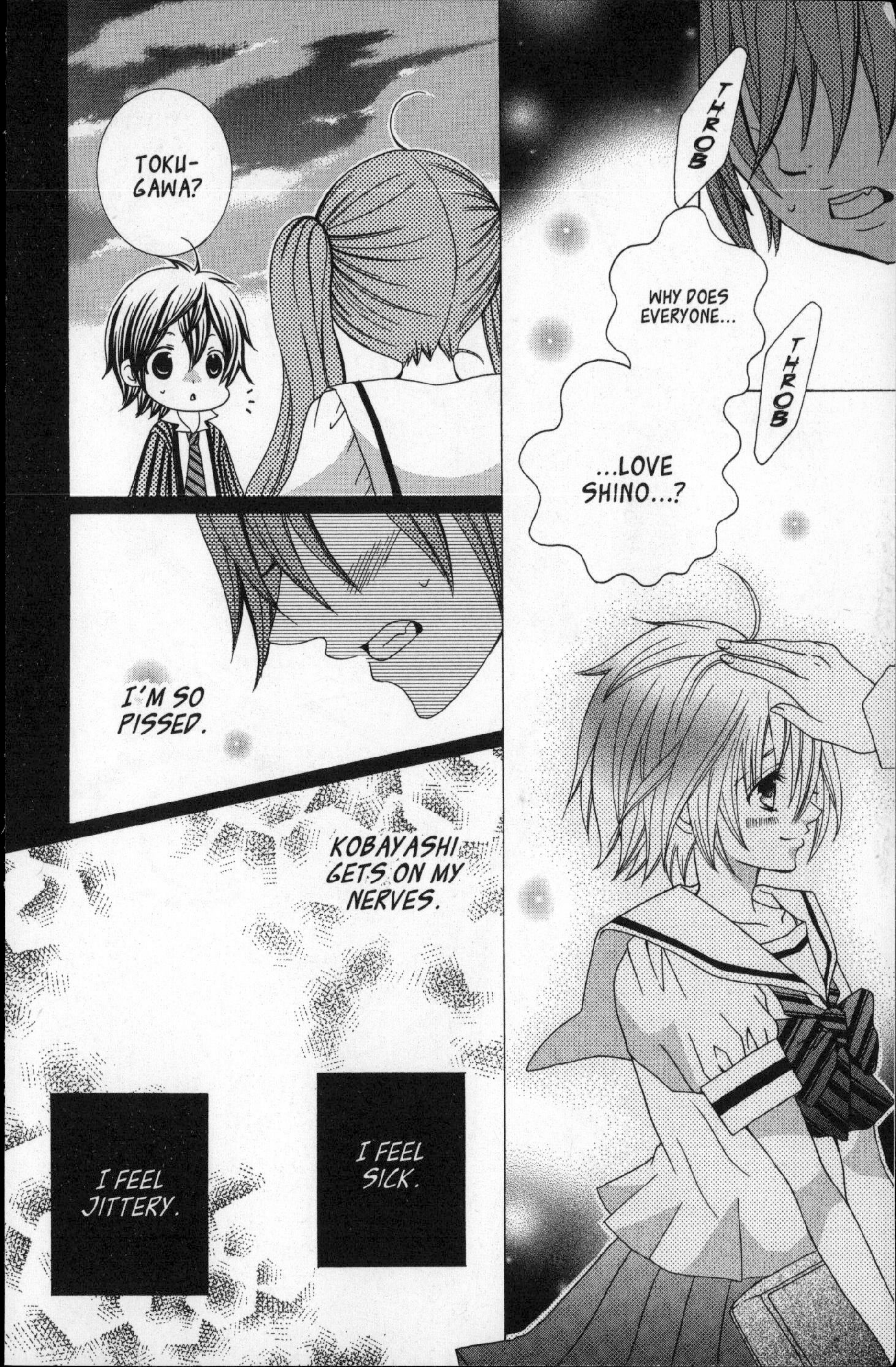
THROB
WHY DOES EVERYONE...
THROB
...LOVE SHINO...?
TOKU-GAWA?
I'M SO PISSED.
KOBAYASHI GETS ON MY NERVES.
I FEEL SICK.
I FEEL JITTERY.

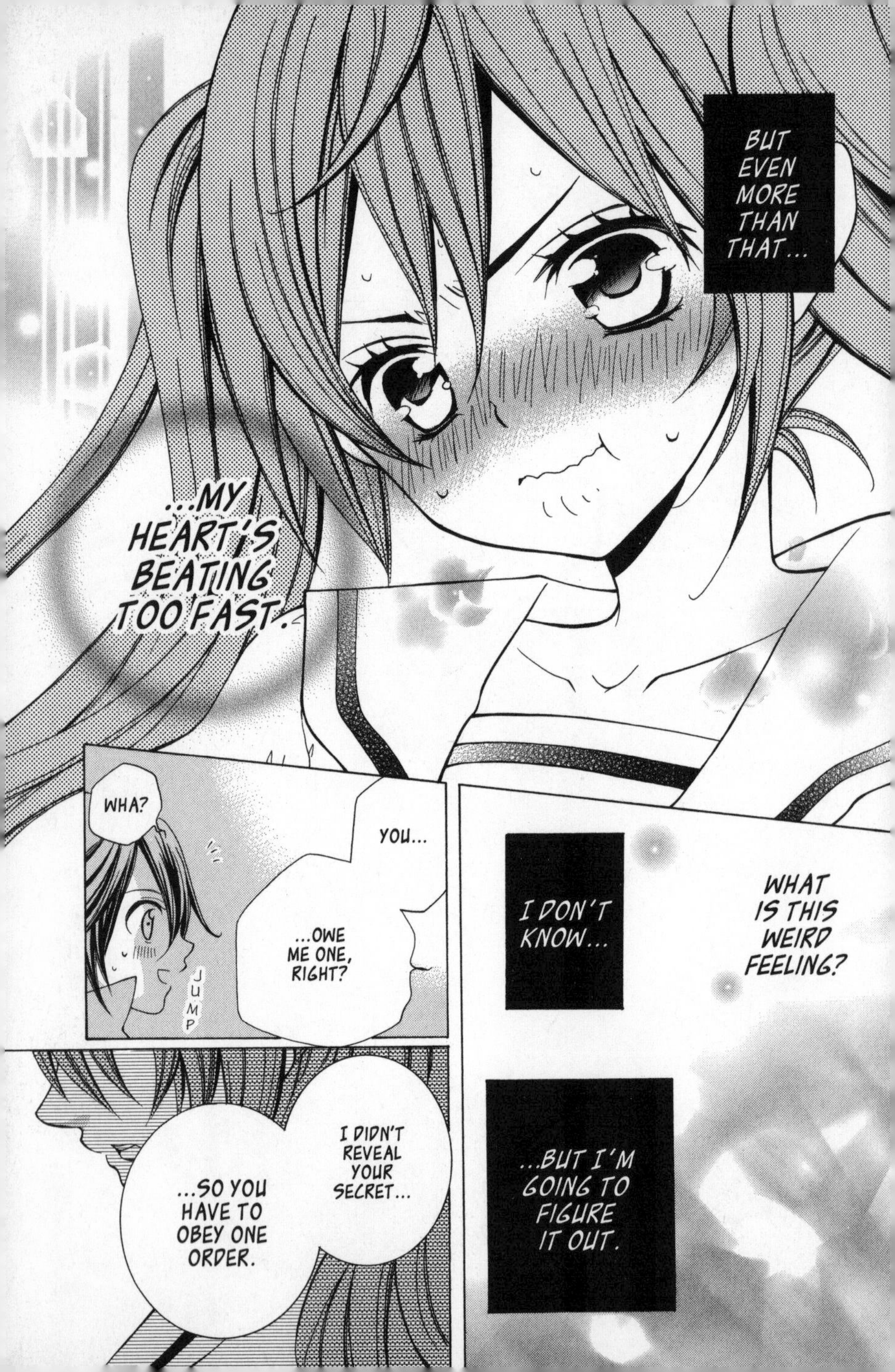

BUT EVEN MORE THAN THAT...
...MY HEART'S BEATING TOO FAST.
WHAT IS THIS WEIRD FEELING?
I DON'T KNOW...
...BUT I'M GOING TO FIGURE IT OUT.
YOU...
...OWE ME ONE, RIGHT?
WHA?
JUMP
I DIDN'T REVEAL YOUR SECRET...
...SO YOU HAVE TO OBEY ONE ORDER.

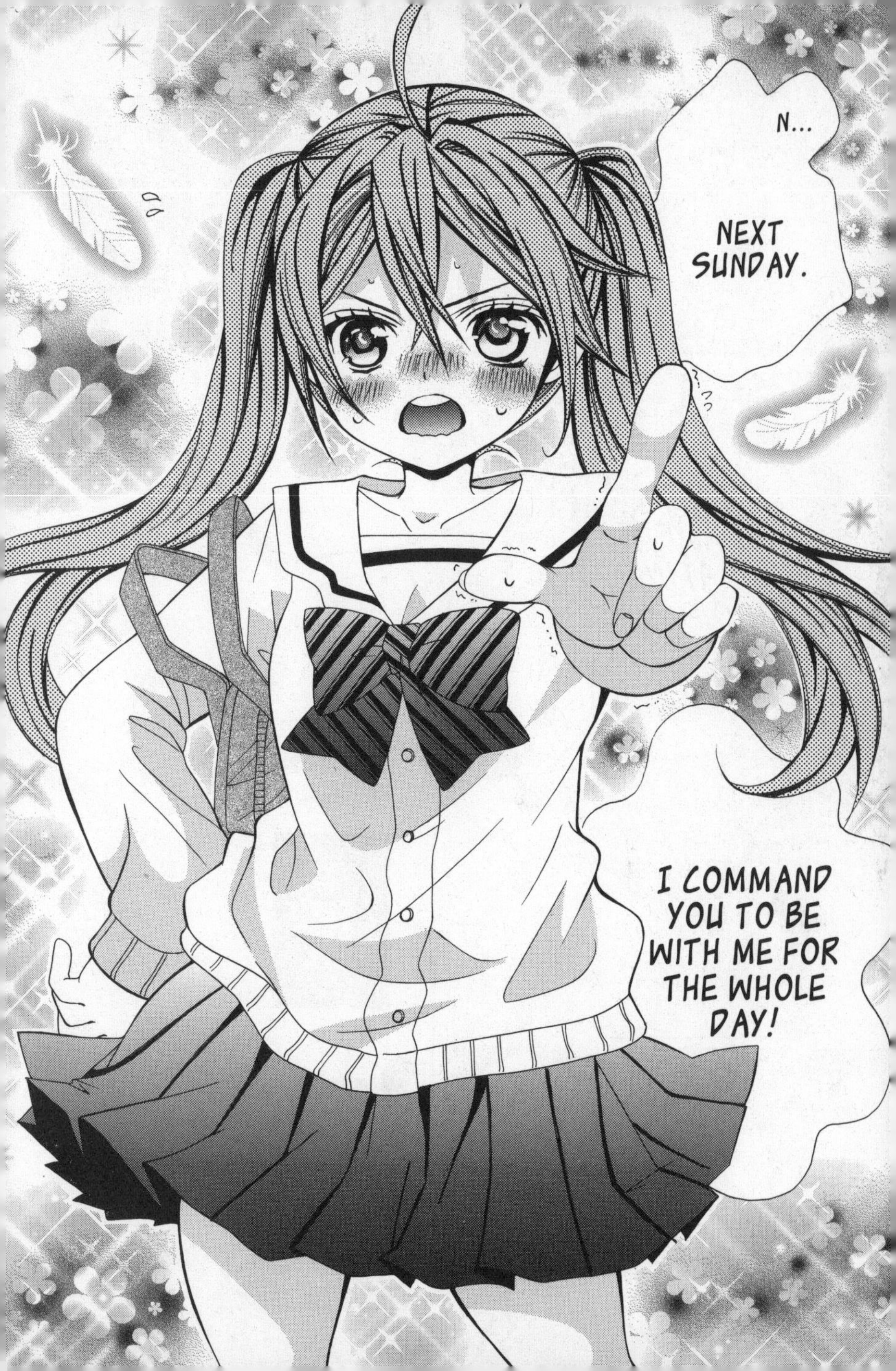
N... NEXT SUNDAY.
I COMMAND YOU TO BE WITH ME FOR THE WHOLE DAY!

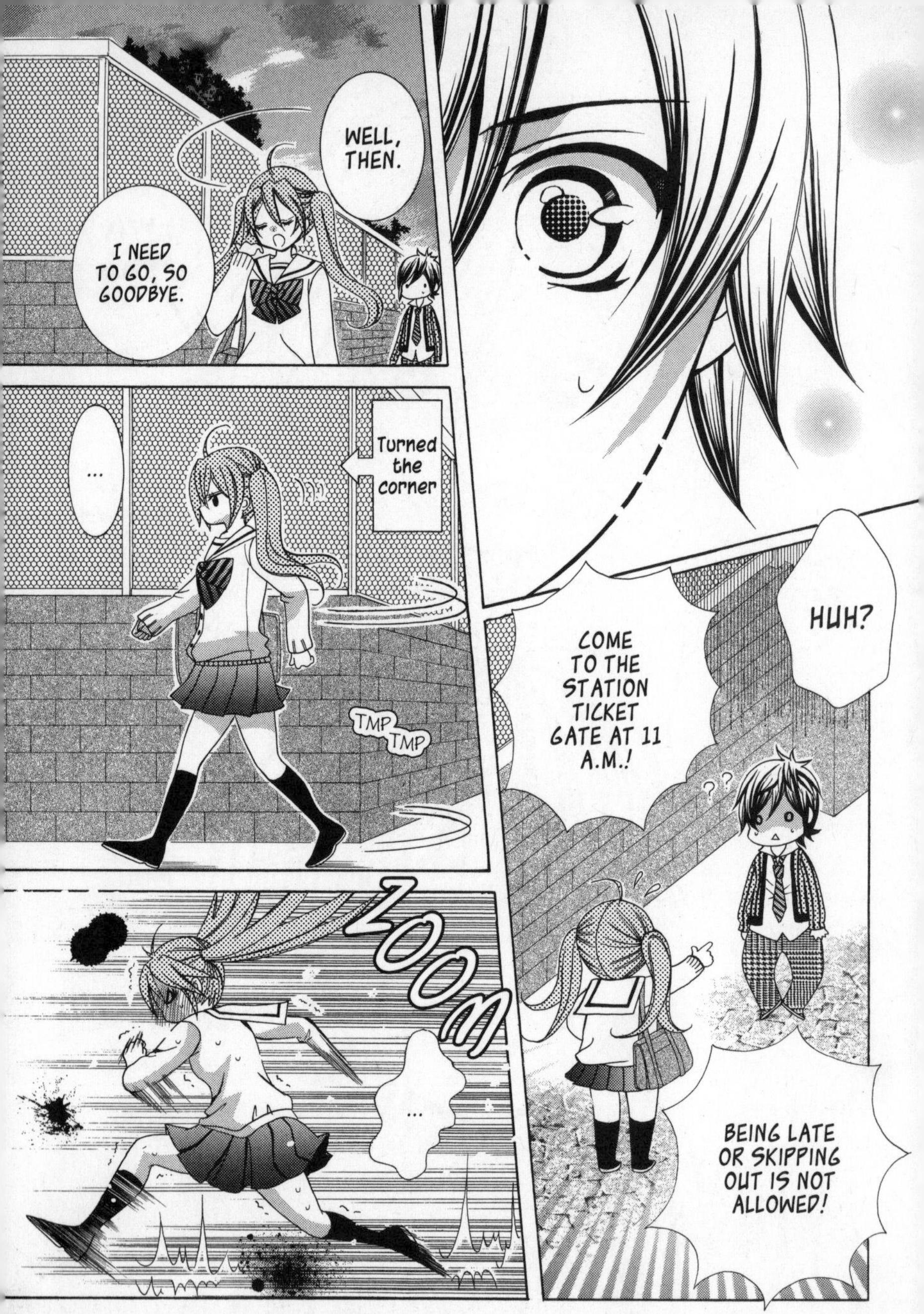
WELL, THEN.
I NEED TO GO, SO GOODBYE.
Turned the corner
...
TMP TMP
HUH?
COME TO THE STATION TICKET GATE AT 11 A.M.!
BEING LATE OR SKIPPING OUT IS NOT ALLOWED!
ZOOM
...

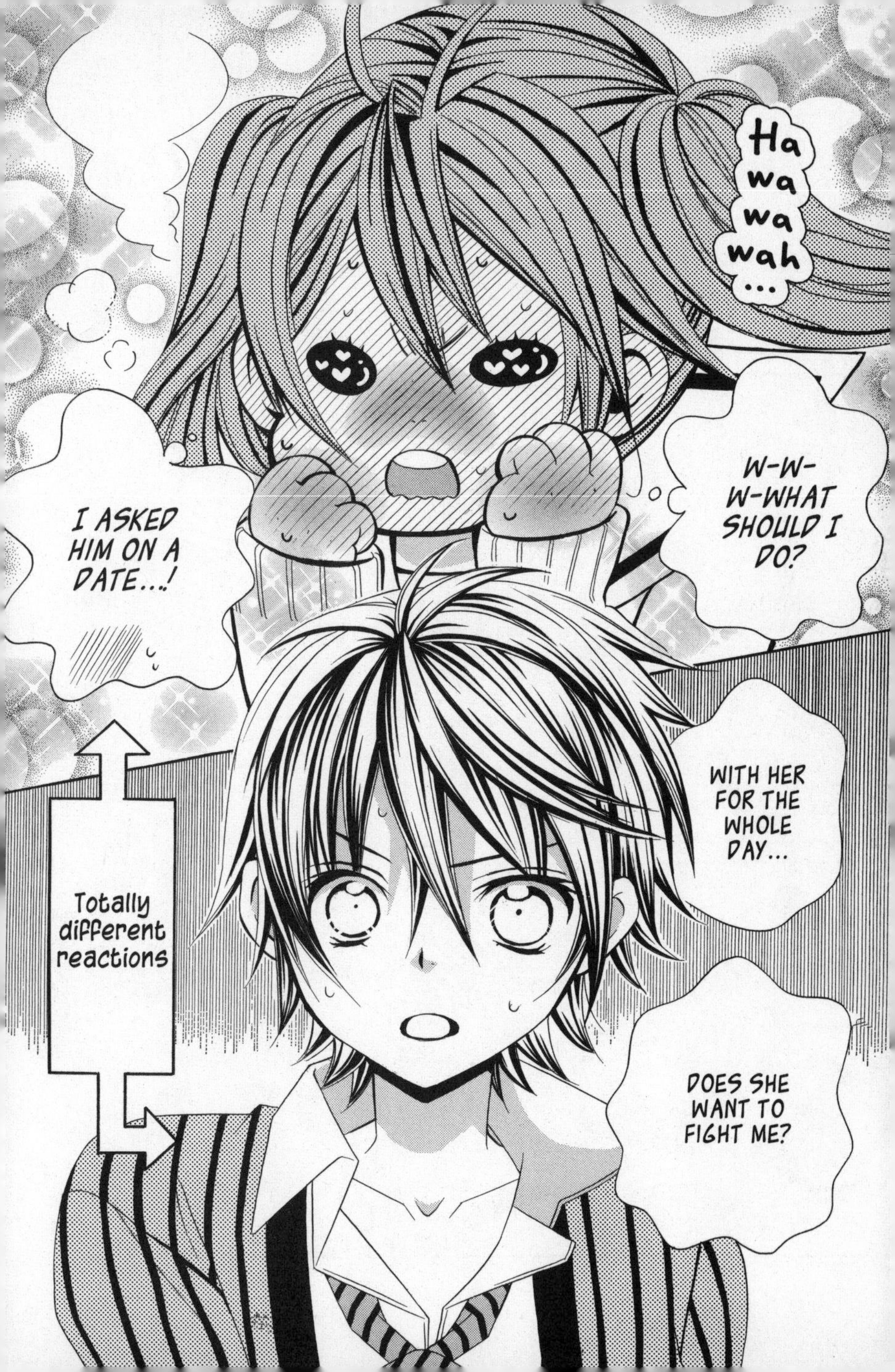
Ha wa wa wah...
W-W-W-WHAT SHOULD I DO?
I ASKED HIM ON A DATE...!
WITH HER FOR THE WHOLE DAY...
DOES SHE WANT TO FIGHT ME?
Totally different reactions

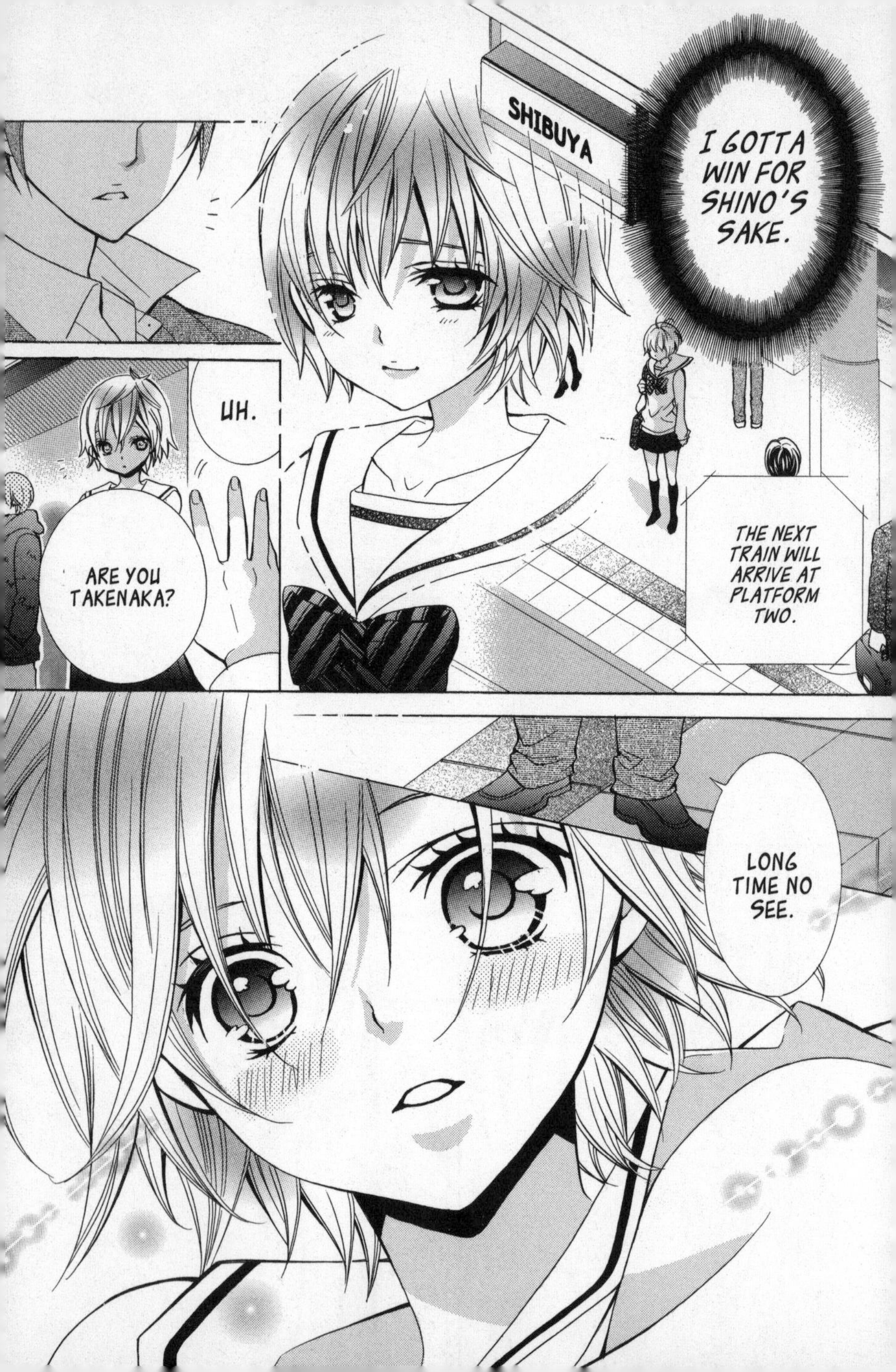
SHIBUYA
I GOTTA WIN FOR SHINO'S SAKE.
THE NEXT TRAIN WILL ARRIVE AT PLATFORM TWO.
UH.
ARE YOU TAKENAKA?
LONG TIME NO SEE.

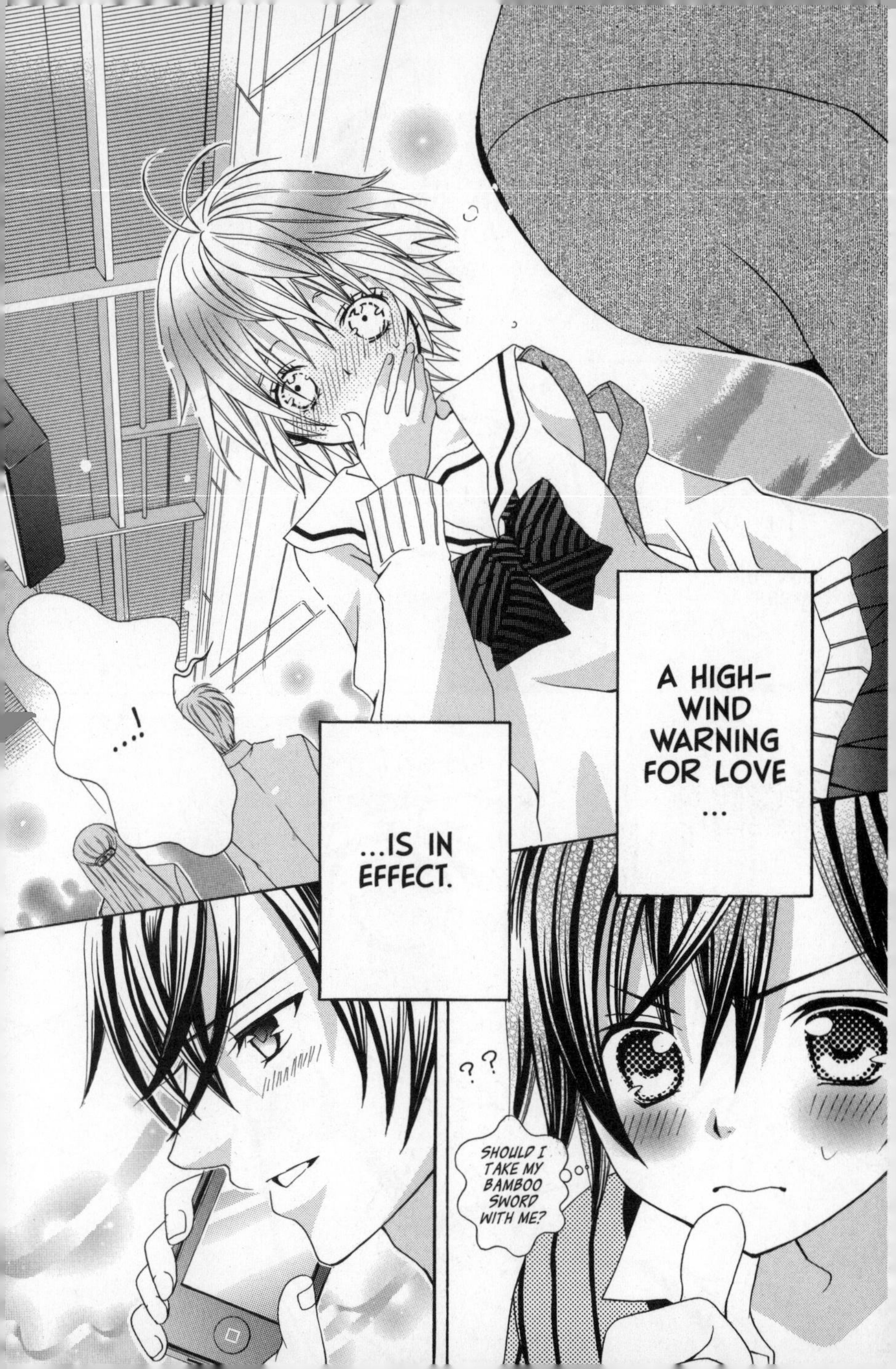
...!
A HIGH-WIND WARNING FOR LOVE...
...IS IN EFFECT.
??
SHOULD I TAKE MY BAMBOO SWORD WITH ME?

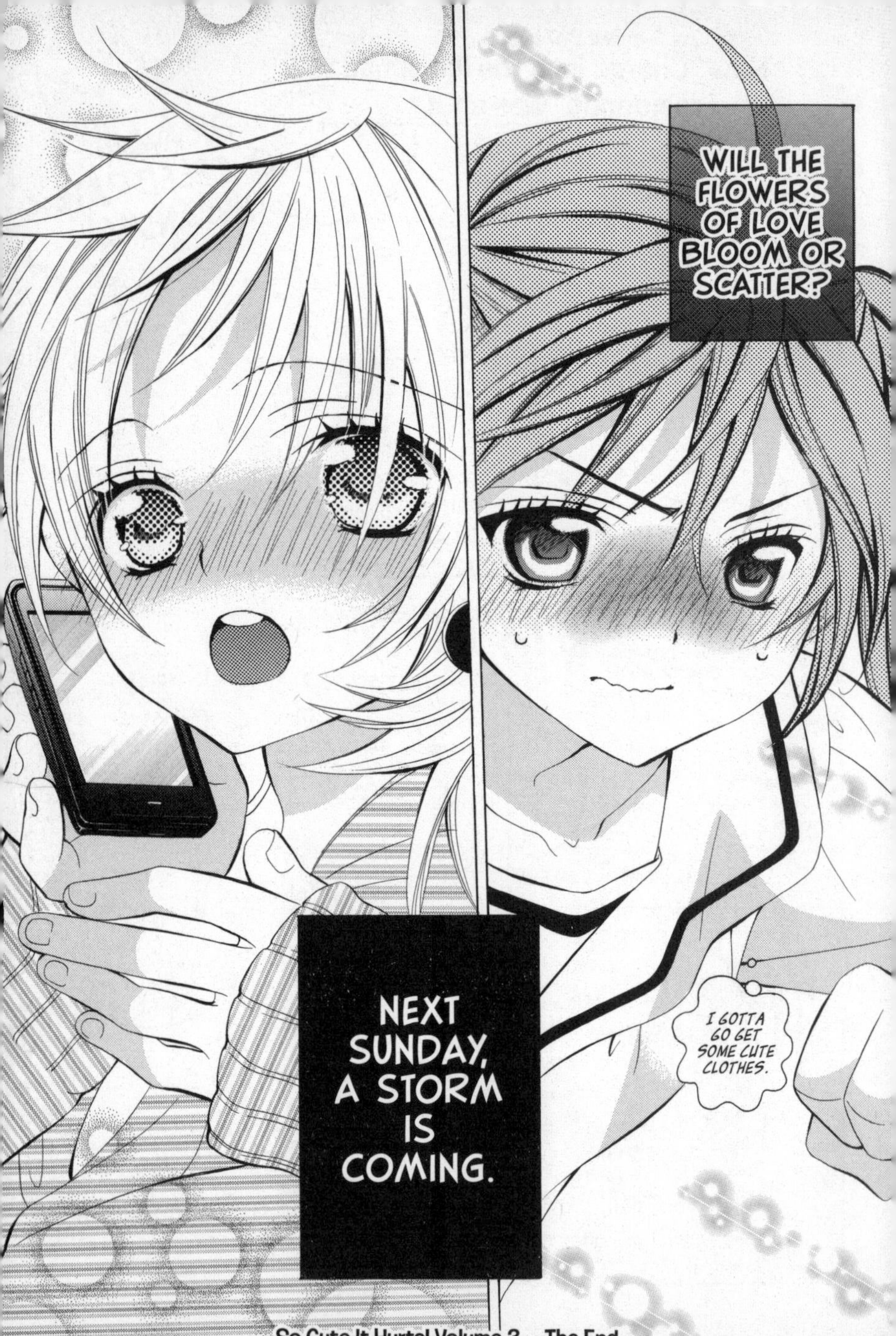
WILL THE FLOWERS OF LOVE BLOOM OR SCATTER?
I GOTTA GO GET SOME CUTE CLOTHES.
NEXT SUNDAY, A STORM IS COMING.

So Cute It Hurts! Volume 3 ~The End~

Volume 3 anime DVD bonus

~How "Charge into the Ikeyamada residence" was shot~

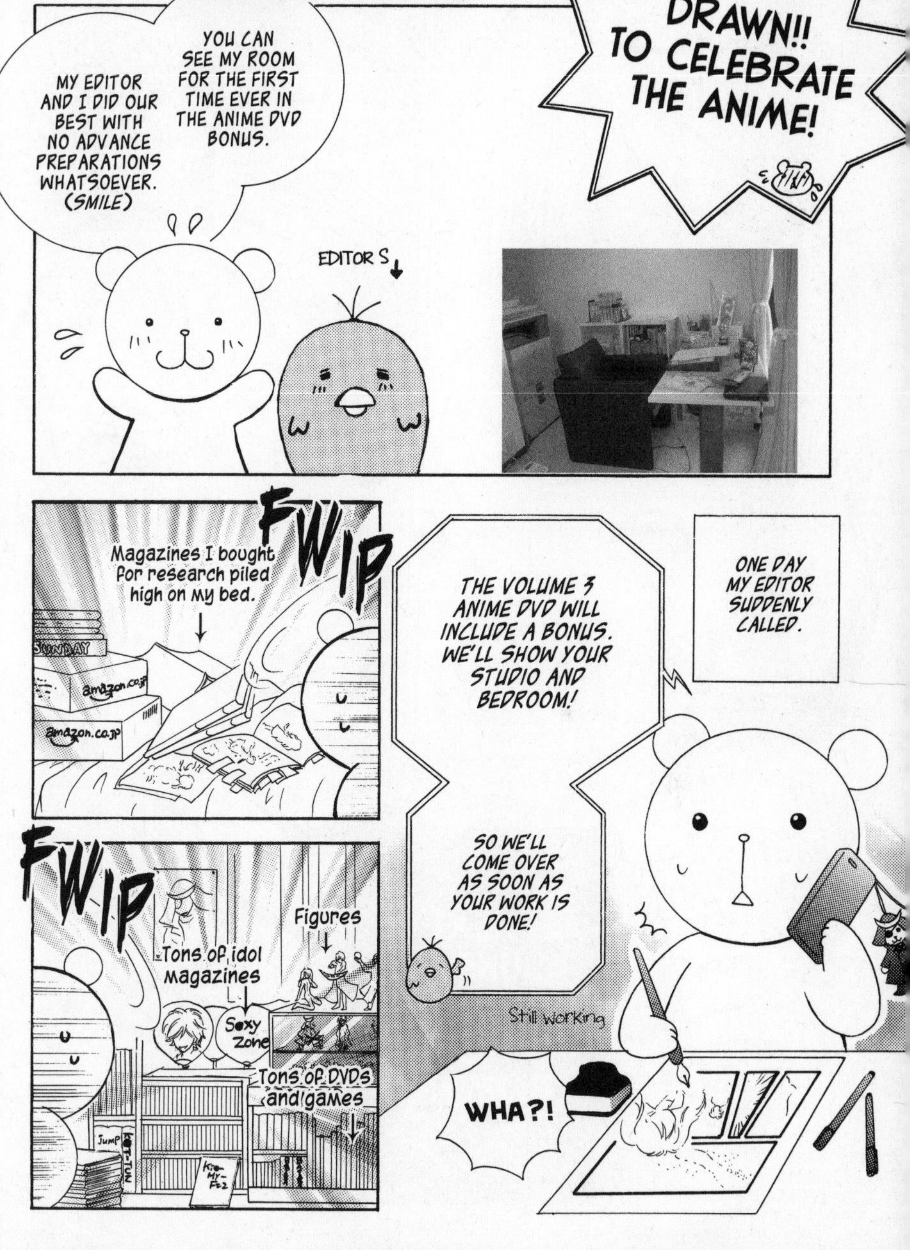
DRAWN!! TO CELEBRATE THE ANIME!
YOU CAN SEE MY ROOM FOR THE FIRST TIME EVER IN THE ANIME DVD BONUS.
MY EDITOR AND I DID OUR BEST WITH NO ADVANCE PREPARATIONS WHATSOEVER. (SMILE)
EDITOR S
ONE DAY MY EDITOR SUDDENLY CALLED.
THE VOLUME 3 ANIME DVD WILL INCLUDE A BONUS. WE'LL SHOW YOUR STUDIO AND BEDROOM!
SO WE'LL COME OVER AS SOON AS YOUR WORK IS DONE!
Still working
WHA?!
FWIP
Magazines I bought for research piled high on my bed.
SUNDAY
amazon.co.jp
amazon.co.jp
FWIP
Figures
Tons of idol magazines
Sexy Zone
Tons of DVDs and games
Jump

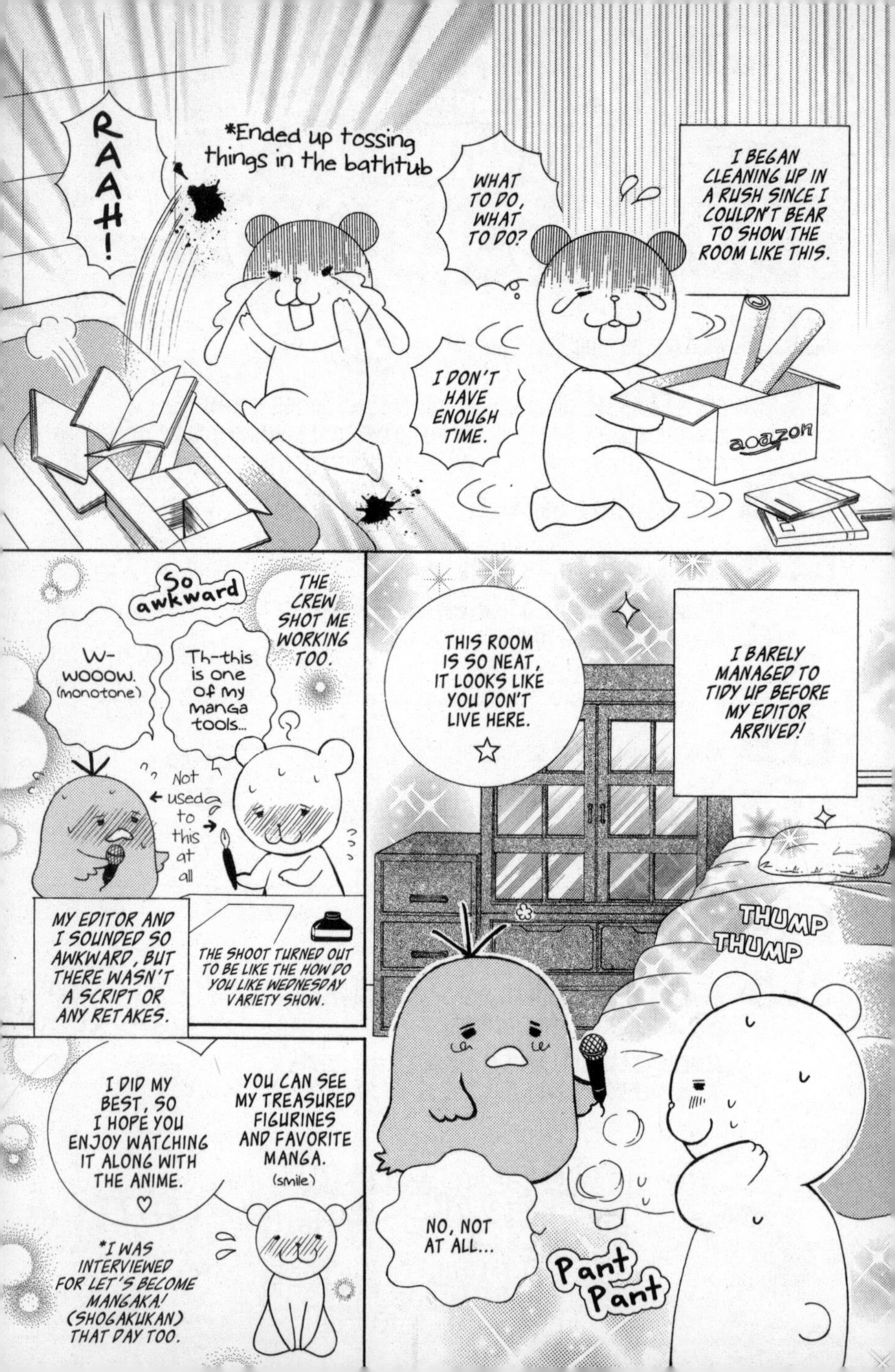
I BEGAN CLEANING UP IN A RUSH SINCE I COULDN'T BEAR TO SHOW THE ROOM LIKE THIS.
WHAT TO DO, WHAT TO DO?
I DON'T HAVE ENOUGH TIME.
*Ended up tossing things in the bathtub
RAAH!
I BARELY MANAGED TO TIDY UP BEFORE MY EDITOR ARRIVED!
THIS ROOM IS SO NEAT, IT LOOKS LIKE YOU DON'T LIVE HERE. ☆
THUMP THUMP
NO, NOT AT ALL...
Pant Pant
THE CREW SHOT ME WORKING TOO.
So awkward
Th-this is one of my manga tools...
W-WOOOW. (monotone)
Not used to this at all
THE SHOOT TURNED OUT TO BE LIKE THE HOW DO YOU LIKE WEDNESDAY VARIETY SHOW.
MY EDITOR AND I SOUNDED SO AWKWARD, BUT THERE WASN'T A SCRIPT OR ANY RETAKES.
YOU CAN SEE MY TREASURED FIGURINES AND FAVORITE MANGA. (smile)
I DID MY BEST, SO I HOPE YOU ENJOY WATCHING IT ALONG WITH THE ANIME. ♡
*I WAS INTERVIEWED FOR LET'S BECOME MANGAKA! (SHOGAKUKAN) THAT DAY TOO.

GO-CHAN INTERVIEWS MR. DAISUKE ONO!!

 PLAYED AOI

Q1 WHAT DO YOU THINK ABOUT THE MANGA?

A1 THIS IS **CLASSIC** SHOJO MANGA. I CAN PROUDLY SAY THIS IS WHAT ROMANTIC COMEDY SHOULD BE AND WOULD LIKE TO RECOMMEND IT TO EVERYONE.

Q2 WHAT WAS IT LIKE PLAYING AOI?

A2 AOI LOOKS COOL, BUT HE'S **PURE** INSIDE. I MADE SURE I PLAYED IT **STRAIGHTFORWARD** WHENEVER HIS HEART WAVERED.

Q3 WHO'S YOUR FAVORITE *SO CUTE!* HEROINE?!

A3 **MEGUMU**'S CUTE NO MATTER WHAT SHE DOES! SHE'S **TOO CUTE IT HURTS!!** (*SMILE*)

Q4 A MESSAGE TO THE READERS PLEASE!

A4 AN ANIME DVD WAS MADE BECAUSE EVERYONE SUPPORTED THIS SERIES! THANK YOU SO MUCH!

SOMETHING **MUCH, MUCH BIGGER** MAY HAPPEN IF YOU KEEP ROOTING FOR IT! KEEP READING *SO CUTE!*

YOU GOTTA SEE THE "MEGO AND AOI'S FIRST KISS♡" SCENE!!

MR. ONO'S LOW VOICE ECHOES IN THE READERS' #1 FAVORITE SCENE!!

So Cute It Hurts!! volume 3 special version with anime DVD 1,350 yen (sales tax included) on sale in Japan now!

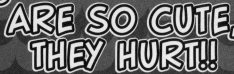

EVERYONE'S DRAWINGS ARE SO CUTE, THEY HURT!!

So Cute! Fan Art Feature ♥

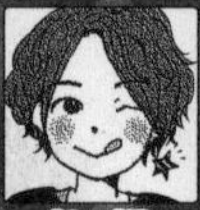

Shojii

Editor Shojii has commented on each one this time too!!

We received so many super-cute drawings, we'll show you more than last time! (>_<)

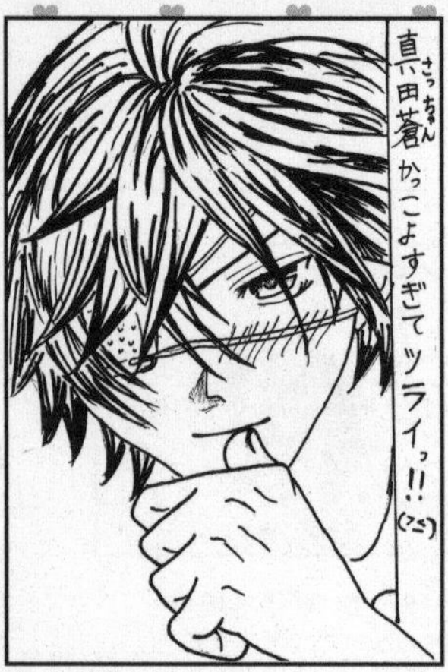
真田蒼 かっこよすぎてツライッ!!
(>_<)

Uppie (Hyogo) ↑

Ed: Hey, Aoi is so sexy it hurts!!

Micchie (Yamaguchi)

Ed: A passionate message for both So Cute! & GO-chan. ♡ →

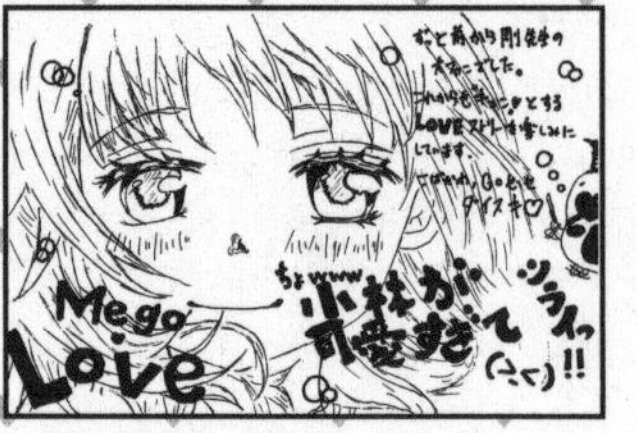
Mego Love
小林が可愛すぎてツライッ!!

Snow Rabbit (Nagano)

Ed: So Cute's two heroes face each other. ♥ ←

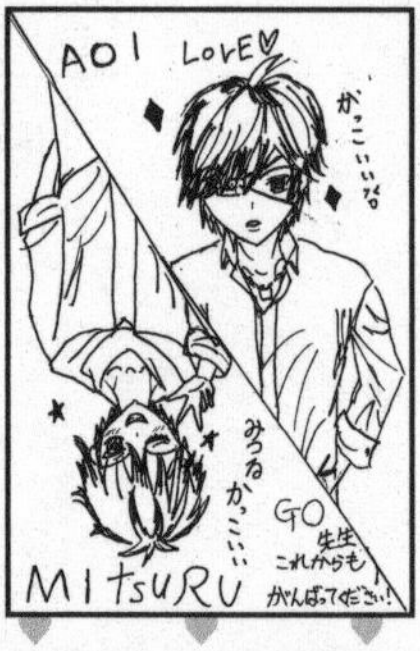
AOI LOVE♡
MITSURU
GO先生 これからもがんばってください!

H·M (Nagasaki)

Ed: Aoi's struggling expression is so moe! ↓

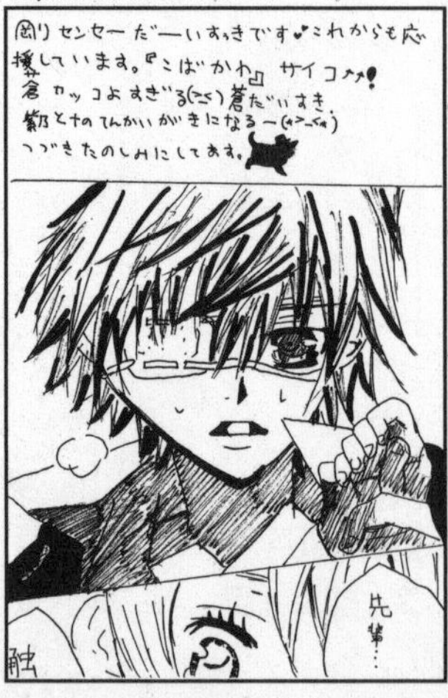

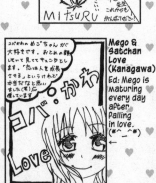

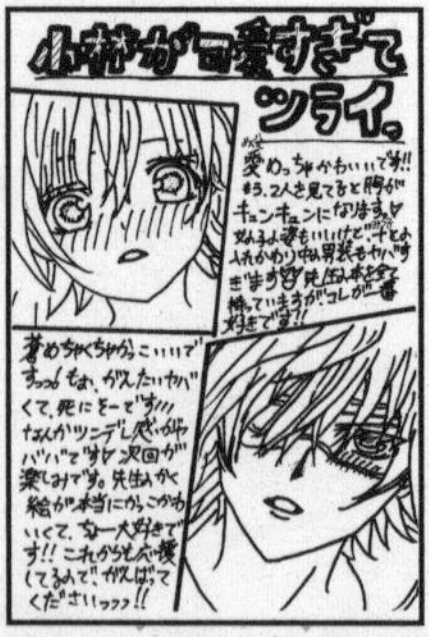
小林が可愛すぎてツライ。

Mizuki Tomizawa (Kanagawa)

Ed: Mego & Aoi are the best!! ↑

Mego & Satchan Love (Kanagawa)

Ed: Mego is maturing every day after falling in love. (*^_^*) ←

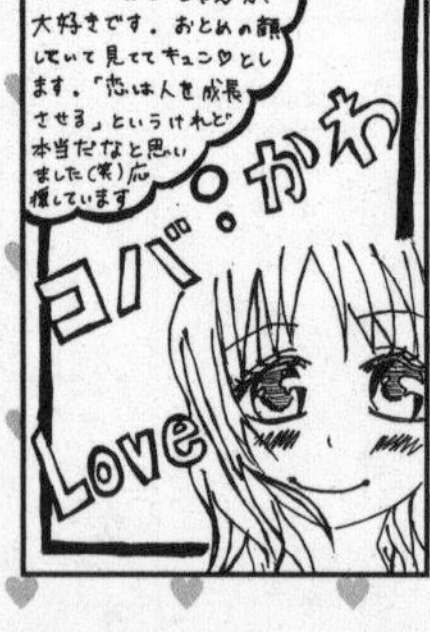
コバ。かわ
Love

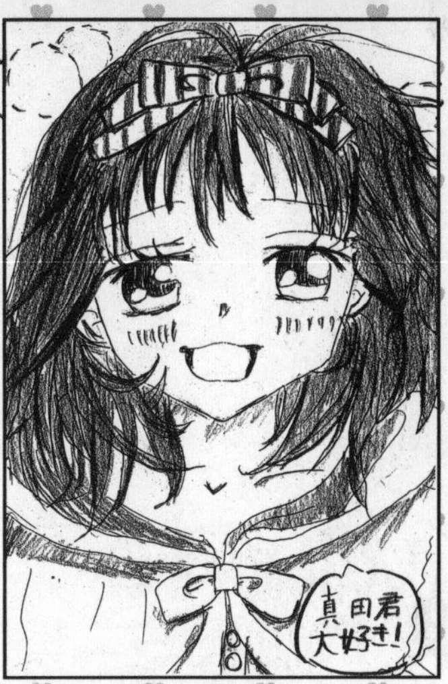
真田君大好き!

Sayaka Tosaka (Aichi)

Ed: Mego's smile makes everyone smile!

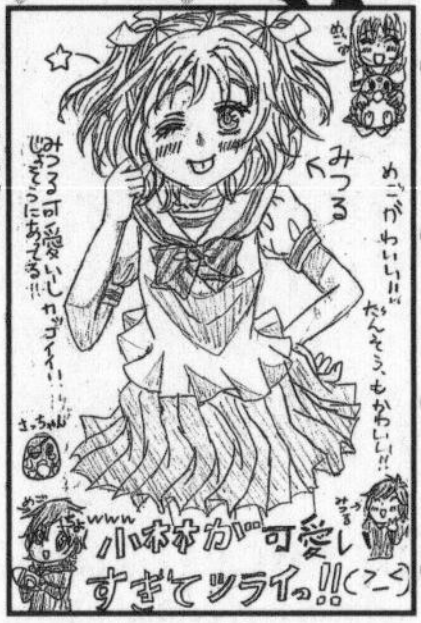
みつる
めごかわいい!!
小林が可愛しすぎてツライっ!!(>_<)

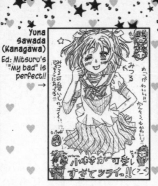

Yuna Sawada (Kanagawa)

Ed: Mitsuru's "my bad" is perfect!!

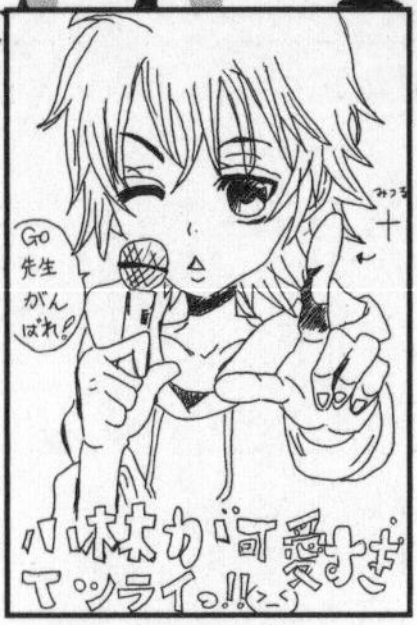
GO先生がんばれ!
小林が可愛すぎてツライっ!!(>_<)

Mitchan (Ehime) ↑

Ed: The karaoke scene was such a party!

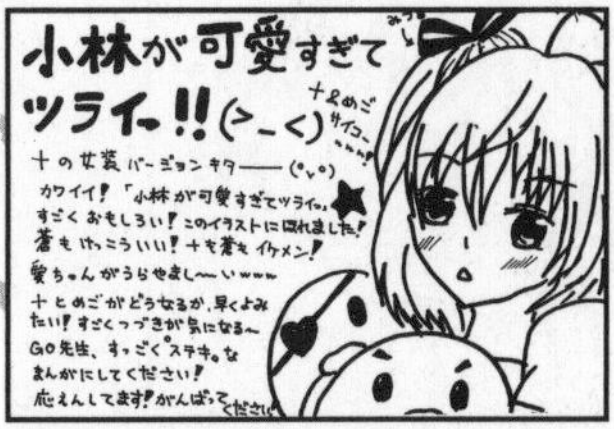
小林が可愛すぎてツライ!!(>_<)
十の女装バージョンキター
カワイイ!「小林が可愛すぎてツライ」すごくおもしろい!
GO先生、すごくステキなまんがにしてください!

Yuri (Mie)

Ed: Mitsuru's particular about wearing ribbons?!

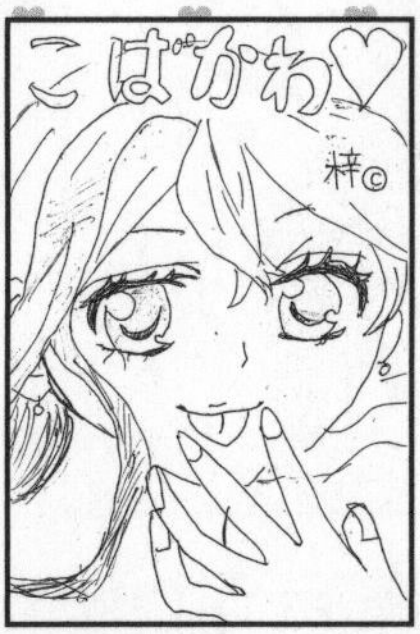
こばかわ♡

Kaori Tsutagoshi (Toyama)

Ed: Heeeereeee's what the queen looks like in public...!!

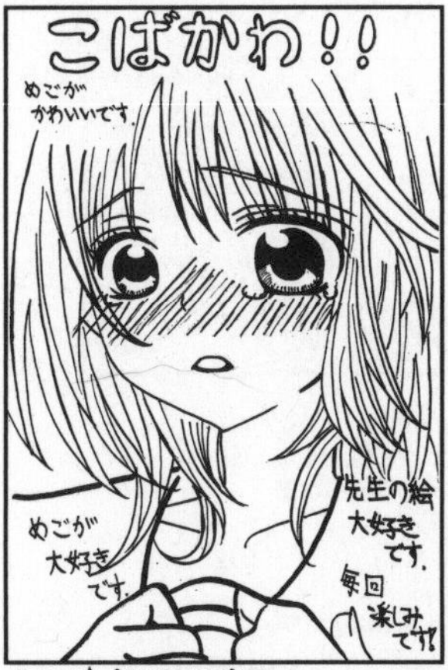
こばかわ!!
めごがかわいいです。
先生の絵大好きです。
めごが大好きです。
毎回楽しみです!

Pako☆ (Saitama) ↑

Ed: Mego's teary eyes look too cute!!

Princess Bea (Shiga)

Ed: A full-length portrait has punch. ♪

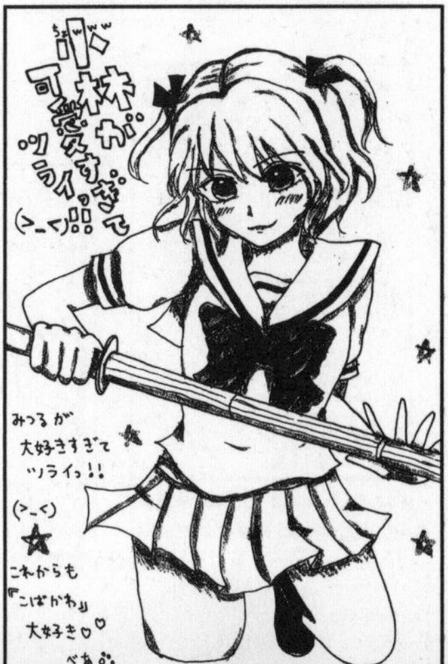
小林が可愛すぎてツライっ!!(>_<)
みつるが大好きすぎてツライっ!!
これからも「こばかわ」大好き♡
べあ

Kyosshii★ (Saitama)

Ed: Eye patch and cat ears?!

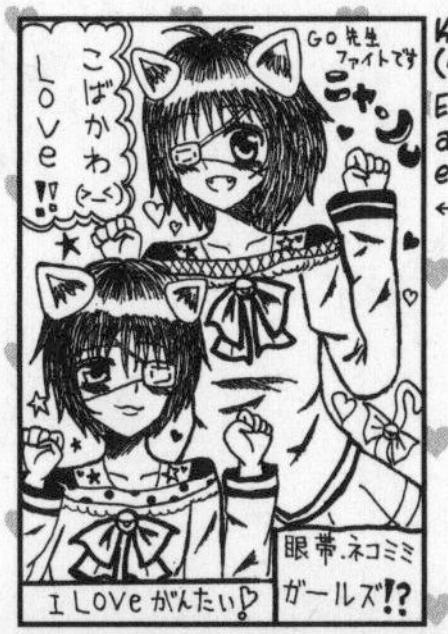
GO先生ファイトです ニャン
こばかわLove!!
眼帯ネコミミガールズ!?
I Love がんたい♡

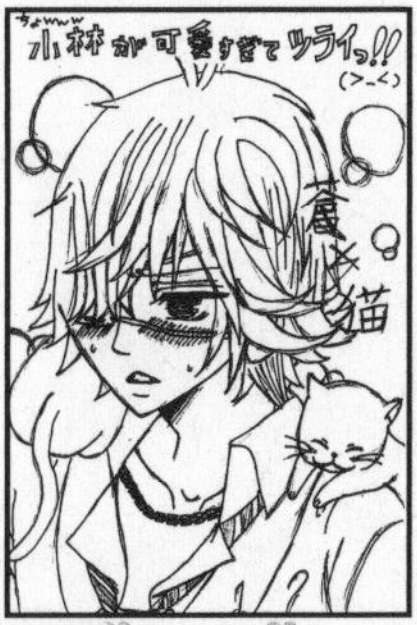
小林が可愛すぎてツライっ!!(>_<)

Misa (Osaka) ↑

Ed: Cats and yanki... a classic combo!

Nanami Asano (Gifu)
Ed: Do you really love Azusa...? (smile) →

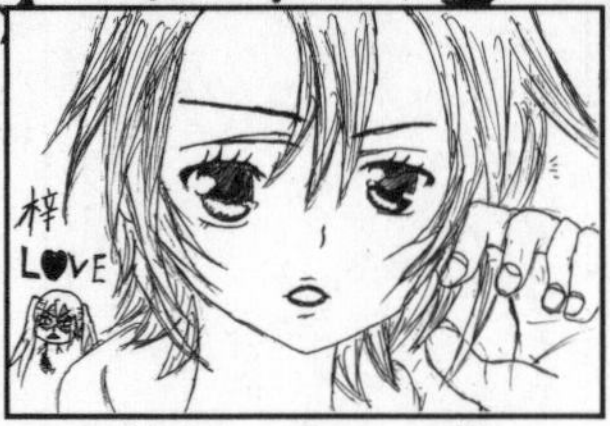
梓LOVE

Okamikan (Nara)
Ed: Otaku friends forever!! ←

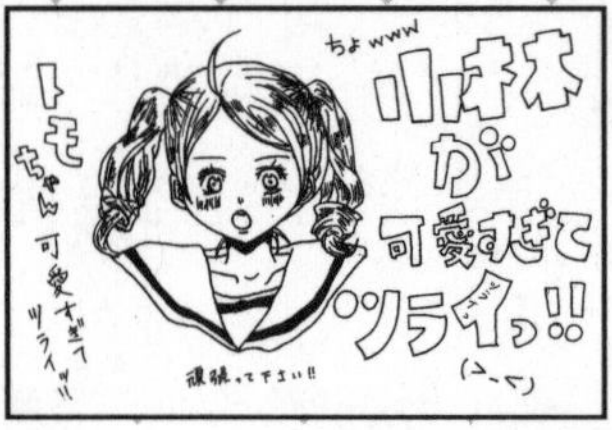
ちょwww
小林が可愛すぎてツライっ!!
トモちゃん可愛すぎてツライッ!!
頑張って下さい!!

Rio Kimura (Kanagawa)
Ed: Azusa the tsundere has suddenly become very popular! ←

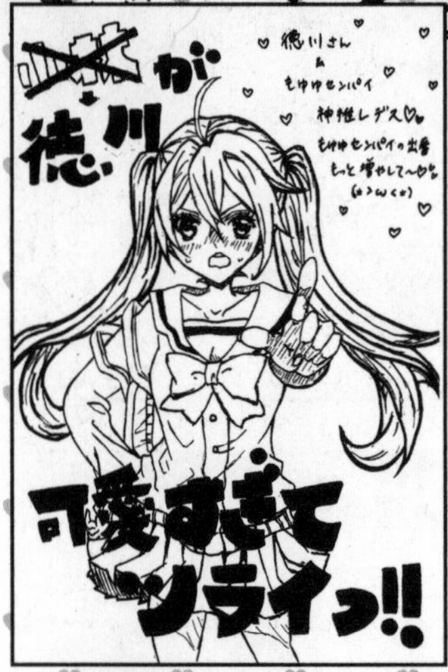
徳川が
可愛すぎてツライっ!!

Yuzuha Ishii (Osaka)
Ed: Mitsuru's wink ↓ got me. (>_<)

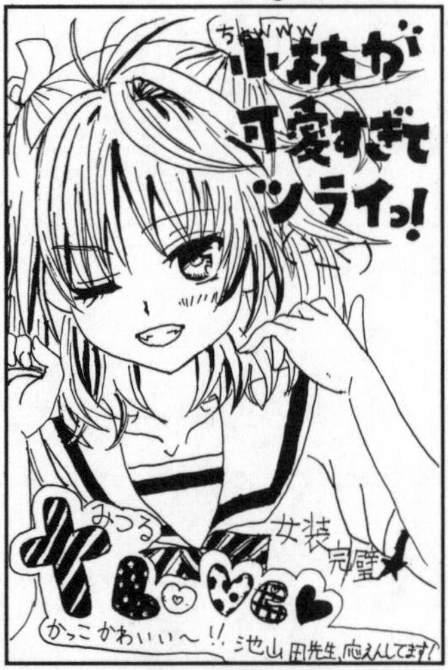
ちょwww
小林が可愛すぎてツライっ!
みつる
女装完璧★
かっこかわいい~!! 池山田先生、応えんしてます!

Ura (Tokyo) ↓
Ed: The next volume is scheduled to come out 8/26!

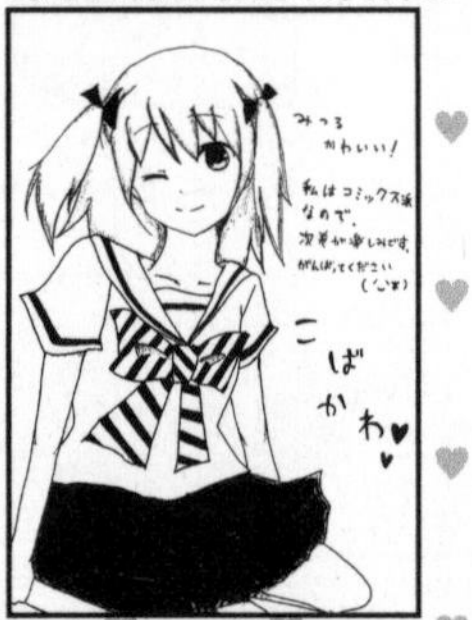
みつるかわいい!
こばかわ♥

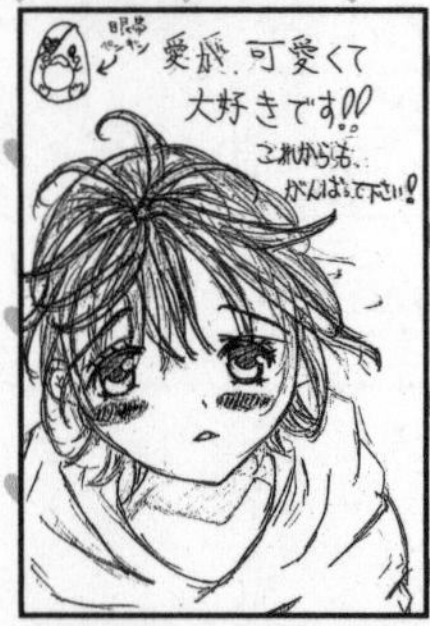
愛ちゃん、可愛くて大好きです!!
これからも、がんばって下さい!

↑ **Megumu LOVE (Saitama)**
Ed: The eye-patch penguin is lovely too. ♥

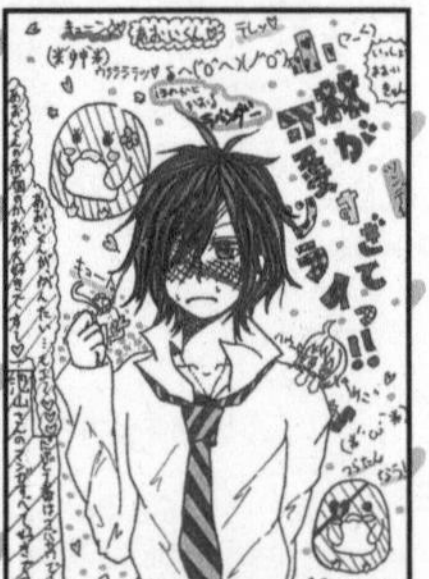
小林が可愛すぎてツライっ!!

↑ **Fushigi Kokoro (Chiba)**
Ed: Aoi looking shy tastes so sweet!!

Mitsuru Love ☆ (Iwate) ↓
Ed: A miraculous sync with the karaoke drawing on the previous page?!

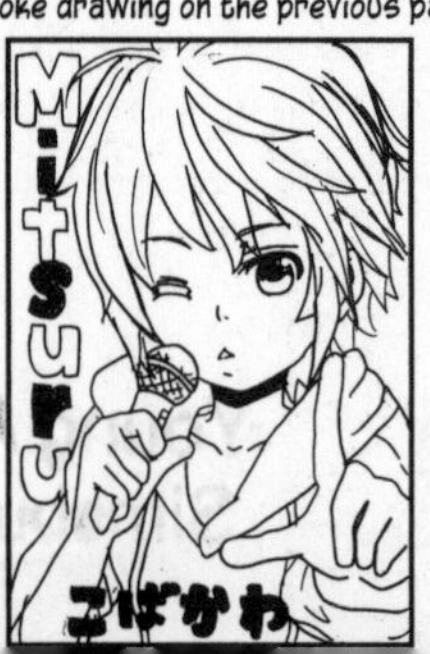
Mitsuru
こばかわ

yuma (Kagoshima)
Ed: Mitsuru's signature pose, penguins in the back. ♥ ←

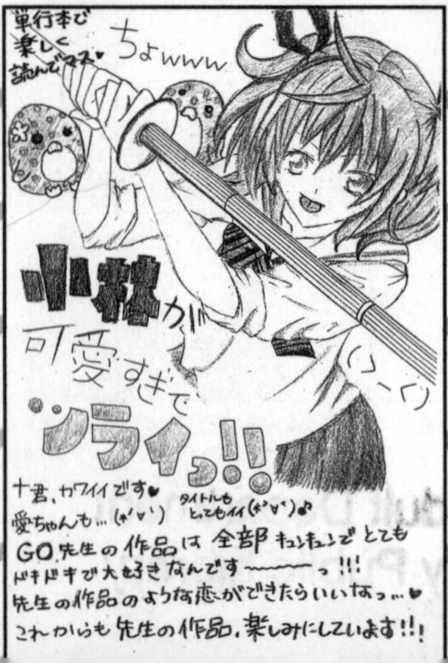
単行本で楽しく読んでマス。
ちょwww
小林が可愛すぎてツライっ!!
十君、カワイイです♥
GO先生の作品は全部キュンキュンでとてもドキドキで大好きなんです~~っ!!!
先生の作品のような恋ができたらいいなっ…♥
これからも先生の作品、楽しみにしています!!!

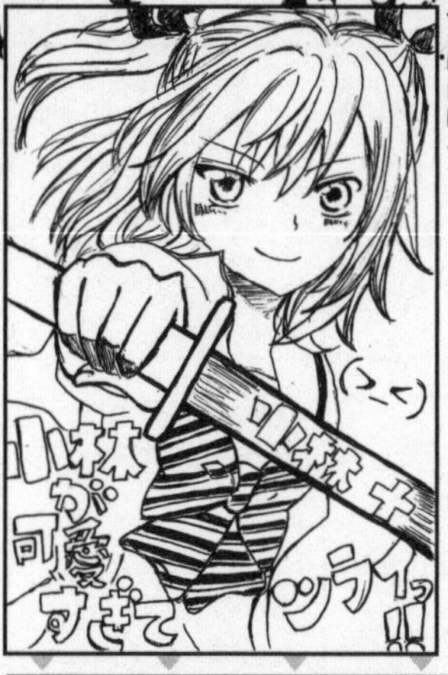
(>_<)
小林が可愛すぎてツライっ!!

Yuu Takahashi (Fukuoka)

Ed: Mitsuru's engraved name goes well with the bamboo sword. ♪

←

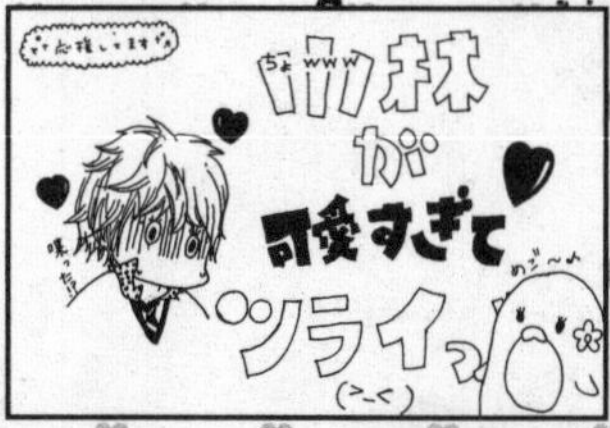
ちょwww
小林が可愛すぎてツライっ
(>_<)

→

Riko (Nara)

Ed: The penguin can speak?! For real...?

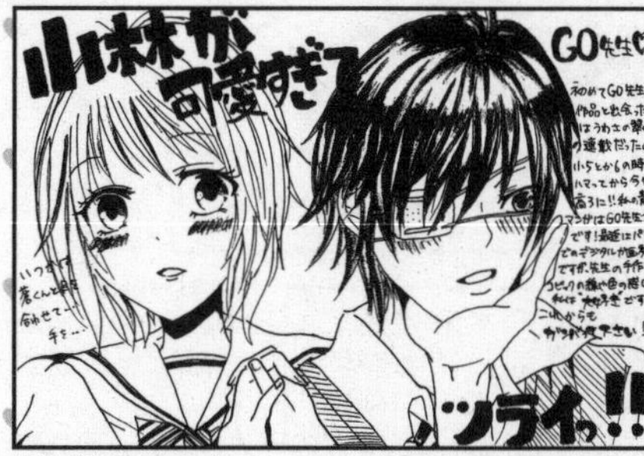
小林が可愛すぎてツライっ!!
GO先生♡

Kiho (Kagawa) ↑

Ed: Aoi looks cool even when looking away...

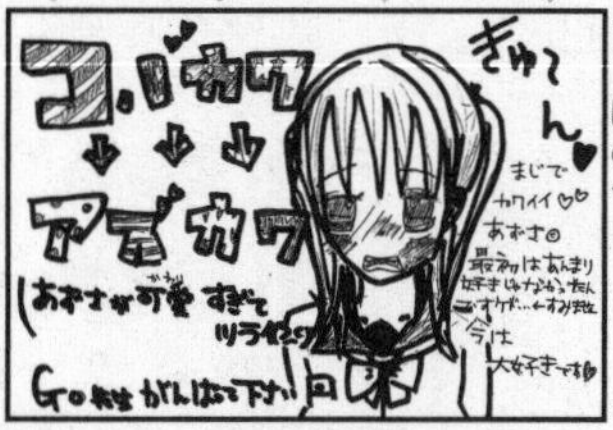

Rina Suzuki (Chiba)

Ed: Azusa's so cute it hurts?!

←

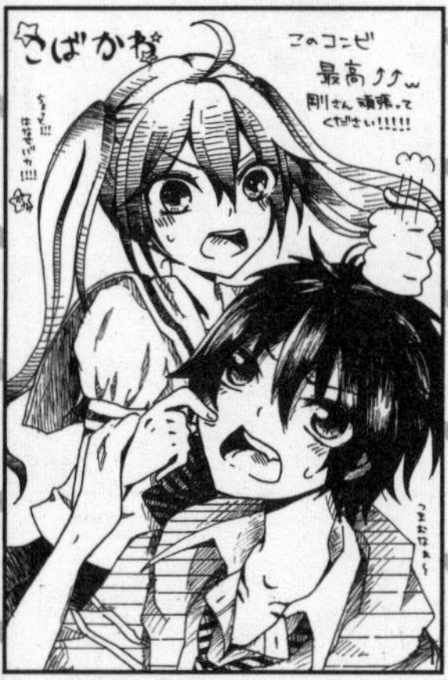

Megumi (Chiba) ↑

Ed: What'll happen to these two...?!

Hiichan ☆ (Tokyo)

Ed: The twins have grown... (^^)

↓

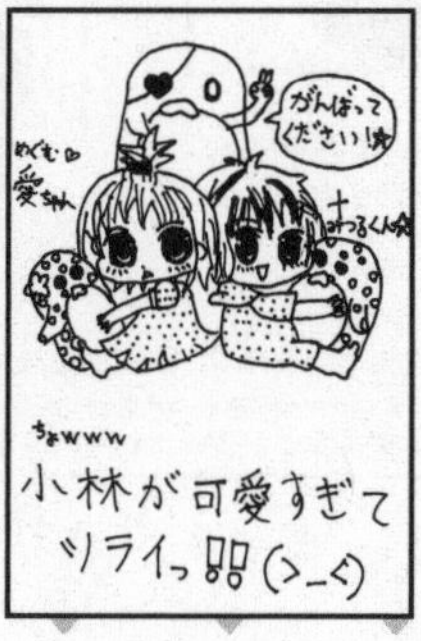
がんばってください!
ちょwww
小林が可愛すぎてツライっ!!(>_<)

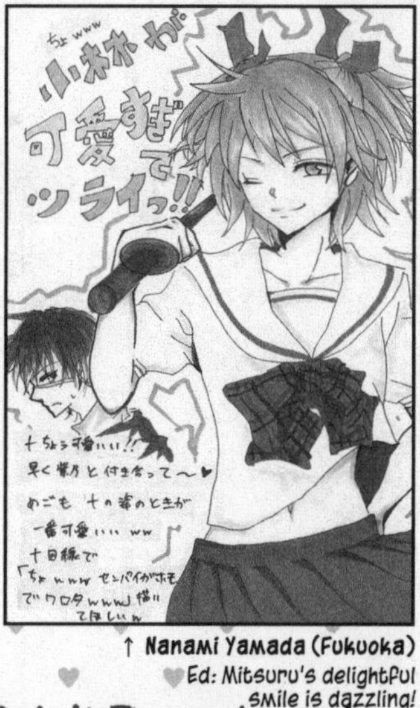
ちょwww
小林が可愛すぎてツライっ!!

↑ Nanami Yamada (Fukuoka)

Ed: Mitsuru's delightful smile is dazzling!

Send your fan mail to:

Go Ikeyamada
c/o Shojo Beat
VIZ Media, LLC
P.O. Box 77010
San Francisco, CA 94107

GLOSSARY

Page 48, panel 4: Darubisshu
Darubisshu Kenji is a member of the band Golden Bomber.

Page 72, author note: Furoku
Free gifts that come with magazines.

Page 157, panel 1: LINE account
LINE is a messaging app that's very popular in Japan.

Page 161, panel 4: Tsundere
Tsundere is a term that combines two Japanese words—*tsuntsun* (which means "unfriendly") and *deredere* (which means "lovestruck"). It is used to describe people who can be unfriendly one second but sweet the next.

AUTHOR BIO

So Cute! is being made into an anime DVD. I've loved anime since I was a kid, so I'm very, very happy. ♥♥
The most popular scene in volume 2 will be featured in the anime. (*smile*)
Thanks to my favorite voice actors, the episode will really make your hearts thump and throb, so please look forward to it. ♥♥
And my editor and I might make an appearance?? In the extras... (>_<) (*smile*)

Go Ikeyamada is a Gemini from Miyagi Prefecture whose hobbies include taking naps and watching movies. Her debut manga *Get Love!!* appeared in *Shojo Comic* in 2002, and her current work *So Cute It Hurts!!* (*Kobayashi ga Kawai Suguite Tsurai!!*) is being published by VIZ Media.